The Army of the Pacific

PLATE 1

FORT UNION, NEW MEXICO, 1866

By permission of the U. S. Army Signal Corps, Washington, D. C.

THE ARMY OF THE PACIFIC

Its operations in California, Texas, Arizona,
New Mexico, Utah, Nevada, Oregon,
Washington, plains region,
Mexico, etc. 1860-1866

by

AURORA HUNT

THE ARTHUR H. CLARK COMPANY
Glendale 4, California, U.S.A.
1951

To

All who have volunteered to serve our Nation

and especially to my nephews

Harold A. and W. George Hunt

Volunteers and Veterans of World War II

in the Pacific theatre

Contents

PREFACE 13
THE PACIFIC COAST ALERTED 19
CALIFORNIA'S QUOTA 24
THE BOOT CAMPS OF THE 1860's 29
THE CONFEDERATES INVADE THE SOUTHWEST . . 52
THE WEST OUSTS THE INVADERS 62
THE LAST CALIFORNIA POLITICAL DUELIST . . . 69
THE ADVANCE GUARD 77
THE COLUMN PREPARES TO MARCH 96
TO RECAPTURE TUCSON 109
OLD GLORY AGAIN FLIES OVER THE RIO GRANDE . 117
ON DUTY IN ARIZONA 129
ON DUTY IN NEW MEXICO 154
TROUBLE ON THE MEXICAN BORDER 175
THE MAIL GOES THROUGH 186
GENERAL CONNOR COMMANDS THE DISTRICT OF THE
    PLAINS 209
TO THE PACIFIC NORTHWEST 220
CALIFORNIA BLOCKHOUSES 238
DR. SAW-BONES – THE ARMY SURGEON . . . 266
THE CALIFORNIA FIVE HUNDRED 281
THE PACIFIC SQUADRON – 1861-1866 301
THE SOLDIERS' RELIEF FUND 324
THE LOYAL AND THE DISLOYAL 336
PEACE 355
BIBLIOGRAPHY 365
INDEX 421

Illustrations

	PLATE
FORT UNION, NEW MEXICO, 1866 . . *(frontispiece)*	1
DRUM BARRACKS, WILMINGTON, CALIFORNIA . . .	2
LIEUTENANT-COLONEL WILLIAM A. MCCLEAVE . .	3
WHITE'S MILL, PIMA VILLAGE, ARIZONA . . .	4
From *Harper's Magazine.*	
FORT WHIPPLE, ARIZONA, 1864	5
FORT TUBAC, ARIZONA	6
"KIT CARSON" AND BRIGADIER GENERAL JAMES H.	
CARLETON	7
Courtesy of Torch Press.	
FORT CHURCHILL RUINS, NEVADA	8
PATRICK EDWARD CONNOR, BREVET-MAJOR-GENERAL	
U.S. VOLUNTEERS	9
From V. C. Martin collection of historical photographs.	
BLOCKHOUSE AT FORT YAMHILL, OREGON . . .	10
OLD BLOCKHOUSE, FORT MILLER	11
FORT YUMA AND COLORADO RIVER	12
From C. C. Pierce collection of historical photographs.	
MEDICINE WAGON	13
"THE COOLIDGE CART" AMBULANCE WAGON . . .	13
NATIONAL COLORS CARRIED BY CALIFORNIA BATTALION .	14
PENNANT ON WHICH IS LISTED 24 BATTLES IN WHICH	
THE CALIFORNIANS FOUGHT	14
THE BEAR FLAG CARRIED BY THE CALIFORNIA HUNDRED	14
THE U.S.S. "CYANE"	15
Courtesy of F. W. Reif.	
THE "AQUILA"	16
THE U.S.S. "CAMANCHE"	17
MAP OF ROUTES USED BY THE ARMY OF THE PACIFIC .	END

Plates 2 to 17 follow page 386 of the text.

Preface

During the great struggle between the North and the South, the Union armies were designated according to the location in which they operated. Familiar, indeed, are the histories of the Armies of the Potomac, the Shenandoah and the West (Mississippi).

Yet there was another army which served longer, fought as bravely and died as valiantly. This was the *Army of the Pacific*. It was composed entirely of volunteers who fought over a territory one-third larger than the total area of all the seceded states.

Search as diligently as you may, there is no complete history of the service of these men other than that found in the official war records. The author of this volume might also have overlooked this rich field of research had she not met the daughter of one of these volunteers. A sword, a faded blue uniform and a photograph unlocked this treasure chest of information. Then, one by one, the discovery of one hundred fifty letters written by these volunteers, served to enhance the interest in this account of the *Army of the Pacific*.

Grateful acknowledgment is hereby made to more than a hundred individuals who have contributed information for this volume and made its completion possible.

Foremost among all others, I wish to express my gratitude to Dr. Herbert E. Bolton, University of California, Berkeley, who directed my first serious efforts in research during the summer of 1938. In later years, 1946-1948, he advised me in the selection of the most important information that I had collected and suggested a plan for its organization in order to present as complete a history as possible from present available sources. It was my good fortune to have him read and appraise my finished manuscript.

From the descendants of the California Volunteers I have received much valuable information which I gratefully recognize. Dr. Thomas C. McCleave, Berkeley, supplied detailed description of the services of his father, Lieutenant Colonel William A. McCleave, first cavalry, as well as photographs, letters and original manuscripts. He also read my manuscript and offered helpful suggestions as he is a veteran of two wars, the Spanish-American and World War I. He served as assistant surgeon and retired with the rank of major.

Miss Leantina Murphy, Oakland, also made an outstanding contribution of a three-year diary of Hiram S. Tuttle, company K, third infantry, who was a member of her family.

Others shared their information with invariable generosity. Miss Florence Calderwood, Phoenix, Arizona; Martin H. Calderwood, Culver City; Rudolph A. Bagdons, Santa Maria; F. E. Conway, Trinity Center; Mrs. E. R. Geries, Fresno; Miss Della Kidder, Redding; Mrs. Ed Meiers, Campo Seco; and Mrs. Jessie Weslow, Sacramento, are among those members of the volunteers' families to whom I owe my gratitude.

Many of the photographs in my collection of more than a hundred were donated by friends and by strangers who became friends. I regret that more of them cannot appear in this volume but I deeply appreciate the gifts of V. Covert Martin, Stockton; the late C. C. Pierce, Los Angeles; Frank E. Cotter, Los Angeles; F. W. Reif, San Diego; Dr. A. T. Leonard, San Francisco; Mrs. Gertrude McDonald, Trinity Center; Bill Conway, Wilmington; and Irving Lee Palmer, Descanso.

It is not possible to list all others who have helped me but the following deserve special mention: the late Thomas F. Keaveny, Drum Barracks, Wilmington; Roger N. Howe, county recorder, San Diego; James D. Forward, president Union Title Insurance and Trust company, San Diego; the late Mrs. Ella Robinson, San Diego; Mrs. C. A. Campbell, Red Bluff; Miss Doris Treat, San Andreas; Mrs. Theresa Leonard, San Andreas; the late Miss Ella Creighton, Campo Seco; August Costa, Downieville; James Stewart, Auburn; Major Fred B. Rogers; and the late Mrs. Amelia Spayd, Stockton, who was friend, companion and guide for me as we located many of the historic spots of the Mother Lode country and at whose home I was a welcome guest during my research in that community.

To Gilbert Grosvenor, editor, *National Geographic magazine,* I am especially grateful for the information he so generously furnished regarding the city of Washington, D.C.

The California librarians and their staffs rendered inestimable help which was freely given and I wish to thank those of the following libraries for their interest and friendly service: California state library, Sacramento; University of California at Berkeley, including the Bancroft and the Boalt Law libraries; Sutter Fort Historical museum, Sacramento; Henry E. Huntington library, San Marino; Los Angeles public library; Southwest museum, Los Angeles; Los Angeles county museum; Whittier college library, also the private library of Dr. Paul S. Smith of the history department of the college; Whittier public library; A. K. Smiley library, Redlands; Stockton free public library; Fresno county free library, Fresno; San Diego public library; Nevada City library; Amador county library, Jackson; Junipero Serra museum, San Diego; Riverside public library; Franciscan Fathers Old Mission library, Santa Barbara; Pasadena public library; and also to the out-of-state libraries including the public library, Boston, Mass.; Provincial library, Victoria, B.C.; Albuquerque public library, and public library, Santa Fe, both New Mexico; public library of Salt Lake City, Utah; Wyoming state library, Cheyenne, Wyoming; Library and Archives, Phoenix, Arizona; San Antonio city library, Texas; and Library association of Portland, Oregon.

Without the assistance received from the national archives in Washington, D.C., this volume would be lacking in much of interest and value. To the following I offer my sincere acknowledgments: Library of congress; Naval records and library; Photographic division of signal corps, War department; Old records division, adjutant general's office, War department; office of chief of engineers, U.S. Army, War department; and Engineer department of the government of the District of Columbia.

The county archives of California contain much information of value and to those in charge of the following I am especially indebted: Calaveras county, San Andreas; Tuolumne county, Sonora; Mariposa county, Mariposa; Siskiyou county, Yreka; San Mateo county, Redwood City; Sierra county, Downieville; and Solano county, Fairfield.

The work of the historical societies cannot be overestimated and the following were especially helpful: Colorado State Historical society, Denver; Oregon Historical society, Portland; Arizona Pioneers' Historical society, Tucson; Kansas State Historical society; Nebraska State Historical society; California Historical society, San Francisco; Historical society of southern California, Los Angeles; San Diego Historical society; San Joaquin Pioneer and Historical society, Stockton; and the Shasta Historical society whose president, Mrs. Gertrude Steger, furnished a vast amount of information about northern California.

To the newsmen of California a very special recognition is due. They are to be commended for the care bestowed on the old news files and for their generosity in making them available.

By reading these old newspapers in the towns where they were published, I was able to more clearly visualize the scenes of activity in the 1860's. By walking the same streets, viewing the sites of the old "armory halls," tramping across the meadows where the volunteers drilled and listening to the tales told by their contemporaries, I was able to more fully understand the cause for which they gave their lives on the western frontier.

Sometimes a seemingly insignificant piece of information finally developed into a complete chapter. Diligently I followed each clue to discover the story of these soldiers whose lives and deeds seem almost fictional.

I commend most highly Miss Neva Turner of Whittier, my typist, reader and cartographer, and extend her my sincere appreciation of her many hours of work.

I humbly accept all assistance that was so freely given. With candor, I can say that I could not have compiled all this information without their help.

There are still many missing pages of this history of the *Army of the Pacific* but I hope that some of the descendants of these volunteers will read this first volume and be prompted to contribute to another. Again I acknowledge the value of the contributions of my co-workers.

AURORA HUNT

Whittier, California, May, 1950

The Pacific Coast Alerted

During the pre-Civil war period, nearly seventy-five per cent of the United States peace-time army was stationed in the west to garrison the frontier posts which were scattered from Canada to Mexico and from the Pacific coast to the eastern slope of the Rocky mountains. This was an area of more than a million square miles and was divided into the five military departments of Texas, New Mexico, Utah, Oregon and California. But the Federal soldiers could not be counted by millions then, for their incredibly small total was only 12,984.[1]

When the guns of Fort Sumter ceased firing april 13, 1861, the War department realized that the feeble numbers of the army were totally inadequate to meet the crisis that threatened the nation. The urgency of the situation increased when nearly all the military posts in Texas were either abandoned by federal troops or captured by the Texans who had adopted an ordinance of secession early in february. In april and may the last of the forts in northwestern Texas were evacuated and by the end of the summer the Arizona forts as well as those in New Mexico south of Fort Craig were deserted by the Union soldiers.

The alarm had been sounded! The Pacific coast was seized with a war panic and convinced that there would be fighting on two fronts—east and west. Clamors for

[1] Report of Secretary of War, june 20, 1860, 36 Cong. 2 Sess. Sen. Ex. Doc. no. 1, p. 209, vol. II. (1079)

protection came from all parts of the nation. Postmaster
General Montgomery Blair asked for men and guns
to guard the Pacific steamers carrying mail and gold
between San Francisco and Panama. The venerable
Winfield Scott, general-in-chief of the army, ordered
the commander of the army of the Pacific "to act in
concert" with the Pacific squadron to prevent the
secessionists from gaining a foothold on Lower California. The navy commander promptly responded by
sending three warships to patrol the coasts of California
and Mexico.[2]

Fort Yuma on the Colorado river was alerted. The
Confederate army must not pass! Greater protection
was ordered for the Overland Mail during its removal
from the southern to the central route. Two 24-pounder
guns were forwarded to San Diego to protect the
southern California border. Shipment of arms to
Mexico was forbidden lest they fall into the hands of
the enemy.

Guns and ammunition were needed for the protection of the national capitol. From the arsenal at Benicia
30,000 stand of arms were shipped. A guard of thirty
men accompanied the shipment as far as Panama. Extra
guards were then stationed at the depleted arsenal and
at Mare island navy base in San Francisco bay.[3]

Warnings were issued to the effect that if any vessel,
sailing under the flag of the Confederacy, attempted to
enter any waters of the Pacific, it would be immediately
captured. Vessels which failed to come to or surrender
on being duly warned, or which would attempt to
escape, would be fired on, and if necessary, sunk. All

[2] *War of the rebellion*, Series I, volume L, part I, p. 476, 498, 531, 534-535, 539.

[3] *Ibid.*, p. 474, 493, 574, 518, 541, 628.

vessels were required to show their colors when they entered San Francisco bay.[4]

Officers in the federal army were required to renew their oath of allegiance. Resignations were restricted thereafter and all leaves of absence curtailed. Any citizen who voiced his opposition to the Union while in the employ of the army was discharged.[5]

Meanwhile steamers were crowded with men returning east. Some to join the Union, others to cast their lot with the Confederacy. Across the Colorado river another group of Californians returned to Texas. Among the latter was General Albert Sidney Johnston who on april 9 resigned his position as commander of the department of the Pacific. However, he retained his office until General Edwin V. Sumner arrived to relieve him april 25.

By mid-august, General-in-chief Winfield Scott, "telegraphed to outer station, thence by pony express and telegraph" to General Sumner that he was to command an expedition into Texas, via Mazatlan. The strength of the invading force assigned to his command consisted of "ten foot" companies of regulars, one regiment of volunteer cavalry, four regiments volunteer infantry and two batteries. General Sumner was especially instructed to regain the government property in western Texas and draw off insurgent troops in Arkansas and Missouri.[6]

The secretary of war hurriedly telegraphed the quartermaster at San Francisco to make all arrangements including transportation for the expedition to Texas. An extra supply of coal for the troop vessels was to be placed in the depot at Mazatlan. Sumner's

[4] *Ibid.*, p. 494, 533.
[5] *Ibid.*, p. 486, 498.
[6] *Ibid.*, p. 572-574.

preference for his beach head was Guaymas but he agreed that it would be determined by the route taken by the Confederates.[7]

The route selected looked feasible to the officials in Washington but to the experienced frontiersman and surveyor, General Edward F. Beale, it was entirely impracticable and he advised General Sumner accordingly. The report was referred to the War department and shortly afterwards General Scott, with the assent of the secretary of war, ordered Sumner to suspend preparations for the expedition against western Texas.

Included in the above communication was an order to prepare the regular troops, except four companies of artillery, "to come by steam to New York. Two regiments of volunteers will replace the regulars." This order was later modified and the ninth infantry was retained on the Pacific coast.[8]

This further increased the alarm of the Pacific coast states. Again official Washington was beseiged with protests from Washington, Oregon, Arizona and California. Indian troubles, foreign invasion and domestic dissension occupied the attention of the press and increased rather than allayed the anxieties of the frontier. The public argued that if the past necessities required the presence of the federal troops on the frontier, the present dangers confronting the Pacific coast were far greater and demanded more rather than less protection.[9]

A tense situation prevailed in foreign affairs. Even as the federal troops were sailing up the Atlantic coast, a flotilla of French, Spanish and English warships, and transports carrying more than ten thousand men, was

[7] *Ibid.,* p. 593-594.

[8] *Ibid.,* p. 605, 610-611, 641, 613, 644-645, 663, 701.

[9] *Ibid.,* p. 631-632.

on its way to Vera Cruz, Mexico, to seize and hold the Mexican coast until satisfactory settlement of the Mexican foreign loans could be accomplished. The policy of these nations was opposed by the State department which settled down to "watchful waiting" of the outcome. The Pacific coast was too close to the situation to regard it dispassionately and was alarmed by the prospect of an alliance between the Confederacy and Mexico, abetted by one or all of the foreign powers at Vera Cruz.[10]

To the north, English and United States troops occupied San Juan island jointly as the northern boundary dispute had not yet been settled. To the south, Spain jealously eyed her lost colonies in South America and by 1865 she had turned her guns on Valparaiso and Callao. The vulnerability of the Pacific coast was readily apparent. San Francisco harbor was the only fortified point on the entire Pacific coast and its loss meant the surrender of the long coast line.

The general-in-chief of the army emphasized the urgency of the situation when he ordered the commander of the department of the Pacific to send by telegram the condition of the troops. Report by letter "fully and frequently." The national struggle, or as Lincoln called it, the "Great trouble" of the nation was prosecuted on two fronts, east and west, linked by a slender wire over which flashed the orders from Washington that co-ordinated the efforts of the troops on both fronts.[11]

---

10 Herbert Ingram Priestley, *The Mexican nation*, p. 335, 340, 347.
11 *War. Reb.* Ser. I, vol. L, pt. I, p. 697.

California's Quota

It was imperative that the federal troops be withdrawn from the west for service on the eastern battlefields and it was equally urgent that others be supplied to substitute for these trained soldiers. An increase in the army was provided for by the Volunteer Employment act passed by the thirty-seventh congress, july 1861. According to this act the service was not to exceed three years nor to be less than six months. The volunteers were subject to the rules and regulations governing the army of the United States and were placed on the same footing as to pay and allowances of similar corps of the regular army.[12]

Simon Cameron, secretary of war, promptly telegraphed to Governor John G. Downey of California for one regiment of infantry and five companies of cavalry to guard the Overland Mail from Carson City, Nevada, to Salt Lake, Utah. California was the first western state called upon for volunteers and supplied the greatest number. The United States census of 1860 credits California with a population of 379,994 and of that number 169,975 or 44.46% were of military age. One-tenth of the men in this group enlisted, for this was then a young man's state. The total population of Washington, Oregon, Arizona, Utah and Colorado was

[12] Volunteer Employment act, 37 Cong. 1 Sess. H. Misc. Doc. no. 20, vol. I. (1115)

Richard H. Orton, *Records of California men in the war of the rebellion*, p. 12. (Calif. State printing office 1890)

only 145,466 or 24,509 less than the military age group of California.[13]

Political opinion was sharply divided at this time and it appears paradoxical that a state that gave Lincoln the small plurality of less than eight hundred votes in 1860, would a year later, stand staunchly behind the president by supplying troops without a draft and continue to do so for the duration of the war and for nearly a year after its close.

The call for volunteers found California eager to respond. As soon as General Sumner could select qualified officers, move them to their respective stations and supply them with the necessary instructions and muster rolls, enlistments began with surprising rapidity. It should be remembered that these recruiting officers and supplies had to be transported hundreds of miles by stage or on horseback. Consequently, the more remote sections of the state were a week or more late in beginning but they made up the time lost by the speed of their enlistments. Within two weeks from the first call for troops, 91 Oroville boys had signed their names on the muster roll; Nevada City supplied 87; Amador County placed next on the list with 74 recruits.[14]

On august 14, 1861, four additional regiments of infantry and one of cavalry were ordered mustered into service. Some of these young soldiers received little or no training before being dispatched to conduct a rigorous campaign against hostile Indian tribes. Five companies of the second infantry reached Fort Vancouver in mid-october and a month later were followed by five companies from the fourth infantry.[15]

13 Eighth U.S. Census, 37 Cong. 2 Sess. H. Ex. Doc. no. 116, vol. IX. (1137)

14 Richard H. Orton, *Records of California men in the war of the rebellion,* p. 336-380. (Calif. State printing office 1890)

15 *Ibid.,* p. 12. *War. Reb.* Ser. I, vol. L, pt. I, p. 697-698, 674, 701.

Companies A and H, second cavalry, received a few weeks training and then were ordered to Fort Churchill to replace the federal troops. The California cavalrymen made the ride across the Sierra before the first heavy snowfall and took over patrol duty in Nevada.[16]

So rapidly were the volunteer regiments filled that the first order for the withdrawal of the federal troops was issued as early as september 9 and the first contingent sailed october 21. The last of the federal troops left on december 21, just five months after the first call for California volunteers. The ninth U.S. infantry, four companies of the third U.S. artillery and a detachment of ordnance were retained on the Pacific coast at San Juan island, Fort Vancouver, and San Francisco.[17]

True to United States army tradition, the California volunteers represented the best of their respective communities. They were husky young sons of pioneers and but a short decade previous some of them had trudged beside the family covered wagon as it pitched and tossed over the same roads they were now ordered to protect. Others were among the sea-farers from around the Horn who came with the New York volunteers under the command of Colonel Jonathan D. Stevenson aboard the "Loo Choo", the "Susan Drew" and the "Thomas H. Perkins". Some of these experienced officers trained the volunteer regiments and led them half way back again across the continent. The officers were well-fitted for their tasks. A few were graduates of West Point. Others obtained their military training in campaigns extending from Maine to Florida and from Jefferson Barracks to Mexico City.

California furnished a total of 16,231 men, which

---

[16] *Ibid.*, p. 652, Gen. Order no. 25.

[17] *Ibid.*, p. 701, 645, 649, 650, 642-643, 620-621, 658, 772; Pt. II, p. 272-273.

included two full regiments cavalry, one battalion native California cavalry, eight full regiments of infantry; one battalion infantry, the Mountaineers; besides eight companies in Washington's only regiment; and in addition to all these, five companies of the second Massachusetts cavalry, who were enrolled in California and credited to Massachusetts. A requisition for an additional regiment of infantry, the ninth, was made on Governor Low of California in april 1865 but the order was countermanded. The total number including those serving in Washington state and in the east, was approximately 17,500, or about 5,000 more than the pre-Civil war army.[18]

The Military department of the Pacific assumed various shapes and sizes according to orders from the War department. Its boundaries were extended only to be constricted later, but during most of the Civil war period, it included all the states and territories from the Pacific ocean to the Rocky mountains and from Canada to Mexico.

The officers in charge were changed almost as often. There were four different commanders during a four year period. Colonel Albert Sidney Johnston, second United States cavalry, brevet brigadier general, served for three months (january 15 to april 25, 1861) and then resigned to join the Confederate army.

General Edwin V. Sumner, who succeeded Johnston, remained six months, april 25 to october 20, 1861, when he was relieved by Brigadier General George Wright who remained in charge of the department of the Pacific for two years and eight months, a longer period than the combined length of service of the other three

---

[18] 38 Cong. 2 Sess. H. Ex. Doc. no. 77, vol. XIII. (1229)
Report of Sec. of War, june 1860.
War. Reb. Ser. I, vol. L, pt. II, p. 1191.

commanders. Major General Irvin McDowell assumed command in july 1864, and for a year directed the military affairs of the Pacific coast.

To supervise the military operations of this vast frontier was a large assignment for General Wright, who was then sixty years old, but his thirty-nine years of service had prepared him for the job. He had able officers and troops of sterling worth to help him.[19]

As though the volunteers of the army of the Pacific had foreseen that their services would be forgotten by the future generations, they left their own record. In the far outposts, they "powdered their ink and took up their pens" to tell the folk at home about their service on the western front. Their news was so important that many of these letters were published in the early California newspapers on whose yellow and crumbling pages the intimate story of the volunteers has been preserved.[20]

---

[19] Brig. Gen. George Wright, born october 21, 1801, Norwich, Vt. Graduated West Point, july 1, 1822. Served: Fort Howard, Wis.; Jefferson Barracks, Mo.; Fort Leavenworth, Kan.; Seminole Indian War, Fla., 1840-1842; War with Mex.; at Fort Columbus and Fort Ontario, N.Y., 1848-1852. Dist. Calif. 1852-1855; Ore. and Wash. Indian wars, 1856-1861, Dept. of Ore.; Dept. of Pac., oct. 20, 1861-july 1, 1864. Dept. of Calif. 1864-1865. Transferred to Dept. of Columbia but died in wreck of s.s. "Brother Jonathan", july 1865.
35 Cong. 2 Sess. Sen. Ex. Doc. no. 32, vol. X. (984)
Maj. Gen. Geo. Washington Cullum, *Biographical register officers and graduates of* U.S. *military academy,* West Point, N.Y.

[20] Calif. Stats. 13 Sess. Calif. legislature, p. 141. April 8, 1862, provided for the preservation of California newspapers and fines and penalties fixed for neglect in collecting said papers or for destroying, mutilating or defacing them. The recorders of the counties were charged with the duty of preservation, but the board of supervisors of the respective counties chose the newspapers that should be preserved. Half of the fines collected was paid into the state school fund and the other half went to the prosecutor.

The Boot Camps of the 1860's

From the valleys and the mines,
From the redwoods and the pines,
From the cities we can't be naming—
The boys have left their all
At their country's call. . .

Their army song rang true when they sang, ". . . From the cities we can't be naming. . ." Listed on the old muster rolls are more than a hundred towns and cities which designate the residences of these volunteers. They came from towns whose present day population is far less than the number of men who responded to Lincoln's call in the 1860's.

The distribution of California's population is strikingly exemplified by these military records. It was then thirteen years after the discovery of gold but Coloma could supply 56 volunteers; Columbia, 63; Downieville, 119; Mokelumne Hill, 154; Volcano, 71; Watsonville, 80; Visalia, 30; Dutch Flat, 61; Los Angeles County, 276; San Francisco, 6,290. Tuolumne county boasted that she furnished one thousand volunteers who served in fourteen different companies.[21]

There were no troop trains nor motor coaches to transport these recruits to their training camps. They willingly walked long distances from some of the remote mining camps, paid their own tolls on the bridges and their fares on the river boats. They crowded aboard the stage coaches making it impossible for the

[21] Richard H. Orton, Adj. Gen. California, *Record of California men in war of rebellion.* (State printing office 1890)

"Six Horses" to pull them up the steep grades. They walked uphill and pushed but had the privilege of riding downhill.

Occasionally a free ride was provided by a loyal Union steamboat company, as in the case of the Red Bluff volunteers who made the trip down the Sacramento river on the "Swan". However, the "Swan" belied her name for instead of floating gracefully, she got stuck in the mud twice but the boys accepted the delays without too many "growls".

The Shasta volunteers traveled the River route also and were towed in a barge behind the "Gem". When the river was low, these old steamboats tied up to the bank at night to avoid the snags and sand bars in the darkness. Slowly they glided between the green banks. The willows dipped their yellow green branches to the water's edge and wild grape vines, festooned from the cottonwood trees, seemed to wave farewell to these young soldiers from Horsetown, Whiskeytown, French Gulch, Trinity Center and Shasta.

They enjoyed the trip but the memory of Shasta produced nostalgia in varying degrees according to whom or what they had left behind. Many could not forget their last night at home when a full moon etched the hills against a clear sky crowded with stars. Others could not blot out the flag presentation ceremony.

While the snowy peak of Mount Shasta still reflected the sun's inimitable artistry, the new recruits marched from their camp near town and formed a hollow square around a platform in the middle of the main street. Then 33 girls, led by a goddess of liberty, ascended the little rostrum. Each girl wore a white dress with a sash of red, white and blue, and in her crown was a star to represent a state of the union. The goddess of liberty presented a silk flag to Benjamin R. West, captain of the Shasta volunteers. He was a veteran of the Mexican war and was engaged in mining at Horsetown when the war began. Anvils rang, Bengal fires of red, white and blue flared in the twilight, while the band played and everybody sang *America*. The rest of the evening was spent in dancing and feasting.

The volunteers left the next morning and spent their first night at the William Ludwig hotel on Cottonwood creek where Mrs. Ludwig baked bread the whole night long to satisfy the appetites of these mountain boys. As they marched away in the early morning, they proudly unfurled their new silk flag. This was the flag that was destined to fly over the island of Santa Catalina two years later, when the Shasta volunteers, company C, fourth infantry, became the "army of occupation" and Captain West was appointed "civil and military governor" of the island.[22]

When Captain West's company reached Sacramento they boarded the train for Folsom where they were transferred to wagons, which hauled them up the grade to Auburn. Here they were mustered in by Colonel Henry Moses Judah at Camp McClellan, october 1861. The Auburn residents welcomed the volunteers and treated them so cordially the mountain men felt quite "at home." In fact, so much so that they visited a neighbor's poultry yard expecting to steal a turkey. It was a dark night and since turkeys and peacocks differ but little in size, they made the mistake of capturing a peacock. The irate farmer reported his loss to Colonel

[22] Information furnished through the courtesy of Mrs. C. A. Campbell, daughter of Mrs. William Ludwig, Red Bluff, California.

Captain West was the original owner of the Washington mine at French Gulch.

War. Reb. Ser. I, vol. L, pt. II, p. 714.

Judah who ordered every tent searched. Not one proud feather could be found!

It was a hard winter to live in tents with straw for bedding. However, the volunteers were soon moved to Sacramento but conditions were worse there, as the city was flooded. Undaunted and debonair, the boys joined the citizens in making a carnival of the flood. With gaily painted boats, colored lanterns and music, they rowed through the streets as though to dramatize a *Night in Venice.*

Training in their wet camp was boresome, and the young soldiers petitioned Colonel Judah to obtain permission from General Wright to send them East for duty. Eight months' pay was due and they agreed to forfeit all of it to pay their expenses to the Atlantic coast. General Wright wasted no words. He said, "The men do not know what they ask. They are needed far more here than in the East."

They welcomed the order that sent them to Camp Latham on Ballona creek near Los Angeles. Here their commanding officer demanded sobriety and prohibited the sale of liquor within three miles of camp. Nevertheless, some of the soldiers continued to procure whisky. The colonel soon discovered the source of supply. A fruit peddler, who had been permitted to enter the camp, had ingeniously cut the rind of some of his watermelons, poured in liquor and then plugged the opening. The colonel bought one of these melons in spite of the protest from the peddler, who offered the excuse that the melon was not good enough for an officer. It proved to be a good enough one to catch the culprit.[23]

23 Edward Carlson, *Overland Monthly,* vol. VII, 2nd series p. 480-496.
Shasta *Courier,* Shasta, apr. 28, 1866; nov. 29, 1862.
Red Bluff *Beacon,* Red Bluff, Calif., oct. 3, 1861.

Not only Shasta, but nearly every town gave its volunteers a flag or guidon. Quite often, one or both were handmade by the girls at home and always were presented by one of the most charming "belles." Such a flag was the one received by the soldiers at Jackson, Amador county. The five-pointed stars were a bit out of line but as the volunteer said, "They were made by loving hands." For three years this flag was carried by company C, first infantry. When Laura Meek handed it to their captain that night in the town hall at Jackson, she could not predict how far it would travel nor where it would wave.[24]

When the column from California entered Tucson in may 1862, Laura's flag was carried at the head of the column. It was the first Union flag to wave over Fort Breckinridge after its occupation by the Texans. On the fourth of july, 1862, it was unfurled over Fort Buchanan; it went with company C up the Rio Grande valley, crossed the Jornada del Muerto, the Journey of Death, past the battleground of Valverde and onward to Fort Wingate. It also waved over Fort Whipple, as this company erected the buildings.[25]

This flag has been preserved and now hangs in the rotunda of the state capitol at Sacramento. Seventeen other flags, with records as colorful, drape their silken folds there to remind us of the service of the California volunteers in the 1860's.

The volunteers' training camps were located at Sacramento, Stockton, Benicia, Oakland, San Francisco, Wilmington, and on the Ballona Rancho on the present site of Culver City. Camp Wright, Oak Grove, was a sub-depot, but here the troops often put the

---

[24] *Weekly Ledger*, Jackson, Amador county, Calif., oct. 15, nov. 11, 1864.
[25] *Ibid.*, march 26, 1864.

finishing touches on their training before starting across the desert to Fort Yuma.[26]

In some of the temporary training camps the officers and men lived in tents and when they moved on there was little left to mark the spot. Camp Union was first located at the Yolo race track across the river from Sacramento, but within a few weeks it was moved to a site a half mile east of Sutterville. On Sutterville road just south of William Land park, a solitary two-story brick house remains to mark the location of the town founded and named by John Augustus Sutter in 1844. Here Colonel George W. Bowie trained the fifth regiment of infantry, California volunteers, for their long desert march to the Rio Grande. This was the year of the great flood and in addition to drilling, the soldiers found much to do in the flood-stricken capital city. Their camp was on high enough ground so that they were not greatly inconvenienced, especially after the floors were laid in their tents.[27]

Camp Halleck at Stockton occupied the site of the present fair grounds which was formerly known as Agricultural park. The "tented village" was regularly laid out with streets twelve to fifteen feet wide. The tents faced west to catch any stray breeze as well as the dust from the parade grounds when Colonel P. Edward Connor drilled the third infantry in preparation for their three years service in Utah, Nevada, Idaho and Wyoming.[28]

Camp Alert, named by General Edwin V. Sumner, was established on the old Pioneer race track, San Francisco. The race track was then located on an undeveloped tract of land north of Bernal heights between

[26] *War. Reb.* Ser. I, vol. L, pt. I, p. 648, Special Order no. 2, (oct. 7, 1861).
[27] Sacramento *Daily Union,* oct. 3, 8, 14, 17, 1861.
[28] *War. Reb.* Ser. I, vol. L, pt. II, p. 55. Order no. 1.

Mission and Folsom streets and Twenty-fifth and Twenty-sixth streets. While in camp, the volunteers of the second cavalry could hear the horses' hoof-beats on the plank pavement as the market wagons rumbled down Folsom street and when off duty, they entertained themselves by checking the traffic. The highest record in a day was 34 horsemen, 66 double teams, and 177 one-horse vehicles. Highway 101 now passes a few blocks east of the camp site with much more traffic in an hour than the old plank street had in a day—and a strangely different kind of traffic.[29]

While in training at Camp Alert, the second cavalry was presented with some of the most costly and beautiful flags. The ladies of Sacramento gave the "Sacramento Rangers" a silk flag with a spear head of solid silver valued at two hundred and fifty dollars. Company G of the same regiment boasted that for neatness and beauty their flag far exceeded anything else in the regiment. It was of silk, a yard long and two feet wide, with the letter "G" and the number of the regiment, "2 C.V.," encircled with a wreath of laurel. It also had a spear head of solid Washoe silver and was a gift from the boys' friends at Downieville. The volunteers were speechless with surprise and gratitude and decided that it was easier to make an uphill charge than to describe all the beauties of their flag.

Then as now, the women did not forget the soldiers. The members of the Unitarian church, San Francisco, gave each volunteer a sewing kit; but the Ladies Dashaway society appeared to be the most generous, as their gifts could be counted by hundreds and included a

<hr>

[29] *Ibid.*, pt. I, p. 617, Special Order no. 169, Series 1861.

miscellaneous assortment, from tooth brushes to shoe blacking and buttons to butcher knives.[30]

At Camp Alert, San Francisco, Reverend Thomas Starr King addressed the young soldiers, who were greatly impressed with the manner in which the famous clergyman could present common every day duties so that they all seemed vital to religion. He told them that negligence of the laws of health was a species of treason. "A sick soldier," said he, "sick through his own negligence, is a diluted, indirect traitor. He not only deprives his own country of his services, but he is a clog and hindrance to his comrades." [31]

By Christmas eve the moral teachings of the good "Shepherd" were forgotten. Evidently there was no prospect of either a chicken or a turkey Christmas dinner, so a few of the fellows slipped past the guard after taps and went on the prowl for poultry. Yes, they were caught when they returned to camp but the spokesman for the boys had an alibi. "We went for a walk to view the country by moonlight but so many ducks and chickens pestered us and blocked our path that we had to wring their necks." They were marched off to the guard house but permitted to keep the fowls. In the morning when the culprits were released, the tolerant colonel warned them that when they went on a foraging expedition again they should get home before taps or else be a little more sly about it.[32]

The cavalry camps at Oakland were located on the shores of Peralta lake, now called Lake Merritt. One camp was named Merritt in honor of Dr. Samuel Merritt, the "Father of Oakland." The volunteer, who

---

30 *Sierra Democrat,* Downieville, nov. 30, 1861.
Sacramento *Union,* sept. 21, 1861.
31 Sacramento *Union,* oct. 15, 1861.
32 *Sierra Democrat,* Downieville, jan. 19, 1862.

sat idly by Lake Merritt when daily camp routine was over, could not then envision the changes since 1861. Then he found forage, wood and water—all the requisites for satisfactory camping. Now his parade ground supports tall hotels and business buildings from which the occupants look down upon the same lake.

As early as august 22, 1861, General Sumner ordered the first infantry moved into camp at some point near San Antonio landing and instructed Captain Kirkham, assistant quartermaster, to select the site. The following day, by special order no. 153, he named it Camp Downey in honor of Governor John G. Downey.[33] San Antonio Landing was located at Washington and Broadway according to the old maps, but Washington has been renamed East Twelfth and Broadway is now Seventeenth avenue. All trace of Camp Downey has disappeared and a city stands on parade instead.

Benicia Barracks was enlarged to take care of the increasing numbers of volunteers. By january 15, 1862, the new quarters were completed and the third regiment infantry "struck tents" and moved in out of the rain. Two weeks later snow fell and the boys rejoiced in their comfortable barracks while their comrades in other training camps shivered in their canvas shelters as the heavy rains of the winter of 1861-1862 flooded the state.

The daily routine at Benicia was the same as at other camps and for diversion the soldiers crossed the bay to San Francisco to attend the theater, where they paid as much as two dollars for a ticket. Often the paymaster failed to arrive on time or failed to pay when he did, as one Sierra boy related. "The paymaster was here and

33 *War. Reb.* Ser. 1, vol. L, pt. 1, p. 578-579, Special Order no. 152-153, series 1861.

Oakland *Directory,* Henry G. Langley, 1869-1872.

all hands expected to jingle a little coin in their pockets. For some reason the paymaster didn't *ante* and we shall have to wait four or five weeks longer before our itching palms are soothed by the application of Uncle Sam's coin."

However, the boys managed to get along without much money. Said the volunteer, "during the evenings we can have all the 'high old fun' we want. We have several violinists in our company who play for our stag dances. Our quarters sometimes present the appearance of a gigantic 'hurdy shop.' The boys play bean or tobacco poker, these articles being a basis of operations in lieu of cash, which, by the way, is very scarce in this locality." [34]

Not every day of the army life of the young soldier was filled with fun and constructive duties. There were days when dishonor and tragedy invaded the ranks. Days when a comrade was "drummed out" and his company was obliged to assist in the ceremony. The regiment was drawn up at dress parade and the prisoner marched out in front of the battalion where the charges, findings and sentence were read. The prisoner was then escorted by a "cordon of bristling steel beyond the borders of the camp to the tune of the *Rogue's March*." Army regulations required that the culprit be drummed out, but occasionally there was no drum on hand so the trumpet was used instead, and as reported by the volunteer, "The prisoner was blown out of the army." [35]

Drumming out a comrade was a solemn occasion but the execution of one was tragedy. It happened at Benicia Barracks in july 1863. A private of company E, fourth infantry, was found guilty of murder and

[34] *Sierra Democrat,* Downieville, oct. 10, 1863.
[35] *Tuolumne Courier,* Columbia, may 14, 1864.

desertion and sentenced to be shot. Ten companies of young soldiers were obliged to witness the execution while twelve of them took active part in the stark drama. The soldiers were formed on three sides of a square in two ranks. The prisoner was then placed near the open side and seated on his coffin. His eyes were blindfolded and twelve men drawn up ten paces in front of him; the command to fire was given and twelve musket shots broke the tense silence. One of the muskets contained a blank cartridge so that each man who fired could hope that he was not the one who took a fellow soldier's life. That proved to be but slight consolation as eleven bullets hit the mark.[36]

Hope and disappointment alternated at Benicia. Rumors that the boys were soon to witness the mysteries of the new art of photography infiltrated the barracks. It was reported that the government had employed a "landscape artist" to take photographs of the permanent posts on the Pacific coast. The hopes of the boys were fulfilled one may morning in 1864 when they were ordered out for dress parade and learned that they were to be included in the photograph of the barracks. The photographer selected his point of observation on a neighboring hill and took but one picture, as the cost was exorbitant—reported by the soldiers to be one hundred dollars each.

The boys waited eagerly, hoping to buy a print, but they were bitterly disappointed. To save expense Captain William A. Winder, in command at Alcatraz, had given Bradley & Rulofsen, photographers of San Francisco, permission to sell those photographs, which would be of no particular use in the hands of an enemy. The proofs had been submitted to Colonel René E.

36 *Sierra Democrat,* Downieville, july 25, 1863.

DeRussy, U.S. engineer, and he had agreed there could be no harm in selling some of them to recompense the photographers for their great expense.

The War department objected and immediately telegraphed orders to suppress the publication and sale of the photographs, especially those of Alcatraz. When General John S. Mason called on Bradley & Rulofsen he learned that thirty different views had been taken of Alcatraz, including every road and battery on the island. The photographers held General George Wright's own order for the work, the contract price being four hundred dollars. They claimed that the work had cost them fifteen hundred dollars.[37]

To accommodate the increasing thousands of soldiers in training, it became necessary to establish more camps in the neighborhood of San Francisco. Hunter's Point was chosen as a suitable site and the post established there was duly named Camp Lyon. At Camp Sumner near the Presidio, four companies of the second regiment of infantry received a month's training before being sent to Washington and Oregon to serve in the campaign against the Indians.

The training period of all the recruits was brief, and many of them were ordered to southern California to prepare for the march to Arizona and New Mexico to drive back the Confederate forces. They made the trip on the old wooden steamers "Oregon", "Senator", "Pacific" and the U.S.S. "Shubrick" and "Active". If the weather was stormy, it often took as long as fifty hours to make the voyage. The first contingent, which consisted of seven companies of the first infantry, arrived at San Pedro, september 18, 1861.

The following day they marched to Don Augustin

---

[37] *Tuolumne Courier,* Columbia, may 14, 1864.

Machado's Rancho Ballona, where a site on a high bench bordering Ballona creek had been selected for a training camp. The camp was named in honor of Milton Slocum Latham, the man who had been governor of California for less than a week. He was inaugurated january 9, 1860 and two days later elected United States senator to fill the vacancy caused by the death of Senator David C. Broderick, who was killed in a duel by David S. Terry, chief justice of the supreme court of California.

Over twelve hundred California boys were in training at Camp Latham by october 6. The camp was first under the command of Colonel Joseph R. West who was succeeded by Colonel George Washington Bowie. The volunteer described Bowie as a "fine looking, portly gentleman with gray hair and a fancy little mustache as gray as his hair. He was gentlemanly in his manner and stepped off as light as a youth of twenty." [38]

Camp Latham served as a training camp for just a year, when the troops and property were ordered to Drum Barracks at New San Pedro (Wilmington).[39] For many years the only reminder of Camp Latham was the ruins of a brick oven where bread was baked for the volunteers. Yet for a year this had been a busy spot. Here the cavalry drilled on foot and on horseback and the infantry improved their aim with their Colt revolvers and Sharp carbines. Here too, their friends came to watch them during dress parade and enjoy their band concerts and "promenade" at Willow grove across Ballona creek. The place where old Camp Latham stood is near the moving picture studios at

38 *Sierra Democrat*, Downieville, apr. 5, 1862.
39 *War. Reb.* Ser. I, vol. L, pt. II, p. 116-117.

Culver City. There the thrilling exploits of the pioneers are re-enacted and filmed. Yet in spite of the valuable and hazardous service rendered by the California volunteers, they have not received just recognition by the producers of historical pictures of the West.

For a short time the volunteers were stationed at Camp Fitzgerald, Los Angeles, but the location presented too many disadvantages for a permanent camp and supply base. The camp (Fitzgerald) was moved to three different sites, each in turn being abandoned on account of the lack of water and pasture for the horses. All supplies were then shipped by boat from San Francisco and a location on the water front was urgently needed. In those pre-railroad days Los Angeles was too far from the port.[40]

Soon after General Carleton was placed in command of the district of southern California, october 14, 1861, he decided to move the supply depot to New San Pedro (Wilmington). No doubt the ambitious and enterprising young merchant, Phineas Banning, influenced his decision. The first site chosen for a camp was a half mile from New San Pedro on a low sandy plain where the old and leaky tents gave little protection from the wind, sand or rain.

A better location was selected on higher ground about a mile from the new town and on january 13, 1862, the site was named Camp Drum in honor of Richard Coulter Drum, adjutant general of the department of the Pacific. Phineas Banning and Benjamin D. Wilson proved to be the "dollar a year men" of the 1860's but not according to the modern interpretation of that "dollar." For the consideration of one dollar, Phineas Banning and Benjamin D. Wilson deeded to

---

[40] *Ibid.,* pt. i, p. 521, 479, 582, 476.

the United States three parcels of land where all necessary buildings could be erected for the new depot and training camp.[41]

For that dollar Banning obtained an enviable business advantage over his competitors. Banning's wagon trains hauled army supplies for the California column; Banning's boats sailed to the Gulf of California with cargoes for Fort Yuma, and with soldiers for Arizona and New Mexico. The town grew and prospered. A volunteer quite aptly described New San Pedro (Wilmington) in 1862. "The town consists of Banning's residence, blacksmith shop, soap and tallow factory, coal and lumber yard, jerked beef jerkery, and a steam 'crawfish' that totes soldiers, baggage and mules five miles from the boats to his wharf when the tide is up. When the tide is out, he waits for the moon to work on the water. . . The soldier sits in his Sibley a mile away in an alfalfa field where the wild geese pasture." [42]

The total cost of the government buildings erected at Drum Barracks, Wilmington (*Plate* 2), has been estimated at a million dollars. The lumber was shipped around the Horn and since the average wage of California carpenters was then from four to five dollars a day, a million dollars was probably the correct figure in consideration of the size and number of buildings. The soldiers' quarters included five buildings, thirty by eighty feet. Each building had a veranda in front and a large wing in the rear for kitchen and mess hall. The hospital was two-story, eighty by forty feet, with two wings, thirty by fifteen feet. The officers' quarters, a two-story sixteen room house, was located on the west side of the camp grounds. In addition to these buildings

41 *Ibid.*, p. 682, 805. Pl. II, p. 136, 156, 178.
42 *Semi-Weekly Southern News*, Los Angeles, apr. 18, 1862.

there were others for the commissary, quartermaster, and granary, each 80 by 40 feet, a hay room, 270 by 70 feet; a shed, 385 by 15 feet; two corrals, 194 by 96 feet; and besides there was the magazine, blacksmith shop, wheelwright, storeroom, and guard house all enclosed by a picket fence 1,638 by 1,480 feet.[43]

Lack of water for the camp was a handicap for a time but a remedy was provided by assembly bill no. 442, approved april 1, 1864. This act authorized Phineas Banning to construct a water course from the San Gabriel river to Camp Drum and to secure a right of way through the Rancho de San Pedro. He was also permitted to construct a dam on the river high enough to divert the water. The dam site was described as being at a point where a due east line, drawn three miles north of the houses of Dominguez, would intersect the river. By april 15 two hundred soldiers were engaged on the project. They worked without extra pay but preferred it to camp routine. Banning furnished one hundred thousand feet of lumber for fluming the ditch where it was necessary on the seven mile course from the river. (San Gabriel river then joined the Los Angeles and flowed as one to the harbor. The stream bore the name of San Gabriel at the lower end of its course and the Los Angeles river was represented on the old maps as a branch of the San Gabriel until the latter changed its course and flowed as a separate river to the sea.)

Drum Barracks has been graphically described by Captain E. C. Ledyard of company A, first cavalry, California volunteers. He said, "We were astonished to find Drum Barracks one of the finest we had ever seen. Some of the men in our company who had seen

---

[43] Report of Surgeon W. F. Edgar, U.S. Army, march, 1872.

service in the East said that they had never seen anything like it. The camp is bountifully supplied with
clear, cool water for camp purposes and a large surplus
for irrigating the gardens and orchards. It runs in small
ditches in front of all our quarters and through and
around the parade grounds." [44]

Regardless of the fine appearance of their camp, the
volunteers were always glad to get a furlough so that
they could visit Los Angeles. They traveled by stage
and described the country between San Pedro and Los
Angeles as a prairie where hundreds of horses and
thousands of Spanish cattle grazed. They said, "Los
Angeles looks like the ruins of a fine city. The three
and four-story brick buildings in the heart of the city
and the one-story adobes in the outskirts present a queer
contrast. Some of the adobes are so old that only one
room remains of what was once large buildings." [45] The
volunteers' furlough was for only forty-eight hours so
they were soon back at camp training for their grueling
service on the desert. Captain Antonio Maria de la
Guerra and his company C, native California cavalry,
were also in training at that time and were greatly
admired by the rest of the volunteers.

Everything was not always pleasant and the volunteers had days of troubles and "growls." There were
meat troubles—not in the quantity but in the quality
as is intimated in the following epitaph written at
Drum Barracks. "Here lies the body of the poor old
ox named Spot who faithfully served his master while
crossing the plains. Had he lived until the coming
fourth-of-july he would have been ninety-nine years,

[44] Marysville *Appeal,* Marysville, april 9, 1865.
[45] *Sierra Democrat,* Downieville, mar. 15, 1862.

two months and four days. This monument is erected to his memory by the soldiers of the garrison.

> Ye Gods, protect his soul
> While time its cycle roll;
> While we inter this ghostly beef
> And thus relieve our jaws and teeth.

> Farewell, farewell, old ox,
> Your end was orthodox.
> Your ghost, pray never come
> To haunt us braves in good Camp Drum.[46]

There is nothing in the records to show that the soldiers were reprimanded for stealing some of the beef and burying it but soon after the incident the *Los Angeles Star* carried an advertisement for *fresh* beef, *good* and *wholesome,* for the troops at Camp Drum.

Many important events were crowded into the short space of time that the California volunteers occupied Camp Drum. The old United States army camp was the terminal of the telegraph line and the first message was sent november 11, 1862. "Another telegraphic line is completed to the Pacific coast. The port of New San Pedro is linked into the endless electric chain." But New San Pedro retained its name for but a few years as it was changed to Wilmington by legislative act in 1863. Likewise Camp Drum was re-named Drum Barracks.

Only the building once used for officers' quarters now remains to mark the site where the thousands of California volunteers trained. It stands at 1053 Carey avenue, Wilmington, and is owned by Mrs. Thomas F. Keaveny, who carefully preserved the few remaining

---

[46] *Alta California,* San Francisco, apr. 10, 1863.

relics. A solid brass knocker decorated with the United
States coat of arms is still attached to one of the doors;
two andirons with their spread eagles have served one
of the fireplaces for more than 85 years; an old cannon
ball lies inert on the hearth; a two-spouted kettle torch
hangs on one of the porches but the old oaken bucket
has slumped into the ivy-covered well in the patio in
the rear.

The old building was substantially built; each room
was 18 by 20 feet with 14-foot ceilings; there are four
fireplaces and mahogany balustrades on two long stair-
ways. The building has been designated by the Native
Daughters of the Golden West as State Historical
shrine no. 169 but is now used as an apartment house
and not open to the public.

Oil derricks now stand as sentinels on the old parade
grounds usurping the guard duty of the volunteers of
the '60's. The rhythmic lift of their walking beams now
mark time in lieu of the drum corps that accompanied
the young recruits so many years ago. Probably every
man, from private to general, who served at the old
army post has long ago answered the last "taps."

For ten years after the war most of the buildings
stood intact although used infrequently. The donors of
the site decided that they would like to repossess the
property but there was no provision in the conveyance
that required the government to return the real estate
that had grown more valuable during the decade. Three
deeds were of record, bearing the dates october 3, 1863,
february 12, 1864, and february 28, 1865.

Phineas Banning went to Washington as a one-man
lobby to engineer a bill through congress so that the
property could be returned to him and Benjamin D.
Wilson. The bill was introduced in january 1873, and

the senate referred it to the Military committee. In Banning's correspondence with Wilson he naively remarked, "The members of that committee favored passing the bill just as it was introduced which would give us (Banning and Wilson) all the buildings but they feared it would be impossible to pass it. Consequently they propose to give us the land and instruct the secretary of war to sell the buildings." The bill as amended passed and was approved february 25, 1873. The buildings were sold at public auction july 31, and netted the government $6,357.00. Banning and Wilson bought most of the buildings. Wilson bought the hospital building for $600.00 and later donated it to the Methodist Episcopal South college and to acknowledge appreciation of the gift the college was renamed Wilson college.

Banning bought the officers' quarters for $1,025.00, the depot for $1,000.00, a storehouse for $60.00, and the fencing, presumably the picket fence, 6,220 feet for $76.00. He paid $60.00 for the blacksmith shop and $75.00 for the wheelwright shop. Yet two cavalry corrals were sold to B. H. Downing for $510.00.[47]

To further facilitate the movement of troops and supplies, General George Wright ordered a camp and supply base established at Warner's ranch. Major Edwin A. Rigg, who was instructed to select the site, left camp at New San Pedro, with four companies of the first infantry on october 10, 1861, and arrived at Warner's ranch within a week. The first camp site

[47] Benjamin D. Wilson, MS, (Huntington library).

Report Secretary of War, Vol. V, pt. I, p. 116, 181, (1873-1874).

Report of sale of buildings, Los Angeles *Star,* aug. 2, 1873.

Record of deeds, Los Angeles county records, book 6 of deeds, p. 286, 387; book 7, p. 112. Book of maps, p. 66-67.

Wilson was grandfather of the late General Geo. Patton, Jr.

chosen was about a mile from the old Warner adobe house and named in honor of General Wright.

The location proved to be ill chosen when the winter storms swept across San Jose valley. A high wind and snow storm caused considerable damage to the new military camp. The officers' tents, the kitchen, and the ammunition tents were blown down. The hospital tent was saved by lashing and tying it securely with heavy ropes. Major Rigg managed to protect the sick volunteers from the storm and their buddies relinquished their own blankets to save the invalids. Surgeon James M. McNulty refused to recommend the site so a request was forwarded to General Wright to obtain permission to move the camp either to Temecula where there was good grazing for the cavalry or to Oak Grove near the Overland Stage station where the large adobe building could be used for officers' quarters and hospital. Permission was readily granted and Oak Grove was finally selected for the camp and supply depot.

Tents were pitched in the shade of the aged oaks at the edge of the meadow; quartermaster and commissary supplies stored away; and then the soldiers looked around for a flagpole. They felled a sixty-foot pine, snaked it down from the mountain, and in a short time "The stars and stripes were waving over their camp in the hills." [48]

Camp Wright was an important post as nearly all the California troops, destined for service in Arizona and New Mexico, stopped here before starting across the desert. Here too, large herds of beef for the army grazed overnight in the meadow. It was also a strategic point as all the important trails over the mountains

[48] *War. Reb.* Ser. I, vol. L, pt. I, p. 706-707, 888-889.
San Jose *Mercury,* feb. 20, 1862.

were but a short distance away and could be easily blockaded if any trouble-makers tried to pass.

The first Californians to occupy Camp Wright were companies D, E, F and H of the first regiment of infantry, commanded by Major Edwin A. Rigg. While company D was en route from New San Pedro to their mountain camp, they picked up a stray cat which they christened Tom. Not to be outdone in the "pet show," another company acquired a crow as a mascot. The two pets became such good friends and their antics caused so much attention during dress parade that Major Rigg was obliged to order Tom and the crow confined to quarters so that the raw recruits could concentrate on their orders. The life of Tom was brief for on the way across the desert he was crushed beneath the wheels of one of the freight wagons. He was buried with military honors and the company marched on to Fort Yuma.[49]

When their camp fires flickered in the desert night they sang the song their comrade wrote while stationed at Camp Wright, october 1861.

From the valleys and the mines,
From the redwoods and the pines,
From the cities we can't be naming—
The boys have left their all
At their country's call,
And rallied for the happy land of Canaan.

Chorus: Oh, oh, oh, oh.

Away, away, down below,
Where they say there's no snow,
The Secesh all have been training.
But the California boys
Will take away their toys,
And send them to the happy land of Canaan.

[49] Captain Hugh A. Gorley MS, (Bancroft library).

Chorus: Oh, oh, oh, oh.

Now we'll soon go down
And take their little town
Across the Colorado without straining.
Major Rigg has gone before,
He's knocking at their door,
To take them to the happy land of Canaan.

Chorus: Oh, oh, oh, oh.

Our Union we prize
Far above the starry skies,
Our Union that's now in danger,
And we'll rally round our flag
While there yet remains a rag
To follow to the happy land of Canaan.[50]

DIXIE
(California volunteers' version)

The bugles are now merrily sounding reveille
   Away, away, away, away.
We've got our marching orders, away, away,
   For Dixie's sunny borders.
   So boys we march today
Away, away, away down south in Dixie.
Away, away, away down south in Dixie.[51]

---

[50] San Jose *Mercury*, feb. 6, 1862.
Song written by George W. Bond, Co. D, first infantry.
[51] *Semi-Weekly News*, Los Angeles, june 6, 1862.

The Confederates Invade the Southwest

July 1861 was a fateful month for the Southwest as well as for California. The Federal troops in the interior of Arizona were transferred to the Rio Grande to re-enforce the garrisons at Fort Fillmore and Fort Craig. From Fort Stanton, New Mexico, the officers and men were ordered to Albuquerque. Army supplies were burned to prevent them from falling into the hands of the Confederate forces which at that time were moving up the Rio Grande under the command of Colonel John R. Baylor, mounted rifles, Confederate States of America.[52]

On july 24, 1861, Baylor's troops were reported just twelve miles from Fort Fillmore and on that same day a pony was racing across the hot plains from Fort Kearny with President Lincoln's call for California volunteers.[53]

The Confederate States government planned the conquest of Arizona and New Mexico and even California and her gold. Major Henry H. Sibley was commissioned brigadier general of the Confederate army and sent to Texas to organize an expedition to take possession of these territories.[54]

But before Sibley arrived in Arizona with his troops, Lieutenant Colonel John R. Baylor started his campaign. Early in july he occupied Fort Bliss and soon

[52] *War. Reb.* Ser. I, vol. IV, p. 3, 22, 49, 59, 62-63.
[53] *Ibid.*, p. 4, 13-14.
Ibid., vol. L, pt. I, p. 543.
[54] *Ibid.*, vol. IV, p. 93, 141.

afterward took possession of Mesilla. At this time Fort Fillmore was occupied by Major Issac Lynde in command of seven companies of the seventh U.S. infantry. Major Lynde gave orders for the evacuation of the fort and marched his troops toward Fort Stanton. Baylor started in pursuit and overtook the Federal troops at San Augustin's Springs. Although Lynde's command outnumbered the Confederates, he surrendered his entire force.[55]

It was agreed that the enlisted men be disarmed and given the liberty of the post at Fort Bliss until instructions for their disposition were received from the department headquarters of Texas. After receiving parole, the Federal officers were permitted to select any route they preferred in leaving for any part of the United States. Prisoners of war were usually released during this struggle for the Southwest, as it cost too much to feed them on this frontier.

Federal drafts totaling $9,500 were captured by Baylor at Fort Fillmore and the Confederacy succeeded in cashing $4,500 drawn on the assistant United States treasurer at New York.[56]

Baylor issued a proclamation establishing the territory of Arizona, declared himself governor, and took possession in the name of the Confederate States of America. Mesilla was selected as the seat of his government, which as organized by him, consisted of but two departments, the executive and judicial. He appointed most of the officers and the executive authority was vested in the army which he commanded. (A dictatorship of the 1860's.) [57]

[55] *Ibid.*, p. 14.
Ibid., p. 16-20.
[56] *Ibid.*, p. 157-158.
[57] *Ibid.*, p. 20-21.

While Colonel Baylor was establishing his government in the Mesilla valley, a second call for additional regiments of California volunteers came from President Lincoln (august 14, 1861). Within a month's time seven companies of California volunteers had arrived at San Pedro to prepare for their march to the Rio Grande.[58]

The officers of the Confederate army realized that the conquest of the Southwest depended upon having sufficient materiel to maintain an army on the desert so far removed from the base of supplies. So while Colonel Baylor awaited the arrival of Brigadier General Sibley, he employed his time in securing supplies and all possible information about the Federal troops under command of General Canby on the upper Rio Grande. Baylor's spies reported that General Canby was at Fort Craig with 2,500 men and planned to move down the river and drive the Confederate army from Mesilla.[59]

Since General Sibley had not yet arrived from Texas with re-enforcements, Baylor decided to retreat. He advised his followers to be calm and collected. He appealed to Judge Simeon Hart, the miller, to send a pony to Chihuahua to ascertain whether or not troops were coming from California by the way of Mexico. He begged Hart to obtain all possible transportation to move the supplies at Fort Bliss to Fort Quitman or even as far south as Fort Davis.[60]

Colonel Baylor was not too happy. Smallpox had broken out in his camp and he had lost several men. General Sibley had expected to join him early in

[58] *Ibid.,* vol. L, pt. I, p. 569.
Ibid., p. 625. Cos. A, B, C, E, G, H, 1st Inf., c. v.
[59] *Ibid.,* vol. IV, p. 128.
[60] *Ibid.,* p. 129.

september but lack of funds and scarcity of supplies disrupted his plans.

Nevertheless, General Sibley was not idle. He negotiated with Simeon Hart for supplies for his own brigade. Hart reported that he had from forty thousand to fifty thousand pounds of flour in storage in a place of safety in El Paso, Mexico, and from $40,000 to $50,000 to pay for the purchase of more flour, beans, salt, beef, corn and soap.[61]

When the government first built Forts Thorn, Fillmore, Bliss, Quitman and Davis, Simeon Hart secured the contract to supply the troops with flour and built a mill on the north bank of the Rio Grande opposite El Paso, Mexico. He purchased wheat from the Mexicans at such a low price that he was able to accumulate a fortune. "He ground the money from good natured Uncle Sam while he ground the wheat—bolting the 'eagles' as fast as he bolted the flour."

By november 8, 1861, General Sibley was able to report from his headquarters at San Antonio that Colonel James Reily's regiment was already en route and had marched 250 miles toward the Arizona border. The third regiment, commanded by Colonel Steele was making ready to start soon.[62]

Undoubtedly the approach of re-enforcements from San Antonio encouraged the worried colonel at Fort Bliss as he feared the arrival of General Canby from the north and the Californians from Fort Yuma. He was correctly informed about the movement of the troops from California for by the time the Confederate forces left San Antonio, the California volunteers were in their barracks at Fort Yuma.[63]

[61] *Ibid.*, p. 134 135.
[62] *Ibid.*, p. 132, 151.
[63] *Ibid.*, vol. L, pt. I, p. 137, 710-714.

General Sibley assumed command of all the Confederate forces on the Rio Grande at and above Fort Quitman on december 14, 1861. A few days before Christmas he issued his proclamation to the people of New Mexico but it was not entirely a message of "Peace and good will to men." He said,

An army under my command enters New Mexico to take possession of it in the name of the Confederate States. . . Upon the peaceful people of New Mexico, the Confederate States wage no war. To them, we come as friends to re-establish a government, to liberate them from the yoke of a military despotism erected by usurpers upon the ruins of the former free institutions of the United States; to relieve them from the iniquitous taxes; and to insure and to revere their religion and to restore their civil and political liberties. . .

The army under my command is ample to seize and to maintain possession of New Mexico against any force that the enemy now has or is able to place within its limits. It is my purpose to accomplish this objective without injury to the peaceful people of the country. Follow quietly your peaceful avocations and from my forces you have nothing to fear. Your persons, your families, and your property shall be safe and secure. . .

Sibley warned those who co-operated with the Union forces that they would be treated as enemies and share the same fate. He appealed to his former comrades in arms, still serving in the Union army, to drop their arms, renounce the service, and array themselves under the colors of justice and freedom, the stars and bars of the Confederacy. He furthermore promised,

By virtue of the powers vested in me by the president and government of the Confederate States, I abrogate and abolish the law of the United States levying taxes upon the people of New Mexico.[64]

After issuing his proclamation, General Sibley turned his attention to Mexico. He ordered Colonel

[64] *Ibid.*, vol. IV, p. 89-90, 157-158.

James Reily, fourth regiment, Texas mounted volunteers, to proceed to the capitals of Sonora and Chihuahua to enlist the aid of those two governments in the cause of the Confederacy.[65]

Reily soon departed for Hermosillo, Sonora, where he expected to meet Governor Don Ignacio Pesqueira and convince him that he should deny the use of the port of Guaymas to the Federal government and forbid the transport of troops across Sonora.[66]

Through the vigilance of R. L. Robinson, United States consul at Mazatlan, and Farrelly Alden, vice consul, both Sibley's and Reily's letters were intercepted and copies forwarded to San Francisco to General George Wright. Copies were sent to Flag Officer Charles E. Bell of the Pacific Squadron who ordered the U.S.S. "St. Marys" to Guaymas.[67]

W. G. Moody, a news correspondent for the *San Francisco Bulletin*, is credited with the scoop. He heard about Reily's mission to Sonora and at once began to ferret out information for his newspaper. He learned that the Confederate officers' correspondence was being translated by Manuel Escalante, so called on him and requested copies, which were readily promised him by the translator.

When Escalante left his office to take his Spanish copies to the governor, Moody and his friend, F. H. Waterman, quickly made copies of the originals and then left. Later they returned to find that Escalante had taken the original correspondence away with him not knowing that copies had already been made by the news correspondent.

---

[65] *Ibid.*, p. 167. (vol. L, pt. I, p. 766-768.)

[66] *Ibid.*, vol. L, pt. I, p. 1032-1033.

[67] *Ibid.*, p. 988-990, 1013.

Ibid., p. 1050-1051.

When Governor Pesqueira discovered that his official correspondence was about to be published, he ordered Escalante to prevent it if possible. Escalante appealed to Moody saying, "I have promised the governor that you would not send the copies until the next steamer. I am very 'tight in the moment' I write the present." He probably meant that at the present moment, he was in a tight spot.[68]

When General Wright received the copies of the letters procured by the resourceful news correspondent, W. G. Moody, he addressed a communication to Governor Don Ignacio Pesqueira and diplomatically expressed his views on the Mexican situation. He said,

By the last steamer from the Gulf of California, I received a copy of a communication addressed to your excellency under date of december 16, 1861, by H. H. Sibley in command of a body of insurgents in New Mexico. Although I did not receive a copy of your excellency's reply, yet I was much gratified to learn that you had declined to enter into any arrangement proposed by him. . .

Considering the friendly relations existing between the government of the United States and that of the Republic of Mexico . . . any other decision . . . would have been deeply regretted. . . I beg your excellency to rest assured that under no circumstances will the government of the United States permit the rebel hordes to take refuge in Sonora. I have an army of ten thousand men ready to pass the frontier and protect your government and your people.[69]

Soon after New Year's day, General H. H. Sibley and his brigade started for old Fort Thorn; from here he continued up the Rio Grande to within seven miles of Fort Craig. On february 16, a reconnaissance in force reached a point just a mile from the fort but three days later fell back from this advanced position and crossed to the east bank of the river.

[68] Ibid., p. 990.
[69] Ibid., p. 1047-1048.

Sibley then maneuvered for a better position. The terrain was traversed by ridges of drifting sand broken in places by protruding beds of lava that paralleled the general direction of the river valley. These ravines offered shelter from attack. So the Confederate commander selected one of the deepest ravines through which he could move his men with safety past Fort Craig.

A few miles above the fort, the Mesa del Contadero rises to a height of about three hundred feet. At both ends of the mesa there were favorable camp sites where the river was accessible. Sibley chose Valverde about six miles north of Fort Craig.

At last General Canby found his adversary in a vulnerable position. He threw his main force across the east bank but postponed engaging Sibley's brigade as it was then too late in the evening. However, in order to keep the Confederate troops in position, a demonstration was ordered on their right flank. The strategy proved to be successful and morning found them in their same position.

The battle began early in the morning february 21, 1862, and continued throughout the day. It was conceded a victory for Sibley's brigade and the Confederate cause. A two day truce was declared so that both armies could remove their wounded and bury their dead. Thus 101 young soldiers, 65 wearing the Blue, and 36 the Gray, were laid to rest by the Rio Grande where it begins to curve westward as though to shun the Jornada del Muerto, the Journey of Death. It was indeed a Journey of Death for the gallant hundred.

As the last clear saddening note of taps lingered, echoed and re-echoed on the silent battlefield, the two armies marched away, each with its wounded. The 160

Federal wounded were moved to Fort Craig. The Confederate army carried about 150 wounded up the Rio Grande to Socorro where all possible care was given them.

It was february 22 on the Rio Grande but there was no celebration of Washington's birthday. At Pacific headquarters no word of the losses at Valverde was received that day. The mail steamer was preparing to sail and General Wright prepared another one of his frequent reports to the War department. "In this state we have peace but I cannot say that we are very quiet. . . ." A telegram announcing the Union victories of the army and navy had reached San Francisco and "universal rejoicing" was greatly in evidence. At this opportune moment, the general ordered the "army of the Pacific" to cease all labor and a salute of 130 guns fired from Alcatraz to celebrate the 130th anniversary of Washington's birth.

As late as march 10 there was still no news from the battlefield on the Rio Grande. General Wright again reported,

> . . . Nothing special has transpired on this coast. . . My information from New Mexico is meager. The strength of Sibley's force of rebels on the Rio Grande, as rumored forth in the papers, I regard as fabulous. With Canby in his front and Carleton in his flank, I cannot doubt the results. . .[70]

General Sibley continued his successful march to Albuquerque which had been abandoned by the Union troops. Before leaving, Captain Herbert M. Enos, assistant quartermaster, in obedience to the command of General Canby, ordered the ammunition wagons taken to Santa Fe and the rest of the supplies burned.

---

[70] *Ibid.*, vol. IX, p. 487-493, 502-503.
Ibid., vol. L, pt. I, p. 883, 917.

Among the buildings destroyed were twelve houses and seven corrals belonging to Colonel James H. Carleton, later brigadier general of volunteers. The buildings had been rented to the Federal government for military purposes and were used as shops, stables, storehouses and hospital.[71]

Santa Fe surrendered to Sibley with but little resistance. The Confederate commander had now grown confident over his victories which extended the length of the Rio Grande from the Texas border to Santa Fe. On his march he had acquired sufficient materiel to supply his army for three months.[72]

Colonel Baylor at Mesilla was equally confident and issued an extra-ordinary command to Captain Thomas Helm of the Arizona guards soon after the capture of Santa Fe: "The congress of the Confederate States passed a law declaring extermination to all hostile Indians. You will, therefore, use all means to persuade the Apaches or any other tribe to come in for the purpose of making peace and when you get them together, kill all the grown Indians and take the children prisoners and sell them to defray the expense of killing the Indians. Say nothing about your orders until the time comes and be cautious how you let the Mexicans know it." [73]

But these Confederate commanders did not know that they had won their last major victory in the Southwest.

---

[71] 37 Cong. 3 Sess. vol. I, Sen. Report no. 106 (feb. 1863) (1151)
42 Cong. 3 Sess. vol. I, Sen. Report no. 441 (feb. 1873) (1548)
[72] *War. Reb.* Ser. I, vol. IX, p. 506-512.
[73] *Ibid.,* vol. L, pt. I, p. 942.

The West Ousts the Invaders

General Sibley was unaware of the strength of the forces that would so soon oppose his conquest of New Mexico. He did not know that on the day following his victory at Valverde, a rugged army of Fighting Pike Peakers commanded by a fighting parson was even then on the march from Denver.

Sibley was about to be subjected to a pincer movement. The California column was ready to march from the west to re-enforce General Canby on the Rio Grande while the Colorado volunteers, together with detachments from the first and third United States cavalry, were marching down from the north and were approaching Fort Union.

General E. R. S. Canby had realized his urgent need of re-enforcements ever since he had assumed command of the department of New Mexico on june 11, 1861. Since the California column had not yet begun its march for the Rio Grande, General Canby sent a request for troops to Governor William Gilpin of Colorado. Two companies of Colorado volunteers had already been organized and were officered by Colonel J. P. Slough and Captain Samuel F. Tappan.

Living at Cherry Creek at this time was Parson J. M. Chivington who traveled from mine to mine preaching to all who would give him audience. He became so popular that a saloon owner offered his barroom for a meeting place. The parson covered the bar and gambling devices with awning and arranged seats for his congregation. He said that he preached the best he could and had reason to believe that it was a profitable season of worship.

When the war broke out a recruit was shot because he refused to drink in a saloon owned by a Southern sympathizer. Parson Chivington preached the funeral sermon with so much patriotic fervor that Governor William Gilpin offered him a commission as chaplain in the Colorado regiment. To this offer the parson replied, "If I go into the army at all, I must have a fighting commission. . . Chaplains are not supposed to fight." The governor retorted, "By Jove, I will make you a major and a chaplain both."

Major Chivington spent his sundays preaching and the rest of the week recruiting. He encountered many difficulties as he relates:

We did not have any money nor did we have the sanction of the War office. We did not have the prestige of a governor elected by the people, but one appointed by the president. (Colorado was then a territory.)

But, we did have one thing that was of great benefit in that time of trial—a man not afraid of responsibility. If any one doubts this, let him look up one of those Gilpin drafts drawn at sight on the secretary of the United States treasury by Governor Gilpin for half a million or more. These drafts were sold for gold dust and with them supplies were purchased.[74]

The Colorado volunteers left Denver february 22, 1862, the day following General Canby's defeat at Valverde. Two companies from Fort Lyon joined them when they crossed the Raton mountains. While camped on Rio Vermejo, a messenger from Fort Union arrived and urged them to hurry as the Conferedate army was then at Santa Fe and on its way to Fort Union.

---

[74] Pac. MS. Colonel J. M. Chivington. (Bancroft library).

The fighting parson lined up his men and asked them to step two paces to the front to signify their willingness to make a forced march. Every man stepped forward. They marched 64 miles on foot in 24 hours and the following day, march 11, 1862, they reached Fort Union, a 16 days' march from Denver through winter snows and rains. This was also the day following Sibley's arrival at Santa Fe.

After a ten day stop at Fort Union, Colonel John P. Slough ordered his command to march toward Santa Fe. He planned to arrive at night and spike the enemy's guns. The Colorado volunteers followed the old Santa Fe trail and in three days reached Bernal springs.[75]

The following day Colonel Slough ordered Major Chivington with two hundred cavalry and 180 infantry to advance toward Santa Fe. Fighting Parson Chivington reports his encounter with his adversary:

We marched from Bernal springs at three o'clock in the morning of march 25 (1862) intending to surprise the enemy. After a march of about thirty miles, we learned that we were in the vicinity of the enemy pickets. We halted at midnight and at two in the morning (march 26) I sent out Lieutenant Nelson with twenty men to surprise the pickets. They did and captured them.

The detachment again moved forward and just as we entered the canyon we discovered the advance guard of the foe and captured two lieutenants. In a few minutes the enemy planted their battery and began to throw grape and shell among us. In double-quick, companies A and E were deployed as skirmishers on the mountain side to the left and company D to the right side.

Soon our men on the mountain side made it too hot for the enemy gunners and they fell back about one and a half miles and took a more advantageous position. They completely covered the mountain sides with their skirmishers to support their guns in the canyon below them.

We assembled our skirmishers in the canyon and again deployed company D on the right and companies A and E on the left. We dis-

---

[75] *War. Reb.* Ser. I, vol. IX, pt. I, p. 534-535.

mounted all cavalry. Since we did not know how near the enemy's re-enforcements might be, and not having any cannon of our own to oppose theirs, we hastened to gather up our dead and wounded, together with several of the enemy's, and fell back to Pigeon's ranch to camp for the night. In this engagement five of our men were killed and fourteen wounded. The Confederate loss was 32 killed, 43 wounded and 71 prisoners.[76]

Two days later Colonel Slough sent Major Chivington with about 430 picked men to Johnson's ranch. With the remainder of his force, about 770 men, Colonel Slough entered Apache canyon. He engaged the enemy in a fierce battle which continued from ten o'clock in the morning until four in the afternoon. From his command of Fighting Pike Peakers, his loss totaled a hundred. Of these, twenty were killed, fifty wounded and thirty reported missing. The Confederates lost almost twice that many. From forty to sixty were killed, over a hundred wounded, and twenty-five taken prisoners. In addition, three pieces of their artillery were damaged and sixty wagons destroyed.[77]

The fighting parson was equally victorious. He reported to General Canby,

We left Camp Lewis near Pecos church at half-past eight in the morning, march 28, 1862. An hour later we left the main road and took the trail leading to Galisteo. We followed this trail for about eight miles then without a road we traveled about another eight miles. At half-past one in the afternoon we reached an eminence overlooking Johnson's Ranch.

After reconnoitering the position, it was ascertained that there were corraled in the canyon, eighty wagons and one field piece in charge of about 200 men. The wagons were heavily loaded with ammunition, clothing, subsistence and forage. . .

We routed the enemy, burned all his wagons on the spot or else rendered them useless. During the engagement one of the wagons

---

[76] *Ibid.*, p. 677-680.
[77] *Ibid.*, p. 533.

containing ammunition exploded and wounded one of our men. We took seventeen prisoners, captured thirty horses and mules and returned to Camp Lewis at ten o'clock in the evening.[78]

The old adobe ranch house is still standing and the adobe corral, loopholed like a fort, is just east of a steep bluff. The United States flag floats above the heights where a marker has been placed to commemorate these battles. United States highway 85 leaves Apache canyon at Cañoncita where the detachment of Colonel Chivington's Union troops captured and destroyed Sibley's supply train.[79]

After the battle of Apache canyon, a 48-hour truce was declared to bury the dead and remove the wounded. Sibley and his Confederate troops retreated to Santa Fe and the Colorado volunteers joined General Canby's command and pursued the Southerners down the Rio Grande river.

Sibley's brigade was a two-day march ahead of the Union forces and by the end of the second night had reached Peralta. The Confederates followed down the west bank of the river while the Union troops occupied the east side; both armies were in full view of each other, the river alone intervening.

Sibley planned to reach Fort Craig ahead of the Union troops, but the latter were so close upon his heels that he (Sibley) decided to go around the fort. He abandoned his wagons and heavy artillery, and with seven days rations packed on mules, his entire force struck out after dark on the hazardous route through the hills. They succeeded in reaching Dona Ana safely and proceeded across the border to Fort Bliss.[80]

[78] *Ibid.*, p. 538.
[79] *Colorado Guide Book*—Federal Writers' Project.
[80] *War. Reb.* Ser. I, vol. IX, p. 506-512; Brig. Gen. H. H. Sibley's report battle of Valverde.

They were not able to move their sick or wounded so left them at Santa Fe, Albuquerque and Socorro. Mrs. Canby and the wives of other Union officers cared for these soldiers for several months, as it was not until the arrival of the column from California that the last patient and captured soldier was escorted to San Antonio.[81]

During the Confederate occupation of Albuquerque, several United States howitzers were captured by General Sibley. When he retreated, he buried them near the home of Major H. R. Whiting. Many years afterwards, they were unearthed and two of them have long been in the possession of the Grand Army of the Republic at Albuquerque. They occupied a prominent site in Robinson park until World War II when they were given to the salvage committee for scrap. However, they were not used and may again be returned to the park. The old Whiting home, a large two-story adobe, gabled roof, still stands on the southwest corner of Rio Grande boulevard, one block south of Perea road.[82]

Another reminder of the Confederate invasion stands in the center of the plaza at Santa Fe. Here the people of New Mexico, through their legislatures of 1866-1868, erected a monument in honor of the soldiers who died in the battles of Cañon del Apache, Pigeon's Rancho (La Glorieta), Peralta, and in the various battles with the Indians.

The monument is of sandstone with the inscriptions carved in a marble background on all four sides of the shaft. The ceremony for the laying of the cornerstone was under the directions of the Masons of Santa Fe. The committee in charge was headed by Colonel John

81 *Ibid.*, p. 583.
82 Information supplied through courtesy of Lillian Vance, Albuquerque public library, Albuquerque.

P. Slough who commanded the Colorado volunteers
during the final battles.[83]

[83] Santa Fe *Weekly Gazette*, Santa Fe, oct. 5, 12, 1867. (Huntington library).
Inscriptions on monument:
1. "To the heroes of the Federal army who fell at the battle of Valverde
   fought with the rebels february 21, 1862."
2. "Erected by the people of New Mexico through their legislatures of
   1866-1867-1868. May the Union be perpetual."
3. "To the heroes of the Federal army who fell at the battles of Cañon del
   Apache and Pigeon's Rancho (La Glorieta), fought with the rebels
   march 28, 1862, and to those who fell at the battle fought with the rebels
   at Peralta april 15, 1862."
4. "To the heroes who have fallen in the various battles with savage
   Indians in the territory of New Mexico."
(Information furnished through the courtesy of Salome Anthony, librarian,
public library, Santa Fe, New Mexico.)

The Last California Political Duelist

Dueling was prohibited by the California state constitution but that seemed to have had little influence on either the duelists or the local authorities in the "dueling fifties." The duelists included a newspaper editor, state legislators, a judge and a United States senator.[84]

The last political duel in California was fought six weeks after the first shot was fired in the Civil war. The duel had its inception at a meeting of the state assembly to consider the resolution to support President Lincoln, the Union and the Constitution; and to defend the United States against any foes.[85]

The vote was taken by roll call, and when Assemblyman Amyx's name was called he asked and was granted permission to explain his vote "no." When Assembly-

---

[84] Article xi, section 2, California state constitution: Any citizen of this state who shall fight a duel, send or accept a challenge to act as a second or aid in any manner, shall not be allowed to hold any office of profit or enjoy the right of suffrage under this constitution.

Duels: (A) Judge David S. Terry, chief justice Supreme Court of California — vs. David C. Broderick, United States senator, september 13, 1859.

(B) William L. Ferguson, California state senator — vs. George Pen Johnson, editor Sacramento *National,* september 21, 1858.

(C) J. W. Denver, California state senator also secretary state of California — vs. J. A. Gilbert, assemblyman.

[85] Joint resolution of senate and assembly (may 17, 1861).

No. xviii — Resolved by the senate, the assembly concurring: That the people of California are devoted to the constitution and Union of the United States, and will not fail in fidelity and fealty to that constitution and Union now in the hour of trial and peril.

That California is ready to maintain the rights and honors of the National government at home and abroad, and at all times to respond to any requisition that may be made upon her to defend the Republic against foreign or domestic foes.

man Blair asked to explain his vote "yes," permission
was refused. Dan Showalter's name was called next and
he also asked to explain his vote "no" and said that he
would like to see the man who would rise and make the
objection. Charles Piercy, a Douglas Democrat, rose
and said, "I make the objection. If it is just to refuse
one member the privilege of explaining his vote, it is
equally just to refuse another."

Showalter, a Breckinridge Democrat, said that no
man ever heard him object to any gentleman's explanation of his vote. Piercy started to reply but Showalter
continued, "It is a right which I have always maintained and I have nothing but contempt for any gentlemen who does object." Showalter then voted "no."

Piercy replied that he emphatically objected to the
language used by the gentleman from Mariposa (Showalter) and insisted that no disrespect was intended and
that he only wished to save time in voting. Piercy continued, "I regret exceedingly that the gentleman from
Mariposa has seen fit to use the language he did. I ask
him now as an honorable gentleman, if he wishes to
explain."

Showalter said that if he had violated the rules of the
assembly, he regretted it, but as far as what he had said
to the gentleman from San Bernardino (Piercy) he had
nothing to retract.

"Then," said Piercy, "I hurl it back in his teeth with
all the contempt that language can express and I have
not language strong enough to express it." (Mild language in comparison with that which resounds in the
halls of congress now.)

A few days later, Piercy again asked Showalter if he
had intended his remarks as a personal insult. Showalter
replied by assuring Piercy that the language was plain

and had but one interpretation. Piercy then left the assembly in a vengeful mood.

According to the outlawed and outmoded "code of honor," Piercy was the gentleman who had been insulted, so to vindicate his honor, he sent a challenge to Showalter. The latter accepted and chose the weapons, rifles at forty paces. Showalter preferred to fight in San Joaquin county but Piercy chose San Francisco so they compromised on Marin county.

Early on the morning of may 24, 1861, Showalter with his surgeon and seconds boarded the steamer "Petaluma" for the opposite shore of San Francisco bay. He could not guess the fate that awaited him. His tall figure stood erect, his red whiskers shone redder in the morning light as his steady black eyes watched the approaching shore.

Charles Piercy chose a sail boat to carry him on his momentous journey. The white sails filled in the fresh breeze from the Golden Gate while the little craft zigzagged her way across the bay. Did the tall slender assemblyman from San Bernardino have a premonition of the fate that awaited him and did he then question the merits of dueling? Did his young life mean more than a political quarrel? Who can say? Perhaps his thoughts were all concentrated on the girl at home whom he had so soon expected to call Mrs. Charles Piercy.

Piercy stayed over night at San Quentin while Showalter remained at an hotel in San Rafael. Early the next morning Showalter started for the McDuffie ranch but the Marin county officers felt that they should at least make a pretense of law enforcement so Showalter was arrested on a warrant sworn out by District Attorney Haralson. Showalter was taken before Judge Frink, county judge at San Rafael, but for some unexplained reason there was no one present to testify against him so the case was dismissed.

He then hurried to keep his appointment with Piercy and perhaps with Death. The ground chosen for the duel was about six miles from San Rafael in a green meadow surrounded by thick chaparral where cattle grazed contentedly and a small stream trickled lazily through the grass.

Preliminaries for the duel were arranged. The articles of agreement provided that the contestants were to fire between the word "fire" and the count of "three." After much delay, all were ready. Both duelists were dressed in black, coats buttoned closely, and their black hats pulled well over their foreheads.

The sun's level rays rested momentarily on the summit of Mount Tamalpais when the signal to fire was given. Showalter fired on the word "one" and Piercy on the word "two." Both missed so the orders were again read, the rifles reloaded, and once more the order of "fire" given. Piercy was instantly killed and Showalter lived to carry on his opposition to the Union, President Lincoln and the United States Constitution.[86]

Six months later he armed and equipped a group of men and planned to flee to Texas to engage in open warfare against the Union army. The plot was discovered, the troops in southern California were alerted, and all trails to the desert blockaded.

Major Edwin A. Rigg was then in command at Camp Wright, Oak Grove, San Diego county, and his vigilance was soon rewarded. The Showalter party succeeded in reaching Temecula without being discovered

[86] Sacramento *Daily Union* — may 27, 28, 30, 1861.
San Francisco *Daily Alta* — may 25, 26, 1861.

so they grew over confident. A hundred miles was a long distance in 1861 so the "Secessionists" spent the evening at Temecula writing letters to their friends urging them to join them and explaining the route they expected to take to avoid the troops at Oak Grove and Warner ranch.

But their perfect plan had its flaw. One of the members of the party, E. M. Morgan, hired a man to take his letter direct to Camp Wright where his accomplice, E. B. Sumner, was waiting to join the party. The messenger failed to pass the blockade and was arrested and searched. The letter was found and turned over to Major Rigg. It disclosed the number of men in the party and their probable location.

Major Rigg immediately detailed Lieutenant Chauncey R. Wellman, company B, first cavalry, California volunteers, and a detachment of his men to search the road to Temecula. It was eleven thirty P.M. when Lieutenant Wellman arrived at Temecula, the old Overland station, and learned from storekeeper John Magee that sixteen men had spent the previous night there but had left the following morning at about ten o'clock.

The Showalter party left their letters at Temecula to be forwarded by the next mail, which was at that time carried by the California volunteers who were designated vedettes. These letters were confiscated and furnished the clue to the route taken by the correspondents.

Early the next morning the California cavalrymen followed the old trail of the padres to Pala Mission. It was a well worn trail that the faithful fathers had followed for nearly half a century as they journeyed to the Temecula Rancho to supervise the harvesting of grain, the building of the rancho buildings in Temecula pass, and to conduct services in the chapel.

The Showalter party, traveling a day's journey in advance of their pursuers, followed the trail from Pala Mission up the San Luis Rey river. Before reaching the valley of San Jose (Warner ranch), they ascended one of the trails on the right, presumably Temescal Lusardi, that led to Mesa Grande where they camped for the night on John S. Minter's ranch.

They were discovered at midnight and when they broke camp at sunrise, the California volunteers started after them. Lieutenant Wellman soon overtook them and placed them under arrest. They were well outfitted with pack mules and good horses and each man was armed with a pair of revolvers and a rifle. All their property was confiscated and a careful inventory made of each man's belongings.

The prisoners were escorted to Camp Wright where each was obliged to make a written statement regarding his former residence, his birthplace and proposed destination. The oath of allegiance was administered to each one by Major Rigg, who reported that he had on hand no particular form of oath so he wrote one to suit himself.

General Wright ordered the prisoners confined at Fort Yuma until further notice. There was a rumor afloat that a group of Southern sympathizers had conspired to release them so an extra guard of fifty cavalrymen was hurried to Camp Wright to re-enforce Captain Parvin's infantrymen who were ordered to escort the prisoners to the fort. The cavalrymen continued their escort to Carrizo creek then turned back as the long hot stretch of desert was protection enough. In order to prevent any future attempt to free the men,

General Carleton ordered Major Rigg to refuse any writ of habeas corpus issued for them.

They were imprisoned but five months when orders came from headquarters to release nine of them. They were supplied with a six-mule team and ten days rations for the return journey across the desert to Camp Wright. Surprisingly, the order read, "This party need have no other guard than their word of honor that they will move with the wagon to Camp Wright."

Prisoners of war they had been, but the greatest consideration seems to have been tendered them. Major Rigg was instructed to return their horses and supply any needy men with shoes or clothing and any other necessary supplies. When they left Camp Wright, they were given another ten days rations to enable them to reach Los Angeles. A few days later Dan Showalter and the remainder of the prisoners were released under similar conditions.

Two years later his friendship for Ann, the daughter of Colonel Ferris Foreman, fourth infantry, California volunteers, betrayed some of his activities. A Confederate spy named Skillman was killed during an encounter with some of General Carleton's scouts on the Texas border. When he was searched a letter from Dan Showalter to Ann Foreman was found and forwarded to headquarters at San Francisco.

Ann had sent a message to Dan by Mrs. David Terry and it called forth an immediate reply from Dan. He said,

I had abandoned hope, so fondly cherished, of hearing from you during the present war. I would have written long ago but feared it might bring your parents into serious trouble if it were known that you corresponded with an arch rebel like myself. Silent as I have been, I have often thought of you while walking my lonely beat at night, and on the battlefield where my comrades were falling around me. I am truly grateful to hear of your father's resignation. You know we were always firm friends and it pained me to think that we should be arrayed against each other. . .

I would be delighted to see you. Indeed, if I had only twenty years to live, I would give up ten years of that time to see and talk with you for one hour. I may survive this war. If so, we may meet again; but should I fall, you will have my last kind thought, my last fervent prayer of your devoted friend.[87]

Ann did not wait too long for Dan. Ten years later she married J. D. Peters, the well known pioneer of Stockton.[88]

Dan continued to fight for the Confederacy and was promoted lieutenant colonel of the C.S.A. He served in Arkansas and Texas with the "Ladies rangers", as his battalion was chivalrously designated, and he also fought in the battle of Galveston. He was mentioned as one of the abettors of the Hasting's scheme to recapture the Southwest.

---

[87] *War. Reb.* Ser. I, vol. L, pt. I, p. 32-35.
Ibid., pt. II, p. 1078-1080.
[88] Guinn & Tinkham, *History of the state of California,* vol. II, p. 120.

The Advance Guard

The advance guard of the California volunteers arrived on the border of Arizona five months before the main army was equipped and ready to march. As early as november 3, 1861, Colonel Joseph R. West with three companies of the first infantry (B, H, I), arrived at Fort Yuma, California, to relieve Lieutenant Colonel George Andrews, U.S.A., who had been ordered East for duty.[89]

Colonel West immediately ordered his troops to build breastworks at the fort and to repair the water system. He improved the old southern Overland road by cutting down the hill five miles west of Vallecita so that the mules could more easily pull their loads over this hump. The desert wells were cleaned out, dug deeper and walled with boards to conserve the meager supply of water.[90]

However, Major Edwin A. Rigg relieved Colonel West before the end of a month (november 26) as the latter was scheduled for a promotion having been placed second to Brigadier General James H. Carleton in command of the expedition to the Rio Grande. When Major Rigg reached Fort Yuma, he found plenty to do. From the Colorado to the Rio Grande was a long journey for the cavalry but a longer one for the foot soldier and every possible provision had to be made for the men and animals. Much of the hay needed at the

---

[89] War. Reb. Ser. I, vol. L, pt. I, p. 137, 661.

[90] Ibid., p. 710-714, 932-933.

stations near the fort was supplied by L. J. F. Yager who agreed to sell to the government at the same contract price that he had had with the Overland Mail company when it operated on the southern route. He also agreed to furnish beef for the troops at the fort as he owned a large herd at San Felipe which could be driven to the Colorado and slaughtered when needed.[91]

The volunteers were detailed to cut grass along the Gila river for hay and haul it to the corrals of the Overland stations. Second Sergeant William Wheeling, company F, first infantry, reported that he had marched to a place fifteen miles above Gila City where he arrived january 11, 1862. Here he and ten of his men cut five tons of hay and hauled it to Gila City only to have it all washed away during a storm.[92]

The flood reached its peak at Fort Yuma where the Gila then joined the Colorado. The river rose six inches in three hours and the troops worked until one o'clock in the morning to save the corrals and hay as well as the quartermaster and commissary supplies. The water works were submerged but the pumps were kept in operation until the water covered the feet of the mules employed in pumping. The machinery was then removed and but little damage resulted as the river soon began to fall.[93]

But while the California volunteers were making hay on the Gila, rumors and more rumors of the advance of the Confederate troops infiltrated the garrison causing considerable anxiety among the officers. Reliable information was difficult to obtain as it necessitated sending government spies to Tucson and it then took three weeks or more to make the round trip on horse-

[91] *Ibid.*, p. 742, 780, 869, 808-811.
[92] *Ibid.*, p. 868.
[93] *Ibid.*, p. 815-818, 841.

back. At Yager's ferry on the Colorado, an enlightening bit of news was received from Peter Brady, writing from Altar, Mexico, on january 1, 1862. He reported that Palatine Robinson of Tucson had posted a notice declaring Colonel Samuel Colt's Cerro Colorado mine confiscated. Van Alstein, Colt's agent at Arivaca, objected, pistols were drawn; the usual compliments, "————— ————", "————— ————— ———", were exchanged but the name-callers separated without bloodshed.

A month later Ami White sent word to Major Rigg confirming the report about the confiscation of Colt's mine and implicated a man named Washburn. The men acted on their own initiative and not from orders from the Confederate commander. These confiscators threatened to mob Major Lally, superintendent of the Poston mine at Tubac if he returned to Tucson. Major Lally was in Magdalena at the time and said that he would remain there "to see the turn that events might take."

Other rumors from Tucson indicated that the residents were offering bets as to whether the Texans would reach that city or not. Nevertheless it was quite definitely established that Colonel John R. Baylor, company A, first cavalry, C.S.A., was at Fort Fillmore with seven hundred or eight hundred troops and was expecting re-enforcements soon.[94]

In order to verify the many rumors, General Carleton ordered some of the experienced frontier scouts to ride forward to Tucson and ferret out all possible information regarding the movement of the Southerners. Frederick C. Buckner was sent to Tucson to interview Solomon Warner, merchant and trader of that city. Carefully disguised and mounted on a government mule without a brand, Buckner crossed the Colorado at

---

[94] *Ibid.*, p. 824-826.

night and took the trail for Tucson via Sonora. He made the round trip in twenty-two days and reported that protection was very much needed in Tucson and would be welcome from any quarter provided that it could be accomplished without the horrors of a battle-field.[95]

J. J. Warner of Warner's ranch was also employed as a special army scout and although entrusted with secret orders and advised that a hurried trip was vital to the Union cause, he could not resist stopping long enough to trap a beaver on the Colorado near Fort Yuma.[96]

Each secret Union agent was kept in ignorance of the others and sent by a different route. One was paid the sum of fifty dollars and, in addition, a receipt for the mule that he rode. The messages were in secret code and the key retained by Major Rigg who was cautioned to lock it up.

At the time General Carleton was issuing orders to his own scouts and secret agents, he had an order for the capture of the Confederate spies. ". . . Have an eye on spies. Seize them quietly and confine them—each by himself until further orders. . . We may have to hang some of these fellows to let them know that the government troops on the Pacific coast are in earnest.—Even our own expressmen may be bribed. If spies are found guilty by a military commission, shoot them. . ."[97]

Colonel Baylor at Mesilla was able to obtain information about the Union troops from citizens of California who had joined his forces in november 1861. These

95 *Ibid.*, p. 854, 867.
96 *Ibid.*, p. 784.
97 *Ibid.*, p. 861 (feb. 12, 1862).

Californians reported that there were no troops then marching toward the Rio Grande but that Fort Yuma was being re-enforced. Therefore Baylor advised stationing a strong force in western Arizona. By so doing, he believed that he could get hundreds of good Southern men already armed and mounted who would be able to watch Sonora and prevent the United States troops from crossing Sonora or using Guaymas or any other port on the Mexican coast.[98]

Having become convinced that the Confederate forces under Captain Sherod Hunter, company A, first Confederate cavalry, were on the march for Tucson, General Carleton ordered extra guards posted at Fort Yuma and all steamers tied on the California side of the river. He encouraged Major Rigg and his small force by telling him that he could whip any force that would menace him as he had command of the river. Pasqual, chief of the Yumas, was asked to keep a sharp lookout and report the presence of any Confederate soldiers. As a reward for his services he was promised trinkets and blankets.[99]

A few picked troops as an advance guard were ordered to scout up the Gila to watch for the enemy and prevent the destruction of the government's stock pile of wheat and flour at White's mill near the Pima village. For this job General Carleton selected his old friend, Captain William A. McCleave, company A, first cavalry, who had served under him for ten years. McCleave was stationed at Camp Carleton, San Bernardino, when he received his orders to start for Fort Yuma on february 11, 1862. Taking with him thirty

[98] *Ibid.*, p. 716 (nov. 10, 1861).
[99] *Ibid.*, p. 810, 847.

of his men, he made the trip through the San Gorgonio
pass to the Colorado in five days. In his detailed description of this road, he recommended it as being
shorter than the one by the way of Warner's pass and
quite practicable for cavalry during the winter months.

This old route through San Gorgonio pass followed
the general direction of the Southern Pacific railroad
as far as the White Water river. There the road turned
southward and followed the foot of the San Jacinto
mountains to Agua Caliente (Palm Springs). It then
continued to Indian Wells and Toros; from here it
swung eastward just north of Dry lake (Salton Sea)
to Lone Palm and Dos Palmas. At this point the route
appears to have followed the ancient shore line to
Frink's Springs and Mammoth Tanks, paralleling the
railroad the rest of the way to Yuma. They traveled
the rough desert trail at night and Lieutenant Nichols
was highly commended for his ability to guide the
cavalrymen in the moonlight.[100]

But the Californians had not miscalculated the
arrival of the Confederates. Two days before the re-
mainder of McCleave's company, under command of
Lieutenant James Barrett, left San Bernardino, Cap-
tain Sherod Hunter, with one hundred men entered
Tucson (february 28, 1862). The next day Colonel
James Reily with two subalterns and twenty rank and
file joined Hunter. He raised the stars and bars of the
Confederacy and promised the citizens peace and
prosperity if they would adhere to the Southern cause.
He soon left for Mexico to seek recognition of the
Confederacy by President Juarez.[101]

While Reily was speech making on the plaza at

[100] *Ibid.*, p. 870-872.
[101] *Ibid.*, p. 944-945.

Tucson, Captain McCleave (*Plate* 3) and his detachment of thirty California volunteers were riding up the Gila river looking for their expressmen and their adversaries. And thus the stage was set for an early encounter. The two companies of cavalrymen, each designated A, the one Confederate, the other Union, moved forward across the desert, each uncertain of the others movements and the time or place they would meet.

A few days after the Confederate flag-raising at Tucson, Captain Hunter and his company started for the Pima village. He kept his own scouts well in his advance and so was able to surprise and capture Ami White and one thousand five hundred sacks of wheat. However, he was not able to move the grain so distributed it among the Indians. The mill was damaged to the extent of making it useless until extensive repairs could be made.

Hunter waited at White's mill (*Plate* 4) for a few days as he had been informed that a train of fifty wagons with government supplies was on its way to the Pimas. The wagon train did not arrive but Captain McCleave and nine of his men did. A member of company K, first infantry, California volunteers, furnishes an account of the meeting of the two captains:

It was late in the evening of march 6 when McCleave knocked at the door of White's house and inquired if White was at home. He was answered in the affirmative by one of the band who, in turn, asked where the strangers were from. They said that they were United States troops from the Colorado. The man retired as if to acquaint White with their presence—(White, by the way, was a prisoner elsewhere and in the power of the Secessionists).

Shortly after, Hunter and about thirty of his band made their appearance and leveling a pistol at the breast of McCleave said, "I am

Captain Hunter of the Southern army. Consider yourselves prisoners. Lay down your arms."

McCleave said that he would do nothing of the kind. Then Hunter remarked, "If you make a single motion, I'll blow your brains out— you are in my power—surrender immediately." McCleave realized that it was useless to contend against such an overwhelming number and surrendered himself a prisoner to that guerrilla chief.[102]

News traveled slowly across the desert in 1862. Ten days after the capture of McCleave, General Carleton sat in his tent at Camp Drum writing to his friend telling him,

I have marked out some work for you. If, by forced marches, you can follow trails and unawares fall on Hunter at Tucson and his one hundred men—it would be a coup that would last you all your life. What you do, must be done at once. If your men take only the clothes they stand in, no greatcoat, one blanket and the necessary provisions, they can move swiftly. . . Sacrifice everything to gain success.

If yourself and Calloway can make a dash, so much the more glory for both of you. Rigg, Calloway and yourself may be in on the secret but no other man until you have passed the Pimas. When you leave Yuma, say that you go on a campaign against the Tonto Indians. . . Go either by the copper mines via Tinaja Alta by trail, or by Pima. Take your choice. If you go up the Gila, be prepared to do the work chalked out in my letter to Rigg.

The infantry are much better than uninstructed cavalry on horseback. Once they get Hunter's men under fire, they will make them howl. If I were you, I should depend on having all my men on foot. Hunter's men are mounted on good American horses and can ride you down; but if you get at them at night, I doubt if ever a man gets into his saddle. . .[103]

McCleave was also instructed to select a site near the Pima village that could easily be defended, and speedily entrenched even if the men had to work day

---

[102] Sacramento *Daily Union,* may 23, 1862. (Letter written at Grinnell's ranch (Stanwix), april 1, 1862).

[103] *War. Reb.* Ser. I, vol. L, pt. I, p. 931-932.

and night. All of White's wheat and flour was ordered to be stored inside and defended to the last extremity.[104]

It seemed incredible to General Carleton, when reports finally arrived, that McCleave and Ami White had been captured and that Hunter had possession of Tucson. He endeavored to keep the news a secret but that was impossible; nor could he conceal his anxiety over the situation in Arizona. "A whole staff," said he, "could not compensate for the loss of McCleave." Had Carleton known about the defeat of the Union forces in New Mexico, he would have been doubly anxious. Even though the battle of Valverde had been fought and won by the Confederate forces a month previous, february 21, the news had not yet reached Camp Drum, Wilmington.[105]

Hurried plans were then made for the re-capture of McCleave before he was carried off to the Rio Grande. The main force of the California volunteers were mobilized at Camp Drum, Wilmington, and at Camp Wright, Oak Grove, where they impatiently waited for their orders to march. Only an advance guard of a few hundred men had reached Fort Yuma but from these, two companies of cavalry, one of infantry and two mountain howitzers, a fighting force of 272 men, were selected to rescue McCleave. Of course, one of the companies was McCleave's own who "were pawing for the advance." [106]

Great secrecy preceded the movements of the Califor-

---

[104] *Ibid.,* p. 929-930.

[105] *Ibid.,* p. 940.

[106] Company A, first cavalry — Lieutenants Barrett and Nichols.

Company D, first cavalry — Captain Nathaniel J. Pishon; Lieutenants Wellman and Baldwin.

Company I, first infantry — Captain William P. Calloway.

Company K, first infantry (detachment) — Lieutenant Phelan.

nians. The interpid Captain Calloway,[107] company I, first infantry, was ordered to march direct to the Pima village to "show face enough to keep the Confederates near while the first cavalry, companies A and D, rode to the south to get in the rear of the enemy." General Carleton relied upon Paulino Weaver to scout ahead to locate Hunter's cavalrymen as "Weaver knew every foot of the country and was almost an Indian himself, having helped the Maricopas against the Apaches." [108]

A soldier of company K, first infantry, writes of the results of their attempts to rescue McCleave.

At nine P.M. we were arranged in two lines in front of our quarters, answered to our names, marched to the Colorado and crossed. We were brought to attention on the Arizona side and addressed by the commanding officer, Edwin A. Rigg, who had accompanied us that far. The major was serious and brief in his remarks which may be summed up as follows:

"Men, you have now crossed the Rubicon and emerged into the great field of labor spread out before you. The first duty of the soldier

---

[107] Company I, first infantry enrolled at Marysville under Captain William P. Calloway. This was one of the "star" companies of the regiment as there was not a single desertion during their three years of service in the southwest.

At the age of twenty-two, Calloway was serving in the Mexican war. When twenty-seven, he had command of a wagon train known as the "Odd Fellows' train" bound for California in 1852. Three members of his family died of cholera while en route.

They avoided an attack from the Indians but were able to rescue one survivor of a massacre, a fifteen year old girl who had hidden in the brush and miraculously escaped. Yes, he married the girl when he reached Marysville.

Captain Calloway was mustered out with his company at Fort Union, New Mexico, september 30, 1864. In 1874 he was engaged by the board of supervisors of San Diego county to survey a new road from San Diego to Fort Yuma. He later aided in the development of the Palo Verde valley where he was killed by an Indian in 1879. (Information furnished through the courtesy of his daughter, Mrs. Jessie Weslow, Sacramento.)

[108] *War. Reb.* Ser. I, vol. L, pt. I, p. 950-951, 958, 764.

Paulino Weaver had been a guide to the Mormon battalion and was one of the first settlers in Prescott where a bronze plaque, mounted on a granite boulder, commemorates some of his exploits.

is obedience. Unaided by the vigilance and cooperation of his men, a commander is powerless. There is work for you to accomplish and you can never return without glory or disgrace."

After a few more remarks, the old gentleman returned to the garrison and left us to continue our march in anticipation of the glory spoken of. Neither incumbered with regrets nor heavily laden with the reminiscences of happy days gone by at Fort Yuma, we marched in silence toward the east.

It was only when the morning star called our attention to the near approach of day that we halted to recruit our failing power of locomotion. Then we became aware of aching all over and stiffness everywhere as the result of the weight of our knapsacks. I have often heard the groans of the heavily loaded pack mules moving past on their way to the mountains, but never did I sympathize with those animals until I threw the burden off my back and rolled in the desert sand after a twenty-mile march from Fort Yuma.

We rested through the heat of the day and at five P.M. of march 23 proceeded to the Lower Mission station. Here we found a picket guard, a detachment of cavalry and infantry who had been employed for some time in cutting and hauling hay for the animals in the service. . . We continued our line of march, stopped at the various stations along the route and in six days arrived at Grinnell's ranch (Stanwix) about eighty miles east of Fort Yuma.

On sunday morning while waiting re-enforcements in order to continue our march, two of the picket guards were shot at. One was severly wounded in the shoulder by a party of rebels who lay concealed about five miles from here. It seems that the rebels (who were, according to the statement of the sentinels, about forty in number) endeavored to take our men prisoners. When they refused to surrender, the rebels shot at them several times but they both made good their escape.

When they arrived in camp and gave the alarm, Captain Calloway ordered the cavalry to hasten in pursuit of the marauders. Company D (first cavalry, Captain Nathaniel Pishon) who were already in their saddles hastened with all speed after the rebels but failed to capture any of them. The rebels burned the hay at Oatman's Flat, fifteen miles from here and were last seen about ten miles in advance of our troops. Owing to the near approach of night and the exhaustion of their horses, our men gave up the pursuit. . .[109]

[109] Sacramento *Union*, may 23, 1862.

The advance guard reached the Pima village april 12 and remained two days to rest and trade with the Indians, giving manta and old fashioned army clothing for flour. At this time Brigadier General James Carleton and the main force of California volunteers were just leaving Camp Drum, Wilmington. He reached the Pima village six weeks later (may 24) which was two and a half months after the capture of his old friend, McCleave. Even the advance guard arrived five weeks too late for his rescue.[110]

The soldier correspondent furnishes an eye witness account of the third encounter with the Confederate forces.

On the 14th we continued our course, marching 24 miles. Next day we were early on the road again and continued unmolested until about four o'clock P.M. when an express returned to inform us that the advance guard was attacked and several men were killed.

The circumstances were as follows: Lieutenant Barrett, in command of a small detachment of cavalry, was instructed by Captain Calloway to move forward and, upon approaching Picacho pass, to turn off the main road and come in from the east by an opening to the left in the mountain. Lieutenant Baldwin, with another detachment, was ordered forward from the west. By this means they could completely cut off the retreat of the enemy's pickets who were stationed in the pass. Lieutenant Barrett unfortunately overstepped his instructions by moving eight miles in advance of the main body. Knowing that the pickets were concealed in the thicket, he charged upon them, discharged his pistol and ordered them to surrender. This was responded to by a volley from the Secessionists (who were nine in number) which told with fatal effect as four of our men fell at the first fire. After this the firing became general and three of the enemy threw down their arms and surrendered. Lieutenant Barrett dismounted to aid in tying them but, in regaining his saddle, a ball took him in the neck and broke it, killing him instantly. George Johnston, company A (first cavalry), was shot in the region of the heart and died in a few minutes. Leonard (William S.), company D (first

<hr>

110 *War. Reb.* Ser. I, vol. L, pt. I, p. 1002-1003.

cavalry), was shot in the back, the ball ranging upwards and passing out at his mouth; he died the next morning. Tobin (William C.), company B (first cavalry), was shot in the forehead but the brasses of his hat caused the ball to glance upwards and left an ugly but not fatal wound. Two others were shot in the arm and shoulder; neither wound is reported as fatal. There were four of the Secessionists severely wounded and one killed. Three were taken prisoners and one escaped uninjured.

If Lieutenant Barrett, in obedience to Captain Calloway's orders, had patiently waited the approach of Baldwin, or had dismounted his command and caused them to deploy and surround the enemy, they would have surrendered without a single shot being fired; but fate decreed it otherwise. Lieutenant Barrett and those who fell with him are buried, side by side, a few paces from where they fell, fifty miles from Pima on the road to Tucson.

After ascertaining as accurately as possible the strength of the enemy, and having but three days provisions left, Captain Calloway deemed it advisable to fall back on Pima and endeavor to obtain some supplies from the Indians. At all events, it was decidedly more prudent to invite attack rather than advance headlong through the thickets and guarded passes where small determined bands could lay in wait and harass the energies of a large advancing corps. The principal object of our expedition to Tucson was to rescue Captain McCleave and his party but we learned from our prisoners that he had been taken to the Rio Grande. . .[111]

McCleave, himself, adroitly tells of his experiences with the Confederates:

We were *looking* for our expressman but *found* ourselves prisoners at White's mill, Pima village. As I had previously served in Arizona, many of this company (Confederates) were known to me as men hailing from the States—not of the South but those who had passed most of their manhood in the mines of Arizona and elsewhere on the borders.

The northern men in this company told me of speeches made to them at the Patagonia mines and other mines by Mowry and his rebel friends setting forth the miserable condition of the Union army and

[111] Sacramento *Union*, may 23, 1862. Letter written at Pima village, april 30, 1862.

(that the Southerners) only waited for favorable opportunity to capture Washington and take control. . .

I gave them the true statement of facts which caused many to desert—some to Mexico, others to New Mexico. After a short delay, I was taken to Tucson to await the return of Colonel Reily from Mexico. He had been sent by Jef Davis to interview President Juarez relative to recognition of the Confederacy by Mexico. I continued to the Rio Grande—but my men were paroled at Tucson and left to take care of themselves; and I regretted being separated from my men.

On the way to the river, a halt was made at old Fort McLane where news was received of the battle near Fort Craig (Valverde). To publish the news of the great victory, the company was formed in line and a bombastic order read setting forth the great gallantry of the Texans over the Union troops after which three cheers were given for the heroes of Valverde.

Just then an officer approached me and remarked, "You are not cheering, Captain."—I answered shortly, "No sir, my time to cheer will come bye and bye." At this a scowl overspread all the men's faces, with remarks that no prisoner should be allowed to talk so about their victory.

Our march continued to Mesilla and we camped nearby. While there, our expressman, Jones, with dispatches from Tucson for General Canby, was captured a few miles above Mesilla. This caused great commotion for it told of the coming of the Californians. The town was at once guarded on all sides and I, instead of being allowed to remain in camp, was placed in jail to keep Jones company.

About this time the troops who had gone north with Sibley began to return in straggling parties. Then it was soon known that they had been defeated above Santa Fe with loss of supply train of eighty wagons.

The rebels then knew they had to get out and started for El Paso. When they abandoned Mesilla, I was taken from prison and turned over to Colonel Philip Herbert and the notorious Ned McGowan. These men treated me kindly and furnished me a horse en route to El Paso.[112]

It was april 19 when the retreating advance guard returned to Pima village to begin the work of fortifying

----

[112] Captain McCleave papers — courtesy of his son, Dr. T. C. McCleave, Berkeley, Calif.

that place. Slowly the second contingent of volunteers marched to their assistance. Colonel West with two companies of cavalry and five of infantry were on their way from Camp Wright but it would take them ten more days before they could join the advance guard.

General Carleton and remainder of the companies had progressed only as far as Temecula and had just received the news of the defeat of the Confederate forces in New Mexico. Carleton complained about the delay in keeping him informed about the movements of the enemy and suggested that he receive the news either through the papers or by telegram. The newspapers appeared to be first with the news as they had ready access to the telegraph—when it was in working order—whereas the soldier on the march was obliged to rely on his expressman and his army mule or horse. There were no "walkie-talkies" for the frontier general. Considering this, his consternation was understandable when he remarked, "From the report of the battle at Pigeon's ranch, it would seem that the Texans had already been masters of Santa Fe." [113]

Colonel West arrived at the site of the new fort at the Pima village, april 29, with Surgeon John H. Prentiss, two ambulances, a medicine wagon and three hospital tents. Surgeon William Kittridge was stationed at Grinnell's ranch. But the doctors were too late. The dead had been buried where they fell, the wounded cared for by their companions and borne in freight wagons back to camp.[114]

Reports reached Colonel West that the audacious Captain Hunter and his cavalrymen remained in Tucson until may 4 seemingly in defiance of the advance

[113] *War. Reb.* Ser. 1, vol. 1., pt. 1, p. 986, 1922, 1949, 1918.
[114] *Ibid.,* p. 969-970.

guard of the Californians. However, at about the same time that Carleton and his "column from California" left Fort Yuma, Hunter started for the Rio Grande to join the departing Southerners who were retreating down the Rio Grande from Santa Fe. Colonel West said that if Hunter "played bopeep in the neighborhood a while and flickered around the candle a little longer, he might get his wings singed." [115]

The post at the Pima village was used as a sub-depot and supply station and when it was completed, General Carleton issued the following command: "The post just established by Lieutenant Joseph R. West, first infantry, California volunteers, at the Pima village, Arizona territory, is hereby designated as Fort Barrett in honor of the memory of Lieutenant James Barrett, company A, first cavalry, California volunteers, who fell in defense of his colors near that point on april 15, 1862. The names of Privates George Johnson, company A, William S. Leonard, company D, first cavalry, who fell by his side, will until the end of the war, be called at every stated roll-call of their respective companies, and a comrade shall always respond, 'He died for his country.' " Here, in Picacho pass, the Arizona Pioneers Historical society has erected a monument in memory of him and his comrades.[116]

Captain McCleave was a prisoner for four months and it was not until after the California column reached the Rio Grande and Colonel E. E. Eyre raised the Union flag over Fort Thorn, july 5, 1862, that an exchange of prisoners was effected. Then it was a trade of "two for one"—two Confederate lieutenants for one Union captain—the fighting Captain McCleave.

115 *Ibid.*, p. 1078.
116 *Ibid.*, p. 1061.

Captain McCleave tells us how he outwitted his captors:

Shortly after reaching El Paso, Colonel Reily sent for me and said he was going to release me on parole but that I must sign a paper not to take up arms against the Confederate government until exchanged. To this I objected, saying I had sworn to fight for the United States and no earthly power could make me take any other obligations.

Several days afterwards, I was sent for again and was handed another paper signed by the adjutant which stated that I was released on my own parole of honor.

To this I replied that so far as I was concerned, the honor consisted in my getting to Fort Craig and reporting for duty as soon as possible.

To reach Fort Craig was now my objective and I started at once for Mesilla. When I crossed the Rio Grande near Mesilla, I cut the ferry rope and let the boat drift down stream to prevent the Texans from following and again arresting me as they had heard that I was on my way to Fort Craig.

This information was given me by one of their own men whom I had formerly known and who ran through the chapparel to avoid being seen and overtook me near the river. This man overheard the officers discussing the propriety of sending the d----- northerner back to El Paso and keep him from giving Canby the news.

The journey up the west bank of the Rio Grande was continued, my party numbering five, three of whom had deserted from the rebels. When about forty miles above Mesilla, Fort Thorn was seen in the distance and our glorious flag—the dear old stars and stripes—waving in the breeze.

This grand and unexpected sight caused a halt. Hats off, cheers were given. It was impossible to express our feelings—only those similarly situated could appreciate our feelings on that occasion. We now knew that friends were at the fort. Our California comrades came to meet us.[117]

Carleton, in a report to General Halleck, explains "what manner of man" was McCleave:

I write this direct to you because I believe you will desire to mark the man to whom I refer as one deserving your notice. Captain

---

[117] Captain William A. McCleave MS — *op. cit.*

William McCleave of company A, first cavalry, California volunteers, served ten years under my command, nearly all that time as a first sergeant in company K, first dragoons. When the California volunteers were organized, he became the ranking captain in the first cavalry.

While on a scout last spring, he was taken prisoner by the Texans and was not exchanged until four months later. When he came to draw his pay he presented $582.50 to the United States stating in his letter of transmittal, "I am not here for pecuniary purposes and respectfully ask that the amount revert to the Federal government whose servant I am." This was the pay which accrued while he was a prisoner.

In a letter to me, Captain McCleave said: "I prefer a clear conscience rather than possess anything the ownership of which is doubtful, and especially in times like these when the government is engaged in such a desperate struggle, I can but render my humble assistance in the noble work."

The devotion of this noble Irishman to the country of his adoption should be known. If you can give him a helping hand you may rest assured you cannot assist a finer soldier or one whose heart is in all respects without fear and without reproach. He should belong to the regular service. He possesses all the elements of which heroes and patriots are made.[118]

It was not courage and devotion to his country alone that won recognition for McCleave but his sincere regard for the men under his command. Wherever his men went, he rode in the lead.

The advance guard alone bore the brunt of the three encounters with the Confederate forces within two hundred miles of the California border. They prepared

[118] *War. Reb.* Ser. I, vol. L, pt. II, p. 222-223 (nov. 14, 1862).

Ibid., vol. IX, p. 585-589, 707-708.

William A. McCleave — First Sergt. Co. K, first dragoons, 7 oct. 1850 to oct. 1860; capt. first California cavalry 23 aug. 1861; major, 1 may 1863; breveted lt. col. vols. 13 march 1865 for his successful pursuit of, and gallantry in an engagement with Apache Indians; honorable muster out 19 oct. 1866.

Received commission in the regular army, second lt. eighth cavalry 28 july 1866; first lt. 6 march 1867; capt. 10 aug. 1869; retired 20 march 1879 — twenty-nine years and five months service. He spent the remainder of his life in Berkeley, Calif.

the way for the army of Californians who were then
ready for their march to the Rio Grande and their three
years service in Arizona and New Mexico.

The Column Prepares to March

While the struggle between the North and South continued in Arizona and New Mexico, more than seven thousand California volunteers had been mobilized and almost two thousand were preparing to march for the Rio Grande.[119]

Colonel James Henry Carleton (later brigadier general) was placed in command of the expedition. He had already served twenty years on the frontier, five of those years having been spent in New Mexico and Arizona. His long service had taught him the difficulties his young Californians would face and he realized the full extent of his responsibility. Said he, in his letter to General Wright,

I cannot venture to put all these troops in motion out upon the desert without seeing beyond a doubt what they are to eat. Once upon the desert, these mouths must eat or we have disaster. . . I do not intend to arrive on the Rio Grande in disarray if I can help it, and if not in disarray, I trust with God's help to be able to strike one good blow for our country.[120]

To prepare for an expedition like this took months of careful planning; months of waiting for the winter floods to subside; many days to bargain for cattle fit to be herded over the long desert trail and more time to select others to be slaughtered for jerked beef and pemmican.

Some of the beef was supplied by Francisco

---
119 *War. Reb.* Ser. I, vol. L, pt. I, p. 836-837.
120 *Ibid.*, p. 973-974.

O'Campo who agreed to deliver beef at six cents a
pound at Camp Wright and at Warner's ranch. He
also offered to drive his cattle with the troops and kill
the beef when required for nine and three-eighths cents
a pound. Abel Stearns also supplied cattle, but when
the troops reached Fort Yuma, L. J. F. Yager contracted with the government to furnish beef at eleven
cents.[121] As the troops continued eastward through
Arizona and New Mexico, Grinnell, Rhodes and
Beard furnished the cattle.

Adequate supplies of hay and grain were equally
important. When Colonel Joseph R. West arrived at
the Pima village he made arrangements with the
Indians to furnish the government with hay, grain and
flour in exchange for manta (shirting, calico, etc.) as
it was the staple article used by the Indians in bartering.
Therefore, the government supplies were paid for by
the yard. It was agreed that a yard of manta was worth
each of the following amounts of supplies: 4½ pounds
flour; 13 pounds wheat; 50 pounds hay; 150 pounds
green fodder; or 5½ pounds pinole.[122] It was further
agreed that the runners of the Indian express between
the Pima village and Grinnell's station should be paid
forty yards of manta for each round trip.[123]

The memorandum of supplies needed for the expedition included pork, flour, beans, coffee, sugar, vinegar,
and pemmican—a diet quite different from that of the
modern soldier. Nevertheless the value of vitamins was
not overlooked although they were not widely ad-
vertised at that time. Orders were issued to the men at
Camp Wright to gather and cook plenty of greens,
nettles, mustard, lamb's quarters and other varieties of

---

[121] *Ibid.*, p. 819-820, 869, 943.
[122] *Ibid.*, p. 1051
[123] *Ibid.*, p. 1054.

plants that make good greens. Attention was called to the mesquite beans as feed for horses and even for men in a pinch.

No detail of camp or army duty was neglected by the commanding officers. Instructions were given for making adobe ovens as well as the recipe for bread. A supply of charcoal was burned as it would be needed for shoeing horses and mules and for repairing wagons.[124] Horse and mule shoes were important items and were handmade by the firm of Nelson and Doble and fitted with steel toes. Ten thousand horse shoes and over four thousand mule shoes were included in the army order.

That great expense was involved in outfitting Colonel Carleton's troops is revealed in General Wright's communication to the quartermaster general at Washington: . .

Since I have been in command of this department, I have used the utmost economy consistent with the interest of the public service; but my troops are dispersed over a vast extent of territory, my extreme positions being two thousand miles apart, and during the last month I have been organizing a large expedition to move from the southeastern frontier of this state. All this involves heavy expenditures for the transportation of troops and supplies; and in addition we have been compelled to purchase about seven hundred mules.

I have made contracts here for the manufacture of all the clothing required for the whole army on this coast. This with the purchase of tents and camp equipage, and the indispensable outlay in erecting temporary shelter, and flooring the tents to preserve the health of my men during a winter of unprecedented severity, together with the purchase of horses to mount seventeen hundred cavalry, will give you an idea of the expense necessarily incurred here. . .[125]

Expense was not the only trouble confronting the commanding officers. Reports of the success of the Con-

124 *Ibid.*, p. 961, 975, 1033, 1049.
125 *Ibid.*, p. 813-814.

federate army in Arizona and New Mexico reached California and the delay in moving forward the troops caused considerable criticism of Colonel Carleton and his plans.

But criticism had to be borne as well as his personal sorrow over the death of one of his children at Los Angeles where his family had moved so that they might be near him.[126] But a soldier and a commander must carry on. So he left nothing to chance but planned every detail with the greatest care. At that time, 1861-1862, there were but two places between Fort Yuma and the Rio Grande where supplies could be obtained. The Indians at the Pima village furnished hay, grain and beef, and at Tucson the Mexicans sold some food and a little clothing.[127]

Consequently each wagon was carefully loaded, each package weighed and a list of such weight made up against every load. Each wagon master was given written instructions as to the hour and day when his train should leave camp. Cavalry and quartermaster trains were divided so that not more than eighty animals would travel twenty-four hours in advance of the next eighty.

The barley was soaked so the horses would not suffer so much from thirst as only one gallon was allotted to each animal and sometimes that had to be drawn up by buckets which were filled by dipping a cupful at a time as fast as the water ran into the desert wells. It often took a full day's steady work to water the animals.[128]

The commanders of the cavalry were instructed to

---

[126] Los Angeles *Semi-Weekly News*, dec. 13, 1861 (Los Angeles public library).

[127] *War. Reb.* Ser. I, vol. I, pt. I, p. 773-779.

[128] *Ibid.*, p. 1033.

walk their men at least half the time by the watch and practice the saber exercise one hour each day as they marched. The infantry was required to march with knapsacks on and carry one greatcoat, one blanket, one cap, one shirt, one pair drawers, one pair socks, one towel, two handkerchiefs, one fine and one coarse comb, one sewing kit, one piece of soap, and one toothbrush. Each soldier whether of cavalry or infantry carried one canteen, one haversack and one tin cup. In his haversack he carried a fork, a spoon and a plate.[129]

The modern soldier's equipment is comparable to the old army pack except that he carries in addition a steel helmet, a shelter half, tent pins, rope, pole, and a first aid pouch. The medium pack weighs forty-five pounds but for extended field maneuvers his pack approximates sixty pounds.

The progress made in the preparation for this expedition to Arizona and New Mexico is reported by General Wright to the War department at Washington, december 31, 1861.

I am throwing forward supplies to Fort Yuma as rapidly as possible. Tomorrow, janury 1, 1862, a steamer will leave for the mouth of the Colorado river laden with subsistence and other stores required for the movement of Colonel Carleton's expedition. It is two thousand miles to the mouth of the Colorado at which point the stores must be reshipped on small river steamers for Fort Yuma. I have also embarked on the steamer, a guard of one company of the fifth California volunteer infantry, 88 strong, commanded by a reliable officer who has received special instructions.

Additional supplies and means of transportation are also being forwarded to San Pedro to be sent by land to Fort Yuma. I am gradually moving a portion of the second cavalry to southern California to replace the troops designated for Colonel Carleton. The latter will not advance to Fort Yuma until advices are received of the arrival of the stores shipped by sea.

129 *Ibid.*, p. 858-859.

The expedition is one of considerable magnitude and operating on a long line remote from its source of supplies. It cannot advance from Yuma until fully prepared for the campaign. Fort Yuma is being fortified and will be securely held by a strong reserve. Under the command of Colonel Carleton, an officer of skill, experience and sound judgment, we have the strongest assurance that the expedition will be successful.

The weather for many days past has been tempestuous in the extreme. The floods east and north of this city have destroyed a vast amount of property and almost entirely suspended our mail communications. The telegraph has not been in operation for several days.[130]

General Wright's instructions to Captain Joseph Smith, company A, fifth infantry, California volunteers, stresses the importance of the duty of that company. It enlisted at Yreka, California, october 30, 1861. Captain Smith was later promoted major of the fifth infantry, California volunteers. No doubt he obeyed these instructions:

The vessel on which your company will embark at Wilmington, january 1, 1862, carries a very large amount of government property and stores and you are to provide a sufficient guard during the time you are passing up the Gulf of California. The general is particularly anxious that no cause of complaint should be given the Mexican authorities, and, therefore, desires that no one belonging to your command should land at Guaymas.

When the stores are transferred from the steamer to the sail vessels you will divide your force and place a platoon on each schooner. On your arrival at the mouth of the river, or wherever the second transfer may be made, you will ascertain the number of trips the riverboat will have to make, and then so dispose of your force so that you will have a sufficient guard with each load.

Having been selected for your discretion and prudence, the general expects you to afford every assistance in your power in transporting and guarding the government property, and as far as is consistent, to respect the authority of the Mexican government.[131]

---

130 *Ibid.*, p. 792.
131 *Ibid.*, p. 791.

The Colorado River Navigation company, which had been organized by Captain George A. Johnson, contracted to carry government supplies from the mouth of the Colorado at Fort Yuma. Captain Johnson was the pioneer river boatman who as captain of the "General Jessup" navigated the Colorado in 1858, ascending as far as Black canyon. He also conveyed the Beale surveying party across the river at the junction of Beale's road. After the explosion of the "General Jessup", Captain Johnson secured another vessel and held control of the river transportation until the coming of the Southern Pacific railroad to Yuma.[132]

The water route to Fort Yuma via the Gulf of California presented many difficulties for the army officers. The steamer "Republic" while en route to Guaymas in december 1861, encountered a severe gale off Monterey and the captain ordered her deck load thrown overboard to lighten her cargo. A statement of the jetsam included thirty-four sacks of barley, one barrel rice, one barrel powder, three wheels of gun carriages, two boxes sponges, one box merchandise and 56 boxes of ammunition.[133]

One delay followed another, and disappointment after disappointment vexed the officers in command. When the long awaited supplies did arrive, the indispensable necessities were often lacking while the non-essentials showed up. Colonel West reported that at Fort Yuma there were picks but no handles, and not a single long handled shovel. Yet two storm flags had been included in the freight and the much needed scythes did not arrive.[134]

---

[132] *Arizona-American guide series,* p. 109-110. (Federal Writers)
[133] *War. Reb.* Ser. I, vol. L, pt. I, p. 822-823.
[134] *Ibid.,* p. 987.

A tandem ambulance without the harness, which had to be especially made, was useless on the desert. Nevertheless two such vehicles were hauled behind the already overburdened freight wagons all the way from Wilmington to Fort Yuma. Carleton said they were about as useless as old lumber.[135]

After having overcome seemingly unsurmountable difficulties and delays, General Wright was finally able to report to the War department at Washington, that *Colonel Carleton was on the march* (april 13, 1862) from Drum Barracks, Wilmington, and that he had been supplied with everything deemed necessary for a successful campaign.[136]

There were two hundred wagons in his train, each loaded to three thousand pounds and drawn by six mules. The train was divided into four divisions of fifty wagons each, with a wagon master for each division. Joseph Winston, William S. Veck, Gabriel Allen and N. L. Roundtree were appointed wagon masters and each was allowed three assistants selected from the teamsters. Each wagon master was held responsible for his train and was required to see that it was properly cared for at all times, and accounted for at stated periods to insure the government against loss. Each wagon was furnished with two six-gallon water kegs to prevent a shortage in case of the failure of the supply in the desert wells en route.[137]

The responsibility of the expedition rested heavily on Colonel Carleton's shoulders. Although he had personally supervised the purchase of much of the supplies, he had delayed moving his troops until sufficient stores had arrived at Fort Yuma, and hay and

---

[135] *Ibid.*, p. 869.
[136] *Ibid.*, p. 1014.
[137] *Ibid.*, p. 853.

grain had been hauled to the stations along the way by the advance guard.

So it was more than five months after the first contingent of California volunteers had left for Fort Yuma before Colonel Carleton issued orders for the movement of his main body of troops. He ordered his men forward not knowing that the brief success of the Confederate forces had terminated with the battles at Apache Canyon and Glorieta (march 26-28, 1862). The Union forces had already re-occupied Santa Fe and the Confederates were in full retreat down the Rio Grande when Colonel Carleton left Drum Barracks, april 13. Four days later when he reached Laguna Grande (Elsinore) he received the news of the battle of Glorieta but the *news* was then three weeks old.[138]

The itinerary of the California volunteers was carefully outlined: El Monte, San Jose, Chino Ranch, Temescal, Laguna Grande (Elsinore), Temecula, Dutchman's (Aguanga), Oak Grove, Warner's, San Felipe, Vallecita, Palm Springs, Carrizo Creek, Sackett's Wells, Indian Wells, New river, Norton's Wells, Gardiner's Wells, Cooke's Wells, Algodones, Fort Yuma, Gila City, Mission Camp, Antelope Peak, Mohawk, Texas Hill, Stanwix ranch, Burke's station, Oatman's Flat, Kenyon station, Gila Bend, Maricopa Wells, Casa Blanca, Pima village, Oneida station, Blue Water station, Picacho, Point of Mountain, Tucson, Cienega, San Pedro, Dragoon Springs, Apache Pass, San Simon, Steen's Peak, Soldier's Farewell, Vaca springs, Mimbres river, Cooke's springs and Mesilla.

Thus the old Overland Stage route was aroused from its lethargy as the heavily laden supply wagons rumbled

[138] *Ibid.,* p. 1009.

along. Vaqueros hurried their herd of long horns across the spring pastures and through the rough canyons to the desert edge. Cavalry mustangs bore semblance to pack animals, for if the commanding officer's orders were obeyed, the mounts carried one hundred pounds of barley in lieu of cavalry men who had been commanded to walk at least half of the time. Infantry with knapsacks securely strapped to their backs straggled along in ranks as broken and uneven as the land over which they trod.

Colonel Carleton reached Fort Yuma may 1 and remained there two weeks to make final arrangements for the departure of the balance of his troops and supplies.[139] While here he issued his general order number one on may 15, 1862, proclaiming: "The forces belonging to the United States which are now moving from the department of Pacific toward Arizona and New Mexico will hereafter be known as the 'column from California.' "[140]

BRIGADIER GENERAL JAMES HENRY CARLETON

James Henry Carleton, the fighter, peacemaker, and writer, was born in 1814 at Eastport, Maine. He rendered his first service on the Aroostook river, Maine, during the boundary dispute with Great Britain in the winter of 1838-1839.

He was appointed second lieutenant of the first U.S. dragoons october 18, 1839; promoted first lieutenant march 17, 1845. He served on the western frontier at Jefferson Barracks and Fort Leavenworth, patrolling the emigrant trails to the Rocky mountains and back until ordered to join General John E. Wool's column which was being organized for the Mexican campaign.

139 *Ibid.,* p. 1045-1047, 1057-1060.
140 *Ibid.,* p. 1075.

He was appointed aid to General Wool in november 1846 and served throughout the war. He was breveted major february 23, 1847 for meritorious conduct at the battle of Buena Vista where he had commanded a company of the first dragoons. He was later appointed acting inspector on General Wool's staff and remained in Mexico eight months after the war ended.

After the troops were withdrawn from Mexico, Carleton resumed his frontier duty. For this service he received special commendation from General John Garland in his report to the secretary of war, june 30, 1854. While he was stationed at Santa Fe, he was placed in charge of a hundred dragoons from company H and his own company K and ordered to explore the country around Gran Quivira and Los Puerto Abo to select a possible route for a railroad.

He is reported to be the first American to give a detailed written description of Gran Quivira which is now a national monument. His report was published in the *Ninth Annual Report* of the Smithsonian Institution.

In 1856 Carleton and four companies of the first dragoons were stationed at Tucson under command of Major Steen and by 1859 Carleton was serving at Fort Tejon in California. In april 1859, he was sent to Salt Lake City as escort to Major Prince, United States paymaster. He was also ordered to bury the bones of the victims of the Mountain Meadow Massacre (september 1857).

In discharging this duty he again had an opportunity to use his ever ready pen to good advantage. He reported his findings to Major W. W. Mackell, U.S. assistant adjutant general at San Francisco and the information was later embodied in a report published by the U.S. Senate, 36 Cong. 1 Sess. Sen. Ex. Doc. no. 42, Vol. XI. The monument he erected consisted of a conical pile of stones fifty feet in circumference and twelve feet high. A roughly hewn cross from a red cedar tree was placed on top of the mound. Carved in the cross were the words, "Vengeance is Mine, I will repay." A further record was made—"Here 120 men, women and children were massacred in cold blood early in september 1857. They were from Arkansas."

In the spring of 1860, Major Carleton was ordered to the new post, Camp Cady, to protect the travelers on the Salt Lake and Fort Mojave routes. Here he made peace with the desert Indians and built redoubts at Camp Cady, Soda springs and Bitter springs.

Upon his return to California he was stationed at Fort Tejon until may 3, 1861, when General Edwin V. Sumner ordered him to Los Angeles where Camp Fitzgerald was established. On august 7, 1861 he was made colonel of the first regiment of infantry, California volunteers. On october 14, 1861, he was placed in command of the district of Southern California which position he held until may 15, 1862. He was breveted brigadier general april 26, 1862.

He led the California column on the expedition to Arizona and New Mexico, april 12 to september 20, 1862. On september 18, 1862 he assumed command of the department of New Mexico and carried on a campaign to protect the settlers and travelers. The detailed account of his services is embodied in the chapters following.

He was mustered out of the volunteer service april 30, 1866 and appointed lieutenant colonel of the fourth U.S. cavalry. On july 31, 1866 he was promoted colonel of the second U.S. cavalry and ordered to Texas with

his regiment. He died at San Antonio, Texas, january
7, 1873 at the age of fifty-nine.

To Recapture Tucson

The G.I. of the 1860's depicts the road to Tucson as the road to a new adventure. They followed the Gila river to the Bend then turned eastward to Maricopa Wells. The Southern Pacific now follows this route from Yuma to Maricopa.

Said the soldier correspondent,

When we left Fort Barrett at the Pima village, our road kept along the Gila for two days and then we left it for good. The second day out, some of our party saw a few Apaches but these American Arabs never troubled us.

About twenty-seven miles from Fort Barrett, our road passed over the ruins of an old city (Casa Grande) which was supposed to have been built and occupied by the Aztecs. Time has made a desert place of what was once a populous city. Old foundations, mounds, and pieces of broken pottery scattered for miles over the plain, are all the evidences that remain to tell the tale of a past people.

The Cañada del Oro is situated in a high broken range of mountains north of Tucson. In the bed of the canyon flows a beautiful stream and the mountains in the background ascend to curiously shaped summits suggesting the form of old castles. One or two years ago considerable gold fever existed in this territory and several parties prospected the banks of the stream with success, but the Apaches have always been too strong and troublesome for small parties, consequently, it has never been worked to any great extent.

As we did not leave camp until eleven o'clock the following morning, our whole party turned out prospecting with tin pans and buckets. The fever ran pretty high for two or three hours. All got "color" and they came to the conclusion that rich diggings could be found. One waggish fellow, in order to express his idea of its richness, said, "The national debt could be paid out of Cañada del Oro."

Of course, all the prospecting was on the surface. Arizona is certainly a rich mining district and I believe that the marching of this expedition, which is composed of old Californians and experienced miners, will eventually be the means of developing it. The entire route has been prospected and it was quite interesting to witness the California column examining the ledges and turning over the dirt. . .

Tucson may be properly described in these words: A little old Mexican town built of adobe and capable of containing about fifteen hundred souls. The Santa Cruz runs within a mile of town and feeds the numerous ditches that irrigate the beautiful little valley that extends to the high hills to the westward and which was, until a week ago before harvesting commenced, one vast field of fine grain. The climate of Tucson is dry and healthful and the soil will produce almost anything planted. The peach, quince, fig, and pomegranate grow to perfection.

Upon our arrival in Tucson, we found it lively with California volunteers but abandoned by its former population. Since then, they have been returning daily and a better pleased set of people cannot be found. Some who have returned have been required to take the oath of allegiance. That portion of the community, which could be best spared, left with Hunter a few weeks ago and will be sure not to come back unless forced to.

Immediately upon his arrival, General Carleton went to work to renovate and straighten out the affairs of the territory. His first move was to arrest eight or ten suspicious characters who had been prowling about the place ever since Hunter's departure.

On the day of our arrival, may 20, 1862, Captain Emil Fritz, company B, first cavalry, dashed through the town at full speed and in five minutes it was surrounded. Shortly after, the prisoners were marched to the guard house and later sent to Fort Yuma. They are a set of bad men who had scorned the law and had their own way. Affairs have taken a turn and I think their jig is up. The general (Carleton) has taken hold with a firm hand and not one of these outlaws against the civil or national authority will escape his vigilance.[141]

General Carleton proclaimed martial law in Arizona on june 8, 1862. His proclamation follows:

[141] *Alta California,* San Francisco, july 10, 1862 (Bancroft library).

The congress of the United States has set apart a portion of New Mexico and organized it into a territory complete in itself. This is known as the territory of Arizona. It comprises within its limits all the country eastward from the Colorado river, which is now occupied by the forces of the United States known as the column from California, and as the flag of the United States shall be carried by this column still farther eastward, these limits will extend in that direction until they reach the fartherest geographical boundary of this territory.

Now, in the present chaotic state in which Arizona is found to be, with no civil officers to administrate the laws, indeed with an utter absence of all civil authority and with no security of life or property within its borders, it becomes the duty of the undersigned to represent the authority of the United States over the people of Arizona as well as over those who compose or are connected with the column from California.

Thus by virtue of his office as military commander of the United States forces now here, and to meet the fact that wherever within our boundaries our colors fly, there the sovereign power of our country must at once be acknowledged and law and order at once prevail, the undersigned as military governor assumes control of this territory until such time as the president of the United States shall otherwise direct.

Thus it is hereby declared that until civil officers shall be sent by the government to organize the civil courts for the administration of justice, the territory of Arizona is hereby placed under martial law.

Trials for capital offenses shall be held by a military commission to be composed of not more than thirteen nor less than nine commissioned officers. The rules of evidence shall be those customary in practice under common law.

The trial shall be public and shall be trials of record, and the mode or procedure shall be strictly in accordance with that of court-martial in the army of the United States.

Unless the public safety absolutely requires it, no execution shall follow conviction until the orders in the case shall be known by the president (Lincoln).

Trials for minor offenses shall be held under the same rules, except that for these, a commission of not more than five nor less than three commissioned officers may sit, and a vote of a majority determines the issue. In these cases the orders of the officer organizing the commission shall be final.

All matters in relation to rights in property and lands, which may be in dispute, shall be determined, for the time being, by a military commission composed of not more than five nor less than three commissioned officers. Of course, appeals from the decisions of such commissions can be taken to the civil courts when the latter have been established.

There are certain fundamental rules for the government of this territory which will be rigidly enforced:

I.   No man who has arrived at lawful age shall be permitted to reside within this territory who does not, without delay, subscribe to the oath of allegiance to the United States.

II.   No words or acts calculated to impair that veneration which all good patriots should feel for our country and government, will be tolerated within this territory or go unpunished if sufficient proof can be had of them.

III.   No man who does not pursue some lawful calling or have legitimate means of support shall be permitted to remain in this territory.

Having no thought nor motive in all this, but the good of the people and aiming only to do right, the undersigned confidently hopes and expects in all that he does to further these ends, that he will have the hearty co-operation of every good citizen of Arizona.

All this is to go into effect from and after this date (june 8, 1862), and will continue in force unless disapproved or modified by General Wright, u.s. army, commanding the department of the Pacific, under whose orders the column from California has taken the field.

General Carleton levied taxes on the merchants of Tucson as well as on the keepers of gambling houses and bars. He also fixed the amount of their fines for failure to comply with his orders.

I.   That from and after this date a monthly tax of five dollars for license to trade shall be levied on all merchants in Tucson, Arizona, including those who shall traffic within a mile in every direction from its suburbs, whose monthly sales of merchandise amount to five hundred dollars or under, and an additional tax of one dollar per month for each additional sale of one hundred dollars.

II.   That every keeper of a gambling house . . . pay a tax of one hundred dollars per month for each and every table . . . whereon any banking game is played.

III. That every keeper of a bar . . . shall pay a tax of one hundred dollars per month to keep said bar. . .

The fines for non-payment of licenses was fifty dollars for the first offense and one hundred dollars for the second. The commanding officer of Tucson was empowered to grant licenses under the above rules and collect all taxes, fines and forfeitures. The money thus collected was turned over to the medical director to be used exclusively for the benefit of the sick and wounded soldiers belonging to the column from California.[142]

After General Carleton had established military law in Arizona, he issued orders for the arrest of all persons suspected of aiding the Confederate troops during their occupancy of Arizona. He dispatched Colonel J. R. West to the Patagonia mine to arrest the owner, Lieutenant Sylvester Mowry, a former U.S. army officer and graduate of West Point.

Colonel West was instructed to seize all papers and documents of a political nature and confiscate the mine as well as all arms and ammunition. To protect the mine owner, a detailed inventory was taken of all movable property, mining implements, machinery, cattle, horses and provisions.

General Carleton had acted under the orders of General Wright, department of the Pacific, who in turn was merely obeying the regulations of the "Confiscation act". This act made the real estate and personal property of individuals liable to confiscation if they were proved guilty of holding office under the Confederate government or aiding or abetting the enemies of the United States.

[142] *War. Reb.* Ser. I, vol. L, pt. I, p. 96-97. (june 18, 1862).

A military board of investigation appointed by
Carleton reported that witnesses had testified that
Mowry had given aid to the enemy and recommended
that he be brought to trial. Mowry was confined at Fort
Yuma from july 2 to november 4, 1862 when he was
unconditionally released.[143]

His release came through the adjutant general's
department, Washington. An order was sent to Judge
William F. Turner, Arizona, requesting that Mowry's
case be investigated and that he be retained or released
according to the evidence available. A board of ex-
aminers was appointed but no evidence was presented
that would incriminate Mowry, so it was recommended
that he be released and his mine returned to him.

Yet this was just the beginning of Mowry's troubles.
For the remainder of his life he tried to re-establish his
fortune. He first filed suit against General Carleton
and the officers who acted under his orders in the
seizure of the Patagonia mine. The suit was filed
december 12, 1863 in the fourth judicial district of
California and Carleton responded by forwarding all
papers relative to the case to Washington.

No settlement appears to have been made, as the case
became the subject of a United States senate investigation through its resolution of may 20, 1864. The case
was reviewed and reports from Adjutant General E. D.
Townsend and Secretary of War Edwin M. Stanton
were read before the senate. The report was ordered
"to lie upon the table and be printed." [144]

[143] *Ibid.,* vol. IX, p. 693. Spec. Order no. 17. (june 16, 1862).
Board: J. R. West, lt. col. 1st. Cal. inf.;
    Chas. A. Smith, capt. 5th. inf. c.v.
    Nicholas S. Davis, capt. 1st. inf.;
    Secy. of board, Erastus W. Wood, 2nd. lt. 1st. inf. c. v.
[144] Mowry brought suit for $1,129,000 against General James H. Carleton;

Mowry lost his health as well as his fortune and died in London, England, october 1871.

THE RIDE OF THE PAUL REVERE
OF THE SOUTHWEST

While General Carleton and his column from California were restoring order in Tucson, General Canby, re-enforced by the Colorado volunteers, was pursuing the Confederate forces down the Rio Grande. General Carleton had repeatedly tried to get a message through to General Canby but without success. It was imperative that the latter should know the strength of the column from California.

Since the two Union armies were now converging upon the retreating Texans, it seemed likely that a messenger could avoid the Indians and get through the enemy lines. Expressman John Jones, Sergeant William Wheeling, company F, first California infantry, and Chávez, a Mexican guide, were the men picked for the job.[145]

They left Tucson june 15, 1862 and traveled three days without hindrance. As they left Apache pass on june 18, they were discovered by a band of eleven mounted Indians and seven footmen who sent up smoke

Colonel Joseph R. West; Theodore Monimann; Abraham Cutter; and Frederick Berkner.

He placed a value of $40,000 on his personal property;

400 bars silver and lead, $4,000

150,000 adobe bricks, $3,000

He claimed his mine grossed from $600 to $1,000 a day.

Daily Call, San Francisco, dec. 15, 1863.

38 Cong. 1 Sess. Sen. Ex. Doc. no. 49, vol. I. (1176)

War. Reb. Ser. I, vol. IX, p. 690, 694.

Ibid., vol. XLI, pt. II, p. 662, 674.

[145] Sergeant William Wheeling enlisted at La Porte, California, in company F, first infantry, California volunteers. 54 other men from La Porte also enlisted in company F.

signals. The soldiers traveled rapidly to get out of the brush before the Indians attacked.

But suddenly the Indians jumped up from their hiding place, mounted their horses, and rode forward at a full gallop. The army messengers dismounted, tied their animals, and prepared to fight. Jones reported,

The Indians came on at a furious rate. Three of our animals broke away. Some of the Indians went after them leaving the others on foot. The Mexican was wounded in the hip but was able to mount. Then we all mounted but the sergeant was thrown so we tied our mules again. The mounted Indians came back, leaped from their horses, and began crawling on us. I told the sergeant that our only chance was to mount and make a rush. The Mexican begged not to be left behind. We told him that we could not save ourselves. I think the sergeant never got out from among the Indians.

They followed after me on horseback yelling, "Now let's have a race. Mucha buena mula! Mucho bravo Americano!" I shot one in the side and another in the shoulder. Six pursued me until sundown. I lost all my pinole and $84.00 in cash.

I struck Cow springs about eleven the next morning and stayed all day in the station. I made arrangements to fight from the chimney but the Indians did not come. Starting out after dark, I reached the lower crossing of the Mimbres river where the Confederate army had a picket stationed. I succeeded in passing him and went on to Cooke's springs.

At sundown june 20 (1862), I reached the Rio Grande at Picacho which is five or six miles above Mesilla. Here I was taken prisoner by some of the Confederate soldiers and brought before Colonel Steele.

Messenger John Jones was examined, his dispatches confiscated and then he was imprisoned. In spite of this, he managed to get word to General Canby that he had been captured and the *Column from California was really coming.*[146]

---

[146] *War. Reb.* Ser. I, vol. L, pt. I, p. 89, 119-120.

Old Glory Again Flies Over
the Rio Grande

"The column from California was coming!" That was discouraging news for the retreating Texans but welcome, indeed, to the commander of the department of New Mexico, General Edward E. S. Canby, and his small force of Federal troops and Colorado and New Mexico volunteers.

General Carleton's Californians were on their way yet there were still many miles of rough marching between the Rio Grande and Tucson where the troops were then concentrating. Carefully Carleton planned this last lap of his journey across the unsettled territory.

It was expedient to make a reconnaissance in advance and Colonel Edward E. Eyre was detailed for this duty. With a detachment of 140 men from companies B and C of the first cavalry, and Surgeon William Kittridge, he left Tucson june 21, 1862.[147]

Four days later, while his troops were dipping water by the cupfuls from the spring at Apache pass, a group of Indians waving a white flag came in sight. Colonel Eyre took a white flag of his own and went to meet them. At the end of an hour he succeeded in getting near enough to talk to them through his interpreter, Newcomb.

When the colonel met the chief he tried to explain the presence of the soldiers by saying, "We are Amer-

---

[147] *War. Reb.* Ser. I. vol. L. pt. I. p. 98.

icans and our great captain lives at Washington; we wish to be friends with the Apaches; at present we are only traveling through your country and desire that you do not interfere with our men or our animals; a great captain is at Tucson with a large number of soldiers; he wishes to have a talk with all the Apache chiefs and make peace and give them presents."

The Apache chief said that he wanted to be friends with the Americans and promised the colonel that neither his men nor his animals would be molested. He asked for tobacco and food and promised to meet the colonel again at the same place at sunset.

But the scheduled meeting never took place for when the colonel returned to camp at the springs, he learned that three of his men were missing. A searching party was immediately organized and about an hour later they found the nude bodies of the California volunteers. They had been scalped and their clothing, firearms and horses stolen. The Indians were pursued but it was impossible to overake them.

The three murdered soldiers, John Maloney, Albert Schmidt and James F. Keith were buried in Apache pass, june 25, 1862. The rest of the command, deeply moved by their first loss, moved out of this danger spot to San Simon springs. Yet they were not entirely safe here as the Indians returned at eleven o'clock in the evening to again attack. Surgeon Kittridge suffered a head wound but was able to continue the march to the Rio Grande.

Extra pickets were posted the next evening. At midnight the camp was awakened by a shot from one of them who had heard a rustling in the bushes. There was no return fire and investigation disclosed that he had shot a large desert coyote.

Colonel Eyre proceeded to the Rio Grande without further trouble with the Indians. He met several parties of miners returning from the Pinos Altos mines and detained them temporarily so that his troop-movements would not be disclosed. On july 4, he made camp on the Rio Grande a short distance from Fort Thorn and immediately raised the United States flag "amid the wildest cheering from the volunteers." This was the first time the stars and stripes had floated over the lower Rio Grande since the occupation of the country by the Confederate forces a year before.[148]

Scouts were sent down the river for the double purpose of finding a suitable crossing and to look for Confederate pickets who might still be in the vicinity. Meanwhile, a hundred men under Captain George W. Howland, third U.S. cavalry, arrived from Fort Craig to re-enforce Eyre's command.

The crossing of the Rio Grande was delayed by the high waters, the time consumed in building a raft, and repairing a road on the west side of the river to the ford eighteen miles from Fort Thorn. By the time the California volunteers were safely across, a messenger arrived from Colonel Marshall S. Howe, commanding the southern military district of New Mexico, ordering them to remain at Fort Thorn. Since they had already left the fort, Eyre decided to march to Robledo or Dona Ana and sent word to Howe that he would await further orders there. Finding no camping facilities at either location, Eyre moved on to Las Cruces. At the latter place he learned that the Confederates were still at Franklin (El Paso), Texas, and only his reluctance in disobeying orders from the department headquarters

---

[148] *Ibid.*, p. 120-124.

prevented his continuing down the Rio Grande to overtake the retreating army.[149]

About a week after Colonel Eyre reached the Rio Grande, the advance guard left Tucson under command of Captain Thomas L. Roberts, company E, first infantry. He was especially instructed to guard a 22-wagon train and to scout far in advance, as much as fifty miles, to watch for hostile Indians or Confederate spies. He was expected to do this with detachments of infantry from his own company and company H, totaling 82 men. Captain John C. Cremony, company B, second cavalry, boasted cavalrymen to the number of 24 who were detailed to escort the wagon train. Two mountain howitzers, mounted on prairie carriages, in charge of Lieutenant W. A. Thompson and 20 more men, made a total of 112 volunteers.

Captain Roberts reached Apache pass at noon july 15. When half a mile from the springs, the Indians attacked the rear of his command and killed Charles M. O'Brien who was attached to Thompson's battery. One of the teamsters, Andrew Sawyer, was wounded. Skirmishers were then deployed on both sides of the pass and supported by the prairie howitzers. The Indians kept up a rattling fire until four P.M. when they were finally driven out of the pass by the old "Napoleons", but this was not accomplished without further loss of life—John Barr, company E, first infantry.

As soon as all the animals were watered, Captain Roberts withdrew his men as he did not have a large enough force to hold the pass and at the same time go to the aid of Cremony's wagon train which was camped fifteen miles in the rear. He sent Sergeant Titus B.

149 *Ibid.,* p. 126-128.

Mitchell, second cavalry, with five men to warn Cremony of the danger.

The cavalrymen had ridden but a short distance when the Indians again attacked. Jesse T. Maynard was wounded and two horses shot. At this time, John Teal was leading his horse about 250 yards in the rear when he suddenly realized that he was separated from his companions and surrounded by about forty Apaches. He mounted and struck off at a gallop closely pursued by fifteen Indians who fired repeatedly. One of the bullets passed through the heart of his horse. Teal flattened himself on the ground behind his dead mount while the Apaches encircled him. The uneven contest lasted for an hour and a half. Teal finally made his escape and at half past ten the same evening reported to Cremony who immediately corralled the train and held it securely.

Captain Roberts with the remainder of his men succeeded in eluding the Indians and reached the wagon train in safety. After this experience, he decided to avoid Apache pass and escort the train through Railroad pass, a safer but longer route. The cavalry was dismounted and one man was stationed on each wagon. A line of infantry marched in front of the train; the wagons were placed next in line; then the cattle, followed by a second line of infantry. By marching in this order the greatest possible protection was provided for the supply line of the column from California.[150]

With the arrival of Colonel Eyre's reconnaissance party on the Rio Grande and Captain Roberts's advance guard well on its way with the first section of the wagon train, General Carleton issued orders for the column at Tucson to march. The first contingent was

[150] Ibid., p. 128-133.

scheduled to leave july 20, the second on july 21, and the third, two days later. Captain John B. Shinn and Lieutenant Franklin Harwood, third U.S. artillery, moved forward with the second contingent. Caravans had traveled over the Colorado desert ever since Anza's memorable march but no battery of artillery had ever before attempted to cross and its success was heralded as an outstanding military achievement. Yet the battery consisted of only four guns, two 12-pounder howitzers and two 6-pounders.

General Carleton accompanied the third contingent and the wagon train with forty days' subsistence followed a week later. It was august 7 when he reached Fort Thorn where the United States flag had been raised a month previous. The strength of the command when it reached Mesilla totaled 1,400 men including teamsters and other civilian employees.[151]

The commanding generals meticulously kept their records of the expedition to the Rio Grande but the G.I.'s of the 1860's kept a different kind of record—one not included in the official government records but nevertheless of some importance. Of the dreaded Apache pass, one volunteer wrote:

As we marched through, they pointed out the place where company

151 *Ibid.*, p. 772, 94.

Ibid., p. 90-91. Gen. Orders no. 10, Tucson, july 17, 1862.

First command—leave july 20—Col. West commanding; Co. B, C and K, first infantry; Co. G, fifth infantry; Co. E, first infantry and Thompson's mountain howitzers ordered to join this contingent at Rio de Sauz. Maj. Theodore A. Coult, fifth infantry. Surg. James McNulty.

Second command—leave july 21—Lt. John B. Shinn, third U.S. art., Co. A, first infantry and Co. B, fifth infantry. Surg. John H. Prentiss.

Third command—leave july 23—Col. Edwin A. Rigg, Co. I, F, D, H, first infantry. Surg. David Wooster.

Wagon Train—leave july 31—Co. A, first cavalry and Co. A, fifth infantry. Co. D, first cavalry, Capt. Nathaniel J. Pishon, advance guard to column. Capt. John C. Cremony, Co. B, second cavalry, act as vedettes and flankers.

E, first infantry, was attacked by the Indians and where (Charles M.) O'Brien, company G, was killed. O'Brien was one of my first acquaintances and was generally liked by all the regiment. He is buried at the station near the springs where a crude headboard with his name, age, and company marks his grave—"He died bravely and was loved by all."

We left the springs the next morning and in the pass we saw the new-made graves of the men from Captain Fritz's company B, second cavalry, and of Sergeant William Wheeling. (The latter lost his life when he rode with expressman Jones, the "Paul Revere of the Southwest," to carry to General Canby the message that the *Column from California was coming*.)

. . . We passed Cook's springs where the U.S. troops had destroyed a great deal of government property to prevent its falling into the hands of the Secessionists. The next day we marched forty miles and reached the Rio Grande. During the night the Indians drove off the beef cattle but since they were nothing but skin and bones on account of our long marches, the Indians were not pursued.

The following day we passed Fort Thorn. It was in a horrible condition as it had also been abandoned. The walls and roofs of the quarters were almost torn down but the flagstaff was still standing and we were rejoiced to think there could be nothing but the glorious stars and stripes raised from it.

After a short rest, we resumed our march and reached the ford where we were to cross the Rio Grande. Here we camped and the next morning we commenced to unload all the wagons and transfer the freight to the boats. Our company was ordered into the river to float the wagons across. Lieutenant George H. Pettis (company B, first infantry), was constantly in the water, leading and cheering the men regardless of danger. While uttering some encouragement, he would sink out of sight, rise, finish the sentence, and sink again, until the work was finished. The boys regarded it as great sport but regretted to find that the lieutenant was laid up for three days on account of exposure and over exertion in swimming the river to get the ropes across for the boats. After three hours of hard work, everything was safely over the river and although the men were pretty nearly worn out we managed to march ten miles in the afternoon. . .

We have splendid quarters in the buildings of the Overland Mail company which had been occupied by the Texans. There is a printing office here where once was published the treasonable sheet, *The*

Mesilla Times. It is an old office, a regular one-horse concern, brought here from Illinois.[152]

While Carleton was at Las Cruces he served a notice to the people of New Mexico but did not want said notice to be called a "proclamation" as that term had too frequently been used by the Texans and might result in misunderstandings.

I. Commanders of towns will at once establish sanitary regulations and require them to be observed by the inhabitants and by the troops. Frequent inspection will be made by commanding officer or by a medical officer under his direction. . .

II. It is expected that all the inhabitants living along the Rio Grande southward from the Jornada del Muerto to Fort Bliss, Texas, will at the earliest practicable moment, repair their dwellings and clean up their streets. . .

The people may now rest assured that the era of anarchy and misrule . . . has passed away; and that now, under the sacred banner of our country, all may claim and shall receive their just rights. Therefore, . . . let them once more pursue their avocations with the full confidence that protection will be given them.

The general commanding this district . . . appeals to every man in the confidence that he will have his support to preserve the peace of his neighborhood and the tranquillity of the country; to forget all feuds; to cultivate good fellowship one with the other; to make honesty, industry and sobriety cardinal points always to be kept in view. And in doing this, there will be little necessity . . . for the application of force to make this country prosperous and the people happy.[153]

After stationing his troops on the Rio Grande at strategic points, Fort Fillmore, Las Cruces and Mesilla, General Carleton left for Fort Bliss, El Paso, Texas. "There", he said, "are many matters of moment which require attention." [154]

152 *Alta California,* San Francisco, nov. 1, 1862. (Bancroft library).
153 *War. Reb.* Ser. I, vol. L, pt. I, p. 144 (Gen. Order no. 15, aug. 14, 1862.)
154 *Ibid.,* p. 110-111.

It was near there that Simeon Hart operated his flour mill for the benefit of the Confederate army in Texas. A volunteer from company A, first California infantry, contributes an eye-witness account of the mill where he was stationed october 4, 1862:

. . . El Molino del Norte, or Hart's mill, as it is more frequently called, is situated on the eastern bank of the Rio Grande, about a mile above and opposite the Mexican town of El Paso del Norte . . . and in sight of Monument no. 2, erected by Major Emory's boundary commission. The mill is operated by water power and runs four French stones. The largest one is three and a half feet in diameter.

Attached to the mill are four large storehouses which were, in prosperous times, filled with wheat, corn, flour, etc. These storehouses are now occupied by the men of company A, first infantry; contents not quite so bulky perhaps, but far more valuable for a finer set of men never marched to battle for their country's rights. . .

The mill on one side, a storehouse on another, the private residence of Hart on the third side, a wall connecting the house and the mill, form a spacious courtyard in the center of which is a large sun dial.

After the mill was built he procured contracts from the u.s. Government and supplied flour to almost all the territory of New Mexico and part of Arizona and Texas. The rate at which he made money may be gleaned from the fact that he bought wheat in the surrounding country at about three dollars for one hundred and fifty pounds, and sold the flour at from nine dollars all the way up to twenty-five dollars per hundred pounds. He had a train of twelve ten-mule wagons so that he paid very little for outside transportation.

At the time when Texas was surrendered by General Twiggs and the United States troops were withdrawn, Hart declared for secession. Having formerly been acquainted with Jeff Davis in Mississippi, Hart wrote to him on the subject of the territories of New Mexico and Arizona and begged him to send a force to take possession of them, offering to have a supply of provisions on hand upon their arrival. He furthermore offered to loan him three hundred thousand dollars in cash without interest.

When the Texans left, Hart went with them but he left his furniture and valuable library in El Paso, Mexico. That he did not destroy the mill is a matter of some surprise, but he fully believed that another Secesh force would arrive in a few months to retake the country. He left the mill in charge of his miller, Mr. H. H. Cooper, of Rome, New York. This gentleman is a strong Union man and upon hearing of the arrival of our column immediately sent for a force to take possession in the name of the United States.[155]

The Californians probably remembered their stay at Hart's mill, and undoubtedly their commanding officer, Colonel Edwin A. Rigg, never forgot as he married the daughter of H. H. Cooper, the mill superintendent. She was described by the soldiers as a beautiful black-eyed bride of seventeen summers.

The soldier correspondent expressed great admiration for General Carleton and although the march to the Rio Grande was a gruelling experience there was not too much complaint from the first infantry. This particular regiment held a remarkable record during its term of service. Even though some of its members re-enlisted and spent over five years in Arizona and New Mexico, five companies held a hundred per cent record in that there were no desertions and only one discharge for which there was no reason cited in the record.

Even the retreating Confederate soldiers must have respected the commander of the column from California for his consideration of the prisoners of war. His letter to the commander of the Confederate forces at San Antonio offers evidence of his compassion as well as the lack of subsistence.

Sir: I found upon my arrival here, twenty or more sick and wounded soldiers of the Confederate States army whom I was ordered by General Canby, commanding the department of New Mexico, to make prisoners of war.

155 *Alta California,* San Francisco, dec. 6, 1862. (Bancroft library).
A total of 1,855 California volunteers deserted.
39 Cong. 1 Sess. H. Ex. Doc. no. 1, vol. IV, part 1, p. 234-235. (1251)

These men, at their earnest solicitations, I sent to San Antonio on their parole. They have been furnished with rations for forty days and with medicine and hospital stores necessary on the road. I have also furnished two wagons for those who cannot walk, and have sent an escort of one lieutenant and twenty-five rank and file of the first cavalry to guard them from attack by Mexicans or Indians until a sufficient force of your army is met to whom they can be transferred; or until they reach some point near San Antonio from which they can travel with safety. From that point the lieutenant is ordered to return with his party and all the means of transportation belonging to the United States with which he was intrusted for the use of his escort and for the benefit of the prisoners.[156]

Another group of prisoners, numbering 93, were supplied with U.S. arms for their protection and ordered to keep moving toward San Antonio. They were instructed to surrender the weapons to Lieutenant French who had already left for Texas with another group of prisoners of war. Surgeon E. N. Covey of the Confederate army accompanied the second group and Carleton warned his officers to prevent the surgeon from learning the size of the force from California. Carleton also suggested to Colonel West that "if you can swoop up other people about you who had better travel to Texas, now is a good opportunity to send them to that country."

A large amount of the government's hospital and quartermaster supplies had been captured by the Confederates and secreted in buildings belonging to the customhouse authorities at El Paso, Mexico. Twelve wagon loads of these stores were recovered by the California column and sent to the supply depot at Mesilla.

General Carleton with two companies of cavalry then proceeded one hundred miles down the Rio

[156] *War. Reb.* Ser. I, vol. L, pt. I, p. 114, 117.

Grande to Fort Quitman, Texas, where on august 22 Captain John C. Cremony, company B, second cavalry, hoisted the stars and stripes. Captain Edmond D. Shirland marched farther into Texas and raised the flag over Fort Davis.[157]

These flags, which symbolized the return of that portion of the nation to the Union, were, by order of General Carleton, sent to General Wright at the headquarters of the department of the Pacific at San Francisco.

General Carleton relieved General Canby in command of the department of New Mexico and in september began his four years' service as commander of the New Mexican forces.[158]

---

[157] *Ibid.*, p. 102.
[158] *Ibid.*, p. 116.

On Duty in Arizona

When the column from California left Tucson for
the Rio Grande, Major David Fergusson, first cavalry,
was assigned to the command of the district of Western
Arizona which, although named Western, was in
reality the eastern section of that territory and extended
from Tucson to Mesilla. In addition to this responsibility, Fergusson was made chief of the commissary
department.[159]

His first consignment went to the starving people at
the Pinos Altos mines. To the troops who were building
defense works at Apache pass, he forwarded sperm
candles, lime juice, whisky, molasses, desiccated vegetables, compressed potatoes, pickles, dried apples and
a hundred bed sacks. The latter were filled with dry
grass or straw for the soldiers' beds. The chief of commissary was plagued by the lack of supplies, transportation and communication. Trains and vedettes from
Yuma and the Rio Grande were frequently long over-
due. When flour eventually arrived, "it was moldy and
tasted as though it had been buried in the ground.[160]

Major Fergusson was temporarily relieved from his
command so that he might survey a route from Tucson
to Point Lobos and La Libertad on the Gulf of California. The government expected to use this road to
expedite the transportation of troops and supplies.
Permission had been granted by the Mexican congress

[159] *War. Reb.* Ser. I, vol. L, pt. I, p. 92.
[160] *Ibid.,* pt. II, p. 36, 47-48, 109-110.

in june 1861 but in the interim French troops had invaded Mexico and international complications arisen.[161]

With a small escort of infantry, Major Fergusson left Tucson, october 10, 1862. When he reached the Cerro Colorado mine near Arivaca, he exchanged his infantrymen for a detachment of cavalry from company E. Among them was twenty-one year old Sergeant Edward Everett Ayer who was then just another GI of the 1860's. While on duty at the mine, he read his first book, the *Conquest of Mexico* by W. H. Prescott, which had been loaned from the library of Colonel Samuel Colt, one of the owners of the mine. This was the book that opened a new world to Ayer. From this beginning he became one of the most prominent collectors of books and art. Today his fine collection may be seen in the Newberry library, Chicago.

Major Fergusson carried with him a boat frame which had been built in Tucson by the mechanics of the quartermaster department. When he arrived on the Gulf of California, the boat was completed and used in making soundings.

He gave a flattering report of La Libertad and maintained that with the exception of San Francisco and San Diego, California had no harbor comparable to it. The harbor was full of many varieties of fish—bass, mullet, sardines, flounders, rock cod, shark, turtles and very large gold fish. At Lobos bay he saw more than three hundred seals and succeeded in killing one of them.

A survey of the available food supply was made but it was difficult to obtain accurate statistics from the Mexicans. In reporting on the road, Fergusson said that a loaded wagon, even drawn by a poor team, would

---

[161] 39 Cong. 1 Sess. Sen. Ex. Doc. no. 17, may 7, 1861. (1237)

not encounter the slightest difficulty and could make
the trip without using an ax, spade or crowbar, or by
moving a single obstruction.

When General Carleton reported the survey to
Washington, he recommended that the government buy
a strip of land through Sonora to the Gulf of California as he believed it to be the most practicable route
for a railroad from the Rio Grande to the Pacific and
advocated its purchase before the French took possession of it.[162]

Hope persisted that Libertad could be used to great
advantage so a second trip was made from Tucson in
the spring of 1863. P. R. Brady proceeded to the port
with "all possible dispatch" but discovered that no
vessel had arrived with government stores and Fergusson's boat was "exactly as he left it." He made the
journey to Libertad and back to Tucson in thirteen
traveling days.[163]

Fergusson also surveyed the road from Tucson to
Mesilla and reported the distance to be 261.87 miles.
Besides his numerous surveys he found time to make
a map of Tucson and take a census of his district. In
order to accomplish so much he must have heeded the
advice of his commanding officer—"What is to be done
must be done without delay; figure closely but figure
quick." [164]

Logistical troubles continued throughout the war

162 Fergusson's route: Mission San Xavier del Bac, Sahuarita, Sopori,
Cerro Colorado mine or Heintzelman's, Arivaca, Sasbe (Zazaba), Altar,
Pitiquito, Laguna Mosca, Libertad; 225.24 mi.; arrived oct. 20. He retraced
his route to Pitiquito and Caborca then turned westward to Lobos, 60 mi.
from Pitiquito. Returned via Altar, Oquitoa, Tubutama, Saric and Arivaca.
Arrived at Tucson, nov. 11.

War. Reb. Ser. III, vol. III, p. 24-35.

163 *Ibid.*, Ser. I, vol. L, pt. II, p. 353-354.

164 *Ibid.*, p. 362, 690, 171.

Ibid., pt. I, p. 937.

and Tucson appeared to be the bottleneck according to orders from the commissary department there. "Keep your business snug, push everything forward this way (Mesilla) that should come and see if you can relieve Tucson of the unfortunate reputation . . . of being the sink that swallows up everything intended to come to the front." [165]

The vedettes formed a very important arm of the service. The best horses and riders were selected for this task for theirs was a perilous undertaking. Usually they were permitted a small escort but often rode alone. Some were killed by Indians, others by highway robbers.[166]

General Carleton reported to Postmaster General Montgomery Blair in october 1862 that he had a line of vedettes operating from Tucson to Los Angeles and said that he was prepared to open the Southern Overland route from Independence or Fort Leavenworth via Santa Fe, down the Rio Grande to Mesilla and thence over the old Southern Overland route to Los Angeles. He repeated his request to the postmaster general in the following spring but evidently without success as the California volunteer vedettes continued to carry Uncle Sam's mail and served twice as long as the much heralded "Pony Express" on the Central route.[167]

Governor John N. Goodwin's report to the first legislature, Prescott, Arizona, september 1864, reveals the extent of this soldier vedette service: "Since the discontinuance of the Overland Mail in 1861 and until action of the present congress (1864) no mail routes

165 *Ibid.*, pt. II, p. 279.
166 *Ibid.*, pt. I, p. 1075, Gen. Order no. 9, par. III.
Ibid., pt. II, p. 348, 784, 352, 391.
167 *Ibid.*, p. 181, 419.

have been established in any part of this territory. We have been indebted to the courtesy of the military authorities for the means of communication between the principal points in the territory and the mail routes in New Mexico and California." The first public mail that reached Tucson after the war came from California on horseback september 1, 1865.

Occasionally escort duty was enlivened by the presence of a traveler of rare wit and intelligence as in the case of J. Ross Browne, correspondent for *Harper's Magazine* and special agent for the department of the Interior. He evidently found the volunteers equally agreeable or he would not have said, "I may here be allowed to say that a better set of men I have never traveled with. They are good humored, obliging and sober and not one of them stole a pig or a chicken on the entire trip." Browne's escort consisted of thirty men from company G, first cavalry, commanded by Lieutenant George W. Arnold.[168]

Escort to a wagon train or a band of one thousand cattle on the long road from California to the Rio Grande could not have been an easy assignment. The mules gave out, the cattle lost weight and died along the way, and the officers lost their tempers. However, the vedettes enjoyed a few advantages that were not cited in general orders. They surreptitiously read the newspapers and were accused of reading the letters also until new mail sacks were made and extra padlocks provided to avert further tampering with Uncle Sam's mail.[160]

The territory along the Rio Grande extending from Fort Thorn to Fort Quitman constituted the district of

168 *Ibid.*, p. 740.
169 *Ibid.*, p. 137, 171, 396-397.

Arizona. Colonel Joseph R. West was placed in command in september 1862 and first established his headquarters at Mesilla. The following month he was promoted brigadier general.

Remembering the old adage that an army fights on its stomach, General West appealed to the farmers on the Rio Grande to sell all the corn, wheat and flour not required for immediate family use. He warned them that if more than two months' supply was found in their possession, they would be considered an enemy of the United States and treated accordingly.[170]

In order to encourage an increase in the production of the farms, General West issued a proclamation advising the owners to return to their abandoned homes and begin planting their crops. In the event the farms were not re-occupied within thirty days after this notice, permission was granted to any person who would occupy and cultivate the land on condition that it would revert to the rightful owner on december 31 of that year. The occupant was also expected to comply with the laws regulating labor upon the acequias.

Brigadier General West assured the people of the ability of the troops to protect them and advised them to fear not and to produce their crops for Uncle Sam with the assurance of a larger market than ever before offered upon the Rio Grande.[171]

In the early spring of 1863, General West moved his headquarters to Hart's mill, Franklin (El Paso), where better pasturage and more commodious living quarters were available at the mill. There was also the advantage of "free" rent during the enforced absence of the miller as his buildings were occupied under the provis-

[170] *Ibid.*, p. 239-240.
Ibid., pt. I, p. 115, Gen. Order no. 20, par. VI.
[171] *Ibid.*, pt. II, p. 274.

ions of the Confiscation act or at least until the federal courts would again be established in Texas.[172]

General West was relieved of his command of the district of Arizona in february 1864 to report for duty at the headquarters of the department of Arkansas. The Arizona district was transferred back to the department of the Pacific the following year and Brigadier General John S. Mason assigned its command.[173]

It cannot be affirmed that the government subsidized the mining industry, but usually the United States army followed the miner and forts were built for his protection. Nor was this all. The California column was ordered to prospect in the new gold fields of Arizona and New Mexico. General Carleton detailed company D, first cavalry, for this duty and ordered Captain Nathaniel Pishon to report the exact time each soldier worked and the amount of gold obtained in return for his labor. In addition, a few samples were requested for the War department.

While company D prospected, companies C and F, first infantry, began construction of a new fort in the gold fields of Arizona. A board of officers consisting of Major Edward B. Willis, Captain Joseph Hargrave and Captain Herbert M. Enos were ordered to select the exact site for a two company post. The responsibility for the plans and the estimation of the cost rested upon these officers.[174]

These California volunteers left Fort Wingate, New Mexico, on november 7, 1863, and started for Chino valley, Arizona. It took them over a month to travel

---

[172] *Ibid.*, p. 329-330.

[173] *Ibid.*, p. 1137.

West breveted Maj. Gen. jan. 1866; died oct. 1898.

[174] *War. Reb. Ser. r, vol. r, pt. II, p. 653 654, Gen. Order no. 27, par. IV* (oct. 23, 1863.)

that far and it was december 17 when they arrived at old Camp Clarke and selected this site for Fort Whipple. The name, Government Corral, also appears on the old military maps as a near-by camp site.

The permanent site of the fort was destined to be built in another valley to the south. Just twelve days after the California volunteers pitched their tents in Chino valley, the new governor of Arizona territory, John N. Goodwin, arrived at Navajo springs, raised the United States flag, and took his oath of office as the governor of the new territory. He came overland from the east but the other officers came by steamer to San Francisco and were furnished with a military escort of California volunteers to Arizona.

Governor Goodwin made his headquarters in Chino valley at the army camp. There existed some doubt about the desirability of this site for the new fort and for the capital of Arizona. We are indebted to a volunteer from company C, first infantry, for the following information regarding the selection of the present site:

An expedition left here a few days ago (his letter dated february 12, 1864) to explore the country in the direction of the Salinas river and to find, if possible, a better location than this for the capital of Arizona and for the establishment of a military post. Governor Goodwin accompanied the expedition and upon him devolves the important duty of locating the capital.[175]

The site of Fort Whipple selected by the California major, Edward B. Willis, eventually determined the location of the capital of Arizona. For when the California volunteers moved to the present location of Fort Whipple (*Plate* 5), Governer Goodwin went with them and chose a site a mile farther up Granite creek

[175] *Amador Weekly Ledger,* Jackson, Calif., march 26, 1864. (Bancroft library).

and named it Prescott in honor of the historian, William Hickling Prescott.[176]

Goodwin was also considered as a name for the new capital according to a report from Major Willis to General Carleton: "The site of the new post (Whipple) selected by me by order of Colonel Nelson H. Davis, is about one mile and a half northeast from the town now being built on Granite creek and laid down upon the map forwarded to department headquarters as Goodwin." [177]

The volunteer then assumed a new duty and became lumberjack, quarryman and carpenter. The timber was cut with a whipsaw, a two-man saw, five to seven feet long. It cost $150 per thousand feet at the sawpit which was twenty-four miles from the fort.

In spite of the primitive building methods, the work, progressed rapidly. The soldier correspondent reports on february 12, 1864: "We are soon to have a paper published here to be called the *Arizona Press*. I believe the building is already up and in a few days more the slick click of the type will be heard among these wilds for the first time. I will send you a copy by the next mail if possible." [178]

Evidently the Californians made the headlines. The *Arizona Miner* of may 11, 1864, published an account of the work being accomplished on the new post by Captain Joseph P. Hargraves and Lieutenant Edgar Pomeroy, company C, first infantry, who had been selected to build the quarters. (The correspondent evidently was misinformed regarding the name of the paper as it was *Miner* not *Press*.)

176 39 Cong. 2 Sess. H. Misc. Doc. no. 24, vol. I, jan. 21, 1867 (Prescott Town Site). (1302)

177 *War. Reb.* Ser. I, vol. L, pt. II, p. 869 (may 27, 1864).

178 *Amador Weekly Ledger,* Jackson, Calif., march 26, 1864. (CU-B)

On june 1, 1864, it was reported that great preparations were being made to get the necessary buildings
completed for the session of the territorial legislature.
Governor John N. Goodwin was still the guest of
Major Willis.[179]

The building program continued over a period of
several years. When General John S. Mason arrived
in Prescott, august 3, 1865, he was quartered in the
governor's house and his soldier escort in the state
house. After making a tour over the territory to inspect
the forts and troops, General Mason made his headquarters at Fort Whipple.[180]

Plans were promptly made for his house and work
began at once. Even before the building started, a
garden was planted to supply fresh vegetables for his
table.

Although the general was made comfortable, the
volunteer had a rough time of it. The official roster and
journal of company C, seventh infantry, kept by Charles
A. Wyckoff, supplies a few intimate details that were
not intended for the public since he wrote:—

> Steal not this book for fear of shame
> For here you see the owner's name.

He seems to have had many extra duties—he was
soldier, clerk and builder. Day after day through the
winter of 1865-1866, in snow and rain, he worked on
the general's house. He hauled the rock, went to the
woods for the timber, split the shingles and when
Veck's train arrived from Fort Mojave with the bricks,
he was hod carrier and mason too.

[179] *San Jose Mercury,* july 21, 1864. (In office of Mercury-Herald co.—by
courtesy J. O. Hayes, Ed.) Letter written by Lt. Edgar Pomeroy, Co. C, first
inf., Calif. vol.
[180] *War. Reb.* Ser. I, vol. L, pt. II, p. 1137, 1181.

Young Wyckoff did not hesitate to say that it was cold as hell and the general was cross as the devil. In december it was snowing but the stables were unfinished and the work went on as usual.

By Christmas, 1865, he had finished the oven in the volunteers' house, but he scribbled in his journal, "Christmas day and nothing to eat.—Some of the boys got drunk." New Years was a little brighter as he received over eight months' pay and in addition, he was able to collect most of the money he had loaned to his buddies.

Fort Goodwin, also built by the volunteers, was named in honor of Governor Goodwin. The site was selected by Lieutenant Colonel Nelson Davis, inspector general of the United States army, and the expedition to the new location was under the command of Colonel Edwin A. Rigg, first infantry, and Major Joseph Smith, fifth infantry.[181]

They left Fort Craig, New Mexico, may 16, 1864, and arrived june 18. Colonel Rigg was well pleased with the spot chosen for the new post and said that it was in the most beautiful valley he had seen in Arizona. He continued:

The spring heads far up (the valley) and furnishes water sufficient to irrigate all the lands fit to be cultivated. It has evidently been a place of great resort for the Indians. Trials lead to it from various directions and have the appearance of being much used. The main trail to Sonora passes here via Graham pass. I explored the lower end of the valley on foot and camped my command on the west side of the stream under a fine shade made by large mesquite trees—the largest of the species I have ever seen. Some of them are as large and wide spreading as the oaks.

I detailed First Lieutenant John Lambert, fifth infantry, to survey

181 *Ibid.*, pt. 1, p. 360-370, Gen. Order no. 12,—1864.

and define the boundaries and limits of Fort Goodwin, . . . to be six square miles in area, taking the site of the fort as a center.[182]

The troops were ordered to clear off the underbrush and build brush houses for their comfort and to cut timber for quarters and storerooms. They were not permitted to cut any of the ash or the walnut trees.

The frontier army commanders were indeed men of vision. After exploring the Gila river and its main tributaries carefully, Colonel Rigg reported that the banks of the Gila were so steep that by means of dams the whole valley could be irrigated.[183]

Sixty-six years later the Coolidge dam was built not far from old Fort Goodwin but many years too late for the frontier soldier to see his prophecy fulfilled. U.S. highway no. 70 passes over the dam and follows the general direction of the military road constructed by the California volunteers of Colonel Rigg's command.

Since the three year term of many of the California volunteers expired during the fall of 1864, it was necessary to recruit others to take their places. Even though the application of the Enrollment act (conscription) had been suspended in California, two more new regiments, the seventh and eighth, were organized. There were enough re-enlistments from the first and fifth infantry to form a battalion of veteran infantry of seven companies. The cavalry regiments were filled by re-enlistments and new recruits.[184]

To encourage enlistments the California legislature passed an act providing for the payment of a bounty of one hundred and sixty dollars. At the time of enlistment

---

[182] *Ibid.*, p. 364.
[183] *Ibid.*, p. 367.
[184] *Ibid.*, pt. II, p. 1054-1055, 1128-1129.

the volunteers received forty dollars and at the end of every successive six months the sum of twenty dollars.[185]

The federal government allowed a bounty of fifty dollars for those who re-enlisted for one year; twenty-five dollars being paid at time of enlistment and the balance at the expiration of their term of service. Those who re-enlisted for two years received one hundred dollars and were paid twenty-five dollars at time of enlistment and the remainder when they had completed their time.

Another provision of the federal draft law was that the draftee could supply a substitute for the price of three hundred dollars. This was not applicable in California and appeared to meet the disapproval of the legislature as a draftee was excluded from the benefit of the five dollars a month extra pay allowed by an act entitled, Relief of Volunteers, passed during the four-teenth session, april 27, 1863.[186]

THE FAR JOURNEY OF A FLAG

The seventh regiment was organized in january 1865 under the command of Colonel Charles W. Lewis, a veteran of the Mexican war. This regiment was un-officially called the "hungry seventh" and also the "gold diggers" regiment. With the exception of three companies, it was composed of boys from the mother lode counties. Company A were all from Sacramento and the rest from the following locations: company B, Marysville; C, Jackson; D, Auburn and Dutch Flat; E, Calaveras county; F, Sacramento and the San Francisco bay region; G, Placerville; H, Mariposa county;

---

[185] Calif. Stats. 15 Sess. chap. 442, p. 486-491, apr. 4, 1864.

[186] 37 Cong. 3 Sess. Sen. Misc. Doc. no. 41, mar. 3, 1863. Enrollment or conscription act. (1159)

I, Nevada City; K, Downieville, Sierraville, La Porte, Howland Flat and Forest City.[187]

The fact that a number of veterans of the Mexican war enrolled in the seventh may have influenced Colonel Jonathan D. Stevenson to present the flag of the New York volunteers to that regiment. The old flag was twenty years old before it started on its journey around the Horn. After hanging idly for nearly eighteen years, it was again called into service as the veterans, themselves, were.

After Colonel Lewis, later breveted brigadier general, had trained his men for a few months, orders came to start for Arizona. With the old flag flying, the seventh marched from the Presidio through the streets of San Francisco to the wharf then up the gang plank of the s.s. "Senator". The regiment was on its way to Drum Barracks, Wilmington, and the flag began another lap of its long journey.[188]

---

[187] A partial list of the number of mountain men enlisted in all California regiments. In compiling this information, it seemed evident that it would be impossible to determine the exact number from any given community on account of the fact that so many volunteers enlisted at the various training camps and gave no home address.

Auburn 356; Angels Camp 30; Bear Valley 73; Big Oak Flat 24; Campo Seco 39; Chinese Camp 9; Coloma 56; Columbia 63; Comanche 12; Copperopolis 20; Coulterville 43; Downieville 119; Dutch Flat 61; Fiddletown 4; Forest Hill 86; Gibsonville 16; Grass Valley 72; Marysville 745; Mokelumne Hill 154; Murphys 25; Howland Flat 42; Jackson 196; La Porte 59; Mariposa 27; Nevada City 252; Oroville 288; Placerville 483; Quincy 59; San Andreas 72; Sonora 67 and Volcano 71.

Richard H. Orton, *Record of California men in the war of rebellion*, p. 763-795.

[188] Colonel Lewis breveted Brig. Gen. march 13, 1865. Served in the Mexican war; came to Yolo county, Calif. in 1849; mustered out may 22, 1866. Served in Arizona legislature one term. Died in San Diego, feb. 3, 1871.

An article telling about the New York volunteer flag published in *Tuolumne Courier,* Columbia, june 29, 1866. (Deposited in the county archives at Sonora, Calif.)

Francis D. Clark, *First New York Volunteers.*

On the same day that General Lee surrendered at Appomattox Court House, Colonel Lewis with a detachment of the seventh, left Drum Barracks for Arizona but the news had not reached the volunteers on the march. They had left Warner's ranch and were out on the desert at Carrizo creek the day that Lincoln died. Their old flag was not flown at half-mast as they were unaware of that tragedy.

Although the war in the east was over, the flag of the seventh was destined to fly over Arizona for a year longer. By may 11, it was raised over Tubac and the volunteers were busy scouting over the nearby territory for troublesome Indians and outlaws.

At old Fort Tubac (*Plate* 6) these soldier correspondents wrote detailed accounts of their experiences. Postage was free for them but paid for by the recipients of their letters. Perhaps this particular volunteer boasted a bit when he wrote,

Our express line has been started. Yesterday the expressman left with the first mail consisting of 350 letters showing conclusively that the seventh, besides being *hungry,* is literary. If we keep on sending letters in that manner, California will be overrun with them. . .[189]

The few letters that are still in existence furnish many interesting details not found in the official war records. The narrative is continued:

. . . I wrote in my last letter that Captain (Hiram Ashley) Messenger and thirty men had gone on a scout. When they reached San Rafael, about twenty miles from here, Sergeant (William D.) Kelly and Private (John) Henry were sent to look for one of our men and a citizen who had missed camp.

. . . Firing was reported about two miles from that camp, so Captain Messenger with fifteen men started to inquire into it. After

---

[189] *Calaveras Chronicle,* Mokelumne Hill, aug. 12, 1865. (Deposited in the county archives at San Andreas, Calif.)

they had gone a half mile, they were attacked by one hundred fifty or two hundred Indians who surrounded them on all sides. A fight of one and a half hours ensued in which fifteen Indians were killed and one of our men, Private (Abel) Roe, formerly of Jackson, was badly wounded by a minnie ball in his knee.

A thunder storm, coming up suddenly, prevented the Indians from using their arrows which doubtless saved the lives of more of our men. The Indians had only two guns which they had taken an hour previous from Kelly and Henry whom they had killed.

The next morning Captain Messenger went out in search of them and found their bodies stripped and horribly mutilated. Henry had his head pounded in by a rock and there were twenty-seven wounds in his body, evidently made by a blunt lance. Kelly also had a bruised head but less wounds. The Indians took two Springfield rifles and eighty cartridges besides all their clothing and accouterments. . .[190]

In the fall of 1865, the old flag was called upon to give protection to the governor of Sonora when he fled from the French troops that had invaded his country. The flag was flying over Colonel Lewis's headquarters at Fort Mason when Governor Pesqueira called on the colonel for permission to camp near the fort where he might be protected by the volunteers. More than a score of times the flag of the seventh flew at half-mast for the Californians who died while serving at Fort Mason, Arizona.

[190] *Ibid.*, sept. 9, 1865. (Deposited in the county archives at San Andreas, Calif.

One of the swords that belonged to Captain Messenger has been presented to the Louis Terah Haggin Memorial galleries, San Joaquin Pioneer Historical museum, Victory Park, Stockton, Calif.

Another was in the possession of his daughter, Mrs. E. Meier, of Campo Seco, Calaveras county, when the author met her in 1938. It was the latter sword and Captain Messenger's old blue uniform that aroused interest in the GI's of the 1860's and impelled her to search for their complete story.

Captain Messenger came overland to California in 1852. He soon followed the gold seekers to Mokelumne Hill where he picked up enough nuggets to buy a large ranch near Campo Seco, Calaveras county. He discovered and helped develop the copper mines of Campo Seco. He was a member of the California state legislature, twenty-third session.

Not until the spring of 1866 did the seventh receive orders for mustering out. They assembled at Fort Yuma, some to make the trip over the desert to Drum Barracks, while others were shipped to the mouth of the Colorado river to Point Isabel where they boarded the steamers for San Francisco.

Many growls poured forth from this demobilization center. The regulars had arrived at Fort Yuma, six companies of them, and taken over the barracks. When the volunteers reached the fort after a tough trip across the country, they were obliged to camp at the corrals. It was a month before they left for home.

Young Wyckoff still faithfully kept his journal. For a month he waited. Each day he wrote, "Still at camp," or "Same old thing. Nothing to do but fish. Caught one that weighed 18 pounds."

Then on march 9, he had news: "Started for San Francisco." Four hundred California volunteers were finally on their way home. They were delayed three hours by being stranded on a sand bar in the Colorado river and were obliged to leave the boat and spend the night on the bank of the river.

They found the s.s. "Oregon" and three brigs anchored in the slough at Point Isabel when they arrived the following day. It took them four days to reach Cape San Lucas where they stopped to take on sixty-seven casks of whale oil and some beef cattle.

Then they set their course northward in the Pacific where they encountered heavy seas and lost one of the "Oregon's" crew overboard. The soldiers endured the rough passage and their rations of tack and salt horse meat until they docked at the Folsom street wharf, San Francisco, march 25, 1866.

Wyckoff of the seventh regiment closed his journal

the following day—"Went to the city; went to the opera. THE LAST DAY OF MY KEEPING JOURNAL!" [191]

The final muster out of the seventh did not take place until may 22, 1866. The old flag had completed its journey and its service. Colonel Lewis presented it to the Society of Stevenson's California Expedition Survivors.[192]

INDIAN CHIEFS — FRIENDS AND FOES

In spite of the many warlike Indians in Arizona there were many others who were friendly and the volunteers became acquainted with their needs and learned to understand their problems. Peace instead of war seemed to be the general policy of the commanding officers. The presence of a company or two of soldiers at strategic points along the main lines of travel usually kept the Indians from raiding the settlements in the immediate vicinity of the army posts.

A white flag was frequently hung from the flagpole to assure the Indians that peace was desired and that they would not be molested if they would come in and have a "peace talk" with the "white chief".

Chief Iretaba of the Mojaves was one of the Indians who discovered that peace was far better for his people than war. He was the first Indian from western Arizona to make the long journey to Washington to call on President Abraham Lincoln. No doubt, the "great father" received Iretaba with courtesy and expressed the greatest sympathy for the Mojave Indians' prob-

---

[191] MS Charles A. Wyckoff, *Roster and journal of company* c, *seventh infantry, California volunteers.* (Fort Sutter, Museum, Sacramento, Calif.)

[192] *Tuolumne Courier*, Columbia, june 30, 1866. (County archives, Sonora, Calif.)

lems. The chief was presented with a major general's uniform and wore it proudly.

Four months passed before Iretaba returned to his people on the Colorado. He still wore his uniform but had traded off his saber in San Francisco for a Japanese sword; his shoes hurt his feet so he wore them on a string around his neck. While in San Francisco, he "registered" at the Occidental hotel then lighted with gas; there was hot and cold water and marble top wash stands. The rooms were elaborately furnished in rosewood and mahogany and the windows hung with silk damask and with lace curtains. One wonders at the impression all this made on the chief of the Mojaves.

While walking down the streets of San Francisco one day, he met Lieutenant Sylvester Mowry from the Patagonia mine, Arizona. The chief said, "Iretaba know you; me one day catch you and whip you heap; try to kill you; shoot six times at you myself; but the Great Spirit would not let me kill you; me friend now; shake hands; me no more bad." [193]

Chief Iretaba's people still live along the Colorado. Although once at war with the whites, they became friends after Iretaba's conference with Abraham Lincoln at Washington in the early spring of 1864. Perhaps they remembered the words of their chief when he returned from Washington—"Me no more bad; me friend now."

The Pima chief, Antonio Azul, was rewarded for his good behavior by a trip to San Francisco. He was mustered in as an officer and the expense borne by the government. Antonio sailed from Los Angeles aboard

[193] *Weekly Alta California (Steamer)*, San Francisco, may 13, 1864. (Huntington library)

Sacramento *Union*, may 4, 1864.

Daily Morning Call, San Francisco, dec. 4, 1863.

the s.s. "Brother Jonathan" and marveled at the great size of the "canoe". He derived his greatest pleasure from a ride with the engineer on the railroad from San Francisco to Redwood City. He had never seen the white man's "iron horse" before and said that he would like a lot of them to chase Apaches.

Juan Echeverria, chief of the Maricopas, argued that he, too, should have a trip. He offered to furnish one hundred warriors if he might be permitted to go to San Francisco. General John S. Mason, then in command of the district of Arizona, consented and the chief was duly rewarded with his vacation in the city.[194]

Even though the Californians won the friendship of Juan Echeverria of the Maricopas, they could not resist having a little fun at the expense of the Indians. They resorted to a few tricks to impress them with the power of the white man.

Company B, second cavalry, was stationed at the Maricopa village when Chief Juan Echeverria walked into the army camp and immediately recognized Captain John C. Cremony. It had been ten years since Juan had seen the captain yet he remembered his being present when Lieutenant Whipple "killed the moon and brought it to life again."

So, said Juan, "You killed the moon once and brought it to life again. You are a great medicine man. You were among us then. You are here once more. I have told my young people about it but they will not believe. When can you kill the moon again?"

The Indians had bestowed the name of Captain Killmoon on Cremony and credited him with possessing

194 *Ibid.*, nov. 26, 1863. (CL)
War. Reb. Ser. I, vol. L, pt. II, p. 1251.

supernatural powers so he resolved to maintain his reputation if possible.

An eclipse of the moon was due and the Indians were told that if they returned to camp in two days, the moon would be killed once more. Meanwhile Cremony found seven skulls on the grazing grounds and secretly prepared for his prank. He arranged them in a circle and securely tied a string to each. A candle was placed in every one; then a small fuse and some dry powder was trailed from each skull to the center of the circle and to a short distance behind the bony heads.

At the scheduled time, a large crowd of curious Indians crowded the army camp. Their attention was diverted by Sergeant George Shearer while Cremony set the stage. Cremony said,

When the candles were lighted, I took my place in the center of the circle of skulls. With my head and right shoulder bare and armed with a saber, I fixed my gaze on the moon, which was about to be eclipsed.

The signal was given and Sergeant Shearer led the excited Indians towards me. With great ceremony I drew a circle around the candle-lighted skulls and prohibited the already frightened Indians from passing that line. . .

The silence and anxiety of the savages was something fearful. I was undertaking a dangerous experiment. If I failed, the consequences might be fatal; if I succeeded, my influence among them would be almost unbounded. . .

In my hands I held a naked saber which gleamed in the candlelight from the sightless sockets of the encircling skulls. I impatiently waited the time to apply the match to the fuses. It came at last. The brilliant flame fizzed and sputtered, then suddenly terminated in darkness.

The change from intense light to darkness was so great that no one saw Shearer draw in the skulls and hide them. . . In the meantime, the moon began to re-appear. I cannot pretend to describe the effect on the Indians but the sobriquet of Captain Kill-moon was unanimously adopted.[195]

---

[195] John C. Cremony, *Life among the Apaches.*

Chief Mangas Coloradas, Red Sleeves, was both friend and foe—alternately he fought or defended the white man. He maintained his stronghold in the vicinity of the Santa Rita copper mines and was known as the chief of the Copper mine Apaches who were also referred to as the Mimbres Apaches.

One of the early friends of Red Sleeves was Benjamin D. Wilson. While "Don Benito" Wilson was trapping on the Gila river, he was captured by a band of Apaches and robbed of his gun and clothing. It was then that Red Sleeves helped Wilson escape by providing a buffalo robe and hiding him from his captors until night when he was able to elude his pursuers and return to Santa Fe.

On another occasion Red Sleeves proved his friendship for the members of the boundary commission. In order to retain the friendship of the chief, John Russell Bartlett ordered a blue suit of clothes made for him and Colonel Louis S. Craig supplied a new white shirt, a black cravat and a pair of shoes to complete the wardrobe.

The chief strutted around the army camp all that day but on the next he did not appear. However, the following day he arrived with his pants wrapped around his waist, his shirt dirty and torn, his coat buttoned to the neck, one epaulet on his breast and the other on the tail of his coat. In less than a week he had no uniform at all as one of his tribesmen had won it in a gambling game.

But the army men had won the friendship of the Apache chief and later, in july 1851, he helped Bartlett translate a few words of the Apache language. The vocabulary, a manuscript of six pages, is in the library of the Bureau of Ethnology, Washington, D.C. and is published in the *Reports of A. W. Whipple's Explorations and Surveys for a Railroad route from the Mississippi river to the Pacific ocean.*[196]

His friendship was of short duration for when the California column arrived, he formed an alliance with Cochise against the volunteers. Red Sleeves was wounded at Apache pass but his tribesmen took him to Janos, a town in Chihuahua, where a Mexican surgeon succeeded in healing his wounds.

A few years later, Chief Red Sleeves lay dead in the volunteers' camp at Fort McLane. General Carleton had ordered Brigadier General West to send out a detachment of men against the Apaches to put a stop to their depredations. Captain Edward D. Shirland and twenty of his men were detailed for this duty and were instructed to use their own judgment in either fighting or getting possession of Red Sleeves.

Captain Shirland resorted to peaceful and diplomatic means to induce the chief to come in and talk peace. The white flag hung amicably from the army camp for several days before any Indian came into camp. A squaw came in first. She was well treated and told to bring others in. The next day men, women and children came and they were fed and given presents.

Then Red Sleeves came in and Captain Shirland returned to Fort McLane bringing the chief with him. At the peace conference, the Indian claimed entire dominion over all the country usually ranged by his tribe but when charged with the atrocities they committed he tried to evade the responsibility.

Since Red Sleeves had voluntarily come to the army

[196] 33 Cong. 2 Sess. Sen. Ex. Doc. no. 78, vol. III, p. 85. (758)

The vocabulary, the manuscript, is recorded on one of the Smithsonian forms of 180 English words, equivalent to about 150 Apache. It is a copy by Dr. Gibbs.

post, he was promised that his life would be spared. In order to prevent a repetition of these Indian wars, he was told that he would be a prisoner for life in the hands of the United States authorities. He was assured that his family could join him and they would all be well treated. After being warned that he would forfeit his life if he attempted to escape, he was placed under guard.

The guards were changed at midnight and within an hour, Red Sleeves tried to escape three times. The soldiers were under orders to shoot if necessary to prevent their captive from making a dash for freedom. The end came to Chief Mangas Coloradas, Red Sleeves, who for more than half a century had led his tribe.[197]

Controversies over the manner in which the Indian affairs were conducted resulted in the appointment of a joint congressional committee of investigation. James R. Doolittle, United States senator from Wisconsin, was named chairman.

A questionnaire was carefully prepared and sent to various military men and civilians. General Wright's answer to the 23 questions reflected his forty years of experience in treaty making and peaceful attempts, as well as fighting, to settle the Indian problem. He recommended that the Indian department be placed under the War department; that the Indians be collected on great reservations and protected by the War department; that the selling of liquor be prohibited and schools and churches be established.

General Carleton also advocated placing the Indians on reservations. He said, "If they do right, they should, in my opinion, be treated with great kindness and

---

[197] *War. Reb.* Ser. I, vol. L, pt. II, p. 296. (january 1863)

consideration. If they do wrong, I believe in punishing them by war until they promise and do what is right again."

At the Bosque Redondo reservation General Carleton attempted to carry out this principle. When the congressional committee was scheduled to visit there in the summer of 1865, orders were issued for increased activity on this community farm of the Indians:

Keep on planting until it is too late to plant beans. Get in every hill of food possible. From floods, insects, grass-hoppers and hail there is danger of famine in the country. Be sure to have absent Indians at the reservation as Doolittle will want to see them all.

W. P. Dole, Indian commissioner, persistently maintained that it was better for all parties that the simple wants of the Indians be supplied and thus prevent wars rather than fight them.

Although a semblance of peace prevailed while the army of the Pacific served on the western frontier, many long bloody years followed before the last peace treaty was signed with the western Indians.[198]

198 *Ibid.*, p. 1268-1270.
Ibid., vol. XLVIII, pt. II, p. 44, 385-386, 485, 669, 707-708, 800-801, 868, 971-974, 1088-1089, 1163-1164, 1176.

On Duty in New Mexico

A very difficult task confronted General Carleton (*Plate* 7) when he arrived at Santa Fe, september 18, 1862, and assumed command of the Military department of New Mexico. During the time the country was occupied by the Confederate troops, the Indians were without the restraining influence of the Federal troops and the Indian agents.[199]

The Apaches were the most troublesome at this time. Six treaties had been made with them but they were all broken before ratification could be completed, so General Carleton first directed his attention to this tribe.

Before any action could be taken, he found it necessary to repair and garrison the old forts and to build new ones so that he could distribute his troops where they could most effectively preserve the peace.

Many of the forts were named to honor the army officers who lost their lives in the early struggle to develop this section of our country. Among those who gave their *lives* and their *names* to the state of New Mexico are: Captain Henry W. Stanton, first U.S. dragoons, killed by Apaches in the Sacramento mountains, january 19, 1855; Captain George McLane, mounted rifles, killed by Navajos, october 13, 1860; Major Joseph Cummings, first New Mexican cavalry, killed august 18, 1863 by Navajos near Canyon Bonito.

---

[199] 37 Cong. 3 Sess. H. Ex. Doc. no. 50, vol. II (1157)
38 Cong. 1 Sess. H. Ex. Doc. no. 41, vol. III (1182)

(On the old map of the Military department of new Mexico, by Captain Allen Anderson, fifth U.S. infantry, the name Cummings is given to the range of hills where the major lost his life—Fort Cummings at the eastern end of Cooks canyon was also named for him.)

Two officers who fell in the battle of Valverde were also remembered. Old Fort Fauntleroy was given the name Wingate in memory of Captain Benjamin Wingate whose death resulted from wounds received at the battle; and the new fort built to protect the Cimarron route received the name of Bascom to honor Captain George N. Bascom, sixteenth U.S. infantry, who died at Valverde.

Fort Sumner was one of the first forts built in New Mexico by General Carleton and his California volunteers. Early in the fall of 1862, Captain Updegraff, company A, fifth U.S. infantry, and Captain John C. Cremony, company B, second cavalry, California volunteers, were ordered to select a suitable site for a fort and to begin construction as soon as possible.

Although General Carleton modestly refrained from taking credit for maintaining a comparative degree of peace in his department, the official records reveal that his plans were humane even though he could not always successfully follow them. The United States government had established the policy of segregating the Indians from the whites and in some cases advocated their removal from their long established homes. Public opinion was sharply divided on this "misplaced persons" procedure but the policy of providing reservations was generally approved.

The Indian policy of General Carleton is presented in a report published in the *Congressional Globe*:

. . . The purpose I have in view is to send all captured Navajos and Apaches to Fort Sumner and there to feed and take care of them until they have opened farms and become able to support themselves, as the Pueblo Indians of New Mexico are doing. The War department has already approved of this in the case of the Apaches and authorized that Fort Sumner should be a chaplain post so that the chaplain there could educate the Indian children. This year those Indians have been contented and happy. They planted, under the direction of their agent and with a little help, some large fields of corn; and now that they have their *acequia* dug, will, next year, raise quite enough to support themselves. This the Navajos can be persuaded to do. At the Bosque Redondo there is arable land enough for all the Indians of this family.

I would respectfully recommend that now the war be vigorously prosecuted against the Navajos, that the only peace that can ever be made with them must rest on the basis that they move on to these lands, and like the Pueblos, become an agricultural people, and cease to be nomads. . . This should be a *sine qua non* as soon as the snows of winter admonish them of suffering to which their families will be exposed. I have great hopes of getting most of the tribe. . .

They should be collected on a reservation away from the haunts and hills, and hiding places of their country; there be kind to them; there teach their children how to read and write; teach them the arts of peace; teach them the truths of Christianity. Soon they will acquire new habits, new ideas, and new modes of life; and the old Indians will die off and carry with them all latent longings for murdering and robbing. The young ones will take their places without these longings, and thus little by little, they will become a happy and contented people; and the Navajo wars will be remembered only as something that belongs entirely to the past. Even until they can raise enough to be self-sustaining, you can *feed* them cheaper than you can *fight* them.

You will observe that the Bosque Redondo is far down the Pecos on the open plains where the Indians can have no lateral contact with the settlers. If the government will only set apart a reservation of forty miles square, with Fort Sumner at the Bosque Redondo in the center, all the good land will be covered, and keep the settlers a proper distance from the Indians. There is no place in the Navajo country fit for a reservation; and even if there were, it would not be wise to have it there, for in a short time the Indians would steal away into their mountain fastnesses again, and then, as of old, would come a new war, and so on *ad infinitum*. . .

General Carleton's recommendations were approved and a reservation was duly established at Bosque Redondo on the Pecos river, New Mexico. A tract forty miles square was allocated to the Mescalero Apaches and later shared with the Navajos.

Under General Carleton's command were the New Mexican volunteers as well as the California volunteers serving in that department. Colonel Christopher Carson (*Plate 7*) was in command of the New Mexican troops and frequently the Californians formed a part of his force while campaigning against the Indians.

Only a soldier who has participated in one of these scouts can accurately portray the event. A correspondent from company C, first infantry, California volunteers, recounts his experiences with the Apaches:

. . . The order for the campaign against the Apaches was promulgated and company C had a part to take. Leaving our warm and comfortable quarters in the lively town of Mesilla, we took to the mountains in the dead of winter. I shall never forget our first day's march from Las Cruces, New Mexico, to San Augustin springs. The wind blew cold and piercing from the southeast and about three o'clock the rain began to fall in torrents. Of course, we were soon wet through. However, we trudged along enlivening the way with shout and song until night in all its gloom and darkness overtook us several miles from camp, or rather from the spring where we were to make camp for the night. We groped our way along until about ten o'clock, when we reached the place selected. A more miserable crowd I reckon it would be hard to get together. To crown it all, no wood was to be found, except a few pieces of driftwood and this burned in a despairing sort of way. A few of the boys huddled around these dimly burning fires while the majority sought a dry spot on which to spread their blankets.

After an hour or two, all but the guard were asleep, when "Bang!" went a musket and "Indians! Indians!" brought us all out again in the rain and cold. After diligent search no redskins were to be found and once more, wet and shivering, we retired in complete disgust with things in general and Indian expeditions in particular.

Morning dawned clear and cold and we were soon on the road laughing and joking over the occurrences of the past night. For sixty days we followed the Indian trails among the White mountains, sometimes camping amid ice and snow and lighting our fires on the tops of the loftiest peaks and then again snugly hiding ourselves in the little valleys. A few times we caught sight of the wary foe we were pursuing. Once, twice, we made him feel the weight of our metal. We sent them howling with pain, fear and rage, to seek protection of Colonel Kit Carson at Fort Stanton. He sent them to Fort Sumner where they are now under the control of the Indian agent.[200]

The versatile frontier soldier found a way to solve nearly every problem that confronted him—even the translation of the language of the Mescalero Apache Indians. At least, that was what one soldier did with the assistance of Juan Cojo, a Mexican, who had lived with this tribe for more than twenty years before he was released.

Juan was acting as interpreter at Fort Sumner when the Mescalero Apache Indians were brought to the Bosque Redondo reservation. At this same time, Captain John C. Cremony, company B, second cavalry, California volunteers, was stationed there. He had already acquired a rudimentary knowledge of the language from Mangas Coloradas, Chief Red Sleeves, who had taught the members of the United States boundary commission more than a hundred words.

After negotiating a wage increase for Juan as language instructor, Cremony began a two months' course in the Apache language—may-june, 1863. When he had finished, he presented his manuscript to General Carleton who sent it to the Smithsonian institute for

[200] *Amador Weekly Ledger,* Jackson, Calif., march 26, 1864. (Bancroft library).

publication. But it was never published and the disappointed Cremony explains,

I have waited several years for its appearance, but have not yet seen anything of the kind. Perhaps, it will some day come to light.

In the meantime, I received from the institute an acknowledgment of my labors, the chief credit being given to General Carleton—probably because he was a general and I, only a captain subject to his orders.

Let that be as it may, I felt both pride and pleasure in acquiring a language never (?) before spoken by a white man and I took much pains to systematize it as far as practicable. In order to be certain about the reliability of my novel acquirement, I submitted my work to the leading warriors of the tribe. They expressed much delight at my desire to learn and communicate with them in their own tongue and manifested zeal in putting me right on all occasions. Nothing was committed to final record until it had been fully tested four or five times and I believe the work to be as nearly perfect as could be under the circumstances.

Cremony's manuscript was later returned to him with the request that he copy it in ink. He was either short of ink powder or time as he never copied it and today the faded pencil copy is in the Bancroft library, University of California, Berkeley. Nevertheless, his translation corresponds quite closely with the modern version.[201]

---

[201] Apache Language—numbers

	Ceremony	Present accepted
1.	tash-ay-ay	hla-i
2.	nah-kee	na-ki
3.	kay-yay	ta-gi
4.	tin-yay	din-i
5.	asht-lay	ash-tla-i
6.	host-kon-ay	gus-tan
7.	host-ee-day	gus-tsi-gi
8.	hah-pee	tsa-bi
9.	en-gost-ay	ngus-tai
10.	go-nay-man-ay	gu-nez-na
20.	nah-tin-yay	na-din
30.	kah-tin-yay	ta-din

A "close up" of a soldier's life at Fort Sumner and the campaign against the Navajos is furnished by Thornton G. Porter, company B, second cavalry, in his letter of february 6, 1864.

. . . It was one of the coldest days I have seen in ten years, when word was brought to the Fort (Sumner) that there was a large party of (Navajo) Indians lurking around, doubtless for the purpose of stealing the government herds of cattle and mules which are always kept near the post. At that time there were only nine of the cavalry here, the rest being out on a scout. But those present saddled up and in company with forty of the Apache Indians, started on the war path. After a ride, or rather a run, of some ten miles we came upon a party of one hundred and forty Navajos drawn up in order of battle on a level plain about three miles from the Rio Pecos. I am not ashamed to acknowledge, that when we ascended the hill and saw the numbers there to receive us on the plain below, I would rather have been at home than there.

After halting for a few moments to allow the soldiers and the savages (Apache allies) to get rid of everything that would hinder them in the use of their arms, we went at them on the full charge, discharging our carbines in their faces at about forty yards. We did not stop to re-load but drew our "Colts improved" and rode in among them, letting them have it right and left. For a few moments I did not know but that the snow, which had been falling for some time, had changed to something more solid in the shape of bullets and arrows. The fight was too close and too warm to last long; as usual, superior arms and discipline prevailed and the savages broke and fled. After that it was a running fight for ten miles. Then the lateness of the day and the tired condition of our horses compelled us to stop. . .

The most singular thing to me is that none of our party were killed and only a few of our Indian (Apache) allies wounded. Yet those Navajos have long been the terror of this country. For my share of the spoils, I had the honor to be commended for bravery in the official dispatches to headquarters (which is all the reward a soldier generally

40. tish-tin-yay	dis-din
50. asht-tin-yay	ash-tla-din
100. too-ooh	gu-nez-na-din

names

Corn Flower—Nah-tanh   Na-tan

gets, and it means nothing) and the promises of two of the horses, but have not received them as yet, nor do I ever expect to.[202]

During the summer of 1864 there was considerable commerce on the Cimarron route between Fort Larned and Fort Union (*Plate* 1) so the Indians seized the opportunity to supply themselves with horses, cattle and provisions by a concerted raid on the wagon trains.

To prevent such a loss in lives and property, General Carleton ordered a total of three hundred troops to be stationed along the road. Fifty cavalry and thirty infantry under command of Captain Nicholas Davis, first infantry, California volunteers, were placed at the Upper Cimarron springs; Major Joseph Updegraff, fifth U.S. infantry, with fifty cavalry and fifty infantry at the Lower Cimarron springs; and Captain E. H. Bergmann, first New Mexican volunteers, with a hundred men at the Upper Crossing of the Arkansas river. For sixty days these soldiers escorted the slow lumbering ox teams, the ubiquitous covered wagons, and the army supply trains.[203]

After patrolling the Cimarron route during the summer of 1864, a campaign was planned against the Comanches in the fall. Colonel Carson was placed in command of over four hundred men—two hundred fifteen California volunteers, one hundred eight New Mexican volunteers and seventy-five Indian allies. Twenty-seven wagons were necessary to carry the supplies for this extensive scout. Surgeon George S. Courtright accompanied the troops but only one ambulance was provided.

The troops were assembled at Fort Bascom, november 10, 1864, to prepare for their expedition. After

[202] *Solano Press,* Suisun, march 12, 1864 (County Archives, Fairfield).
[203] *War. Reb.* Ser. I, vol. XLI, pt. II, p. 811.

fifteen days' march, they reached Cañada de los Ruedas, or Wheel Gulch, where the Mexican ox-wagon trains laid over to make new wheels from the large cottonwood trees which grew there.

From here, Carson's Indian allies were sent ahead to locate the hostile Indians who were reported to be camped not far from St. Vrain's Fort, also known as Adobe Walls. The scouts soon returned to report that they had found the Indians.

Then Colonel Carson gave his order to march at night. All troops were to travel in light marching order and no smoking or talking was permitted. Just before daylight, Carson halted his troops, dismounted his men and commanded them to remain by their horses and hold their bridle reins. There was a heavy frost that night but the Indians did not mind as they were covered with their heavy buffalo robes which were belted on tightly at their waists and stood high above their heads.

When the bugle sounded the charge, the Indians dashed into a clump of chaparral, disposed of their heavy robes and came out in their war paint and feathers. They needed no further command. They splashed across the Canadian river, through the tall grass, and on toward their enemy.

A thousand warriors opposed the soldiers. Late in the afternoon Carson gave orders to retreat to his wagon train in the rear. The Indians followed and set fire to the dry grass in the rear of the soldiers and by so doing they could hide behind the smoke and get within firing distance. Carson took to the higher ground where the grass was not so high and set fires in his rear to stop the Indians' attack.

Two of the soldiers were killed and twenty-one wounded. The one ambulance could not hold all of them so the injured volunteers were loaded on the gun and ammunition carts—a rough trip. Several of them died on the way back to Fort Bascom where they arrived december 20, 1864. The Indians' loss was estimated at one hundred.[204]

Early in the spring of 1865 General Carleton ordered Colonel Carson, with company F, first California cavalry, and two companies of New Mexican volunteers, to march east on the Cimarron route to a point about halfway between Fort Union and the Arkansas river and establish a post. The exact location was left to Carson but Cedar bluff and Cold springs were both recommended as suitable sites.

By june, Carson reported that six sets of officers' quarters were completed and occupied; a quartermaster building 12 by 20 feet was nearly finished; and the men were sheltered in tents supported by walls. There was little lumber available but plenty of rock. The troops were entrenched behind breastworks of stone banked with earth which inclosed a space 200 feet square. The camp was named Nicholas.

Carson had been instructed by Carleton to talk to the Cheyennes, Kiowas and Comanche chiefs and to tell them, "If the Indians behave themselves that is all the peace we want and we shall not molest them. . . If they do not, we will fight them on sight and to the end. They must not stop the commerce of the plains."

Carleton did not say for what purpose or for whom he wished beaver skins, but he asked Carson to speak to St. Vrain about buying some. Carleton had a wife and

---

[204] *Ibid.*, pt. I, p. 939-944.
Co. B, M, K, first California cavalry—Major (promoted from captain) Wm. McCleave, commanding; Co. A, first California veteran infantry, Capt. Geo. H. Pettis. 2 mountain howitzers. Co. C and D, New Mexico cavalry.

two daughters, Etta and Eva, who had probably inveigled the head of the family to obtain some for them.

With their new camp in order the volunteers were ready for escort duty between Camp Nicholas and Fort Larned, Kansas. Fifty men from company F, first California cavalry, under command of Captain Thomas A. Stoombs and Lieutenant Richard H. Orton left on june 19, 1865. On their first trip they accompanied a train of seventy ox-wagons. Captain Stoombs was warned to proceed with extreme caution and to remember that his first duty was to protect the property entrusted to his care.

As early as march 1, General Carleton had announced to the people of New Mexico that a company of troops would act as escort to all wagon trains leaving Fort Union for Fort Larned on the first and fifteenth of each month. The first company would follow the route through the Raton pass and the second, the Cimarron route. Merchants and travelers were asked to assemble at Fort Union.[205]

Fort Larned was built at the confluence of the Pawnee creek and the Arkansas river, Pawnee county, Kansas. The first fort was built of adobe with a sod roof and it was this one that sheltered the Californians after their long trip from Camp Nicholas. Fort Larned was first established in 1859.

The comparatively bloodless campaign against the Navajos in the summer and fall of 1863 was under the command of Colonel Carson. He was assisted by his New Mexican troops, four companies mounted and two dismounted, and in addition, detachments of California volunteers under the command of Major

---

[205] *War. Reb.* Ser. I, vol. XLVIII, pt. II, p. 317, 344-345, 338, 360, 368, 922, 941. *Ibid.*, pt. I, p. 689, 782-783.

E. D. Willis and Captain Joseph P. Hargraves, company C, first infantry.[206]

It appeared to be necessary to secure approval of the campaigns against the Indians as General Carleton reported his plans to the War department and asked permission to use one hundred Utes because Carson wished to use them as guides.

Evidently the required permission was received as the Utes accompanied Carson on his Navajo expedition. However, they quit their job as soon as they discovered that they could not have all the war booty they acquired. They saw no reason why they could not capture the Navajo women and children and sell them in Mexico. General Carleton refused to permit this traffic in human beings but did agree to pay them a dollar a head for all captured sheep as they could be used to feed the soldiers.[207]

After establishing his headquarters at Fort Defiance, Carson lost no time in starting his campaign. He was a hard riding fighter and expected as much from his men. He had taken his staff, a detachment of his soldiers, together with the Ute guides, and rode west toward the stronghold of the Navajos. The guides sighted a band of them so Carson left his command and rode off with the Utes. For thirty-six hours he sat in

206 *Ibid.,* vol. XXVI, pt. I, p. 250-260 (report of Carson).

Ibid., p. 259 (report Capt. Joseph P. Hargraves).

Christopher Carson, commonly known as Kit Carson, was made lieutenant colonel of the first New Mexican infantry, july 25, 1861, and advanced to the rank of colonel september 20, 1861.

Colonel Carson was breveted brig. gen. volunteers, march 13, 1865, for gallantry in the battle of Valverde and for distinguished service in New Mexico.

Muster out volunteer service, oct. 8, 1866.

Promoted lt. col. first battalion New Mex. inf. and cav., oct. 8, 1866.

Honorable muster out november 22, 1867. Died may 23, 1868.

207 *War. Reb.* Ser. I, vol. XXVI, pt. I, p. 563, 235.

the saddle but finally gave up the chase as he would have been obliged to travel ninety miles without water if he continued to follow the fleeing Navajos.

Upon returning to his command he found a group of disgruntled men—even the chaplain complained. Carson at once asked for his resignation as well as that of Captain McCabe and explained, "I do not wish to have any officers in my command who are not willing to put up with as much inconvenience and as many privations for the success of the expedition as I undergo myself." [208]

It was a gruelling experience to travel over the rough terrain of Navajo land in the mid-august heat. One unnamed volunteer from company B, first New Mexican regiment, carefully recorded each day's events of the campaign.

After a hard scout, he was enjoying a brief respite in a spot that he called "Volunteer canyon". Here, said he, "I found an abundance of wild rose bushes and gathered and prepared some slips for my home on the Hudson."

On august 14, 1863, he wrote, "One of our men was at work yesterday chiseling on the face of a smooth rock on the side of the canyon the legend, '1st. Regt. N.M. Vols., aug. 13th 1863—Col. C. Carson, Comm.' Ages hence this may cause as much curiosity among antiquarians as do now the old names upon the famous Inscription Rock near Zuni, where there are hundreds of names and records of events back to the year 1618." [209]

This canyon is known to the Navajos as Lukadeshjin, meaning "ashy reeds"; to the general public, as Keams

[208] *Ibid.*, p. 233-236.
[209] MS William Gillet Ritch (Huntington library).

canyon named for Thomas Varker Keams, company C, first cavalry, California volunteers. Keams married Gray Lady, a Navajo girl, and for many years owned a trading post in the canyon that the soldier designated as Volunteer canyon.

The expedition to Canyon de Chelly was next on the soldiers' agenda, so preparations were made for leaving camp in "Volunteer canyon". On the first day's journey, the Navajos tried, but failed, to surprise the soldiers and stampede their horses. The diarist recorded, "Mr. Navajo became convinced that he was in the same predicament as the bull was, in trying to butt off the locomotive.

"The heat was past endurance. Nearly every pack horse had to be repacked during the day. More packs came off than I have ever seen in one day. The animals gave out and were shot as fast as they became unable to keep up with the command. Six horses and two mules shot today."

On august 20, 1863, the soldiers left Fort Defiance and after traveling sixteen miles, camped on a high barren bluff overhanging Canyon de los Trizos. They passed many singular and grotesque formations of rock —caves, domes, arches, towers and steeples.

It was an all day's job, so they left camp without breakfast to explore Canyon de los Trizos. After a two mile hike, thirty men were deployed as flankers on each side of the canyon while the main body of troops kept to the middle. For a distance of three or four miles, the canyon was only fifty to one hundred fifty yards wide and the walls rose perpendicularly to two hundred feet.

At two o'clock in the afternoon Captain Pfeiffer ordered all, except thirty, of his men to return to camp. He remained behind with his detachment until dark to ascertain whether the Indians would return. Eight or ten did and were fired upon without effect. The captain returned after dark and prepared to start for Canyon de Chelly the following day.

They continued their journey—"Where to—no one knows but the chief," wrote the volunteer. On august 24, they came in sight of *La Ventana,* the Window.

La Ventana, Window rock, is now the site of the central agency of the Navajo Indians. The buildings were completed in 1935 and about one hundred fifty people, including the Navajos, are employed there. The Navajo radio station, KTGM, which serves forty smaller stations on the Navajo reservation, now supplants smoke signals as a means of communication.

On the same day they examined the nearby petrified trees of all sizes and in all stages of preservation. With the exception of their branches, some of them were as perfect as the day they fell. One tree measured fifty feet in length and two feet in diameter. Most of the trees were broken or seamed into sections from two to four feet long and clearly showed the grain of the wood. The volunteer commented upon the fact that there was no timber of that size growing any place near the spot.

On august 25, (1863), a notable comment was recorded in the volunteer's diary, "We seem to be passing around the mountains and striking for the upper end of Canyon de Chelly."

The next camping site suited the volunteers perfectly. There were rabbits to hunt and they learned from the Indians a novel way to capture them. Mr. Indian dug neat little canals from the stream to the rabbits' burrows, giving his quarry the choice of being drowned or captured when forced to the surface.

Captain Pfeiffer (later colonel) reported to Colonel

Carson that he had passed from the east to the west entrance of Canyon de Chelly without a casualty. The walls were almost perpendicular for the first twelve miles, he reported, and high among the rocks were the forts or castles of the Navajos in this Gibraltar of Navajodom. One structure, in particular, was substantial and of beautiful masonry. He was surprised to find a large peach orchard nearby in the canyon.

The Navajos evaded direct combat with the troops and retreated to the mountains where it was difficult to find them.

Although for twenty years General Carleton had campaigned against the Indians, his admiration for a valiant adversary did not diminish as revealed in his report to the Indian department at Washington:

The exodus of this whole people from the land of their fathers is not only an interesting but a touching sight. They have fought us gallantly for years on years; they have defended their mountains and stupendous canyons with a herioism which any people might be proud to emulate; but when it was their destiny, as it had been that of their brethren, tribe after tribe, to give way to the insatiable progress of our race, they threw down their arms. As brave men and fully entitled to our admiration and respect, they have come to us with confidence in our magnanimity; with the belief that we are too powerful and too just a people to repay that confidence with meanness or neglect. They hope that in return for having sacrificed to us their beautiful country, their homes, the associations of their lives, the scenes rendered classic in their traditions, we will not dole out to them a miser's pittance in return for what they know to be a princely realm. . .

All the main routes of travel were patrolled by the volunteers until the spring of 1866. One of their major tasks was to protect the sheep and cattle. During the year 1863, the Indians stole over twenty thousand sheep and more than four hundred head of cattle. But few army horses were stolen as they could usually outrun the Indian ponies. The soldiers succeeded in recapturing nearly all of the sheep as they traveled so slowly.

From the Pecos to the Rio Grande, and at all the old forts, the volunteers scouted for hostile Indians to either induce them to quite fighting and move to the reservation, or to capture them and bring them in under guard.

The attempt to convert the Bosque Redondo into an agricultural community was initiated more than a half century too soon. Today, the Alamogordo dam impounds sufficient water to irrigate these same lands upon which the Navajos and Apaches reached near-starvation in the years 1863-1868.

During those first years at the reservation, thirty miles of irrigation ditches were dug and a sizable dam built across the Pecos river at a distance of six miles above the post. The winter rains washed out the bank of the river for a distance of 120 feet but the dam held, and instead of holding the waters back, it only served to change the course of the river and destroy the crops.[210]

The food shortage was so critical that General Carleton ordered the soldiers on half rations so that the Indians would not starve. He also instructed three companies of the first cavalry to remain at Drum Barracks as there was not enough food for them in Arizona and New Mexico. Said he, "They cannot come forward and starve on the desert or at Tucson. If troops can get bread, meat and salt, they must hold on."[211]

The already depleted United States treasury could not meet the heavy expense of providing food and shelter for so many Indians who were unable to help

[210] 40 Cong. 2 Sess. H. Ex Doc. no. 248, vol. xv (report for 1868). (1341)
[211] War. Reb. Ser. I, vol. xxxiv, pt. II, p. 674-675, 677, 755.

themselves. General Carleton reported that there were 8,793 captive Indians on the reservation in 1864; and M. Steck, Indian agent, said that $700,000 had been spent—a half million of that amount exclusively for food and the rest for transportation, clothing and the erection of new buildings.[212]

After five costly years, a treaty was made with the Navajos, june 1868, by which they were assigned 5,200 acres in their old country; each Indian was allowed five dollars in clothes, ten dollars, if he farmed or traded; the head of each family was permitted to select 160 acres of his own and was given one hundred dollars in seeds and implements the first year; and twenty-five dollars the second and third years; 15,000 sheep and 500 cattle were alloted to the tribe. Buildings were to be erected at a cost of $11,500; and a school and teacher promised for each thirty children. The sum of $150,000 was appropriated by Congress to pay the cost of the removal of the Navajos.

When General Carleton and the California column first arrived in New Mexico, the people were so grateful for their protection that the legislature passed a resolution thanking them and the Colorado volunteers. However, it was not long before the New Mexicans began to complain about the restrictions of their freedom. Regimentation was not popular on this frontier.

The people objected to the system of passports that had been instituted july 12, 1864, by General Carleton to keep track of all possible enemies. There existed a constant threat of another invasion from Texas and by this method of issuing passports to non-residents he could register those who might be spies.[213]

---

212 *Ibid.*, vol. XLI, pt. II, p. 901.

Ibid., vol. XLVIII, pt. i, p. 899-909.

213 *Ibid.*, vol. XLI, pt. II, p. 168-170.

Liquor dealers and owners of "gaming tables" protested against the high taxes on their business. No doubt, the order to collect the taxes was rigidly enforced as the money thus collected was paid into the hospital fund for the benefit of the California volunteers.

Several of the original tax receipts are now in the Henry E. Huntington library, San Marino, California. One is quoted:

$100   April 10, 1863.
   This is to certify that Joseph Gerrol has paid into the Hospital fund at Fort Craig, New Mexico, one hundred dollars, which entitled him to sell liquors by the glass in the town of Paraje (de Fra Cristobal), New Mexico, for the period of one month from march 19, 1863.
   Edwin a Rigg Commanding, Colonel First Infantry, California Volunteers.
   Headquarters District Fort Craig, New Mexico.   214

Furthermore, General Carleton did not always agree with the civil authorities as he felt that they imposed upon the military personnel when they asked the soldiers to perform the duties that rightly belonged to the officers of the territory of New Mexico.

General Carleton had been in command of the department of New Mexico for only six months when he addressed a somewhat caustic reply to Governor W. F. M. Arny's request for transportation. He agreed to furnish wagons and escort but reminded the governor that the Military department was busily engaged in operations against the Indians and that the unusual burden of having to administer justice between citizens over a large extent of country was very onerous indeed.

He continued, "As the government has sent civil

214 William Gillet Ritch MS (Huntington library).

officers here for this purpose and is paying their salaries, it seems particularly hard that the military should bear this additional burden in all of Arizona and the Mesilla valley because of what appears to be unwarranted procrastination on the part of the federal officers, whose duty it is to perform the legitimate functions of their office or give way to others who will willingly do so." [215]

A year later, the controversy had not yet been settled and an appeal was made to the United States attorney general by Judge Knapp of New Mexico. The opinion rendered by the attorney general upheld that of Judge Knapp and, in addition, the secretary of war ordered General Halleck to inform General Carleton that the military commissions and courts in New Mexico had no jurisdiction over cases between persons not in military service and that such decisions were null and void. Moreover, the individual members of these military commissions rendered themselves liable to punishment and damages.[216]

Even after the end of the war, the controversy between General Carleton and the New Mexicans continued. The general and a few of his friends, including Colonels N. H. Davis and A. B. Carey, coveted a part of the Rio Grande Rancho and negotiated with some of the owners to obtain title to it for a paltry sum.

They were thwarted in their attempt as the New Mexican legislature assembly council addressed a memorial to congress requesting that General Carleton and his associates in the real estate deal be removed from duty and that an investigation be made in regard to their official conduct.[217]

[215] *Ibid.*

[216] *War. Reb. Ser.* I, vol. XXXIV, pt. II, p. 245-246.

[217] 39 Cong. 2 Sess. H. Misc. Doc. no. 16, vol. I, jan. 7, 1867. (1302)

The Spanish grant to Rancho del Rio Grande, Taos county, is dated february 4, 1795, and the act of possession bears the date april 9, 1795. The grant was recognized by Mexico in 1837; and the claim was good and valid under the treaty of 1848 between United States and Mexico.[218]

According to the United States surveys of the years, 1877, 1879, 1890, the Rio Grande grant contained 109,043 acres. The grant was confirmed, not to the military officers but to the New Mexicans.

Through all the war years, General Carleton was ably assisted by Colonel Carson and his New Mexican volunteers and he did not hesitate to express his appreciation of the fighting colonel in one of his communications:". . . A great deal of my good fortune in Indian affairs—in fact, nearly all with reference to the Navajos, Mescalero Apaches and Kiowas—is due to you. It always affords me pleasure to acknowledge the value of your services." Further help was rendered by detachments of the fifth U.S. infantry.[219]

General Carleton was mustered out of the volunteer service, april 30, 1866, and made lieutenant colonel of the fourth U.S. cavalry. On july 31, of the same year he was promoted colonel of the second U.S. cavalry and ordered to Texas with his regiment. He died at San Antonio, january 7, 1873, at the age of fifty-nine.

218 40 Cong. 2 Sess. H. Misc. Doc. no. 97, vol. II, march 1868. (1350)
42 Cong. 2 Sess. H. Misc. Doc. no. 181, april 1872. (1526)
219 *War. Reb.* Ser. I, vol. XLVIII, pt. I, p. 689.

Trouble on the Mexican Border

Although all the Confederate troops had recrossed the Texas border and the sick and wounded escorted back to Fort Davis, rumors persisted that a second invasion was imminent. Letters flaunting, "Department headquarters of Texas, New Mexico and Arizona," were intercepted on the border and revealed the determination of the Texans to make another effort to conquer the far southwest.

Colonel John Baylor, C.S.A., received orders from Richmond, Virginia, to raise four battalions of partisan rangers, three of them to be recruited in Texas and the fourth in Arizona and New Mexico. The men were to receive the same pay and bounty as the volunteers but were required to furnish their own arms, equipment and horses. Judge S. M. Baird, a resident of Arizona for fifteen years, was appointed colonel of the fourth battalion and Dan Showalter the lieutenant colonel.[220]

To prevent a surprise attack, General Carleton concentrated a large number of California volunteers at Fort Bliss, Texas, and at Las Cruces, New Mexico, while spies were dispatched down the Rio Grande to look for the advancing army from San Antonio.

About the middle of october 1862, a notorious Confederate spy known as Captain Skillman arrived in El Paso, Mexico, and reported that a large force of

[220] *War. Reb.* Ser. I, vol. L, pt. II, p. 298, 332-333.
Ibid., pt. I, p. 1108.
Ibid., vol. XLI, pt. II, p. 169.

Texans was within ten days march of the town. His propaganda was so effective that many of the residents, of Isleta, Socorro and San Elizario hurriedly crossed the Rio Grande to Mexico to escape the invaders.

Captain Skillman usually arrived at night and would deliver the mail, secure all possible information, and be away by morning. At one time, he barely escaped capture when he and ten of his men held the plaza at El Paso for two hours before they were able to shoot their way out.[221]

American and Mexican outlaws were then operating on both sides of the border. A gang at Fort Leaton, on the Texas side, crossed to Del Norte and took a peaceful American citizen, named Wolfe, from his bed one night and hanged him until he was almost dead before they released him. He was subjected to this gruelling experience because he had vowed his loyalty to the Union. The chief instigator of this near-hanging was the American desperado, Edward Hall, who lived at Fort Leaton. He claimed to be an agent of the Confederacy and showed papers signed by a notary empowering him to dispose of the United States government property at Fort Davis.[222]

When President Lincoln appointed Reuben Creel as United States consul to Chihuahua, more reliable information was obtainable and before long the activities of the outlaws and the spies on the border were curbed. Creel had lived in Chihuahua for sixteen years and offered his services to the government gratis.

---

[221] *Ibid.*, vol. xv, p. 600, 605-606.
MS *William Gillet Ritch* (Huntington library).
[222] *War. Reb.* Ser. I, vol. xv, p. 675.
Fort Leaton was built in 1849 near Presidio del Norte, Texas, at the junction of the Rio Grande and the Conchos rivers. The old fort has been restored as a memorial.

Major David Fergusson, first California cavalry, was ordered to confer with the new consul and devise plans whereby the movement of the Texas troops could be watched and an invasion of the southwest averted. He also called on Don Luis Terrazas, governor of Chihuahua, in order to adopt some plan to rid the border of desperadoes and the abuses of some of the southern sympathizers who had taken refuge in Mexico. Terrazas agreed to grant passports to American officers and their armed escorts when necessary for their protection. Lack of extradition laws proved harmful to both the United States and Mexico as the outlaws habitually crossed the border after raiding one side or the other.[223]

Creel was able to obtain considerable information from M. M. Kinney, vice consul at Monterey and from citizens of San Antonio, but because mail service was so slow and uncertain, the California troops on the border would receive the information before Creel's letter arrived or Skillman would have come and gone again.

Orders were issued for increased vigilance and unceasing patrol of all border trails. As a further precaution, all supplies were to be moved north of the border if the Texas force proved to be too large to be held back. Furthermore, buildings along the Rio Grande were ordered burned, especially Hart's mill; and all ferry boats and stocks of lumber destroyed. Colonel West was cautioned to retreat rather than permit the Texan troops to advance to a position where they could shut off the Californians' source of supply at Fort Craig.[224]

[223] War Reh. Ser. I, vol. xv, p. 634-635, 638-639, 674-675, 682-683, 687, 701, 708-709, 992-993, 997.

[224] Ibid., p. 578, 599-600.

Letters and newspapers from Texas exaggerated the threat of invasion and Reuben Creel concluded that the army reported moving north was a humbug. However, he did give credence to a rumor that the Jews were fleeing from Texas and pouring into Mexico for safety as they were being violently persecuted.[225]

For almost three years, Captain Skillman, the Confederate spy, rode the border trails, eluding the troops on each trip; but he was destined to take his last ride. It was april 1864, when he reached the Spencer ranch near Presidio del Norte to rest his horse in the hospitable shade. Company A, first infantry, was then stationed at Hart's mill and Captain Albert H. French had ordered his men to keep a sharp lookout for Skillman. Did the daring spy and pony express rider decide to fight his way out, and did he die fighting? Was he surprised and shot when he refused to surrender? The records do not say. Shorn of all details, the official report reads, "One of my scouts killed the notorious spy, Skillman, and confiscated the mail he carried. One of the letters was from Dan Showalter to Ann Foreman, daughter of Colonel Ferris Foreman."[226]

Continued vigilance was the price of safety. Even during the last years of the war, efforts were made to recruit volunteers for an army that would move north from Texas to recapture Arizona and New Mexico and even California if possible.

Judge J. W. Hastings, a former resident of California, made a trip to Richmond, Virginia, to present his proposal to James A. Sedden, secretary of war, Confederate States of America. Sedden appeared to favor the scheme although there was no money available to

225 *Ibid.*, vol. L, pt. II, p. 377.
226 *Ibid.*, p. 1078.

pay the expenses and suggested that money could be raised by the exportation of cotton which could be managed by Major Hart the "cotton king".

Judge Hastings received a commission as major and was ordered to report to Texas headquarters. He was confident that he could raise from 3,000 to 5,000 troops. First, he planned to recruit men in California and send them in the guise of miners to Mexico. They were expected to maintain the character of a mining company and advised not to violate the neutrality of that country as they passed through to Texas. All the men were ordered to come armed and equipped at their own expense but were promised that they would be reimbursed for all money expended.

Dan Showalter and Judge David S. Terry, both survivors of political duels in California, were to assist in carrying out Hasting's scheme. Judge Terry assured Jefferson Davis that if he could open the road from El Paso to California, he would at once have an army of 25,000 men as he expected considerable help from the secret societies, Knights of the Golden Circle and the Columbian Star.

The loyalty of the southwest and the west was no doubt underestimated by the promoters of this scheme as all attempts resulted in failure. Texas troops were soon needed at home to repel the invasion of the Union troops and the plot to recruit troops for the Confederate cause in the southwest and California was abandoned.[227]

The California troops on the Arizona-Mexico border were alerted for any trouble that might result from the French occupation of Mexico. Five companies of infantry and four of cavalry, under the command of Colonel Charles W. Lewis, were stationed at Fort

[227] *Ibid.,* p. 703-705, 700, 710, 721-722, 621, 648, 681.

Mason, Arizona, to preserve the neutrality of the United States.

General Carleton found himself in an embarassing position when the War department warned the California troops against any military action that would jeopardize the friendly relations with France or complicate the United States in the war between Mexico and Maximilian's French troops.

On the other hand, William H. Seward, secretary of state, adhered to the good neighbor policy and maintained that the United States recognized only the republic of Mexico and its president, Benito Pablo Juarez, and not the government of Prince Maximilian.

When the French troops landed at Guaymas and began their conquest of Sonora, Governor Don Ignacio Pesqueira succeeded in eluding them and crossed the international border near Fort Mason. The governor sent a messenger to ask Colonel Lewis's permission to camp near the fort. A soldier correspondent from company C, native California cavalry, furnished an account of this incident:

Colonel Lewis replied that he and his officers would do themselves the honor to wait on the governor of Sonora. This they did and offered him the hospitality and protection of the post.

The next day the governor and his officers paid a visit to Colonel Lewis. The fugitive governor decided to make his quarters on an old ranch nearby where he can pasture his cattle, mules, and donkeys and horses. He brought one thousand head of cattle, one hundred head of horses and mules, besides a large number of sheep and goats. They say that the last place he visited in Sonora was his mine. It is reasonable to suppose that he has money. All his family and servants are here with him.

Shortly after this incident, the French troops were withdrawn from Sonora and Governor Pesqueira returned and once more assumed control of his state.

At about this same time, some of the California troops were having troubles of their own on the Mexican side of the border where they had been intercepted by the French troops and obliged to explain their presence south of the border. When the Californians said that they had deserted from the Native California cavalry, they were held as prisoners and their horses, arms, and equipment confiscated.

Captain José Ramon Pico, company A, and Captain Porfirio Jimenez, company B, with thirty men, crossed the border to obtain the release of their men. They met the French troops in Magdalena and demanded the deserters. They were told that if they would acknowledge the Imperial government in Mexico, the prisoners would be freed. Captain Pico swore that he would not recognize the emperor or the Imperial government; and that the republic of Mexico under President Juarez was the only government he would recognize.

The French officer then replied that he could not surrender the California cavalrymen until he had notified and received permission from his superior officer at Hermosillo. So Captain Jimenez returned to Fort Mason to report to Colonel Lewis. A few days later, Captain Pico and his deserters reached the fort, as the French had agreed to release the Californians and had given them eight hours to leave Magdalena and twenty-four to cross the border.

Colonel Lewis increased the guard on the border to be assured that the French troops would not cross and if they did, they would not be permitted to return.[228]

The presence of French troops so near the border was a continual source of anxiety and resentment to both officers and men of the army of the Pacific. Gen-

[228] *Semi-Weekly News*, Los Angeles, oct. 24, 1865.

eral Wright repeatedly requested permission to occupy the port of Guaymas and prevent either the Confederate troops or the French from occupying the states of Sonora and Chihuahua. He emphasized the importance of maintaining the independence of these two Mexican states or attaching them to the United States. To the War department he wrote, ". . . I can guarantee that the loyal men on the Pacific coast will not be behind their brethren of the Atlantic and will meet them half way in the halls of Montezuma which may once more be occupied by an American army." [229]

As the army of Juarez was driven northward by the French, the retreating president issued orders to Colonel Leaton, formerly of the Confederate army, to raise a guerrilla regiment to repel the invaders. Leaton established his headquarters at Guadalupe on the Mexican side of the Rio Grande about twenty-five miles below San Elizario, Texas, which at that time was occupied by a detachment of the first cavalry, California volunteers, under the command of Richard H. Orton, company F.

Leaton sent recruiting agents to the American side and by offering large bounties, offices in his regiment and high prices for horses that the soldiers might bring with them, induced a number of them to desert.

Lieutenant Orton was ordered to cross the border and capture the deserters. He made five raids into Mexico. Twice he surrounded Leaton's camp and recovered some of the government property and his men. General Carleton sent a complaint to President Juarez who gave orders for the disbandment of the regiment and the arrest of Leaton.[230]

---

[229] *War. Reb.* Ser. I, vol. L, pt. II, p. 788-789.
[230] Richard H. Orton, *California men in the war of rebellion*, p. 76.

Juarez received the plaudits of the volunteers who served near the border. Sanford Bailey, company M, first cavalry, while stationed at Fort Selden, january 13, 1866, wrote to his friends at Weaverville and denounced the French occupation of Mexico.

An order came about two months ago to muster us out of service but it has been suspended by General Pope until troops can be transferred from the east, which I think will be as late as june. We are yet uninformed whether we shall be discharged here or marched home. In this district there are six companies of California veteran infantry and seven of California cavalry.

Being on the Mexican frontier leads us to take some interest in the welfare of that unhappy country. President Juarez with several of his cabinet is at El Paso, Mexico. He has about three hundred soldiers with him and a dozen pieces of artillery. There are a good many French refugees on this side of the river who acknowledge their disgust for the dirty work which they were sent here to perform. The fifth u.s. infantry stationed at Franklin, Texas, has enlisted about sixty of these refugees. Two weeks ago the Liberals released twelve French prisoners who immediately crossed the river and donned the Union blue.

President Juarez is a patriot in the fullest sense of the word. He has struggled nobly to defeat the invaders of his country. He has thrown into the contest his entire private fortune, while an unscrupulous leader might have amassed an immense fortune and retired into exile.

The invaders have not made the headway on the upper Rio Grande which was expected. At no time have they been farther than twenty-five miles this side of Chihuahua. French refugees tell some funny stories of these people who are to civilize the Mexicans. . . . How long will our government permit such scenes to be enacted at its very doors? It seems to me that the French should be notified to leave this soil forthwith and in case of refusal, Sherman or Sheridan should be entrusted with the job of moving them. . .[231]

The communication from secretary of state, William H. Seward, expresses the foreign policy of the United States at this period.

[231] *Weekly Trinity Journal,* Weaverville, feb. 24, 1866. (Bancroft library).

The United States government recognizes, and must continue to recognize in Mexico, only the ancient republic, and it can in no case consent to involve itself, either directly or indirectly, in relation with or recognition of the institution of the Prince Maximilian in Mexico.

. . .

Nations are not authorized to correct each other's errors except so far as is necessary to prevent or redress injuries affecting themselves. If one state has a right to intervene in any other state, to establish discipline, constituting itself a judge of the occasion, then every state has the same right.

General Carleton requested instructions from the War department regarding the admittance of the fugitive president and his protection by the California volunteers. He said,

Does the government desire that greater hospitality be shown the president of our sister republic, who has been driven from his country by foreign bayonets and forced to seek an asylum on American soil, than to any other private gentleman?

It seems to me that if our own president (Lincoln) were compelled to leave his country under similar circumstances, we should feel grateful to Mexico, if she in turn, held out a helping hand and had a cheering word for him. I have ventured to say this, presuming that we, as a nation, are able to do right without an eye to diplomacy, and are able to let the consequences of right take care of themselves.

Just another incident in the world history of political refugees.[232]

It must have mitigated the general's anxiety when he was informed that the United States then had no extradition treaty with Mexico that required the surrender of belligerents to their adversaries.[233]

Less than two years later, june 19, 1867, Emperor

---

[232] *War. Reb.* Ser. I, vol. XLVIII, pt. II, p. 1182-1183, aug. 14, 1865.
Ibid., p. 1242-1243.
[233] 39 Cong. I Sess., Sen. Ex. Doc. no. 6, december 1865, report secy. state, Wm. H. Seward—French occupation of Mexico. (1237)

Maximilian was shot by a firing squad and Benito Pablo Juarez made his prophecy, "The death of Maximilian is the death of the spirit of foreign intervention."

The Mail Goes Through

The Overland Mail was moved from the Southern to the Central route in the summer of 1861 to prevent its capture by the Confederate forces. To afford adequate protection, the War department ordered General Wright, then in command of the department of the Pacific, to assign two or three regiments of California volunteers to patrol the road from California to Salt Lake City. The order was not issued until november 13, 1861, and it was then too late in the season to send troops over the mountains.

After many conferences with Louis McLane, agent of the Overland Mail company, and with Governor J. W. Nye, Nevada territory, General Wright decided that all the Indians needed was an occasional distribution of provisions from Fort Churchill (*Plate* 8) and if this were done, the protection of the telegraph lines and mail would be guaranteed until spring.[234]

To the third regiment of infantry, California volunteers, fell the duty of protecting this long route over desert and mountain. Patrick Edward Connor (*Plate* 9) was made colonel of the regiment when it was organized september 4, 1861. He knew the hardships that were in store for his young volunteers as he had joined the regular army when he was but nineteeen and served at Forts Leavenworth, Atkinson and Des Moines, as well as in the Mexican war.[235]

---

[234] *War. Reb.* Ser. I, vol. L, pt. I, p. 745, 766, 1022-1023.

[235] Louis Pelzer, *March of the dragoons in Miss. valley, Annals of Iowa, third series,* vol. IV, no. 3, p. 167.

The majority of the men in the third regiment enrolled in the Mother Lode counties and among their home towns listed are names that recall the gold rush: Fiddletown, Poverty Bar, Chinese Camp, Chili Gulch, Jenny Lind, Columbia, Angel Camp, Sonora, West Point, Telegraph City, Mokelumne Hill, San Andreas, Don Pedro's Bar and Campo Seco.

Soon after companies A, B, C, and D were organized and they were sent to the Humboldt district to garrison Forts Bragg, Humboldt, Terwaw and Gaston and relieve the Federal troops on duty there. The remaining companies spent five months in training at Benicia Barracks, then moved to Stockton where final arrangements were made for the long march to Salt Lake City.

The arrival of "Connor's third" at Stockton aboard the s.s. "Helen Hensley" was an occasion for a "patriotic rally of all good Union men". The boats in the harbor and buildings along the line of the volunteers' march were decorated in the red, white and blue. "From all the balconies the ladies modestly waved and cheered the fighting men." Salutes were fired, the band played, and the Stockton home guards escorted the volunteers out Main street to Agricultural park to

Jill-Cossley-Batt, *Last of California rangers*, p. 192-193.

John R. Ridge, *Life and adventure of Joaquin Murrieta*, p. 80.

Lewis Pub. Co., *History of San Joaquin co.*, p. 126.

29 Cong. 2 Sess. H. Ex. Doc. no. 119. Spec. Order no. 133, par. 3, vol. IV, aug. 31, 1846.—p. 242. (500)

Ibid., Spec. Order no. 82, p. 47-48.

General Connor arrived in California in 1850 and engaged in various business enterprises ranging from lumbering in Humboldt county, surveying in Kern river valley, establishing Stockton city water works, farming, assisting in the capture of Joaquin Murrieta, to contracting for the foundation of the state capitol at Sacramento. He was released from this contract when he re-entered the army.

their training camp which had been named Camp Halleck.[236]

One hundred tents were pitched and the regiment settled down to routine duty while Colonel Connor obtained the necessary materiel for his expedition. Six weeks passed before he was ready to start across the Sierra and then he had to leave with only seven companies as three had been detained in the Humboldt district and were not returned to his command until the summer of 1863.[237]

All was bustle and commotion that july morning in 1862. There were 45 wagons to load and securely rope lest their supplies slip and fall over some precipice on the mountain road. A ton and a half was packed on each wagon. Additional wagons of provisions, supplied by contractors, accompanied the army train. Two mountain howitzers menacingly drew into line.

The bugle sounded, whips cracked, and the wagons creaked under their heavy loads. The tinkling bells on the lead horses mingled their notes with the band as it played *The Girl I Left Behind Me*. Lustily singing their farewell song, the California volunteers followed behind Colonel Connor at the head of the long procession down Main street and out Weber avenue.

Three ambulances and a number of carriages for the officers' families lengthened the long line. In one carriage rode Reverend J. A. Anderson of the First Presbyterian church of Stockton who had been appointed chaplain of the third regiment. Safely tucked away in his baggage were Bibles, books and magazines

236 *War. Reb.* Ser. I, vol. L, pt. I, p. 693.
MS Hiram Tuttle diary, may 26, 27, 28, 1862.
San Joaquin Republican, Stockton, may 26, 27 ,1862.
237 *War. Reb.* Ser. I, vol. L, pt. I, p. 652, 1110.

that had been donated by the residents of Stockton. Surgeon Robert K. Reid also accompanied the army train. The first night they camped at the Waterloo house about ten miles from Stockton.

The second day's march was hot and dusty for a distance of fifteen miles to Prince A. Athearn's ferry on the Mokelumne river. The old road that led to the ferry branched north from state highway no. 12 (Lockford road) about a mile due east of Clements where the old Polland house was then located. Only a group of sturdy locust trees now mark the site of this old roadhouse past which Connor's third regiment marched.

An entire day was spent in ferrying the regiment and its wagon train across the river. During the day, an Indian, crazed by the white man's fire-water, attacked and severely injured two soldiers with a hatchet. When the man who sold the liquor was captured, he was promptly horsewhipped and his supply of liquor confiscated.[238]

The volunteers continued their journey toward the low rolling foothills to the northeast. They marched about fifteen miles a day, camped at night near one of the old roadhouses, then onward the following day to the higher and cooler altitudes among the pines. After a week of steady walking, they reached Placerville where they camped a mile from the town. A dress parade was ordered on sunday and all Placerville turned out to see the "Boys in blue".

[238] *Ibid.*, pt. II, p. 19.

Calaveras Chronicle, july 19, 1862. (County archives, San Andreas)

Prince A. Athearn's ferry, Sec. 11, T 4, no. R, 8 E.

Reverend John Alexander Anderson entered the service of the United States Sanitary commission in 1863 and served with the 12th army corps. He was later made superintendent of transportation and had charge of half a dozen steamers. After the war, he returned to the ministry and in 1891 was appointed United States consul at Cairo, Egypt.

Slowly they climbed the Sierra. Nine or ten miles a day was their limit as they neared the summit. They followed the South Fork of the American river and if one should drive U.S. highway no. 50 today, he could see the same snowy peaks, the same river tumbling down and splashing the face of every boulder that blocked its course.

When the volunteers reached the Oglesby house, they witnessed for the first time the magic of the new "magnetic telegraph". The operator showed them a telegram and tried to explain the mystery of the "talking wires".

Sugarloaf station was their next stop where some of the more ambitious soldiers climbed to the top of the landmark, Sugarloaf mountain, and unfurled the stars and stripes. Edward Vischer, pioneer illustrator of California, made a sketch of this rugged peak with the flag flying from its summit.

When they reached Fort Churchill, august 6, 1862, Colonel Connor assumed command of the military district of Utah. In his instructions to his officers he insisted that no supplies would be purchased from anyone who had, by word or act, manifested disloyalty to the federal government.

It was mid-august when they left Fort Churchill to cross the Nevada desert. The thermometer registered 122 degrees, the dust was deep and the road rough. By marching in the twilight and the pre-dawn hours, they avoided casualties that otherwise might have occurred. In spite of the heat and other discomforts, dress parades were ordered regularly in the midst of sand and sage.[239]

239 Stockton *Independent,* aug. 5, 1862. (Stockton city library)
MS Hiram Tuttle diary, aug. 16, 1862.
War. Reb. Ser. I, vol. L, pt. II, p. 55.

They followed the Overland Mail route and after two weeks' marching reached Ruby valley where they remained a month. During this time the regiment lost three of its members. Snow began to fall on the mountains and the heavy rains found the volunteers with scant shelter. Colonel Connor ordered timber cut to build winter quarters for the troops who were detailed to garrison the post during the winter. The labor was performed by a few extra duty men and the teams of the command. Thus Fort Ruby was added to the long list of frontier posts.

And here on september 24, Corporal Hiram S. Tuttle wrote in his diary, "Signed $50 toward paying the passage of the regiment to the seat of the war in the East." Likewise Colonel Connor sent word to General Halleck, chief-of-staff, that the third regiment had authorized the paymaster to withhold $30,000 of pay then due if the government would order the regiment East. Private Goldthwaite, company G, subscribed $5,000, increasing his company's total to more than $7,000. The volunteers, furthermore agreed to pay their own passage to Panama if the amount raised was not enough. Their offer was not accepted as other services, equally important, awaited them.[240]

During the building program at Fort Ruby, Colonel Connor took the stage for Salt Lake City to select a site for a camp and to make provision for the troops en route. He examined old Fort Crittenden (Camp Floyd) but most of the adobe buildings were in ruins and the owner's price of $15,000 was too high. His final selection was a site three miles east of Salt Lake City on an elevated spot, which commanded a full

240 *War. Reb.* Ser. I, vol. L, pt. II, p. 133, 143.
MS Hiram Tuttle diary, sept. 10, 15, 24, 29, oct. 1, 1862.

view of the city and Great Salt lake. Here he had the advantage of the new telegraph line and direct mail communication, in addition to being located at the crossing of two roads to Oregon, three to California and one East.[241]

By the first of october enough supplies had arrived at Fort Ruby to warrant the movement of the troops to Salt Lake. Two companies of the second cavalry, California volunteers, marched by the way of the Northern route where they hoped to capture the Indians who took part in the Humboldt massacre of emigrants. Colonel Connor and his men took the more direct Mail route.

Trouble-mongers predicted armed resistance from the Mormons when Salt Lake was reached but Colonel Connor crossed the River Jordan and marched his men through the city without interference. They stopped in front of the governor's house and gave him three cheers, then proceeded to their new camp site.

As soon as the officers laid out the grounds, the volunteers began digging holes—not fox-holes but excavations four feet deep over which they placed their tents. The officers' quarters were built of logs over similar holes covered with boards and straw.

A weather record kept by Corporal Tuttle, company K, third infantry, shows that the winter of 1862-1863 was not a mild one. Six snow storms in the month of december must have caused the troops to feel chilly in their tents if not to actually suffer. As late as april 9 it snowed all night and the last snow of the season fell on april 23.[242]

---

241 *War. Reb.* Ser. I, vol. L, pt. II, p. 97, 119.
242 *Ibid.*, p. 144, 218.
MS Hiram Tuttle diary, oct. 21, nov. 22, 1862; apr. 9, 23, 1863.

Kidnapping was a common practice among the Indians and when the California volunteers heard the call, "To boots and saddles and to horse", little time was lost in going to the rescue. Such was the case when Colonel Connor ordered Major Edward McGarry, second cavalry, Lieutenants George D. Conrad and Albert Y. Smith, and sixty men to Cache valley where Chief Bear Hunter was camped with thirty or forty of his tribe, Soshones, Snakes and Bannocks, and was holding in captivity the ten year old nephew of Zachias Van Orman. The boy's parents had been killed near old Fort Boise in september 1860, and the boy held in captivity until Colonel Connor issued his orders on november 20, 1862. Three sisters, captured at the same time, had died.

Three previous expeditions had been sent out from Oregon for the recovery of the children but all had failed. During the summer of 1862, a friend of the Van Orman family, who had seen the children, attempted to buy them from the Indians, but the price was too high.

So it was a determined group of soldiers that responded to their colonel's orders. By traveling at night they were able to reach Providence where they left their horses. At one o'clock in the morning with the little captive's uncle as guide, they were on their way to the Indians' camp. It was a dark cold night in november and they did not find the camp until daylight. Just two old squaws greeted them. All the rest had fled during the night.

At eight o'clock in the morning the Indians' war-whoops echoed in the clear air as they circled on a nearby hill. The cavalry attacked and in a short time the Indians disappeared into the hills. Chief Bear

Hunter soon returned with a white flag to parley for peace. He and four of his men were held as hostages until the next day when the captive boy was delivered to Major McGarry after being held by the Indians for two years.[243]

Many and varied duties confronted the commanding officer after his arrival at the Mormon city. From every direction came calls for troops. The War department ordered Fort Bridger garrisoned by a part of the California regiment. Colonel Connor protested against the order that would divide his command. The Overland Mail from Fort Ruby to Ham's Fork was under his control and he believed that there was no need for troops at Fort Bridger, but a very definite need at Salt Lake. Nevertheless, the colonel obeyed his superior officer and dispatched Captain Micajah G. Lewis of company I, third infantry, to garrison the fort.[244]

The first major engagement by the volunteers was at the battle of Bear river. Reports had reached Colonel Connor that Chief Bear Hunter and his tribe were camped on Bear river so a winter campaign was planned to prevent further attacks on the telegraph lines and mail stages.

Assured that secrecy was the surest way to success, Colonel Connor sent a small force in advance knowing that they would not be feared by the Indians. Accordingly on january 22, 1863, company K, third infantry, under command of Captain Samuel N. Hoyt, and a detachment from the second cavalry with two howitzers, started for Bear river at one o'clock in the afternoon. The snow was falling but they marched thirteen miles before dark.

243 *War. Reb.* Ser. I, vol. L, pt. II, p. 60-61, 228-229.
   Ibid., pt. I, p. 181-183.
244 *Ibid.*, pt. II, p. 256-257.

They reached the town of Franklin at the end of the sixth day. That same day, after a two nights' ride over the mountains in deep snow and piercing wind, Colonel Connor and Major McGarry with 230 cavalry joined them. The infantry marched for Bear river soon after midnight and the cavalry followed a few hours later. It was dawn when they reached the Indian camp where a four hour battle resulted in the defeat of Chief Bear Hunter's warriors.

Surgeon Robert K. Reid, who had accompanied the troops to the battlefield, gave all possible aid to the wounded. The return journey was slowed down by the storms and muddy roads. When within fifty miles of Camp Douglas, Surgeons Jonathan Williamson and Steel met the caravan, transferred the wounded from sleighs to wagons, and hurried them to the rude hospital where hot soup and coffee awaited them.

On the evening of february 4, the volunteers began to arrive. First, came the cavalry, then the infantry who had suddenly turned cavalrymen as they had mounted the Indians' ponies that had been captured in battle. Colonel Connor made the return trip in a buggy and with him was his Mormon guide, Porter Rockwell.

The next day the saddened volunteers attended the funeral of sixteen of their comrades. Sixteen riderless horses, blanketed in black, were led in the solemn procession as the young soldiers were buried with full military honors. Reverend John A. Anderson delivered his comforting message which was repeated the next day, and for several days following until the number of casualties from the battle totaled twenty-two.

In the frontier hospital, tents placed over excavations covered with boards and straw, Surgeon Reid nursed the fifty or more wounded boys. Frozen toes and fingers were amputated, wounds dressed, and severe colds cared for. It was not long before these rugged sons of the early pioneers were returned to duty.[245]

The disagreement between the federal officers and the Mormons reached a crisis in march 1863. A mass meeting of the Mormons was held in their tabernacle, march 3. After heated debate, resolutions were passed asking Governor Stephen S. Harding and the two associate justices, Thomas J. Drake and Charles B. Waite, to resign and leave the territory. The Mormons alleged that these officers had accused the members of the Mormon church of extreme disloyalty and had recommended the passage of laws that would be detrimental to them.

Governor Harding's reply to these resolutions clearly indicated that he would not resign unless ordered to do so by President Lincoln. The governor said that he had come as a messenger of peace and good will and with a firm determination to discharge his duties honestly and faithfully and nothing would prevent him from carrying out his purpose. He vowed he would not be driven away nor would he cowardly desert his post.

As a signal for another meeting, Brigham Young raised the flag over his residence on march 8, and about 1,500 armed men assembled. Four days later he again called his faithful followers to his residence. His explanation for his unusual act was that he had received word that General Connor intended to arrest him and send him to Alcatraz.

General Connor remained in the district of Utah long enough to see the results of his conciliatory policy.

---

[245] *Ibid.*, pt. I, p. 185-187.

MS Hiram Tuttle diary, jan. 19, feb. 9, 1863.

Pajaro Times, Watsonville, oct. 17, 1862. (Bancroft library).

Alta California, feb. 19, 1863.

He said that the power of the Mormon church was greatly exaggerated and that before many years had passed Utah would contribute a loyal and healthy support to the entire country.[246]

In addition to his many military duties, General Connor assumed the role of colonizer also. On his expedition from Camp Douglas to Soda Springs, Idaho, he conducted a band of one hundred sixty Morrisites, comprising fifty-three families who had expressed their willingness to establish a settlement at the site selected for the new post at Soda Springs. He provided transportation for the most indigent but the others furnished their own teams and wagons.

The Morrisites left Camp Douglas, may 5, 1863, accompanied by company H, third infantry, as escort. The following day General Connor with company H, second cavalry, set out for Soda Springs, but instead of taking the direct route as the infantry and the Morrisites had done, he took the less traveled route and crossed the mountains dividing the Great Basin from the Snake River ferry. Here he held a conference with the Indians and Judge James D. Doty, superintendent of Indian Affairs for Utah. After the customary smoking with the chiefs and a grand dance by the Indians, flour, bacon and sugar were distributed.

Ever anxious to explore and find shorter and better routes, General Connor ordered Lieutenant Clark and twenty-five men to proceed up the Snake river for sixty or seventy-five miles to try to find a pass through the mountains and join the command at Soda Springs. The pathfinders were successful and found a good pass for a future road. They reached Soda Springs, may 17, a

---

[246] *War. Reb.* Ser. I, vol. L, pt. II, p. 369-374.

Richard H. Orton, *Record of California men in the war of rebellion*, p. 510, 513-514.

twelve days' journey from Salt Lake. The infantry and the Morrisites did not arrive until three days later.

A site for the new town was selected on the north bank of the Bear river near the great bend and four miles east of the place where Soda Springs valley opens into Old Crater valley. The settlers were allotted building lots of fair size and they began at once to build shelters for their families. General Connor remained six days to establish the infantry at the new post and to look after the present and future needs of the settlers. The new town was named Morristown and appears as such on the early maps.

The military reservation at Soda Springs was a mile square and adjoined the new town site of the Morrisites. The post was named Fort Connor in honor of General Connor, soldier and colonizer. One hundred and fifty additional Morrisites were sent to Carson City and transportation was furnished by the government wagon trains which hauled quartermaster supplies from Fort Churchill.[247]

Although the Overland Mail had been moved to the Central route to forestall its capture by the Confederates, it was not entirely immune from their attack. Three years passed before any attempt was made to seize the treasure boxes to defray the expenses of the Southern armies and strange military tactics were employed by the Confederate band.

The down stages from Nevada were then carrying heavy shipments of bullion from the Comstock Lode. On the night of june 26, 1864, two stages, the first driven by Ned Blair and the second by Charles Watson, were stopped by a gang of armed men near the Thirteen-mile house above Placerville. When a two-

[247] *War. Reb.* Ser. I, vol. L, pt. I, p. 226-229.

gun man covered Watson, he boldly demanded that the
highwayman hold his guns downward just in case they
went off; and when ordered to throw out the bullion,
Watson said that he couldn't as there was no one to
hold his horses. Nevertheless, the defiant driver was
forced to yield and the two stages lost $20,000 in bullion
and $26,000 in coin and dust from the treasure boxes.

Stage robberies were not uncommon at that time but
it was unheard of for a highwayman to offer a receipt
for his loot. The leader, Henry M. Ingraham, professed
to be a captain in the Confederate army and maintained
that he was collecting money to pay the cost of recruiting volunteers in California for service in the South.
After he handed Watson the receipt for an unnamed
sum of money from the Wells Fargo company, the
"Confederates" disappeared in the mountain darkness.

The local sheriff and his deputies were notified and
within twenty-four hours two of the bandits were
captured at the Thirteen-mile house and another,
Thomas B. Poole, was wounded and arrested at the
Somerset house. When Constable Ranney stepped
inside the Somerset, he asked a group of men in the
room whether or not they had seen or heard any horse
men pass in the night. The men reached for their guns
because just then Sheriff Joseph M. Staples's leveled
gun loomed in the doorway. Three of the men were not
quick enough on the draw so threw up their hands. Two
of the others opened fire and fatally wounded Sheriff
Staples.

Ranney then bolted through the door and hid behind
a tree. The outlaws quickly uncovered him and began
firing as they chased him up a ravine. A bullet struck
Ranney in the chest so he surrendered. As the gang
closed in each one in turn placed his pistol to Ranney's

head. They robbed him of three gold dollars. One threatened to blow his brains out because he had wounded Poole, his accomplice. Another one demanded Ranney to tell how in h--- he found them so soon.

Not knowing how many were in pursuit of them, the highwaymen fled to their hide-out near West Point and later went to San Jose where they looked up an acquaintance named Hill. But Hill proved to be a friend of the law and not of outlaws so he notified the local sheriff who arrested them.

They were returned to Placerville where they were given a jury trial. Thomas Poole was convicted and sentenced to be hanged. Preston Hodges was found guilty of second degree murder and was sentenced to twenty years in prison but the rest of the bandits were eventually acquitted.

Almon Glasby, one of the prisoners, was only nineteen or twenty years old. He did not deny his participation in the robbery but insisted that he acted under the authority of the Confederate government and declared that he should have been treated as a prisoner of war and not as a criminal.

Ingraham, the leader, known as the "Red Fox", came from Missouri where he had the reputation of a bushwhacker and a desperado. He gained the confidence of his associates and induced them to join his so-called company by showing them his commission as captain in the service of the Confederate army.

Louis McLane, superintendent of the Overland Mail company, appealed to General George Wright for soldiers to guard the stages over the Sierra. Lieutenant W. L. McKnight and ten men from his company F, second cavalry, California volunteers, were ordered to ride the stages to assure the safety of the mail and treasure boxes. They were on duty for just a month for by that time the road was free from bandits.[248]

In addition to their military duties, the troops were employed as surveyors and cartographers. With an odometer secured to one of the wheels of a six-mule wagon, the early army surveyor measured the military roads and mapped out shorter and better ones. Some of the present U.S. highways coincide quite closely with these old surveys.

Frequently the route was too rough for a four-wheel wagon. In that case a one-wheel contraption was used. Two shafts were fastened on a wheel to which an odometer was attached. A steady old mule was saddled and then harnessed to the one-wheeler. Then if he did not object too much to being saddled and harnessed at the same time, the surveyor mounted and proceeded to measure off the route assigned to him.

Only a contemporary writer could picture this odometer in action. "To see the odometer on a steep mountain trail is better than a circus. On a precipitous path, strewn with boulders and overgrown with chaparral, it displays the infinite possibilities of its motions. At one moment it bounds from the ground and saws the air; then it swings over the rider's head and assumes the appearance of a patent hair-brushing machine of unusual proportions. In extreme instances, it reverses its normal position and is propelled by the mule instead of being dragged behind that capricious creature's tail." [249]

A surveying party left Camp Douglas in the spring of 1864 to survey the route to Fort Mojave. Captain George F. Price of company M, second cavalry, was detailed for this task and placed in command of a

[248] *Ibid.*, pt. II, p. 895-896, 936.
Sacramento *Union*, june 1, 9, 27; july 2, 7, 21, 29, 1864.
[249] William H. Rideing, *Harpers Magazine*, vol. LV, p. 68.

detachment of sixty men, sixty-four government horses and four six-mule wagons.

He moved his column of Californians over the San Bernardino road by easy marches to Mountain Meadow, a distance of three hundred miles in sixteen days. Here he rebuilt the monument to the victims of the Mountain Meadow massacre. The first one, erected by Colonel Carleton in 1859, had been destroyed. These early monuments were usually large mounds of rocks to which each passer-by added a few more.

After leaving Mountain Meadow, Captain Price's troubles began. His stock began to fail rapidly and he was forced to make short drives. When he reached the Rio Virgin he was compelled to pack his outfit on the cavalry horses and hitch all mules to the empty wagons, also sixty men with ropes, to pull them to the top of the hill.

He was obliged to leave thirty worn out animals and fifteen men at Muddy. By reducing the men to one blanket and their saddle bags, and loading only provisions and water barrels on the wagons, the troops succeeded in crossing the desert to Las Vegas without much trouble. But the surveying party was still a week's journey from their destination. It was now june, the desert springs were almost dry, and the horses were crazy for water. Ten of them gave out completely and had to be shot. They struggled on and reached Rock Springs to find that there was no water for the horses so drove them out to Government hole where there was enough to quench their thirst. Here they found a stray cow and shot her for meat. The next day they reached Fort Piute and realized they were near the end of their journey.

They arrived at Fort Mojave, june 16, 1864, completely worn out. Half the men were barefoot. The horses were scarcely able to walk. The total number of animals unserviceable was sixty-nine, leaving only twenty out of the number with which they started.

In spite of the extreme hardships endured by the exploring party, Captain Price decided that no shorter nor a more practicable route could be run from Camp Douglas to Las Vegas. He said that there was no occasion to run the southern terminus of the road below El Dorado canyon because steam boats could navigate the river that far as easily as they did to La Paz. When Hoover dam was completed more than three quarters of a century later, the Colorado river did become navigable a hundred miles farther up stream from Captain Price's survey and in a manner that probably was inconceivable to the California volunteer.

From the southern terminus of the road at the mouth of the El Dorado canyon the military road was located by the way of Las Vegas, Muddy, Virgin river, Santa Clara river, Mountain Meadow, Cedar, Beaver, Fillmore, then along the west side of Utah Lake to Salt Lake City. U.S. highway no. 91 follows this survey very closely except that it passes east of Utah lake instead of to the west. Where Captain Price reported the condition of the road as being good, heavy hauling, sandy, desert, or turnpike, the one word "paved" tells the story now.[250]

Although Colonel Connor was promoted to brigadier general of volunteers, he had already proved himself more than a military commander. He took a very personal interest, not only in the settlement of this territory but also in the development of its mines. The district of Utah had been under his command since

[250] *War. Reb.* Ser. I, vol. L, pt. I, p. 355-360.

august 1862—long enough for him to discover its many resources. To further the development of the mines he issued orders to his officers to permit the volunteers to prospect in the vicinity of their respective posts when it did not interfere with their military duties.[251]

The Mormons resented the fact that many prospectors and settlers were occupying the land that had been selected for their own colonization. In answer to their repeated threats against the miners and settlers, General Connor issued a circular on march 1, 1864, in which he stated that the territory of Utah was public property of the United States and the people wished it developed as soon as possible; that citizens were freely invited and would be assured of protection. The miners, on the other hand, were ordered not to interfere with the vested rights of the Mormons; and while the troops had been sent to protect settlers from the Indians, they were also there to preserve peace. Since this was the mission of the troops, General Connor declared that he would see that it was fulfilled by kindly warning words if possible, but if not, it would be enforced at every hazard and at any cost. He would not permit the public peace and welfare of all to be jeopardized by the foolish threats or unlawful acts of a few.

The Mormons assumed a belligerent attitude toward the troops but their able commander's strategy resulted in an amicable adjustment of the difficulties and the only war between the Mormons and General Connor's third regiment appeared to be a "war of words".

By constant patrol of the Overland Mail, by continual scouting to keep the Indians away from the emigrant roads, the California and Nevada volunteers

---

[251] *Ibid.*, pt. II, p. 655-657, 774-775.
Connor appointed brigadier general, march 30, 1863.

prevented any large scale outbreak by the Indians. Nevertheless many instances of cruelty were experienced by the young troops. In one of their attacks on the Mail stations, the Indians surprised the guards at breakfast, set fire to the stables, burned seven horses, then threw the wounded and dying soldiers and stable keeper into the flames. One of the soldiers escaped but just as he was passing through the gate his horse was wounded. It traveled three miles before it fell and the soldier lived only long enough to report the attack.[252]

But there was fun and laughter as well as tragedy. Company I, third infantry, California volunteers, was stationed at old Fort Bridger and the old "blotters", (cash books) divulge many interesting chapters of army life at that period. There was no U.S.O. to entertain the boys so they supplied their own entertainment. Charged to the California minstrels' account in the books were all the makings of a good minstrel show. The account ran from march to october so evidently the talent of the volunteers was well appreciated by the rank and file.

While on garrison duty, the volunteers were apparently granted enough hours off duty to carry on a bit of business on the side, for on the back inside cover of the blotter for the year february 1864 to september 1865, the following notation dated october 24, 1864, states: "Let Lieutenant (John W.) Chew have six beaver traps on the condition that he is to give me one-fourth of the beavers caught and return the traps in good order—signed, Judge W. A. Carter."

Another account, may 18, 1864, headed Soldiers' hay party, seemed to reveal the industry of the soldier-farmers. It was recorded that a deposit of twenty dollars had been paid on a scythe and sneath and that the

[252] Sacramento *Union,* may 25, 1863.

hay was cut, then sold, and the net proceeds divided among the seven soldiers of the party.

Other items explain the high cost of clothing. Lieutenant Willard Kittridge, company I, third infantry, had merchandise to the total value of $136.50 charged to his account. Five and a half yards of blue broadcloth cost him $82.50, and his boots $17. Other accounts showed a wide variety of purchases from ink powder and pens, to cabbages and mosquito netting.

When not otherwise employed, the Californians enjoyed friendly visits with the old mountaineers. "Uncle" Jack Robinson, who had lived near Fort Bridger for thirty years was a popular character. One of his favorite expressions was, "Darn a dog that eats soup or a wolf that howls in the daytime."

In the summer of 1864 a new type of emigrant surged westward over the Central Overland route. Among the throng were draft evaders and war refugees. Mrs. John Brown, her two daughters and son were provided with a special army escort as rumors that the son might be assassinated reached the widow of John Brown of Harpers ferry notoriety. Lieutenant Francis M. Shoemaker, company D, first infantry, and five of his men were ordered out from Camp Connor, Soda Springs, Idaho, and gave the protection necessary to assure the safe arrival of the Brown family at Red Bluff, California.[253]

Each company appeared to have a regular correspondent to its home town newspaper and furnished the company news as well as a few "growls" as complaints were then called. The *Union Vedette* was first published at Camp Douglas, november 20, 1863, but early

253 *Ibid.,* sept. 5, 1864.
Shasta *Courier,* aug. 11, 1865.

in 1865 General Connor stopped its publication. It was again published in june 1865 at Salt Lake City and continued until november 27, 1867.

A few quotations from the soldiers' newspaper reveal the character of the efforts of the amateur reporters. The weather on november 7, 1864, is described in the following manner: "Cold weather is all the rage in these parts. Water turns to icicles, hands and toes turn to aching and our general thoughts turn to muffling." The *Union Vedette* of july 20, 1865, published a letter from one of the volunteers from company A, third infantry, written while on the expedition to open a new road from Salt Lake to Denver by the way on Uintah valley: "Dear *Vedette*:- It may appear almost an unpardonable offense in the eyes of some that no communication from the 'Gallant third' has appeared in the *Vedette* since companies A and B left Camp Douglas."

He then explained that the girls they left behind had first claim on their spare time and that the "road" required so much physical energy that they did not have the will to write when they reached camp. Yet he did find time to include in his letter a few items of interest:

Hobble Creek canyon is about twenty-seven miles from Springville. This town enjoys the honor of being the only place in Utah territory, except Camp Douglas and Salt Lake City, which possesses a printing press and publishing office. Here the *Farmers' Oracle* had its birth, still exists and enjoys a limited circulation—much less than it deserves. It is issued monthly, and as its name intimates, is a magazine devoted to the agricultural interests of Utah. . .

Our muskets are much admired by "this people" who seem very anxious to procure some of them. They told us that they would be very useful in catching trout. When this adaption was first named, we were somewhat puzzled to "see the point" and were amused to discover that they thought the bayonet was a spear and that with a minnie musket they could fire at and spear a fish at the same time.[254]

Each day brought new duties for the "Gallant third" and also the prospect of being mustered out as their three year term of service drew to a close. Some of them re-enlisted and it was a year after the close of the war before they received their honorable discharge. Their commander, General P. Edward Connor, was placed in charge of the district of the Plains in the spring of 1865 and led the Powder river expedition.

---

[254] *Union Vedette,* july 20, aug. 11, 1865. (Salt Lake City library)

General Connor Commands the
District of the Plains

His success in keeping the mail stages moving through the district of Utah won for General Connor his assignment to the district of the Plains. This district included the territories of Nebraska, Colorado, Montana and Utah and had been formed to more effectually curb the activities of the Indians.[255] (Utah was removed from this District in july.)

The year 1865 has long been recognized as the "bloodiest year on the plains". The first major attack of that year began early in january when the stage station at Beaver creek, Colorado, was burned. By the end of two weeks, every Overland Stage station and ranch for a distance of one hundred miles was destroyed. Twenty-two wagons loaded with government supplies were either stolen or burned and 1,500 head of cattle driven off. The telegraph lines were demolished for over fifty miles on the Fort Laramie and Denver roads. Over three hundred poles were cut close to the ground and carried away while the wires were left twisted and tangled. Not only was it the duty of the frontier soldier to protect the telegraph lines, but also to repair them when destroyed.[256]

As the fury of the Indian attacks increased, the duties of the small frontier army grew in proportion. There

[255] *War. Reb.* Ser. I, vol. XLVIII, pt. I, p. 1285, Gen. Order no. 80; 568-569. *Ibid.*, pt. II, p. 1111-1112, 1113.
[256] *Ibid.*, pt. I, p. 88-92, 793-794, 40-44.

were over two thousand miles of mail and telegraph roads to keep open and if every available soldier had been detailed along the route, the force would not have exceeded more than four men to each mile.[257]

The greatly increased devastation wrought by the Indians was attributed to the fact that they possessed firearms as good or better than the soldiers. This raised the question as to how and from whom the weapons were procured and prompted President Lincoln to order the arrest and trial by court-martial of any one who supplied firearms to the Indians.[258]

General Connor was confronted with a difficult task when he assumed command of the district of the Plains, march 1865. In addition to the two companies of his own third regiment of Californians, he was expected to organize an effective fighting force composed of men from five other states among whom were former Confederate prisoners. To infuse new life, discipline and effectiveness into the troops under his new command was a much more difficult task than it had been three years previous when he organized his own regiment of California youths. Nevertheless, the undaunted warrior assumed command with his customary vigor and thoroughness.

Realizing that much of his success depended upon the quality of leadership of his officers, he addressed a special circular to them and stressed the fact that he would not tolerate any bickering, jealousy, slander or tattling gossip. He insisted that he desired to be surrounded by men who respected themselves, the honor of their country and the position they occupied. He warned them that if they violated his injunction they

[257] *Ibid.,* p. 807-808, Spec. Order no. 41, (6-12) feb. 10, 1865.
[258] *Ibid.,* p. 1205.

would be promptly dealt with to the full extent of his power.[259]

The Indians concentrated their families on the North fork of the Powder river during their raids on the emigrant roads and it was reported by Mrs. Morton, a former captive, that the Cheyennes, Arapahoes, Kiowas, and the Sioux were forming an alliance and were planning "to make war to the knife".[260]

Consequently the Powder river expedition was planned with considerable foresight as nearly all supplies had to be hauled from St. Louis. All cavalry were ordered to take short rations as troops on special detail, "hay-makers", supplied enough fodder for the stock en route to Fort Laramie.

Bridging the rivers by pontoons saved hundreds of miles yet added an extra burden to the supply bases. A train of fifty wagons and an escort of one hundred troops were necessary to transport the 1,200-foot pontoon of Russian canvas boats. It was july before this work was completed and turned over for General Connor's use.[261]

While Connor was concentrating his troops at Fort Laramie in june, trouble was reported at Camp Mitchell. Colonel Thomas Moonlight was ordered in pursuit of the Indians with every cavalryman he could get—Kansas, Ohio, and companies L and M, second cavalry, California volunteers. They overtook the Indians at Dead Man's fork, Dakota territory, about 120 miles northeast of Fort Laramie.

Colonel Moonlight had marched his men twenty miles before breakfast and camped in a river bed with high banks. The horses were turned loose to graze,

[259] *Ibid.*, pt. II, p. 688-689, Circular no. 5, Julesburg, may 20, 1865.
[260] *Ibid.*, p. 974.
[261] *Ibid.*, p. 947, (june 20, 1865), p. 982, 981, 950, 1064.

many of them without picket ropes. In a short time an alarm sounded as about two hundred Indians attacked. The horses were corralled but the noise of the Indians stampeded them directly toward the Indians who started to run. They soon discovered that the horses were unmounted and quickly surrounded the frightened animals and drove off more than seventy of them—fifty-one belonging to the Californians. It was necessary to destroy the saddles as there was no means of transporting them back to Fort Laramie.[262]

As the season advanced, the troubles of the frontier officers multiplied. The expedition that was planned in april was stalemated the last of july. Stores that should have been at Fort Laramie six weeks previous were stuck in the mud. The troops were mutinous as the war was then over and they demanded their discharge. They complained about traveling on half rations and being mounted on old and worn out horses.[263]

As one difficulty was overcome, others arose to disturb the officers. ". . . It seemed that all the rascals in the West were combined to swindle the government. . . . Fearful gangs operated from the Mississippi river to Denver. These men enticed soldiers to desert, sold the government property and then assisted them in getting out of the country."

When all the columns were ready to move forward, Secretary of War Stanton demanded the reason for such expeditions and insisted upon knowing who planned them. The quartermaster at Fort Leavenworth offered the explanation that the Indian campaigns had been planned since april. "The work is done. The troops

[262] *Ibid.*, pt. I, p. 325-328.
[263] *Ibid.*, pt. II, p. 1132, 1112-1113, 1144-1145, 1122-1123, 1178-1179.

are launched beyond recall. The expenditures for sending forward stores will not again be incurred for they
have enough to last a year if the troops are judiciously
moved. . . It remains to wait for results commen-
surate with the cost of the preparations and the further
daily expense of so large a force. . ." [264]

It would appear that all the officers in command of
the expedition received a reprimand as each in turn
tried to justify his actions. General P. Edward Connor's
reply clarifies his views. "I fear they do not understand
in Washington what the necessities of the service are
here. I require a great many more supplies than I have
troops as the nature of the service keeps troops moving
from posts far distant from each other, and it is difficult to move stores in winter. Unless I can end this
war this fall, the present force will have to be kept up
or the white people leave the country." [265]

When it seemed that all the difficulties had been
surmounted, Major General Pope issued orders to
abolish the district of the Plains, remove Connor from
command, and transfer him to the district of Utah once
more.[266] Furthermore, Connor was charged with violation of the laws and regulations regarding the making
of contracts for quartermaster and commissary supplies.
When notified of the accusation, he assured General
Pope that his instructions would be implicitly obeyed
and that he would make satisfactory explanation of all
his transactions.[267]

But the harassed commander of the Powder river
expedition had a staunch friend in General Dodge,
who earnestly pleaded for his retention and promised

[264] *Ibid.*, p. 1167.
[265] *Ibid.*, pt. I, p. 352.
[266] *Ibid.*, pt. II, p. 1209, 1201, Gen. Order no. 20, august 22, 1865, par. VIII.
[267] *Ibid.*, pt. I, p. 355-356.

that if Connor could be kept in the field with two thousand men the Indian difficulties would be settled. A compromise was effected and Brigadier General Connor was given another month or two to subdue the powerful Arapahoes. It was indeed a brief time to accomplish an objective for which four months' time and thousands of dollars had been spent.[268]

Fort Laramie had been selected as the concentration point for the greater part of the Powder river forces and after all the delays and disappointments, General Connor was finally ready to start. He divided his command into four columns, the right, center, left and west. He accompanied the left and the west columns, which included companies L and M, second cavalry, California volunteers. All supplies were transported with him as the right and center columns were instructed to meet him on the Rosebud river. However, this location proved ill chosen as it was far beyond the actual battlefield.[269]

It was july 30, 1865, when General Connor left Fort Laramie and led his little army of about six hundred men up the North Platte river to the Old Platte bridge. A ten days' march brought them to the Powder river where a site on a hundred foot mesa on the east bank was selected for a post and supply base. Here a stockade was built of roughly hewn timbers twelve feet long and from eight to ten inches thick. These were set four feet

---

[268] *Ibid.*, pt. II, p. 1220-1221.

[269] *Ibid.*, pt. I, p. 335-336, *West column,* Capt. Albert Brown, Co. L, sec. cav., Calif. volunteers; Co. M, Capt. George Conrad, sec. cav., Calif. volunteers, 116 men; Omaha scouts 84 men; total 200. *Left column,* Col. James H. Kidd, sixth Michigan cav., 200 officers and men; seventh Iowa cav., 90 men; eleventh Ohio cav., 90 men; Pawnee scouts, 95 men; total 475. *Center column,* Lt. Col. Samuel Walker, sixteenth Kans. cav., 600 officers and men. *Right column,* Col. Nelson Cole, second Missouri light artillery equipped as cavalry, 797 men; twelfth Missouri cav., 311 men; total 1108 officers and men; 140 six-mule wagons; aggregate 1,400 men.

deep in a trench thus providing an eight-foot barrier
to the marauding Indians. Blockhouses, officers' quarters and quartermaster buildings were constructed and
the new post named Fort Connor in honor of the
commanding general.[270]

The troops broke camp at sunrise august 22 and
marched northwest to Crazy Woman creek, then followed along the base of the Big Horn mountains to
Lake De Smet. From here they continued to the divide
between the Powder and the Tongue river valleys and
marched down to Peno creek, now called Prairie Dog
creek. Their route followed the same general direction
as U.S. highway 87 but at that time there were no
familiar highway markers. Indian scouts and James
Bridger pointed the way along the rough roads and
trails.

It was now a month since they had left Fort Laramie
and still there were no signs of any large bands of
hostile Indians. Yet the soldiers moved forward cautiously and quietly as General Connor had ordered
them not to speak above a whisper. Their secrecy and
caution was rewarded for suddenly as the soldiers in
the vanguard emerged from a deep ravine to the mesa
above them, they saw hundreds of tepees and Indian
ponies. They quickly dismounted and hurried back to
notify General Connor of their discovery.

General Connor took the lead up the steep bank and
at the first sight of the general's horse the Indian ponies
raced toward the tepees. Volley after volley was fired
and the Indians fled in confusion up Wolf creek with
General Connor in pursuit. He followed them for ten
miles when he realized that he had but fourteen men
left so he retreated to the Indian village. By mid-

---

[270] *Ibid.*, pt. II, p. 1193, 1229.

afternoon the soldiers were on their way back to their camp. The troops were greatly outnumbered and traveled all night to avoid another encounter with the Indians who followed them until midnight but did not attack. Approximately fifty Indians were killed, six hundred horses captured and their village and winter supplies destroyed.[271]

Colonel Nelson Cole, commanding the right column, left Omaha july 1, 1865, and followed the Platte river to Columbus where he left that stream and pushed on up the north bank of the Loup. While camped near the mouth of the north branch of the Loup, he received from General Connor a map and description of the route and the rendezvous of the four columns. Until then Colonel Cole had not been informed except that he was to move his column up Loup fork where he would be met by messenger.[272]

General Connor's instructions were probably as accurate as possible considering the lack of general knowledge of the country. Cole was ordered to march north of the Black hills, turn westward until he reached the Powder river, then follow down that stream until opposite the Panther mountains. Then he was supposed to turn northwest until he reached Rosebud creek. Meanwhile to watch for smoke signals from Connor's camp.

At the Pawnee mission, Colonel Cole secured Indian scouts. His only other source of information was a copy of Lieutenant G. K. Warren's map furnished by the Engineer's department. On this map the Panther mountains were clearly marked although they appear to have vanished from the modern maps.

---

[271] *Transactions and reports Nebraska State Historical society,* vol. II, p. 197-229; Capt. H. E. Palmer, Co. A, eleventh Kansas volunteer corps.

[272] *War. Reb.* Ser. I, vol. XLVIII, pt. II, p. 1064.

By august 14, Cole reached Bear Butte. Here after six weeks' marching he was still widely separated from General Connor who on that date was at Fort Connor. Lieutenant Colonel Samuel Walker, commanding the center column, left Fort Laramie on august 2, and joined Cole's right at Red Water. The two columns then moved forward together.

It was august 29 when they reached the Powder river at a point estimated to be fifty miles from the Yellowstone river. This was the very day of the battle on Tongue river where General Connor's forces defeated the Arapahoes.

Colonel Cole sent out scouts to find General Connor and his supply base. They returned in a few days and reported that they had found no supplies although they had gone more than fifty miles west and had discovered Tongue river, Rosebud creek and Panther mountain as laid down on the map. "Panther mountain," they said, "was simply masses of volcanic rock." Upon receiving this information Cole put his troops on half rations.

Late in the afternoon of the same day three hundred Indians attacked them and ran off twelve horses, killed four soldiers, and wounded two others who died soon afterwards. The next day the troops moved down the Powder river hoping to find more grass for the horses and perhaps buffalo and game for the hungry men. A severe storm broke over the weary army, so they again turned northward toward the Yellowstone. Although Captain Walker's rations were also nearly depleted, his column moved rapidly as it consisted entirely of pack animals, while Cole's supplies were transported by 140 six-mule wagons.

The storm continued and so did the attack by the

Indians. Cole then decided to retreat down the river. The Indians attacked in force but Cole succeeded in routing them. Walker was then three miles in advance and turned back to help. The storm increased in fury so the troops moved into the heavy timber. Here they hoped to save their animals by building fires around them but during the thirty-six hour storm, 414 animals died. This necessitated the destruction of wagons, cavalry equipment and everything not absolutely essential. The men suffered greatly and were ordered to march in circles for many hours to keep from freezing.

Meanwhile General Connor had sent out scouts to find his lost columns. It was now september 10 and there was still no news from either his left or center column. The following day hundreds of dead cavalry horses were found. Cole's trail was soon discovered and the rescue party followed it up the Powder river. In a few days they found the ragged barefoot soldiers who since july 1 had marched one thousand miles over a route on which they had built their own roads and had lived eighty-two days on sixty days' rations. Until supplies arrived from Fort Connor on september 19, the troops ate horse and mule meat. The lost columns reached Fort Connor september 20, 1865.

General Connor's total loss in the Powder river expedition was fifty men killed. He would have continued his campaign forty days longer if the right and center columns had been able to join him and if he had not been ordered to return at such an early date.[273]

Although the expedition was a disappointment to the fighting general, he was received with honor at Denver where he was "feted and feasted" at the Planters hotel. He returned to Salt Lake City where he remained in

---

[273] *Ibid.,* p. 1236; pt. 1, p. 329-389.

command of the district of Utah until mustered out april 30, 1866. He was breveted major general of volunteers, march 13, 1865. He lived in Utah for about twenty-five years after the war and greatly influenced the early development of the state, especially the mines. He died at Salt Lake City, december 17, 1891, and was buried with military honors at Fort Douglas.

The services of this pioneer-soldier have been recognized and honored by the erection of a monument to him and his California and Nevada volunteers at Fort Douglas cemetery near Salt Lake City. Likewise the Bear river monument commemorates the last major battle with the Indians in northern Utah. Here General Connor and the third regiment of California volunteers defeated these tribes on january 29, 1863.

The state of Wyoming perpetuates the name of General Connor by naming one of its state parks, Connor Battlefield park. The park is near Ranchester on the Tongue river. On a large stone marker is recorded the date, august 29, 1865, when General Connor and his California volunteers, together with the left column, defeated the Arapahoes under their chiefs, Old David and Black Bear.

To the Pacific Northwest

Cautiously the s.s. "Pacific" sailed out the Golden Gate and set her course northward in the fog. For forty-eight hours her tall masts cut a path through the white cloud and billowed it from her sails. As she approached the mouth of the Columbia river, the transition from fog to rain and then to sunshine seemed almost instantaneous. On one horizon the sun set and on the other the moon rose to begin her night vigil and guide the seafarers across the much dreaded bar of the Columbia where so many of the early ships had been wrecked.

By eleven o'clock the s.s. "Pacific" stood safely in over the bar and at midnight docked at Astoria to unload freight and take on a licensed river pilot. Almost a decade previous, the territory of Oregon had organized a pilot commission to license those who piloted the deep water vessels between Astoria and Portland, thus securing greater safety in the treacherous channel.

On this trip the s.s. "Pacific" was in the hands of an experienced and trustworthy pilot who brought her safely up the river and discharged five companies of the second infantry, California volunteers, at Fort Vancouver, october 21, 1861. The Californians had been ordered to replace the u.s. regular army and protect the frontier of the great Pacific Northwest until a sufficient number of companies from Oregon and Washington could be organized and assigned to duty there. By december 31, 1861, three companies of California volunteers were stationed in Oregon and seven in Washington.[274]

The California volunteers remained but a few days at historic Fort Vancouver and were loath to leave their comfortable barracks to spend the winter in the snowy mountains of the far north. Nevertheless, three companies of cheering soldiers marched aboard the s.s. "Wilson A. Hunt". Their own cheers were muted by the wilder shouting of the two companies left ashore and by the steamboat whistle when Captain John Wolf ordered the gangplank up and started for the Cascades.[275]

The paddle wheels of the old river steamer churned the water to a foam as she met the current, and the october sun jabbed at the ripples in her wake sending myriads of sparklers down the Columbia. The dark green of the forest was high-lighted with splashes of fall colors yet Corporal Jack was depressed and lonely as he sailed up this great river of the North. Fort Colville, near the border of Canada, seemed very far away, a long march for a young infantryman like Jack. He knew that when he landed at Wallula there would still be over two hundred miles to walk. Captain Wolf was extremely kind to the boys and tried to make them comfortable on his crowded little boat, so Corporal Jack tried to forget his own troubles and be grateful for the consideration shown by the captain of the s.s. "Wilson A. Hunt".

---

[274] Cos. A, B, C, D, E, 2nd. inf.: A, B, C, D, E, 4th. inf., Calif. vols. *War. Reb.* Ser. I, vol. L, pt. I, p. 793.

[275] Fort Vancouver, Pacific headquarters of Hudson Bay co., built in 1825. On oct. 29, 1853, the site, 640 acres, was declared a reservation. (*Outline description of* U.S. *military posts and stations,* War. dept. Q.M. general's office, M. C. Meiggs.)

They were received with welcoming cheers when they reached the Cascades, for their arrival meant that these men of the regular army could soon leave for San Francicso where they would take passage for the East. With Major James F. Curtis in the lead, the California volunteers marched the three miles from the Lower to the Upper Cascades. Here they boarded the s.s. "Idaho" for the Dalles.[276]

After they were comfortably settled aboard, rumors began to circulate among the passengers that there were more Secessionists on the boat than Union men. The s.s. "Idaho" flew no u.s. flag and the Californians lost no time in telling Captain John McNulty that they wanted to see the flag flying wherever they went. The captain raised the flag, the boys cheered, the band played *Yankee Doodle* (the band was only a fife and drum) and thus peace was proclaimed on the Columbia river.

They reached The Dalles at nine o'clock in the evening and expected to remain there for the night but the quartermaster met them at the landing and told Major James F. Curtis that they were to march at once for the Deschutes river. The major had made arrangements for his volunteers to sleep aboard the "Idaho" and many of them were already in bed. The Dalles was then garrisoned by u.s. regulars so there was no argument. The major and his Californians landed.

Company A, second infantry, California volunteers, went into quarters as they had been ordered to assume duty here. Companies C and D started in the dark for the Deschutes nineteen miles away. The road was rough and hilly but the boys were in fine spirits and sang and

---

[276] s.s. "Idaho" built at the Cascades in 1860. On july 11, 1881, she was piloted over the Cascades by Capt. J. W. Troup. (*Marine history of Pacific Northwest,* Lewis & Dryden, p. 93.)

yelled as they marched. They said that they wanted to wake all the settlers to let them know that the California volunteers were coming. They rested three times on the road and were tired when they arrived at Deschutes at five o'clock in the morning.

They found the little stern-wheeler "Colonel Wright" lying beside a pile of freight on a rocky shore. She looked as though she could not hold two companies of vigorous young men but they all managed to get aboard and had room to spare. The captain and his mate gave up their berths to Major Curtis and his officers while the privates stowed themselves away in every possible manner all over the boat. At ten o'clock in the morning they started for Wallula. Most of the boys were asleep and this time the boat pulled away as quietly as though there were none aboard.[277]

The s.s. "Colonel Wright" had no trouble in navigating the Upper Columbia except at the mouth of the John Day river where it was necessary to put a hundred men ashore with ropes to help pull the little steamer through the swift current at this point. When they reached Wallula, they camped there for a few days until the government teams arrived from Fort Walla Walla to haul their tents and knapsacks to the fort. The boys made the most of their time and went hunting and fishing.

They reached Walla Walla after a two-day march and camped half way between Walla Walla and the fort. Three or four soldiers came down to see the California volunteers but no officer came near. Corporal Jack said, "The volunteers were not killed by the kindness of the post commander, Captain Wm. T.

[277] The s.s. "Colonel Wright" was launched oct. 24, 1858, at the mouth of the Deschutes river and was the first steamer on the Upper Columbia river. The steamer was named for Col. Wright, later Brig. Gen. Wright.

Magruder. He would not give us an ambulance nor a spring wagon for our sick although there were four wagons at the post. He allowed Major Curtis to start off afoot on a two hundred mile journey without offering him a horse or a mule."

Walla Walla then boasted about 1,500 inhabitants who treated the volunteers cordially. The two companies of volunteer infantrymen remained in town five days before they began their long march for Fort Colville in the winter rains and mud. When they left, Major Curtis walked at the head of his column of Californians and the Walla Walla citizens followed to the outskirts of the town while the fife and drum corps bravely played *Yankee Doodle* once more.

The november days were now shorter and the nights were cold for sleeping on the frosty ground. Each morning the soldiers found the water frozen and it did not take them long to get going after breakfast. They reached the Snake river about four miles above the ferry so Major Curtis bargained with some Indians to take Captains O'Brien, Hull and Lieutenant Henry, and himself down to the ferry in a canoe. The Indians brought out a dugout but it commenced leaking as soon as the officers got into it, so the Indians quickly shoved into the stream for fear of losing their passengers. The pleasure party sat in about three inches of water and it was as much as Captain Hull and Lieutenant Henry could do to keep the dugout afloat. At every riffle the water would come in over the gunwale. The Indians seemed to enjoy it and took the officers over the worst places they could find. Captain O'Brien swore that if they capsized he would hold on to the Indians and drown them. The Indians answered in Chinook, laughed and grunted. Neither understood what the other said, so there was no chance for a growl and they kept on until they reached the ferry. The major paid the Indians well and they separated good friends.

They camped on the Palouse river where they waited over one day for an ox team to bring grain for the command. The following day the guide led the little army on a trail that followed the Palouse for twelve miles. They marched in single file and Corporal Jack lingered far in the rear "to be alone with his thoughts". What were they? Just fantasies of youth. With the hood of his greatcoat over his head, he marched along building castles in the air. As he leaped from rock to rock, he was scaling the walls of a fortress or dodging a cannon ball or firing from behind a bush. He marched to the tune of a great band instead of the raindrops that fell upon his back.

The delusion lasted until he reached camp but it was soon dispelled when the French cook had a hot supper ready. Hot coffee, plenty of biscuits and a big hunk of fresh beef satisfied the hearty appetite of Corporal Jack and he went to bed content, but he thought that the folk at home did not fully realize the hardships of the man who volunteered to fight for his country.

In four days they marched eighty-three miles, crossed the Spokane river and reached the timber country. Here flour was issued, hard biscuits thrown aside and all the boys reveled in the luxury of having "soft tack" for supper.

They reached Fort Colville in three more days, just a month from the day they left San Francisco. When within a mile of the fort, the companies formed and as they came in sight of the barracks, the music struck up and they marched as lively as if they had not been on a long journey. The volunteers were welcomed by

Major Pinkney, ninth U.S. infantry, and entertained at a good feast. The next morning the two companies of the ninth infantry started for San Francisco, and companies C and D, second infantry, California volunteers, took over the task of maintaining peace with the Indians of the far North.[278]

For a week after the volunteers arrived there was no sun. Four inches of snow had fallen so Corporal Jack looked up one of the oldest residents to ask him how often he had seen the sun. He found the old man dressed in beaver skins from head to foot—cap, coat, pants and moccasins. He had been a beaver trapper in the employ of the Hudson's Bay company for twenty-seven years. Jack had to ask him twice as the old man did not seem to understand. He shook his head and slowly said, "I have seen the sun every summer except one and that was fifteen years ago. I was hunting beaver in Flow canyon for eight months. There the sun never shines and here it seldom does. The last time I saw it was nine days ago. It came slowly over the top of the mountain but it seemed displeased with something for it went down in about ten minutes and has not come back since. It must have been disgusted with things generally and made up its mind to stay away until spring." Not a sunny prospect for Jack.[279]

It was a long winter for the ten companies of California volunteers. In addition to Fort Colville, they garrisoned Forts Walla Walla, The Dalles, Vancouver, Hoskins, Yamhill (*Plate* 10) and Steilacoom. There was but little trouble with the Indians during the

---

[278] Fort Colville built in 1826, was named for Andrew Colville, governor of the Hudson Bay co. in London. The old fort was first used as a United States army post, june 30, 1859, and was abandoned in 1871.

[279] *Alta California,* San Francisco, oct. 30, 1861, nov. 12, 1861. Letters written by "Corporal Jack", Co. c, 2nd inf., Calif. vols.

winter months as there were no travelers on the emigrant roads and the heavy snowfall and the floods of that winter of 1861-1862 prevented even the Indians from traveling far. "The weather," said one volunteer, "was just a little more samer as de same."

Among the two companies at Fort Colville, sufficient talent was discovered to give quite creditable performances at the garrison theater which could seat a hundred. "The stage," said the correspondent, "was a mere fisherman's quarter deck—three steps and overboard." [280]

The lack of comfort in their crude log barracks is revealed in the requisition for supplies. Included in the order for hay at $45 a ton, was an order for straw, twelve pounds a month allotted to each officer, private, musician and laundress. Evidently the straw in their bunks was changed once a month and served in lieu of mattresses. The medicine list consisted chiefly of Bourbon whisky, 1812, at $17.60 a gallon, dozens of one and two-ounce vials, and a few pounds of white sugar—no antiseptics or bandages for arrow wounds or other emergencies. Pork at $24 a barrel and beans at $4.80 a bushel were the staple articles of diet. [281]

Recruiting volunteers was slow and difficult in the sparsely settled Pacific Northwest. A combination of circumstances made it almost impossible to get men to serve in the army. When notices were posted offering the rates of pay for soldiers, private companies would post notices right beside them offering forty dollars to fifty dollars a month in coin. Miners were paid as much

[280] Pub. *Alta Weekly California (Steamer)*, nov. 3, 1863. (Huntington library)

[281] MS Thomas R. Cornelius (CSMH).

as five dollars a day so the pay of the soldier was insignificant in comparison.[282]

Washington and Oregon did not receive their call for volunteers until three months after California received hers. Oregon promptly recruited six companies of cavalry but Washington found it quite impossible to find men to fill her quota. Therefore, Colonel Justus Steinberger, commanding the district of Oregon, secured permission from General Wright to recruit men in California for service in the Washington infantry.[283]

He arrived at San Francisco, january 28, 1862, and in three months' time had enrolled four companies of California boys and was on his way back to Fort Vancouver. A total of eight companies was raised in California and served as an integral part of the Washington infantry. Of the ten companies of the first Washington infantry, only two companies were raised in Washington.[284]

Time was needed to train these new recruits so that they could relieve the Californians and it was july 1862, before companies A, B, C and E, fourth infantry, California volunteers, left the district of Oregon for service in Arizona and in the Humboldt district of Northern California. To reach Eureka the volunteers were shipped from Fort Vancouver to Alcatraz then all the way back to Humboldt bay.

Five companies of the second infantry, California volunteers, left in the fall of 1862 but company D, fourth infantry, remained in Oregon for four years.

282 *War. Reb.* Ser. I, vol. L, pt. II, p. 510-511.

283 *Ibid.*, pt. I, p. 663, 848, 900, 987-988, 1038, 1040, 1053, 1124. The War dept. called on Oregon and Washington for troops oct. 12, 1861. By that time the California troops were on their way to Fort Vancouver.

284 *Ibid.*, pt. II, p. 896-898.

In this company seventy-one boys enrolled at old Volcano which is today numbered among the ghost towns of the Mother Lode. Just a few buildings and the old cannon "Abe" remain in this secluded spot and there is nothing left to commemorate the services of these California boys who signed the muster roll october 15, 1861.[285] This company was stationed at Fort Yamhill, Oregon, for two consecutive years when it was transferred to Fort Hoskins for one year then sent back to Fort Yamhill until mustered out.[286]

How they traveled through those dense forests and along the rugged shore is described in the report of Lieutenant Louis Herzer, first Washington infantry, when he commanded a detachment of ten California volunteers from company D, fourth infantry, on an expedition from the Siletz Blockhouse to Coos bay to capture or persuade some of the Indians to return to the reservation at Siletz.

They marched twenty-eight miles to Yaquina bay where they secured a large flat boat, embarked all the men and horses and arrived at the mouth of the bay in time to camp for the night. They started along the beach the next morning at low tide but by eleven o'clock the tide came in and they were obliged to wait until evening so that their tired horses could swim the one-third of a mile across the mouth of Alsea bay to the sub-agency. It rained all night and by morning the road was almost impassable.

They again followed the beach to Cape Perpetua

---

285 *Weekly Ledger,* Jackson, sept. 12, 1862 (Bancroft library).

War. Reb. Ser. I, vol. L, pt. I, p. 793, 1155, 675-676.

286 Fort Yamhill, located at Grande Ronde reservation about 25 mi. so.w. of Dayton, Ore. Fort Hoskins, established by Capt. Christopher Colon Augur, 4th u.s. *inf.* (Co. G), july 25, 1856. Named in honor of Lt. Charles Hoskins who was killed at Monterey, Mexico, sept. 21, 1846. Fort Hoskins was finally built east of the mountains in Kings valley.

which they ascended to take the trail through the woods. Fallen timber blocked their path and they were forced to cut their way through large tree trunks so that the horses and pack animals could get through.

The next day they reached the Suislaw river where the horses again took to the water. At the end of another day they reached the Umpqua river where the soldiers rowed across but the weary horses were again obliged to swim. They camped at Winchester bay and after a twenty-mile march along the beach they reached Coos bay.

They succeeded in capturing thirty-one Indians— some of whom had never lived on the reservation and others who had been absent over two years. Seventeen Indians returned voluntarily and without escort to the reservation as they were assured of food and shelter during the long wet winter.

The little group of California volunteers were absent twenty-one days and had traveled two hundred sixty-two miles. U.S. highway 101 parallels the beach where the young soldiers waited for the low tides so that they could march on the smooth wet sand and substantial bridges now span the mouths of the rivers across which those army horses swam.[287]

CALIFORNIA-WASHINGTON FIRST INFANTRY

Since eight of the ten companies of the first Washington infantry were raised in California, many of the Californians resented being designated as Washingtonians and insisted on maintaining their citizenship in California. They voted in the California state election of 1863 and contended that as Californians they were

---

[287] Expedition to Coos bay, *War. Reb.* Ser. I, vol. L, pt. I, p. 353-354 (april 21—may 12, 1864).

entitled to the extra bounty paid the California volunteers serving in the other western states. (This "absent ballot", known also as the "Soldiers' ballot", was eventually declared unconstitutional.) When they were mustered out, they were recognized as residents of California, the place of their enrollment, and were given their choice of being mustered out either at San Francisco or Fort Vancouver.[288]

The winter floods of 1861-1862 prevented the movement of the Washington first infantry and interfered with their training also. When june 1862 arrived, companies B and C left Fort Vancouver on the Oregon Steam Navigation company boats for the mouth of the Palouse on the Snake river and marched overland to Fort Colville relieving the Californians who had been stationed there since november 1861. Company C, California-Washington infantry, remained there for two years and eight months.[289]

The most arduous service was rendered by companies D, E, G and I. They patrolled the emigrant roads from Walla Walla to Lapwai, Boise, Salmon Falls, Bruneau valley and to the limits of the district of Utah where General Connor's volunteers guarded that territory.[290]

---

[288] *War. Reb.* Ser. I, vol. L, pt. II, p. 1154, Special Order no. 54 by Brig. Gen. Benj. Alvord, march 6, 1865.

Letter written at Fort Colville, oct. 3, 1863. Pub. *Alta Weekly California (Steamer)*, nov. 3, 1863 (Huntington library).

[289] *War. Reb.* Ser. I, vol. L, pt. I, p. 1150 (june 19, 1862).

[290] Companies of Washington 1st inf. (8 Cos. Californians) and stations occupied:

    Co. A, Walla Walla, over 2 yrs.
    " B, Colville and Walla Walla.
    " C, Colville, 2 yrs. 8 mos.
    " D, Fort Hoskins 1862, Boise 1863-1864.
    " E, Lapwai 1862, 1863, 1864, Vancouver 1865.
    " F, Dalles 1862-1865.
    " G, Steilacoom 1862, Boise 1863-1865.
    " H, Dalles 1862, 1863, Vancouver 1864, Dalles 1865.

To afford ample protection to that vast frontier, General Alvord, commanding the district of Oregon, established a post at the Nez Percé reservation and ordered company E, first Washington infantry, and company F, first Oregon cavalry, to erect buildings to protect themselves from the zero weather in the winter of 1862-1863. The post was built three miles from the junction of the Clearwater river with the Snake and twelve miles from Lewiston. It was named Lapwai and served as an advance supply base for the territory to the east.[291]

The Nez Percé Indians were known for their persistent friendship for the whites and it was with grave concern that General Alvord received the news that two white men had been killed by some one of their tribe. For thirty years no Nez Percé Indian had ever been accused of such a crime against the whites. Lawyer, their head chief, surrendered the accused, Wet-too-law-in, to Major J. S. Rinearson, first Oregon cavalry, commanding Fort Lapwai.

General Alvord arranged a meeting with thirty of the chiefs among whom were Lawyer, Big Thunder, Joseph, Looking Glass and all the principal chiefs except Eagle-of-the-Light. From ten thousand to fifteen thousand miners had entered their reservation without authority and in violation of the provisions of the treaty made with the Indians june 11, 1855, and ratified by the United States senate april 29, 1859.

It was regrettable that after seven years there was but little evidence of the fulfillment of the treaty on the part of the government. Lawyer had received but six months' salary as the head chief of the Nez Percé

”   I, Vancouver 1862, Boise 1863-1865.
”   K, Steilacoom 1862-1864.
291 *War. Reb.* Ser. I, vol. L, pt. II, p. 280 (oct. 1862).

and the house promised him had just been commenced. Few of their annuities had ever reached the tribe.[292]

Whether the Indians understood the words of General Alvord or whether he was sincere the "talk" of this pioneer soldier reveals the faith of the early Indians. "When camped near The Dalles ten years ago, in may 1853, your men were seen to kneel on the ground and say their prayers and worship in truth and sincerity the great God in heaven. You won my respect and regard. Could I have had my will, I would have raised a wall as high as the heavens around you to keep out intruders. It is very sad to find that the discovery of gold should have brought such a mass of the very worst white men in contact with you. Better if all the gold found there were sunk in the ocean than such injustice should be done to you."[293]

The new treaty negotiated with the Nez Percé Indians, permitted the whites to occupy Lewiston and other mining towns but the Indians insisted that the sale of whisky be prohibited on their lands. The squatters were ordered from the reservation and an attempt was made to recompense the Indians for their losses incurred in surrendering some of the gold regions.

New Fort Boise was established on a site forty-three miles east of old Fort Boise. As this post was a sub-depot, the troops could patrol the route to Salmon falls, the Bruneau valley and as far east as Fort Hall. The Snake Indians were quiet during the summer of 1863 as a new treaty had just been negotiated with them by General Connor and Governor Doty. By systematically patrolling the roads General Alvord maintained comparative peace in his district during these years.

[292] *Ibid.,* p. 206-209.
[293] *Ibid.,* p. 192, 103.

For three long years these young Californians rode the rough roads and trails of Washington, Oregon and Idaho. Some of them rode south to Klamath lake, others to the north at Fort Steilacoom near the present Tacoma, while others preserved the peace on the Pacific shore, and in the Umpqua and Rogue River valleys.[294]

COASTAL FORTIFICATIONS

At the beginning of the war there were no fortifications whatever in either Oregon or Washington. Not a cent had ever been spent by the government. All money appropriated by congress had been spent in California in fortifying San Francisco bay at Fort Point and Alcatraz.

However, the need of defending the Pacific Northwest was recognized by congress and in july 1862, the Fortification bill was passed. It provided an appropriation of $100,000 for the defense of the Columbia river. The following year $200,000 additional was provided for the further defense of Oregon and Washington. Brigadier General René De Russy, U.S. Engineer in charge of Pacific coast defenses, selected Cape Disappointment as the site for the new fort which was named Fort Cape Disappointment by General Wright. Work began on the fort in july 1863 but it was not completed until the following spring.[295]

[294] *Ibid.*, pt. I, p. 399-401 (feb. 1865); p. 329, 388-389 (oct. 1864).

They were stationed at more than a score of camps and forts of this district: Forts Colville, Lapwai, Boise, Hall, Salmon Falls, Owyhee river, Polk, Watson, Curry, Wright, Alvord, Walla Walla, The Dalles, Cascades, Steilacoom, Hoskins, Yamhill, Siletz Blockhouse, Camp Lyon, and many other camps some of which were quite temporary.

[295] *War. Reb.* Ser. I, vol. L, pt. II, p. 613, 134-135, 259, 301-302, 1182, 140-141, 726.

René de Russy, graduate of West Point 1812. He died at San Francisco, nov. 23, 1865.

In the fall of 1864, California was called on for another regiment of volunteers and the eighth was promptly organized. Company A enrolled at Watsonville and in february 1865 was sent to garrison the new fort at Cape Disappointment.[296]

They had been at the fort two months when the bark "Industry" went on the bar at the mouth of the Columbia. Seven soldiers from company A, eighth infantry, California volunteers, and one man from the ninth U.S. infantry procured a boat from the lighthouse keeper and started for the "Industry". After a hard pull of about eight miles, they succeeded in getting within a half mile of the wreck and picked up five passengers who were floating on a raft. They then started toward another raft on which there had been fourteen persons but when they reached it only two remained. The rest had all been swept away. The soldiers managed to place the victims aboard an oyster sloop which took them ashore.

By this time the tide was so strong that the Californians could not make another trip. They returned to the fort for hot coffee and re-enforcements and soon went out again to look for other survivors. They kept up their vigil until morning when they abandoned their fruitless search and returned to shore. "Out of twenty-six, passengers and crew, only seven survived to bless the brave California volunteers."

The "Industry" had sailed from San Francisco with passengers and cargo for Portland. After she struck, the water rushed in at the bottom and came surging up bringing with it most of her cargo and scattering it along the shore.[297]

---

[296] *War. Reb.* Ser. I, vol. L, pt. II, p. 1059, 1082, 1116-1117, 1128-1129, 1194.
[297] Letter from member of Co. A, 8th inf., Calif. vol. *Pajaro Times*, Watsonville, april 8, 1865 (Bancroft library).

Company A, eighth infantry, remained at Fort Cape Disappointment until august 1865, when it was transferred to Fort Dalles. Company B of this regiment was stationed at Fort Stevens from april 25, 1865, until mustered out in december 1865.[298]

THE MILITARY DEPARTMENT OF OREGON

The department of Oregon as established in general orders no. 10 from the adjutant general's office on september 13, 1858, included Washington territory and that part of Idaho lying west of the Rocky mountains, also all of Oregon except the Umpqua and Rogue river valleys.

On january 15, 1861, the departments of Oregon and California were merged into one department by order no. 1 issued by Brigadier General Albert Sydney Johnston who was then in command of the department of California.

Oregon then came under the command of Pacific department headquarters at San Francisco, and was designated as the district of Oregon. Within the short space of a year, four different officers directed the military affairs of this district.

On september 13, 1861, Colonel Benjamin L. Beall, first dragoons, assumed command and was relieved the following month by Lieutenant Colonel Albermarle Cady, seventh U.S. infantry, who in turn was replaced by Colonel Justus Steinberger, first Washington infantry, may 5, 1862. Two months later, july 7, 1862, Brigadier General Benjamin Alvord, U.S. army, took over and remained in command until called to Washington in march, 1865. Colonel Reuben F. Maury succeeded General Alvord and remained in command

---

298 Fort Stevens was named in honor of Gov. Isaac I. Stevens.

until the department of Columbia was created to include Oregon, Washington and Idaho, and Brigadier General Wright was placed in command. However, he never assumed command as he was drowned in the wreck of the S.S. "Brother Jonathan" while en route to his post of duty.[299]

---

[299] *War. Reb.* Ser. I, vol. L, pt. I, p. I fn; 2-6.

California Blockhouses

A few California cities still bear the names of the old forts that once protected them, as Fort Bragg, Fort Bidwell and Fort Jones. The sites of others are designated by "markers" on which are inscribed the name and a brief account of the men who garrisoned these outposts once known as forts or camps, yet in reality, they were but blockhouses. Built of logs or adobe, or both, they shielded the soldiers from the Indians' arrows and bullets. The California volunteers served at thirty or more of these old blockhouses of the state.

Since many of these boys served beyond the borders of their state, it has often been inferred that they were not needed at home. The great central valleys were comparatively free from Indian attacks but hostile bands harassed the settlers and miners in the foothills and mountains.

To use the troops most effectively in the seven counties of the northwest, the Humboldt military district was created and Colonel Francis J. Lippitt, second infantry, California volunteers, placed in command. In january 1862 he established his headquarters at Fort Humboldt, Eureka, and for eighteen months directed the policing of almost twenty thousand square miles of wilderness.[300]

300 The Humboldt Military district, created by order of Gen. Wright, dec. 12, 1861, comprised the counties of Sonoma, Napa, Mendocino, Trinity, Humboldt, Del Norte and Klamath. (Klamath was then a county.)
War. Reb. Ser. I, vol. L, pt. I, p. 760 (Spec. Order no. 233).

There were thousands of Indians scattered through the forests and mountain gulches and he had but eight hundred California volunteers at his command. It was not surprising that he was a bit nonplused. "Why," said he, "there are so many Indians and they are so hard to find, that to bring them all in by sending small detachments after them would take as long as it would to bring in all the squirrels and coyotes."

The roads were impassable during the heavy winter rains and the new commander was unable to communicate with his troops. Fort Terwaw, on the north bank of the Klamath river and about six miles from its mouth, was completely destroyed. It was one of the oldest in the district and seventeen buildings had been built for the troops and government stores.

According to a soldier correspondent, Terwaw is an Indian word meaning "beautiful spot". Said he, "Terwaw is thirty miles from Crescent City, amidst the grandest old forests my eyes have ever beheld or my fancy conceived. Calaveras boasts of one of her big trees, but the banks of the Klamath river support a forest of mammoth trees where they may be counted by the thousands and thousands, and where every tree one comes to, seems as large or larger than the one just passed." [301]

The winter rains deluged Fort Humboldt so that Colonel Lippitt was obliged to move his troops to the new town of Bucksport where they might find shelter from the heavy downpour. Yet being storm bound

---

Col. Francis J. Lippitt was formerly captain of Co. F, Stevenson's New York volunteers.

Fort Humboldt built in 1853 by companies B and F, fourth U.S. infantry, Lt. Col. R. C. Buchanan, commanding. Gen. U. S. Grant was stationed there in 1854.

[301] *Calaveras Chronicle*, Mokelumne Hill, april 26, 1862.

seemed to be conducive to the formulation of plans for his spring campaign against the Indians. His first policy was to avoid bloodshed if possible. This he proposed to do by concentrating the soldiers at Fort Gaston and inviting the Indians to a "field day". Here he planned to exercise his men in showy and striking maneuvers including the firing of blank cartridges and the discharge of the mountain howitzer. He was convinced that his "field day" would so impress the Indians with the might of the white warriors that all the tribe would agree to move to the reservation.

He submitted his plan to General Wright and asked for additional men including six companies of the ninth U.S. infantry. He also suggested that the Indians be moved either to Fort Tejon or to the Santa Barbara islands so that they could not return to their old homes.

Colonel Lippitt soon learned that an Indian campaign was no field day. General Wright's reply was brief but decisive. "Your plans," said he, "are good but you must not rely on such an increase to your force. The removal of the Indians and the establishment of reservations is a matter belonging entirely to the Indian bureau." [302]

It was not until march that Colonel Lippitt was able to make a hundred seventy mile tour through a part of his district. For the first time this New Englander saw the Northwest. He declared that the country was more Alpine than Switzerland itself and that for hundreds of miles he could scarcely find a level spot. When he saw the charred ruins of many ranch buildings, he fully realized the gravity of the situation.

He ordered a number of new forts built that spring.

[302] *War. Reb.* Ser. I, vol. L, pt. I, p. 842-846, 858.

One was located on the north side of Mad river at Brehmer's ranch opposite the Blue Slide and about twenty miles east of Arcata. This was named Fort Lyon. The site chosen for the second one, Fort Baker, was twenty-eight miles eastward from Hydesville on the north side of Van Dusen fork on Neil's ranch. Fort Anderson was built on the north bank of Redwood creek about a mile from Minor's ranch.[303]

During the summer of 1862 his ten companies of the second infantry carried on an active campaign and engaged the Indians in dozens of skirmishes. In addition to the many hundreds of miles traveled on foot over exceedingly rough country, the soldiers cut new trails from ten to twenty miles in length. All blockhouses and barracks were built by the troops with no additional expense to the government. To fell the trees, erect bullet proof buildings and stockades, and bring in hundreds of Indians to the reservations was a creditable service indeed.

Yet since absolute peace had not been attained and numerous depredations aroused the settlers, a special committee wrote to General Wright charging Colonel Lippitt with incompetence and ignorance of Indian warfare. They alleged that he had lost the confidence and respect of the citizens.

In reply to the charges Colonel Lippitt said that it was true that he was ignorant of Indian warfare, at least the kind of "wolf hunting" that was then practiced in the Humblodt district. He declared that he had tried to acquire all possible information from the settlers and had listened to their advice. "But," said he, "having none of the practical skill of a 'Leather Stocking' in trailing Indians, I have not thought it my duty to scout

[303] *Ibid.*, p. 906-910, 915-916, 169-175.

myself." Whatever the outcome of the inquiry which followed, he remained in command for almost another year.[304]

The futility and disappointments of his first summer campaign is revealed in his report november 13, 1862:

The only effect of the summer campaign has been to transform hundreds of peaceful Indians into hostile ones. Since the Indians left the Smith river reservation, fresh outrages have been committed in every direction—ranches have been burned, their owners killed and mail stations plundered.

To send soldiers in pursuit of any particular party of Indians in this country is as futile as it would be to send a two-horse stage after a locomotive. To send a detachment to the spot where an outrage has been committed simply exhausts the men and spends the government money for that is the only place where the Indians will be sure *not* to be.

I appeal to the department commander that this sort of warfare is better suited for savages than for troops of a civilized and Christian nation, and could be carried on far more effectively by a company or two of wild beasts and Indian hunters as well as far more economically.

Colonel Lippitt requested the withdrawal of his regiment from the odious and thankless task. He even appealed to Lincoln according to the following letter, the original of which is now deposited in the Huntington library, San Marino, California:

Headquarters Humboldt Military District, Fort Humboldt, California, October 12, 1862.
To his Excellency, the President of the United States.
Sir: I have the honor to request a leave of absence from the Department of the Pacific for three months, subject to the approval of the department commander.
With the greatest respect, I have the honor to be
Your Obt. Servt.

---

304 *Ibid.*, p. 60.
Ibid., pt. II, p. 58-59, 66.
Richard H. Orton, *Record of California men in the war reb.*, p. 419-420.

Francis J. Lippitt, Colonel 2nd Inf. c.v. Comdg. Humboldt Military District.

On the reverse side of the letter was the endorsement,

Respectfully referred to the Secy. of War but not approved.
Nov./14   H. W. Halleck, Gen'.l in Chf.
Leave refused, Edwin M. Stanton.

The letter was mailed back to the department of the Pacific with the notation, "Respectfully returned—furlough cannot be granted." The disappointed colonel of the Humboldt military district was ordered to remain and conduct a vigorous winter campaign.[305]

However, the rank and file did not share the anxiety of their commander. On many of their scouts they never caught a glimpse of an Indian. In relating some of his experiences, one volunteer began his narrative with the couplet:

> Our brave young chief with thirty valiant men
> Marched down the coast and then right back again.

They had been ordered to start at sunset.

At dark, said he, we were in the redwoods and a darker prospect I never met. There was no moon and the stars were hidden by the fog. After trying in vain to follow the road, we were suddenly brought to a halt by running our wagon against a log. We had a good supply of candles so we lighted two and carried one in front of the wagon and the other behind. We marched through the forest for five miles as solemnly as a funeral procession.

We arrived at Crescent City at one o'clock in the morning and camped just outside of the town entirely out of range of the rifled battery of "thousand yard whiskey" which has proved so destructive to other detachments of volunteers.[306]

Indian attacks in all sections of the district brought

---

[305] *War. Reb.* Ser. I, vol. L, pt. II, p. 221-222, 154. MS (Huntington library) IIM 23699.

[306] *Alta California,* San Francisco, sept. 18, 1862. (Bancroft)

calls for help. Round valley experienced so much trouble that it was necessary to declare martial law to restrain the whites. Captain Charles D. Douglas, company F, second infantry, was ordered there early in november 1862 but was delayed for a month on account of lack of transportation. Colonel Lippitt chartered the steam tug "Mary Ann" to transfer the company and supplies from Fort Humboldt to Fort Bragg for seven hundred dollars but repeated delays impelled him to cancel his order and hire the "Dashaway" which cost one thousand dollars.

After reaching Fort Bragg, the troops started overland to Round valley. They were hindered by the heavy rains but finally arrived after a week's march. Captain Douglas selected a site in the center of the valley for the fort and named it in honor of General Wright. The stockade and all the buildings were loopholed and bullet and arrow proof. Order was soon restored, the sale of liquor prohibited on the Mendocino Indian reservation, and martial law discontinued.[307]

Colonel Lippitt's continued request for the withdrawal of his regiment from the Humboldt district and the petition of the citizens for permission to organize a battalion of mountaineers resulted in General Wright's appeal to Governor Stanford for more troops. The governor issued a proclamation february 7, 1863, calling for six companies of volunteers for the Mountain battalion. Companies A and B were promptly organized and mustered in within a few months.

On july 31, Colonel Lippitt was relieved from command and Lieutenant Colonel Stephen G. Whipple

307 *War. Reb.* Ser. I, vol. L, pt. II, p. 176, 228-231, 202-203, 310. Martial law in Round valley, oct. 15, 1862—feb. 11, 1863. Fort Bragg established june 1857 by Lt. Horatio Gibson and named for Gen. Braxton Bragg, veteran of Mexican war.

assigned to take his place. When the latter assumed command, he, too, asked for more men. Recruiting for the Mountain battalion did not reach his expectations so he suggested that enlistments be obtained in the more populous parts of the state. It was a year before he could muster in enough men to fill all six companies. Meanwhile he conducted an active campaign although handicapped by lack of men. The december report for 1863 credits the Humboldt district with an aggregate of only five hundred forty-five soldiers.[308]

A new post, named Camp Gilmore, was established three or four miles north of Trinidad to protect the mail route and huts were built to shelter the troops. Fifty miles south of Fort Humboldt on the Eel river, Camp Grant was located to protect the road between the southern part of Humboldt and northern Mendocino counties.

Lieutenant Colonel Whipple remained in command of the Humboldt district just seven months when he was transferred to the Mountain battalion. His headquarters were at Fort Gaston in Hoopa valley about forty miles from Arcata on the west bank of the Trinity river and about fourteen miles above its junction with the Klamath.[309]

According to accounts written by the soldiers, Indian warfare in the redwoods was quite an adventure:

---

[308] Richard H. Orton, *Record of California men in the war reb.*, p. 826-831.

War. Reb. Ser. I, vol. L, pt. II, p. 536-537, 711.

Lt. Col. Stephen G. Whipple, breveted colonel, march 13, 1865. Captain of thirty-second u.s. inf., jan. 22, 1867; in command first u.s. cavalry, dec. 15, 1870; breveted major for service at Clearwater, Idaho, july 11, 12, 1877; retired oct. 3, 1884.

[309] Fort Gaston established december 1858, by Capt. E. Underwood, fourth u.s. inf., named in honor of Second Lt. William Gaston, first dragoons, 24 year old West Point graduate who was killed during the Spokane expedition, may 17, 1858.

Lieutenant Rufus F. Herrick, with a detachment of company D, was sent after the Indians who were making their way in all haste up the steep side of Trinity mountain. The chase was an exciting one as both soldiers and Indians were plainly visible for more than two hours. But as usual, the enemy dodged into dark brush covered gulches and made good their escape.

The Seranaltin ranch takes its name from Seranaltin John . . . who for bravery, daring and intelligence, has no equal in Northern California. For many years he has been chief and head of the Redwood and Hoopa Indians. He is quite tall, dark, and of very light build. When excited he has a strange wildness of expression in his eyes and an odd twitching of the head.[310]

Skillful strategy was needed to make peace with these northern tribes who were at war with each other and with the whites. After a year's campaign, Lieutenant Colonel Whipple began negotiations for peace by sending for Indian Charlie Hostler who appeared to be friendly and desired peace for his band. Seranaltin John also came in for a "big talk" and promised to bring in Big Jim, the leader of the Trinity Indians.

When the latter arrived april 27, 1864, he acknowledged that he was tired of living in the mountains where he was obliged to keep moving to avoid the troops. His people had no homes, no food, nor a place of safety. They wanted to be friends and settle again where they had formerly lived. Big Jim returned to his people and induced Handsome Billy to visit Fort Gaston and make peace.

It was with the greatest satisfaction and relief that Whipple was able to report the results of his "big talk" with these tribes: "The last lot of Indians of the upper Trinity river came to the Hoopa valley (Fort Gaston) and expressed their desire to remain here upon the same conditions accorded the others. Three days ago

310 *Humboldt Times,* Eureka, feb. 13, 1864.

Curly-headed Tom's band arrived. . . This band is the worst in the country and has for years been the terror of the people of the counties of Humboldt, Klamath and Trinity. By their own admissions they have been the ringleaders in all the depredations about Humboldt bay.[311]

Colonel Henry Moore Black, who had succeeded Whipple in command of the Humboldt district, contributed much to the success of the campaign that brought about this peace. Although in command for but four months, february 6 to june 30, 1864, he supported Whipple's campaign and was able to supply an aggregate of a thousand men—four companies of the sixth infantry; the Mountain battalion consisting of six companies; and one company of Native California cavalry.

The latter company, under command of Captain Ramon Jose Pico, was employed the greater part of the time as escort to the government train to Arcata and occasionally to Fort Gaston to protect the herds of cattle being driven there for the use of the troops. His company was also engaged in a skirmish with Seranaltin John's band resulting in the loss of one soldier.

The presidential election of 1864 was vigorously debated in all the army camps where the California boys were stationed and Fort Humboldt was no exception. Captain Pico addressed the following appeal to his company: "I am about to leave this district and may be absent a month or more. . . In my absence it may be attempted to lead or influence you from the path you have voluntarily chosen. I, therefore, ask of you to be steady in the opinion you have formed and expressed in regard to the coming election. Soon will

[311] *War. Reb.* Ser. I, vol. L, pt. II, p. 694, 824, 831, 853, 881-882.

come the day when you will be called upon to exercise your rights as civilians in the selecting of a man for the chief magistrate of the nation. On such a momentous occasion it is hoped that you will sustain the defenders of the Union and the cause of liberty." [312]

When Colonel Black was ordered to West Point, Major John C. Schmidt, second infantry, California volunteers, was placed in command of the Humboldt district and remained on duty there until june 27, 1865. The force under Major Schmidt consisted of but 334 men. The warlike Indians had been subdued and placed on reservations; emigrant roads and mail routes were given adequate protection, and the farmers had returned to their homes. [313]

An account of General Wright's efforts to colonize the Humboldt Indians on Catalina island deserves mention in this chapter. For more than a decade General Wright had tried to maintain peace between the Humboldt Indians and the settlers. He had repeatedly requested the removal of the Indians to some section of the country so far removed from their old haunts that they could not return. The general appeared to be one of the early advocates of the "displaced persons" procedure.

He selected the island of Santa Catalina as the most favorable location for a reservation and military post and was so positive that the Indian bureau would ap-

---

[312] *Humboldt Times, Eureka,* oct. 1864. (Written at Fort Humboldt, oct. 15, 1864.)

Soldiers were permitted to vote while absent on duty but the law known as "absent or soldiers' vote" was declared unconstitutional.

[313] *War. Reb.* Ser. I, vol. L, pt. II, p. 874, 881-883.

Col. Henry M. Black, graduate West Point, july 1, 1847; served on the Pacific coast 1858-1864—Ft. Dalles, Vancouver and Alcatraz; with Calif. vol. 1863-1864. Ordered to West Point as instructor of artillery, infantry and cavalry tactics, june 30, 1864. (*Biog. register officers & graduate of* U.S. *Military Academy,* West Point, N.Y., George Washington Cullum.)

prove his choice that he at once proceeded to occupy the island. He ordered Major Henry Hancock to speedily obtain information of the island's resources and advantages as a military post.

Major Hancock sailed for the island aboard the "Ned Beal", november 21, 1863, and made the trip in six hours. At the end of the fourth day, he wrote a lengthy report enclosing a sketch of the harbor and the isthmus. He said, "The island is capable of becoming a vast military and naval depot and if it were occupied by an enemy it might endanger the safety of California." He recommended that a small force with a few guns should be permanently stationed there. With two guns at Ballast Point, two more on the opposite shore and others at eighty feet elevation overlooking the harbor, the safety of the post would be assured.

Plans for the occupation of the island were rushed and Colonel James F. Curtis, then in command of Drum Barracks, was ordered to select a competent and discreet officer to take possession. Captain Benjamin R. West and his company C, fourth infantry, from Shasta, were chosen for this duty and were designated the "army of occupation" on Catalina island and to Captain West belongs the distinction of having been both civil and military governor of the Island.

On New Year's day, Captain West and his company landed and began construction of temporary quarters and the improvement of the water supply. All camps or posts were formally named so on january 9, 1864, orders were regularly issued to name the main harbor Catalina and the smaller one, just north of the isthmus, Union bay. The latter bay had two coves, Fourth-of-july and Fisherman's.

Orders had been issued for the removal of all persons before the first of february but an exception was made in the case of permanent residents who were permitted to remain; miners were allowed to stay and work their claims.

The islanders objected to the occupancy of their land by the army and sent vigorous protest to the governor. A few adjustments were made and General Wright rescinded his first order by agreeing to let those, who wished, land and work on Santa Catalina island until the Indian department wanted it.

Approval of the Catalina plan was slow in coming from Washington. Two months passed and still no word except a telegram stating that General Halleck had approved the plan. General Wright became impatient and wired Washington to please telegraph the decision of the department of the interior.

All supporters of the plan, including Congressman Conness, were disappointed when W. P. Dole, commissioner of Indian Affairs, disapproved of the location. Mail service had not then taken to wings so it was august when General Wright ordered the withdrawal of the army of occupation from Santa Catalina island. Thus the island was not to be colonized by the "red skins" but to be left to await the pioneer resort promoters who were to sell Americans on "tanned skins".[314]

Although the California volunteers garrisoned a dozen blockhouses in the Humboldt district, the northeastern section of the state was left open to attack. At the beginning of the war, Fort Crook was the only post in that vicinity that was occupied by the Federal troops. When they were withdrawn in october 1861, they

---

[314] *War. Reb.* Ser. I, vol. L, pt. II, p. 686-689, 692, 706, 714, 708, 720, 723, 728, 730, 736, 772, 760.

Report W. P. Dole, Indian Affairs, 38 Cong. 2 Sess. H. Ex. Doc. no. 1, vol. v. (1220)

were replaced by company C, second cavalry, California volunteers, commanded by Captain Henry B. Mellen.[315] The volunteers left Camp Union, Sacramento, aboard the river packet, "Antelope", and sailed up the Sacramento river to Red Bluff. From here they marched to Fort Crook where they remained until 1864 when their three year term of service had expired. The company was then filled up by recruits from San Francisco who garrisoned the fort until the spring of 1866.

For more than four years these California cavalrymen patrolled the emigrant trail that led from Salt Lake to Oregon and California. They carried the mail, escorted the travelers, and extended their protection northward to the Owyhee river, and beyond to the John Day.

It required two days for the cavalrymen to make the trip to Red Bluff with the mail if the weather was favorable. If they encountered a snow-storm, there was certain to be trouble in store for them as the nearest settlement to the fort was sixty miles.

Early in december 1862, Corporal I. H. Wolf and Calvin Hall, company C, second cavalry, left Fort Crook with the mail for Red Bluff. Hall came back alone and stated that Wolf returned with him as far as Bacon's on Cow creek. For two years nothing was heard from Wolf and he was listed as a deserter and so his record stands today but it should be changed from "deserted" to "died in the service of his country". Two years later, december 8, 1864, his body was found in a deserted blacksmith shop at Oak Run on the Middleworth place. He was identified by the corporal cloth-

[315] Report Gen. Joseph K. F. Mansfield, june 2, 1859, National archives, Washington, D.C. (Courtesy Gertrude A. Steger, Pres. Shasta Historical society.)

War. Reb. Ser. I, vol. L, pt. I, p. 794.

ing, his name on his glove, a silver watch, and Colt pistol. There were four loads in the pistol and forty-five cents in his pocket.[316]

Fort Crook was abandoned july 1, 1869, after being of service for more than twelve years. Historical marker no. 355 now identifies the site and a flagpole stands as a reminder of the men who served there.

Fort Bidwell was not established until the close of the War. Major General Irvin McDowell issued his order for the selection of a site and construction of a fort on the same day that President Lincoln died. The war in the East was over but the western troubles were increasing. A new fort was necessary to protect the roads from Chico via Susanville to Surprise valley; from Red Bluff via Fort Crook to the Owyhee river to Idaho; and the road from the Humboldt river to the southern part of Oregon.

Major Robert S. Williamson, U.S. engineer, with an escort from company C, second cavalry, under Captain Henry B. Mellen, located the new post in the northern end of Surprise valley. It was named Fort Bidwell in honor of General John Bidwell, pioneer of Chico.[317]

Ernest M. Woodman, company K, second cavalry, relates a few of his experiences while on patrol duty on the Idaho road. His company left Sacramento in mid-summer, july 25, 1865, and in three days arrived at Colusa. By the end of two more days they reached Chico where, said Woodman,

That enterprising townsman, General Bidwell, gave us permission to go into his garden and gather all the fruit we wanted to eat, for which we were very thankful. . . We left Chico on the first of

---

316 Shasta *Courier,* dec. 24, 1862. (Bancroft library).

317 *War. Reb.* Ser. I, vol. L, pt. II, p. 1195-1196, 1192-1193, 1182-1183, 1177, 1187, 1234-1236.

Ibid., Gen Orders no. 44, june 10, 1865, p. 1259.

august and traveled over the Chico and Idaho route. It is a fine road and we enjoyed the ride very much.

We crossed the summit on the third and while resting our horses, we spied the starry banner floating to the breeze from one of the loftiest peaks in view. Our color bearer, Corporal P. O. Dodge of Bangor, unfurled our flag and we united with him in giving three hearty cheers such as none but true hearted Union volunteers can give. . .

We arrived at Smoke creek on the tenth and found it Smoke creek in reality. It is situated about three miles from the state line and about the stepping off place of God's footstool. We have not seen any Indians yet but our company will start on a scout in a few days. We have sent several small detachments out as escorts to teams en route for Idaho and Humboldt and also an escort for the stage.[318]

The Sacramento rangers, company F, second cavalry, garrisoned Fort Bidwell until may 31, 1866, when they were recalled to be mustered out. The town Fort Bidwell, still bears the name of the old fort that once protected that part of the state.

Fort Reading was the first army post built in northern California. The old adobe fort was named in honor of Major Pierson Barton Reading, early pioneer of northern California, and for fourteen years served the purposes of the army when occasion demanded.

The old fort was seldom used by the California volunteers at the beginning of the war but in 1865 the citizens of Shasta and Tehama counties petitioned General Wright to send a company of soldiers to Black Rock on Mill creek but the general judged Fort Reading to be a more central location and ordered out a company of cavalry from Fort Union, Sacramento. The old fort was no longer used by the army after 1866 and four years later the buildings were sold.[319]

318 *Weekly Union Record,* Oroville, sept. 2, 1865. (Calif. State library).
319 Fort Reading established may 26, 1852. Major Reading for whom it was named came to California with the Chiles-Walker party. In 1844 Reading

Fort Jones was occupied for a brief time in january 1864 when trouble arose between the Indians and the settlers on Salmon river. Just twenty-five men were ordered to the valley to maintain peace. It is commendable that Fort Jones retains with pride the name of the old fort.[320]

No fort or blockhouse guarded the great central valley between Fort Reading and Fort Miller. From 1861 to 1865 the latter was frequently occupied by the volunteers en route from the north to Drum Barracks. Company K, second cavalry, was stationed at Fort Miller (*Plate* 11) from december 26, 1863 until october 1, 1864. Among the members of this company there was quite a skillful artist, C. F. Otto Skobel, who made several sketches of this fort, photostats of which are now in the State library, Sacramento. The sites of both Fort Miller and Millerton, the old county seat of Fresno county, are now submerged beneath Millerton lake.[321]

The establishment of Camp Independence in Owens valley became imperative on account of the uprising of the Indians. Lieutenant Colonel George S. Evans with a detachment of the second cavalry was ordered there to establish a post. The following account written by one of the California volunteers, describes the campaign against the Indians at this time:

I have just returned from a long trip after being out forty-one days from Camp Latham. On march 19, 1862, a detachment of fifty men was detailed to go to Owens river to quell Indian disturbances. I was

received from Gov. Micheltorena a grant to Rancho Buena Ventura, a 34,000 acre tract on the upper Sacramento river near Redding. In 1844-1845 he was clerk and chief of trappers for Captain Sutter.

320 Yreka *Union,* may 4, 1861.

321 Maj. Albert S. Miller, a graduate West Point, served at Monterey, Calif., in 1849, and in 1850 commanded an expedition to the Sierra Nevada mts. He died at Benicia, Calif., dec. 7, 1852.

one of those ordered to go. We had only fifteen minutes notice before starting.

When we reached Owens river we found the Indians troublesome. As we started up the river to find them, we met a detachment from Fort Churchill (company A, second cavalry). We were then over one hundred strong. We proceeded above the place called "the fort," a house built of stone, and sent scouting parties out. . .

I had stood guard the night before so I was in the rear that day, guarding the pack mules and grub. The rest of the soldiers and the citizens were drawn up in line of battle and divided into platoons under command of Lieutenant Colonel George S. Evans. . .

The Indians were in one of the best natural fortifications I ever heard of. The soldiers undertook to advance but the Indians commenced whooping and yelling and firing their guns. No Indians could be seen except those on the top of the hill where our men could not get at them nor within firing distance, so Colonel Evans withdrew his men. . .

Since we could not get the Indians out, we moved down to "the fort" and stayed a day. The people gathered up their stock and left the valley with us and the Fort Churchill party. The Fort Churchill boys lost two men—the only soldiers lost. We returned with every man.

This expedition was not equipped for an extensive campaign and was forced to return to Camp Latham for supplies.[322]

On june 11, Lieutenant Colonel Evans again started for Owens valley. This time he commanded two hundred men from companies D, G, and I, second cavalry, with a train of forty-six wagons, carrying in addition to their garrison equipage and ammunition, rations for the men, and forage for the horses for sixty days.[323]

Lieutenant Colonel Evans reached the "Stone fort" at daylight on june 26 and found that the Indians had destroyed it by burning everything that would burn and throwing down the stone walls. This fort was also

[322] *Sierra Democrat,* Downieville, may 17, 1862.
[323] *War. Reb.* Ser. I, vol. L, pt. I, p. 1140.

known as Putnam's store and was situated on Little Pine creek on the western side of Owens river about forty-three miles above Owens lake.[324]

The first intention of Lieutenant Colonel Evans was to make his headquarters at Big Pine, twenty miles farther up the valley, but instead he chose the site on Oak creek. On july 4, he ordered a flagstaff erected, "And the old flag with 'all' its stars upon it was hoisted to the breeze, with 'three times three' given most heartily by the men, and a salute fired with small arms." He then named the location Camp Independence.[325]

The campaign of the summer of 1862 was fraught with many difficulties, one of them being the lack of adequate communication. By the time an order from headquarters would reach the outpost, conditions there would be so changed that it would be folly to attempt the execution of the order.

Occasionally the orders were quite contradictory. This was the case in Owens valley when Captain Edwin A. Rowe, company A, second cavalry, and Indian Agent Warren Wassen, marched down from Fort Churchill to join Lieutenant Colonel George S. Evans' forces. The two commanding officers had considerable difficulty in getting together.

When Captain Rowe reached the eastern bank of the Owens river, he sent a messenger to ask Lieutenant Colonel Evans to come down to the river and try to talk from bank to bank. It was impossible to hear, so Lieutenant Colonel Evans swam across two sloughs and the river, waded a half mile through willows and tules and finally succeeded in reaching the eastern bank. The

---

[324] *Ibid.,* p. 146.
[325] *Ibid.,* pt. II, p. 125, Gen. Orders no. 10, sept. 16, 1862.
Ibid., p. 88-89.
Ibid., pt. I, p. 152-153.

officers were then as widely divided in opinion as they had been by the river. Captain Rowe, under orders from headquarters of the Pacific, was endeavoring to make peace with the Indians, while Lieutenant Colonel Evans had been instructed to chastise them.[326]

Captain George, the big war chief of the Indians, and forty of his warriors were in Captain Rowe's camp at the time. A "big talk" was held and it resulted in Indian George saying that he was tired of fighting; that it was no good; that he wished to be friends with the white men; that if they would let him alone he would let them alone.

Lieutenant Colonel Evans left Camp Independence the first of october, and in his report to army headquarters, San Francisco, he tells about his one hundred twenty mile trip over the mountains with company D, second cavalry, to Visalia:

. . . They made the trip in four and a half days. The route is almost an impracticable one and great credit is due the men for their fortitude and forbearance in making the trail without a murmur of complaint. The animals were without shoes and so very weak from the lack of grain for two months that the men had to walk two-thirds of the way over the precipitous hills.

The men were barefooted and naked for many of them were as destitute of shoes as they were the day they were born and had no pantaloons except such as they, themselves, had made out of barley and flour sacks. The weather was freezing cold, heavy frost every night, and on the 4th a heavy snowstorm; still the men plodded on and stood guard at night, leaving the blood from their feet upon the rocks and snow.[327]

Camp Independence was garrisoned the winter of 1862-1863 by company G, second cavalry, commanded

[326] *Ibid.*, p. 148.
[327] *Ihid.*, p. 152-153, oct. 7, 1862.
Ibid., pt. II, p. 1081-1082.

by Captain Theodore H. Goodman. The soldier com-
mentator has preserved the news as well as some of his
views on conditions in the Owens valley. His letter
bears the date, october 28, 1862, Camp Independence.

. . . Our prospects are brighter now than I thought they would
be. We will have very good quarters considering the short time that
was allowed to build them. . . Last winter let us out of spending
another in tents, when by a little work we might have good cabins.[328]

There is a vedette line established between here and Aurora, a
distance of 150 miles. It is kept up partly by the command and partly
by subscription from the citizens of Aurora and the valley.

Two of our men made a trip to Aurora. They were not molested
by the Indians on the way there, but on their return they were compelled to run right through a body of three hundred Indians, amidst
a perfect shower of bullets and arrows. They arrived in camp without
a scratch although considerably scared.

Indian Agent Wentworth was here a short time ago and distributed
three or four hundred dollars worth of blankets, clothing, and provisions among the tribe. They were sadly in need of clothing, many of
them being entirely naked.[329]

Unless one reads a first-hand account of Indian warfare it is difficult to evaluate the services of the California volunteers in Owens valley. So once more excerpts
are quoted from a volunteer's letter.

. . . We came on as fast as our horses would carry us, until we
reached a safe place for our horses. Then we dismounted and took it
on foot. The Indians appeared anxious to fight but we could not induce
them to leave the oaks. After feeling our way, we charged them in the
ravine and among the oaks. Our little party was divided. One-half
made the charge while the other guarded the horses.

. . . We drove the Indians from one oak to another until they
found a still better position and we were obliged to halt. . . After
separating into four groups, we charged again and drove the Indians
completely out of the woods, killing several of them. We then chased

---

[328] *Sierra Democrat,* Downieville, nov. 8, 1862. (County archives, Downieville)
[329] *Ibid.,* dec. 6, 1862.

them toward the lake. Some of the Indians got within fifty yards of it, a place of safety, so they thought, but it proved death to them. Of those who went into the lake, but few came out. . . Our loss was one man wounded and the lieutenant's horse, which was killed under him.

About a week later Captain H. Noble with a detachment of company E arrived. Both of our companies, numbering about one hundred men, started in search of the Indians. We saw signs of them the second day out on the foothills west of Big Pine and about thirty miles north of Camp Independence. We dismounted and turned the horses out to feed and scouted on foot. We soon found the Indians and went after them driving them into the mountains. . .

The fighting was all done on foot and the Indians could travel much faster over the mountains than the soldiers, so it was deemed best not to follow them but to patrol the river instead.

The Indians, finding that it was not safe to approach the river, began to come in until nine hundred of them arrived at our camp. The commanding officer sent his report to headquarters and the Indians were ordered to be taken to the reservation at Fort Tejon. The valley is now rid of Indians and there is no more trouble to be apprehended from them unless it is from Joaquin Jim and his party, three hundred strong, who are reported to be in the White mountains. . .

Since Captain George had said that he was tired of fighting and willing to move to the Sebastian reservation near Fort Tejon, preparations were made for their removal. It was august 6, 1863, when he had gathered together all his people, men, women and children, numbering about a thousand, and left his beautiful valley, trusting the soldiers to feed and care for them according to their agreement.

It was a long journey for the very young and the aged and it took nearly two weeks to cross the mountains via Walkers pass and reach their destination. They were accompanied by companies D, E, and G, second cavalry, under the command of Captain Moses Mc-Laughlin.

This early practice of caring for displaced persons resulted in much injustice—not necessarily from the soldiers under whose protection the unfortunate Indians were placed, but from the lack of sufficient funds to care for such a large number of human beings. Provisions were scarce, and sometimes the soldiers were ordered on half rations in order that the Indians might not starve.

Thus the confinement of some of the Owens valley Indians at Sebastian reservation was of short duration. When food became scarce, many of them wandered away from the reservation and returned to their old homes.

In an endeavor to capture the returning Indians, the volunteers were stationed at Camp Leonard in Kern valley and one of these soldiers tells about his experiences:

> This camp (Leonard) is located in a willow swamp and is shady and pleasant during the day. It is about fifteen miles northeast of Keysville on the south branch of Kern river. We are placed here to intercept straggling bands of Indians on their way back to their old stamping grounds and we will probably be moved to some other place in a month or six weeks. Some of the men express the wish that we be transferred to the white settlements as we have been bushwhacking for about a year and a half. . .
>
> There are about thirty-five or forty votes in this camp for Sierra county Union candidates and if they will send us tickets they can rest assured there will be no scratching done. The Copperheads need expect no help, for soldiers are as loyal now as when they joined the service.[330]

As the day of the Presidential election drew near, the interest of the California volunteers was keenly aroused as the legislature had passed an act granting the soldiers, absent on duty, the right to vote. The law was later

[330] *Ibid.*, sept. 5, 1863.

declared unconstitutional but not until after the soldiers had voted.[331]

Camp Leonard was undoubtedly not the only camp occupied by the California volunteers at this time as the outline of earthworks may still be seen on a knoll just below the town of Keysville where a tablet has been placed to mark the spot where these soldiers warded off the attacks from the Indians.[332]

But elections and political controversies did not appease the Owens valley Indians who resisted the settlers' encroachment on their lands. Camp Independence was abandoned in 1864, but the following year, november 30, 1865, it was again reoccupied by company E, second cavalry, who remained until april 30, 1866.

This company spent two years at Camp Babbit, near

---

[331] The "Absent vote" passed by the legislature in 1863 was destined to be the subject of political controversy for three quarters of a century. The act of 1863 was commonly known as the "Soldiers' Vote" and was declared unconstitutional by the supreme court of California. (Vol. XXVI, case 161—vol. XXXI, case 261.)

On march 12, 1872 another Absent Voters' law was enacted. This was designated as legislation chapter XIV and was composed of paragraphs 1357-1365.

By statutes 1899 (p. 48) fifteen new sections were added and numbered consecutively, 1366-1380, and at the same time the Original Code chapter XIV, 1357-1365, was repealed.

By statutes 1901 (p. 606) chapter XIV was again transformed, but no further changes were made for ten years. Then in 1911 all the sections added in 1901 were repealed by statute 1911 (p. 1393).

A new chapter comprising paragraphs 1357-1364 was added by statute 1923 (p. 587) and approved may 31, 1923. New amendments were added by statute 1927 (p. 595). In 1931 another change was made by statute 1931 (p. 1628; p. 429) and this was followed by further amendments that were approved june 28, 1937 and in effect aug. 27, 1937.

Soldiers' Vote—Reports of cases determined in supreme court of California—

   Vol. XXVI, case 161

   Vol. XXXI, case 261 (Boalt library.)

[332] Tablet dedicated june 1937—Bakersfield Parlor no. 42, N.S.G.W., El Tejon parlor, no. 239, N.D.G.W. and Kern co. chamber of commerce.

Visalia, not especially for Indian service but to maintain peace between the two political factions, the Union and Southern sympathizers.

Fort Tejon, another of the early California army posts, was also garrisoned by the volunteers. There was no need for troops at this fort continuously but whenever disturbances arose, they were promptly dispatched there from either Fort Miller or Camp Babbit.

Company D, second cavalry, occupied Fort Tejon from august 1863 until january 1864. They were replaced by companies B and G, of the same regiment, who remained until the post was abandoned september 11, 1864. When the California cavalrymen packed up and moved to Drum Barracks, company G had a little more to pack than some of the other companies as they carried a well selected library with them. These boys were from Sierra and Nevada counties and their record was a creditable one, for after three years' service, their company still numbered seventy-six men.[333]

Fort Tejon is perhaps more widely known than some of the other forts in Southern California as many thousands have seen its ruins as they drove over the Ridge route. Yet of the thousands who passed by, but few knew that here the California volunteers marched on the parade grounds, slept in the barracks and, perhaps, occupied sick beds in the hospital. Here they stopped to rest after their long march from Drum Barracks, Wilmington, to Owens valley—a distance of more than three hundred miles.[334]

For many years the site of Camp Cady was an im-

---

[333] Sacramento *Union*, feb. 2, 1864.
War. Reb. Ser. I, vol. L, pt. II, p. 927. (Spec. Order no. 168.)
[334] *Ibid.*, p. 603-604, 613, 617-618, 645, 647, 658, 696, 710, 727-728, 733-734.

portant camping place and was garrisoned occasionally when outrages occurred along the Mojave river.[335]

During the summer of 1864, Camp Cady was garrisoned by company B, second cavalry, commanded by Captain John Cremony. In the following spring, Captain E. Bale, company D, Native California cavalry, patrolled the desert route from Lane's crossing on the Mojave river (now Oro Grande) to Soda lake. When Captain Frederick Munday arrived with his company K, fourth infantry, there was a total of one hundred twenty men at this desert post.[336]

William S. Kidder, the "fighting parson" from company I, seventh infantry, describes the camp as he saw it while he was en route to Fort Whipple in june, 1865. "The quarters are made entirely of brush and are intended for shelter from the sun only. Here we were obliged to leave one of our boys because the day previous he accidently shot himself. The ball entered his left hand and passing upward came out above the wrist. He has since died, his arm having mortified, and being one hundred sixty miles from any physician, there was no help for him." [337]

Captain Benjamin West, company C, fourth infantry, appeared to be one of the most energetic commanders of the desert post at this time. It was reported that he and his volunteers built thirty-five small adobe houses for which he received commendation from General Irvin McDowell in a special order dated Camp Cady, january 11, 1866.

Old Camp Cady remained in existence until 1868 when it was moved half a mile west where buildings of

---

[335] Lt. Col. Albermarle Cady, West Point graduate, commanded the district of Oregon 1861-1862, retired in 1864.

[336] *War. Reb.* Ser. I, vol. L, pt. II, Order no. 49, july 26, 1864, p. 920.

[337] Shasta *Courier,* sept. 9, 1865. (Bancroft library).

stone and adobe were built. The ruins of the latter may
still be seen on the Cady ranch a few miles south of
U.S. highway 91 near the station of Harvard on the
Union Pacific railroad. The old fort was abandoned
in 1871.[338]

The desert road continuing due east from Camp
Cady to the Mojave river was unprotected except for
crude redoubts built at the desert springs. At Piute
springs in the southeastern corner of San Bernardino
county, the ruins of a stone fort stand on a hill that
commands a view of the three states, Nevada, Arizona
and California. The walls of the fort were loop-holed
for the old Sharps' carbines and the stone platform on
the south may have served for mounting one of the old
Napoleons. On the north wall, a seven foot fireplace
remains intact although its chimney no longer stands.
Adjoining the fort are the ruins of a stone corral which
once protected the travelers' and the soldiers' stock
from being stampeded by the Indians.

The fort takes its name from the springs and the hill
of that name although some of the old residents have
conferred upon it the name of Beale. The ruins of the
old outpost are on the ranch formerly owned by T. W.
Van Slyke. The Metropolitan Water and Power company's line and maintainance road both pass within a
short distance of this unmarked and little known army
post. No doubt, the clear water cascading over the
rocks at Piute springs was a welcome sight to the California volunteers after their long desert march from

---

[338] Wilmington *Journal*, mar. 10, apr. 19, 1866.
Alta California (Steamer), San Francisco, oct. 10, 1865.
Los Angeles *Star*, apr. 14, may 12, july 14, 1860.
Ibid., oct. 6, 1868. (Los Angeles city library)
San Francisco *Herald*, apr. 11, 1860.
Camp Cady, Calif., was not officially declared a military reservation until
october 1870.

Cajon pass to the Colorado river; and probably it was doubly appreciated by the California volunteers' surveying party that marched from Salt Lake via Las Vegas, Camp Cady, and Rock springs to Fort Mojave.[339]

Fort Yuma (*Plate* 12) was the supply base for the California column during the four years while these troops were serving in Arizona, New Mexico and out upon the plains to Fort Leavenworth. Afterwards, it housed the Federal troops until final peace treaties were signed with the Indians of the Southwest.[340]

These old California blockhouses and forts were to the travelers on land what the lighthouses were to the seafarers—a guidepost to safety. Many of them were especially built to prevent the Indians' arrows and bullets from penetrating the walls; others were for living quarters only and would have afforded but little protection in case of attack.

To these outposts came the trader, the trapper, the miner and the farmer. Here also, could be found the Indians who begged for food, clothing, blankets and tobacco.

Little remains of many of these army posts. One frame building at Fort Reading; another one at Fort Humboldt, a flagpole at Fort Crook; Fort Miller lies beneath Lake Millerton; at Fort Tejon a few crumbling adobe walls; Camp Cady has little left as the Mojave river washed most of her adobe walls away and scattered the rock foundations; Fort Piute, built of rock, has suffered less through the many years. Truly, the military service of our pioneers has been overlooked.

---

[339] Information supplied through courtesy of Frank E. Cotter, Los Angeles.
[340] W. G. Spencer, *Hygiene of the U.S. army*, p. 562-563.

Dr. Saw Bones - The Army Surgeon

With his scalpel and his saws, his ipecac and *spiritus frumenti,* the frontier army surgeon followed the soldier wherever he went. His hospital tent was pitched on the desert, the mountain and the seashore. There he soothed blistered feet, bound jagged arrow wounds and amputated frozen toes incurred during the winter campaigns.

At the beginning of the war the army medical department consisted of one surgeon general who received the commission of colonel; thirty surgeons ranking as majors; and eighty-four assistant surgeons who served as lieutenants for the first five years, after which they were promoted to captains.[341]

Their training was far short of the present requisites. Medical colleges then offered two courses of lectures of eighteen weeks each, but before beginning his studies, the student usually served one year as an apprentice to a reputable physician. This procedure was not comparable to that of the present medical colleges, as the doctor of today must complete four years training before he begins his interneship and assumes the personal care of a patient.

---

[341] *Medical and surgical history of war. reb.*—Surg. vol. II, pt. III, p. 899. The rank of each officer was raised and additional ones appointed by congressional act approved apr. 16, 1862. The surg. gen. was promoted to rank of brig. gen.; the asst. surg. gen. and the med. inspector were both raised to rank of colonel. Ten more surg. and ten asst. surg. added; the number of cadets was increased to twenty. Henry Gibbons, Jr., *Training of surgeons,* in *Occidental medical times,* 1893, p. 10.

A list of the instruments used by the old army surgeons resembles that of a carpenter—a chisel, probe, gouge and mallet; six different kinds of saws, a large assortment of forceps, including one known as a gnawing forcep with a spring handle. In addition there were several varieties of hooks. Surgery was then in its infancy and the surgeon was often caricatured as "Dr. Saw Bones".

Whiskey, opium, quinine and ipecacuanha predominated in the supply of drugs; and alcohol, diluted carbolic acid, and soap and water were used as antiseptics. Chloroform and ether were available but the supply was limited and often minor operations were performed without anesthesia.

The old army ambulances differed but little from the "covered wagons of the plains" except that they were equipped with beds and medicine chests. However, a new type, a two-wheeled cart, was introduced in the West at this time to test its mobility and general advantages over the larger four-wheeled ambulance. One type of ambulance cart (*Plate* 13) was designed by Surgeon Richard H. Coolidge and it was this cart that was sent to Fort Yuma for the use of the California column.[342]

Often the freight wagons or the gun carriages of the old mountain howitzers were used to transport the wounded back to camp, which was sometimes a hundred or more miles distant from the battlefield. Down the steep mountain trails the injured were carried on improvised stretchers. The slightly wounded sat grimly on their horses enduring the agonizing pain of infected

---

[342] Surg. Coolidge served in California at the beginning of the war, but was ordered east in the spring of 1862. *Medical and surgical history of war. reb.*—Surg. vol. II, pt. III, p. 947.

War. Reb. Ser. I, vol. L, pt. I, p. 1039.

wounds, for numerous "pain-killers" of the present were non-existent then.

Arrow wounds claimed the attention of the medical profession at that time, and the *American Journal of Medical Science* published a report on the results of the injuries as observed by Surgeon J. H. Bill when he was stationed at Fort Craig, New Mexico, january 1862.[343] Although the arrow was one of the oldest weapons, there had never been any definite or accurate information compiled to guide the surgeon in his treatment of wounds inflicted by it. Surgeon Bill discovered that there was a greater fatality from arrow wounds than from any other weapon. The greatest danger arose when the shaft became detached from the arrow, leaving it so deeply embedded that it was impossible to extract it.

Bill recommended that the arrow be removed by using a forceps as a dentist does in extracting a tooth, with a gentle rocking motion. Cold evaporating lotions were then applied and if the wound was a minor one, the patient would be well within a week. In eighty cases of arrow wounds reported, fifty-one patients recovered and twenty-nine died. Few men were ever wounded by a single arrow—three soldiers shot by Navajos received forty-two wounds. An expert Indian bowman could shoot six arrows a minute, but poisoned arrows were seldom used.

Some of the foremost medical men of the nation served in the West during the sixties. Among them was Surgeon Jonathan Letterman who served on the frontiers of America for thirteen years, including five years in the department of the Pacific—New Mexico, Ari-

---

[343] J. H. Bill, pub. in *American journal medical science*, Philadelphia. N.S. XLIV; 365-387. (U. C. Berkeley library.)

zona and California, 1854-1860. He was stationed at Fort Tejon during the spring of 1860 and in april accompanied the first dragoons under command of Colonel Carleton to the Mojave desert where Camp Cady was established to protect the Salt Lake route. After three months campaign against the Piutes, peace was declared so the dragoons and Surgeon Letterman returned to Fort Tejon.

When Fort Tejon was abandoned by order of General Sumner in june 1861, Surgeon Letterman was stationed at Camp Fitzgerald, Los Angeles, and at San Pedro for a short time before he was assigned to duty with the army of the Potomac in november 1861. Later he was appointed medical director of West Virginia.[344]

The first and most complete ambulance system was established by Surgeon Letterman in august 1862. So carefully was his system prepared that little modification was necessary when it was embodied in an act of Congress march 11, 1864.

He returned to California in december 1864 and for two terms served as coroner of San Francisco. He died in march, 1872 and was buried in the National cemetery at Arlington. The Letterman General hospital at the Presidio, San Francisco, was named in his honor.

David Wooster, a veteran of the Mexican war, was appointed surgeon of the fifth regiment infantry.[345]

---

[344] Los Angeles *Star,* feb. 11, 25, apr. 14, may 12, june 2, 7, july 14, 1860. *War. Reb.* Ser. I, vol. L, pt. I, p. 682.

Jonathan Letterman, *Medical recollections of the army of the Potomac,* 1866. He graduated from Jefferson college, Philadelphia, in 1849, passed the army medical examination the same year and was appointed U.S. army surgeon; served in the Seminole war in Florida; at Fort Ripley 1853; in 1854 marched from Fort Leavenworth to New Mexico; at Fort Defiance during campaign against Navajos; at Tucson with Major Steen.

[345] *War. Reb.* Ser. I, vol. L, pt. II, p. 24.

Dr. Wooster founded the *Pacific medical and surgical journal* with Dr. John Trask as co-editor. The *Journal* was one of the most important early

Early in the spring of 1862 he supervised the hospital at Camp Wright which occupied the old adobe Overland Stage station at Oak Grove, San Diego county. He was soon transferred to Fort Yuma where he expected to remain, as he had taken Mrs. Wooster and their two year old child with him. He was soon ordered forward with the advance column from California and young Mrs. Wooster accompanied him on the long desert journey. She appeared to be a good traveler and a favorite with the volunteers who shared their catch of fish and wild game with her.

Surgeon Wooster served with the Californians until 1863, when he resigned to resume his practice in San Francisco. For two years he was surgeon at the U.S. Marine hospital after which he again returned to his private practice. He died september 20, 1894.

The army surgeon shared the same dangers as the soldier and likewise felt the pain of bullet and arrow wounds. Surgeon William Kittridge accompanied Colonel Eyre's reconnaissance force to the Rio Grande and was wounded at San Simon springs. The injury was slight and he recovered to continue his valuable services to the volunteers.

He was present when Colonel Eyre raised the first Union flag over Fort Thorn after the Confederates had hauled down their colors. His first assignments on the Rio Grande were at Fort Fillmore and at Mesilla. He accompanied the expedition against the Mescalero Apaches in november and december.[346]

California medical journals and continued in existence until 1917. Dr. Wooster contributed many papers for publication and was editor of the *Journal* for four years. He was author of *Diseases of the heart.*

Letter written by Calif. vol. while at Antelope Peak, may 16, 1862, pub. in *Weekly Alta California (Steamer)*, San Francisco, june 14, 1862.

346 *War. Reb.* Ser. I, vol. L, pt. II, p. 212-213, 60, 165,

Ibid., pt. I, p. 98, 122, 969.

Dr. E. L. Watson was commissioned assistant surgeon of the first infantry at Sacramento in 1862, but did not join his own regiment until the following summer as he was stationed at Fort Bowie with the fifth. He made the trip to Fort Craig without accident, and when he left he was furnished with an escort of five or six men and a government wagon. They traveled leisurely as it was mid-summer. The driver, Robert S. Johnson, company G, first infantry, rode his wheel-mule and Surgeon Watson sat on the front of the wagon with his feet hanging down on the whiffle-trees. The soldiers were all lying on their blankets in the back of the wagon with their guns and equipment beneath them.

They felt perfectly safe as there was not a rock, tree or bush as large as a man's head within a distance of five miles. But suddenly all was changed! Ten or twelve Apaches lay buried in the sand within twenty feet of the wagon. They poured a volley of arrows into the doomed party. Some of the Indians attacked the soldiers while others cut the mules loose, mounted them and were on the run for the Rio Grande river out of rifle range before the survivors could get out of the wagon. The driver was shot through the heart and several of the other soldiers wounded. Surgeon Watson was hit by two arrows, one in the right arm and the other in the left thigh, severing the femoral artery. He died within a few minutes and was buried at Fort Craig, New Mexico, where nineteen other California soldiers lie.[347]

When James Madison McNulty was commissioned surgeon of the first infantry, his friends presented him with a four hundred dollar set of surgical instruments.

---

[347] *The National Tribune,* Washington, D.C., june 30, july 7, 14, 21, 28, 1927. (Southwest Museum).

San Jose *Mercury,* june 10, 1864.

War. Reb. Ser. I, vol. L, pt. I, p. 213.

No doubt they were effectively used for when he reached Arizona he was appointed medical purveyor of the district of Arizona. He assumed the office of medical inspector of New Mexico in september 1862 and spent many busy days at Fort Sumner. He was constantly in the saddle. In addition to his medical duties, he was president of the general court martial and on the board to locate new posts. Not only did he administer to the needs of the soldiers but also to the Indians when they were placed on the reservation at Bosque Redondo.

Those first days at Fort Sumner required courage, initiative and diplomacy. The Navajo Indians were being brought to the new reservation by the hundreds. There was no shelter for them and but little food. General Carleton ordered that the old, and sick and the very young be furnished tents, old army blankets and clothing when possible.

Surgeon McNulty shared the responsibility with the officers in command. The crops that were planted failed to mature. The Indians were hungry and threatened to leave the reservation. Trouble was imminent. But the versatile and intrepid Captain John Cremony, company B, second cavalry, offered a solution to the food shortage.[348] He secured permission to accompany the Indians on a hunt. The Indians promised to return to the reservation within forty-eight hours, to take only their bows and arrows with them, and to leave their guns in camp.

Captain Cremony, armed with four Colt revolvers and a Bowie knife, started out with one hundred and ten Apaches. The Indians formed in two lines about

---

[348] John C. Cremony, *Life among the Apaches.*
Alta California (Steamer), San Francisco, oct. 13, 1861; oct. 14, 1863.

six hundred yards apart and when they discovered a
herd of antelope, the two wings of the first line rode
forward at full speed and encircled the herd. They
quickly closed in and the slaughter began. Eighty-seven
antelope were killed on that expedition and for a brief
time there was food enough for all the Indians on the
reservation.

Game was then killed for food and not for "sport".
The California soldiers captured six antelope when
they were but a week old and raised them at Fort
Sumner. They fed them goats' milk and their pets
became domesticated even if they were a bit troublesome. They also succeeded in taming two hawks, a few
crows and several squirrels. The wild turkeys refused
to respond to the boys' overtures for friendship.

Surgeon McNulty remained on duty at the fort until
september 1864, when he was ordered to the army of
the Potomac and appointed surgeon of the first division
of the second army corps. He participated in all the
engagements of the corps and was breveted lieutenant
colonel for his valuable services.

He resigned in february 1865 and returned to San
Francisco where he received the distinction of being
the first health officer of San Francisco when that office
was created in 1865.

The service of the frontier army surgeon was highly
praised by Surgeon McNulty. He reported that the
troops suffered very little from sickness on their march
to the Rio Grande, april 13 to august 8, 1862.[349]

Surgeon John H. Prentiss succeeded Surgeon Mc-

[349] Francis B. Heitman, *Historical register* U.S. *army.*
War. Reb. Ser. I, vol. L, pt. I, p. 144-145.
Ibid., pt. II, p. 24.
San Francisco *Call,* july 1, 1900. (Death of Surgeon McNulty at Santa
Barbara, june 23, 1900).

Nulty in command of the medical service of the district of Arizona in september 1862. He also served with the advance guard of the California column and remained in the service for three years, mustering out december 1, 1864.[350]

Surgeon George Gwyther was examining physician at Camp Downey, Oakland, where he rejected but few of the recruits, as they were all "such stalwart big-bearded men, hardened and bronzed by life in the open." "They were well dressed," said Surgeon Gwyther, "and each carried his carpet bag or valise."

The hardy fighting surgeon accompanied the first cavalry to Arizona and New Mexico and followed his men wherever they fought. No road was too rough, no trail too steep. This was demonstrated on the expedition to Black canyon. Four hundred army horses and mules had been stolen from Fort West, so Captain McCleave, company A, first cavalry, gave orders to mount one hundred men with five days rations. A volunteer remarked, "There is a devilish look in Mac's eye that foretells stiff work for us. He will have those horses again or give good reasons why." And the volunteer was right.

Surgeon Gwyther was ready. For three successive days and nights he rode with the Californians. The horses gave out and before the end of the fourth day seventy horses were killed and their saddles demolished.

When they reached the mouth of Black canyon at sunset, the command was allowed four hours sleep. Captain McCleave then took one half of his men and marched twenty miles in the dark and rain to the higher peaks. At daylight they saw the Indians at the

---

[350] *War. Reb.* Ser. I, vol. L, pt. I, p. 811, 821, 683-684, 969-970.
Ibid., pt. II, p. 24, 102.

foot of the mountains. Then he asked, "Do you know how to whip Indians? Never show them your back." Thus, after having four hours sleep in four days and nights, with nothing but hard tack and salt pork to eat, and with only thirty horses left out of one hundred, the troops moved forward to attack. They forgot their hunger, cold, and fatigue with the first ring of the carbines, seconded by the clear trumpet tones of Captain McCleave's voice as he led the attack.

Within fifteen minutes the soldiers won the battle, recovered three hundred horses, burned the Indian camp and killed forty Indians. There were no casualties among the soldiers in this attack but during a second encounter Private Hall was wounded and died from an infection two days after his return to the fort. Very few men survived a severe case of infection as little was then known about antiseptics and Surgeon Gwyther regretted that he could not save his patient.[351] He was appointed surgeon of the first regiment New Mexican cavalry in december 1864. His original oath of office and pledge of allegiance is now preserved in the archives of the Henry E. Huntington library, San Marino, California.[352]

Although not recognized as a psychiatrist, Surgeon Gwyther knew the mental agony of the man who locked the memory of a great personal tragedy in his mind. He was stationed at Fort Garland, Colorado, with Captain Albert H. Pfeiffer, company H, first New Mexico volunteers, when he became acquainted with the gruff old Dutchman, gained his confidence and respect, and learned why he never mentioned one of his encounters with the Indians. It was june 1863 and Captain Pfeiffer

---

[351] *Scout to Black canyon,* Surg. George Gwyther, *Overland Monthly,* vol. v, 1st series, p. 221, 1870.

[352] William Gillet Ritch MS no. 1390; no. 1409 (Huntington library).

was stationed at Fort Craig when his eyes began to trouble him so he decided to spend a few weeks at Ojo Caliente below Fort McRae where he hoped to be benefited by the spring water. He was accompanied by his wife and child, one servant, and six soldiers. They pitched their tents in a grove of cottonwoods near the spring and in a short time Captain Pfeiffer's health began to improve.

One morning at sunrise, he went down to the spring to bathe and just as he was leaving the pool, he heard the howl of the Apaches followed by the shrieks and groans of his wife and child. He was utterly powerless to save them. The Indians rushed toward him but he ran for the Colorado river. Upon reaching the bank, he plunged from a twenty-five foot bluff into the current and swam across. He reached a heavy thicket in safety and by crawling through it managed to escape.

The Apaches burned all his camp equipment, killed his wife and child, two soldiers, and severely wounded a servant girl, but she hid among the rocks and was rescued by the soldiers from Fort Craig. Captain Pfeiffer was not found until the following day. His body was covered with blood from an arrow wound in his side and from the numerous scratches from the brush and cacti as he had not had time to dress after the Indians attacked. He was blistered from the hot desert sun and delirious from shock and exposure.[353]

Dr. Robert King Reid was appointed surgeon of the third infantry and accompanied General Connor's expedition to Salt Lake. He attended the wounded at the battle of Bear river and was commended for his skill and bravery. It was after this battle that Surgeon Reid's strength was taxed to the utmost degree.

---

[353] *Overland Monthly,* vol. v, 1st series, p. 520, Surg. George Gwyther.

Twenty-two men were sick in the rude log hospital and seventy in their barracks. The hospital tents were placed over excavations covered with boards and straw —a very inadequate shelter for sick and wounded men. More fatalities might have occurred if the boys had not been so robust. Surgeon Reid remained in the service until 1866 when he returned to his private practice in Stockton.[354]

Day after day the army surgeon was in the saddle. No campaign against the Indians was started without him. No site for a new post was selected without his approval. While traveling over northern Nevada with Colonel Charles F. McDermitt to find a suitable location, Surgeon Zetus N. Spalding rode to the top of the hills to survey the country with his field glasses. A frontier post could be located only where there was plenty of water, grass and wood, but all that the surgeon could see was sand, sage and cacti. Finally Quinn River station was chosen as the most desirable spot.[355]

Here the troops subdued the Indians but not without great loss as Colonel McDermitt was killed in Quinn River valley, august 8, 1865. Surgeon Spalding felt his loss keenly as the two men had become close friends while working together at this outpost. The post was named Camp McDermitt in honor of the colonel.[356]

[354] *War. Reb.* Ser. I, vol. I., pt. II, p. 318, 325-327.
Dr. Reid came to California in 1849 and settled in Stockton in 1850. The following year he accepted the position as resident physician at the state hospital and remained in that office until 1858. After his discharge from the army he resumed his private practice. In 1879 he was made president of the Stockton bank. Later he was appointed u.s. examiner and surgeon for the board of pensions and continued in that office until 1889. He died feb. 6, 1891.

[355] Letter from Surg. Spalding, pub. *Mountain Messenger,* Downieville, july 8, 1865. Surgeon Spalding came overland to California in 1852 to Sierra county where he tried mining, farming and a general merchandise store. After his discharge from the army he served as coroner of Sierra county for two terms. In 1871 he was elected superintendent schools of Lassen county.

[356] Colonel McDermitt was a veteran of the Mexican war and came to

Among other prominent surgeons serving in the West at this time was Surgeon Charles McCormick, medical purveyor of the department of the Pacific in 1858. In june 1862 he was relieved from that office and ordered East for duty. Upon his return West, february 1865, he was appointed medical inspector of the department of the Pacific.[357]

From all sections of the nation came these men of the medical profession, yet there was one, perhaps more, who were sons of the early pioneers. Such a one was John E. Klunker, son of Dr. E. A. Klunker, the man who refused all offers to leave Placerville to practice in the big cities. Placerville was his home and there he remained. Son John was first assigned to duty at Camp Halleck, Stockton, where the third regiment of infantry was stationed before leaving for Salt Lake. He was also with Captain West's "army of occupation" on Catalina island. However, his service on the island was brief and he was soon ordered to Fort Yuma and later to Tucson.[358]

In addition to the army surgeons there were many civilian doctors who administered to the needs of the volunteers when they were stationed near the doctors' offices. The regular fee for such service was fifty dollars a month for one visit a day to the army hospitals.

Space forbids a full recital of the surgeons' many

California soon after. He superintended the building of Benicia Barracks. In 1852 he was sheriff of Siskiyou county and in the same year engaged in an expedition to found Crescent City. He built a grist and saw mill at old Etna and later moved to Fort Jones. He served in the California assembly in 1859-1860. In 1861 he was captain of Co. M, sec. cav., Cal. vol. (Daggett Scraps) (California State library).

357 *Dictionary of Am. Med. Biog.*, Howard Atwood Kelley & Walter L. Burrage, pub. D. Appleton & Co., 1928.

War. Reb. Ser. I, vol. L, pt. I, p. 1144.

358 John E. Klunker was asst. surg. first cav., march 2, 1863 to may 29, 1865, when he was promoted surgeon.

exploits; nor has it been possible to list all who served as many were civilian doctors whose names did not appear on the muster rolls.

The following tabulation from the muster rolls furnishes the names of those who served for a year or more. A considerable number enrolled, but before the end of six months they had resigned, or were discharged.

SURGEONS AND ASSISTANT SURGEONS
OF
CALIFORNIA VOLUNTEERS
1861-1866

	Rank	*Regiment*
Brown, Isaac W.	Asst. surgeon	Third infantry
Cassell, Francis M.	Asst. surgeon	Second infantry
Christian, Robert A.	Brigade surgeon	First cavalry
Clark, Jonathan	Surgeon	Mountain battalion
Cooper, James G.	Asst. surgeon	Second cavalry
Cox, Valentine H.	Asst. surgeon	Fifth infantry
Davis, Joseph W.	Asst. surgeon	Seventh infantry
Deans, William C.	Asst. surgeon	Sixth infantry
Elliott, Stephen E.	Surgeon	Fourth infantry
Farley, C. C.	Asst. surgeon	Second cavalry
Geleich, Vincent	Surgeon	Fourth infantry
	(Transferred to first battalion Native Californians)	
Gwyther, George	Surgeon	First cavalry
Handy, John C.	Asst. surgeon	Second cavalry
Hayes, Lewis W.	Asst. surgeon	Fifth infantry
Hayes, William W.	Surgeon	Sixth infantry
Hoffman, David S.	Asst. surgeon	Fourth infantry
Holbrook, C. E.	Asst. surgeon	Second cavalry
Horn, George H.	Asst. surgeon	Second cavalry
	(Promoted surgeon, first infantry and later transferred to second infantry)	
Kirkpatrick, Charles A.	Surgeon	Third infantry
	(Transferred to eighth infantry)	

Kittridge, William	Act. asst. surgeon	First infantry
Klunker, John E.	Asst. surgeon	First cavalry
Lippincott, Henry	Asst. surgeon	Sixth infantry
McKee, William H.	Asst. surgeon	Promoted surgeon fifth infantry
McNulty, James M.	Surgeon	First infantry

(Commissioned surgeon, u.s. volunteers, february 19, 1863)

Parry, Isaac	Surgeon	Second infantry
Phelps, Edward	Asst. surgeon	Second infantry

(Transferred to sixth infantry, promoted surgeon, seventh infantry, january 1865)

Prentiss, John H.	Surgeon	First cavalry
Randle, Peter W.	Asst. surgeon	First infantry
Reid, Robert K.	Surgeon	Third infantry

(Transferred to second cavalry)

Romatke, F. A.	Asst. surgeon	Seventh infantry
Sharples, Abram	Asst. surgeon	Fourth infantry
Spalding, Zetus N.	Surgeon	Second cavalry
Todd, Simeon S.	Asst. surgeon	Second infantry

(Promoted surgeon, fourth infantry)

Tolman, George B.	Asst. surgeon	Sixth infantry

(Transferred to first battalion, Native Californians)

Tompkins, E. A.	Asst. surgeon	Fourth infantry
Watson, E. L.	Asst. surgeon	First infantry
Williamson, Jonathan M.	Surgeon	Second cavalry
Woods, Eugene H.	Asst. surgeon	Seventh infantry
Wooster, David	Surgeon	Fifth infantry

The California Five Hundred

To the Pacific Northwest, to the Rio Grande river, and out upon the Overland route as far as Salt Lake, seven regiments of California volunteers had been distributed to guard the national and local interest of the western frontier. Yet not one organized military unit had been sent East for service on the battlefields.

Many of the volunteers were keenly disappointed and, as has been noted in previous chapters, offered to pay their own expenses if they would be permitted to go.

The loyalty of the young men of the West appeared to match their resourcefulness for they found a way to join in the fight for the preservation of the Union. Early in september 1862, a committee of San Francisco men sent a telegram to Simon Cameron, secretary of war, offering to place a thousand men at Panama if the government would provide passage the remainder of the way. Cameron agreed to this proposal.[359]

At this time Massachusetts was paying large bounties for volunteers so it was suggested that this money be paid into a special fund which could be used for recruiting a company in California and for paying its fare East. A message was sent to Governor John A. Andrews asking him if he would accept a company of Californians under these conditions and credit it to the quota of his state.

---

[359] *War. Reb.* Ser. I, vol. L, pt. II, p. 112, 117.

Committee members: William Lenter, M. Jessup, Eugene Sullivan, Wm. D. Chaplin.

The necessary authority was received from the Massachusetts governor and recruiting began october 28, 1862. Hundreds tried to enroll but only one hundred could be accepted as that was the limit agreed upon. They were mustered in by Lieutenant Colonel George Ringgold and officially designated the California hundred. J. Sewell Reed, formerly captain of the first light dragoons, was appointed captain.

An early writer of verse, J. Henry Rogers, describes these men when he presumes to quote Captain Reed:

> . . . I've gathered from our land
> To go with me, a gallant band.
> Thousands stood forth at my request
> To represent the Golden West.
> But from each thousand warlike men,
> My limit was to choose but ten. . .
> And from their sturdy ranks I took
> One hundred men—each had a look
> Of desperate courage in his eyes;
> There were no two alike in size—
> For tall or short, broad, thick or thin,
> Where courage showed—they mustered in. . .
> They were not measured by their inches,
> But by the nerve that never flinches.
> And from such desperate men as those
> The California hundred rose. . .

After all the hundred were mustered in, there remained another volunteer who insisted upon accompanying Captain Reed. The young officer hesitated—

> Dear one, my muster roll is full,
> Yet something at my heart strings pull.
> A new recruit is speaking now,
> With laughing eyes and sunny brow;
> She whispers in my listening ear,
> "Come, take one female volunteer. . ."

> 'Tis well, I'll keep thee by my side,
> With my brave hundred thou shalt ride. . .

Thus the California hundred was increased to one hundred two as arrangements were made for Mrs. Reed and her young son to accompany her soldier husband.

Before leaving San Francisco the volunteers were reviewed by General Lucius H. Allen. They presented a striking appearance in their new uniforms which had been supplied by private subscription. Theirs was not the conventional army uniform of blue but green adorned with gold.

> Green velvet caps the warriors wore,
> Whose front an eagle's plumage bore;
> Encircled by a golden band,
> On which in silver letters stand
> The word *EUREKA*—underneath
> *ONE HUNDRED* in a laurel wreath.

The patriotic enthusiasm reached a high pitch among the friends of the California hundred. Reverend Thomas Starr King could not attend the festival given for them at Platt's Music hall but wrote a note of farewell in which he said: "If the government desires to see them fitly mounted for duty, it should provide for them one hundred full blood Black Hawks—horses such as Shakespeare describes: 'Horses that trot the air; horses that make the earth sing when they touch it; horses whose neighing is like the bidding of a monarch.' . . ."

Before leaving for the front each member of the company was presented with a Bible and forty-three of the young soldiers joined the Dashaway society, a temperance organization. Captain Reed received a pair of revolvers and a fine saddle from his friends.

Their guidon was a silk Bear flag (*Plate* 14), and on its staff a silver plate bore the inscription, "Presented to the California hundred by Daniel Norcross of San Francisco, december 1, 1862." This flag was especially designed for the California hundred and differs from the Bear flag commonly seen at present. Although the scarlet stripe is faded and the white one torn, the bear and the gilt letters US are clearly discernible. The pine tree, under which the California grizzly bear stands, fades into the background and would not be noticed by the casual observer. The flag is remarkably well preserved considering the years that have passed since it was carried by the California hundred on the battlefields of Gettysburg, Fort Stevens, Winchester, Cedar Creek and Appomattox.[360]

When the day of departure arrived, december 11, 1862, the hundred was escorted through the streets of San Francisco by five companies of home guards, two pieces of artillery, a brass band and many carriages of prominent citizens. As the young volunteers marched aboard the s.s. "Golden Age" in their natty green uniforms, the band played *Hail Columbia, Happy Land!* while a thousand voices joined in the song. Captain Reed, with his wife and young son, waved to the cheering thousands on shore as the "Golden Age" headed toward the Golden Gate. For the gallant young captain there was no return.[361]

After crossing the isthmus of Panama they boarded

[360] *D. Alta Calif.*, s.f., dec. 11, 1862.

[361] Home Guards: Ellsworth rifles, black hussars, Vallejo rifles, light dragoons and first Calif. guard.

Band: Kidd's military band.

Line of march: Post, Montgomery, Washington, Front, California, Sansome, Market, Second, Folsom to wharf.

D. Alta Calif., s.f., nov. 27; dec. 4, 7, 9, 10, 1862.

D. Morning Call, s.f., dec. 4, 6, 12, 1862.

the S.S. "Ocean Queen" en route to New York where they arrived january 4, 1863. The New Yorkers entertained the Californians at the New England Soldiers' Relief association where an excellent dinner was served. After listening to a number of flattering speeches, the hundred marched to the City Hall park where they were reviewed by the mayor and then escorted by the fifty-third Massachusetts regiment to the Stonington steamer and were soon on their way to Boston.[362]

The citizens of Boston entertained them in a similar manner. They were introduced to the mayor, then marched to the old State house where they met the "Executive of the Commonwealth". After this ceremony, the Boston lancers and dragoons led the way to Faneuil hall where they all enjoyed a good Boston dinner.[363]

The Californians were made company A, second Massachusetts cavalry and began training at Camp Meigs, Readville. They received considerable attention from the citizens of Charlestown who were personal friends of Reverend Thomas Starr King. When the California hundred left San Francisco, King wrote to a friend saying, "Our hundred men for the Boston cavalry go by this steamer. They are splendid, perfect fellows. I hope you will see them and speak with their captain who is a friend of mine. I have lectured, preached and prayed and talked for this company. They are my pets. . . "[364]

The response from Charlestown was prompt and

[362] N.Y. *Times,* jan. 4, 1863. (Huntington library).

Speakers: James T. Brady; Charles Gould, Vice Pres. New England Relief Ass'n.; Col. Bartlett; Gen. Wetmore.

[363] Boston *Post,* jan. 5, 1863. (Huntington library).

[364] Charles W. Wendte, *Thomas Starr King, patriot and preacher,* p. 162-163.

hearty for on january 13, 1863, several hundred people surprised the Californians by serving them a fine supper in their barracks. Speech making appeared to be the popular manner in which to entertain soldiers as no less than ten men spoke during the evening.

The most noteworthy event of the evening was the presentation of the United States flag to the hundred. As the Bunker Hill Baptist choir from Charlestown sang *Stand by the Flag,* old glory was unfurled by Miss Abbie Lord. A silver plate on the flag staff bore the inscription, "Presented to the California hundred, Captain J. Sewell Reed, by Miss Abbie Lord." Abbie was a dressmaker from Charlestown and bore the entire cost of the flag herself. She had enlisted as a nurse in august 1862 but was not called into service. Captain Reed expressed his gratitude to Abbie for her flag and to the folk from Charlestown who had entertained his company. At a late hour, the visitors returned to their homes and the soldiers to their bunks.[365]

After spending but a few weeks at Camp Meigs, the hundred was ordered to Gloucester Point near Yorktown and placed under the command of Major Casper Crowinshield. At this camp they experienced their first hardships. Each night they expected an attack and slept in their clothes and boots, with their spurs, Colt revolvers and sabers by their sides. Sixteen men occupied one tent which was heated by a wood burning stove. Many of the men were sick and, out of the hundred, only sixty were fit for duty. There was no epi-

---

[365] Boston *Post,* jan. 14, 1863. (Huntington library).

Speakers: three clergymen, Gardner, Graves, Miles; Gen. Childs; Lt. Hodgkins; Lt. Ripley; Alderman Childs; Councilman Moore; J. Locke; H. Wellington; Capt. Reed; Miss Abbie Lord.

Information from Charlestown directories 1862-1866. (Courtesy Mary E. Harris, librarian, Charlestown branch.)

demic—just colds and minor complaints. Their horses had no shelter and suffered in a foot of snow.[366]

During their first two months at Gloucester Point they performed picket and scouting duty and at the same time perfected their drills so that they made a creditable appearance when they paraded at Falmouth, Virginia in april 1863. They formed a part of the cavalry division of General Joseph Hooker's army of the Potomac which was reviewed by President Lincoln and his party at that time.

The California hundred wore their green uniforms and their color bearer carried their guidon, the Bear flag. J. Henry Rogers describes these men:

> Proudly they looked drawn up in line,
> Though toil and dust had bedimmed the shine
> Of their rich uniforms of green.
> Dark stains upon the lace were seen,
> Whose fretted edge of burnished gold,
> Once brightly back the sunshine rolled.
> The army chieftian gave no heed
> To soil, nor stain, nor dusty steed.
> But viewed with practiced eye
> Each soldier as he passed by. . .

The Bear flag aroused the curiosity of the spectators. They had seen the various flags raised by the Confederacy, the early United States flags and those of foreign countries but none that bore any resemblance to this one.

> Strange was the flag, still stranger seemed
> The small white hand in which it gleamed. . .
> For all among the stranger band
> Wore sunburnt face and roughened hand.
> All, save the youthful standard bearer
> No lady's cheek could be fairer. . .

---

[366] *Alta W. Calif., Str.*, s.f., may 2, 1863. (Huntington)

J. Sewell Reed, captain of the Hundred, signaled his standard bearer to ride from the ranks with him to formally present his company to General Hooker who sat on his white horse by the side of President Lincoln's brown one. The standard bearer's face flushed but the "sable steed" trotted forward with the rider and the Bear flag toward the "chieftains". The young captain from California saluted, then—

> Called to his side the sable steed,
> And there presented MRS. REED.

The California hundred engaged in their first battle at South Anna bridge, june 26, 1863. Seventy Californians and twenty other men from the second Massachusetts cavalry met and captured 123 of the 44th North Carolina infantry in a dismounted charge upon the Confederate earthworks. The California hundred lost one man, Joseph B. Burdick, and two others were seriously wounded.

While the hundred was guarding the approaches to Washington, three hundred more Californians were aboard the s.s. "Constitution" en route for New York. The success attained in recruiting the California hundred encouraged the enrollment of other companies under the same conditions. After considerable negotiations with the secretary of war and with the Massachusetts authorities, permission was received by Major D. W. C. Thompson to raise a battalion of four companies. In less than two months, they were mustered in and three companies sailed from San Francisco, march 21, 1863. The fourth company did not receive uniforms by the time the "Constitution" sailed so were obliged to remain behind and wait for the s.s. "Sonora" which sailed at a later date. The uniforms were paid for by private subscription and were the regulation army blue. The state refused to supply uniforms for men who served for, and were paid by, Massachusetts.[367]

The battalion of Californians had been reviewed by General George Wright, and presented with a large silk flag; they had been cheered by the crowds as they marched through the streets of San Francisco; they had proudly kept step to the inspiring martial music of the bands; and next they were enduring the agony of maldemer. Hiram Townsend was very sick. As the boat tossed in the heavy sea, he lost his balance and plunged into the Pacific. All attempts to rescue him failed.

Food served on the s.s. "Constitution" brought forth plenty of "growls" from the passengers. When they reached Manzanillo, Captains Chas. S. Eigenbrodt and George A. Manning went ashore and brought back a basket of eggs for their breakfast—a most appetizing change in their diet. The two captains, so young and lusty then, were not aware of the fate that awaited them. One fell at Halltown, the other survived fourteen months confinement in Andersonville prison.[368]

It was april the first when they entered the Gulf of Tehauntepec but it was not a day for april jokes to celebrate all fool's day. An exceptionally severe storm struck the seafarers. The chaplain prayed, the ladies wept, but many of the boys who were "salty tars" laughed and cheered as the boat rolled and shuddered from each succeeding battle with the waves.

After safely anchoring at Panama, they made a quick

[367] Cos. A, B, C, sailed mar. 21, 1863; Co. D, apr. 13, 1863.
Officers of Calif. bat. in the 2nd Mass. cav.:

    Co. E—Capt. Charles S. Eigenbrodt
       " F— "   David A. De Merritt
       " L— "   Z. B. Adams
       " M— "   Geo. A. Manning

[368] *Alta W. Calif., Str.,* s.f., apr. 23, 1863. (Huntington)

trip on the Panama R.R. to Aspinwal (Colon) on the Atlantic side where the S.S. "Ocean Queen" was waiting to carry them to New York. From Aspinwal to Cuba they were convoyed by the U.S.S. "Connecticut" to protect them from an attack by the pirate "Alabama" which was reported to be lying in wait for them.

When they arrived at New York, april 15, 1863, they were met by a dozen cab drivers, two newspaper boys, a few old apple women and a deputy sheriff. A bit disappointed in the lack of welcome, they marched rather soberly to Park Barracks. But by evening their gloom was dispelled by an invitation from the manager of the Bowery theater to a free performance.

The next day the California boys in their dress uniforms of blue had an opportunity to exhibit the loyalty of the West. After being received by the mayor of New York and addressed by Governor J. W. Nye of Nevada territory, they marched up Broadway to Union square, around the equestrian statue of Washington, then down Broadway to the Battery where they embarked on one of the Long Island sound boats for Providence. Here they boarded the train for Camp Meigs, Readville, Massachusetts.

The western boys did not mind the cavalry drills and considered it good sport to break their horses. However, one of the boys of company C, Sergeant Gilbert R. Merritt, suffered a broken leg from a vicious kick from his horse and was discharged for disability before he even reached the front lines.[369]

The California battalion remained at Camp Meigs less than a month when they were transferred to Washington, D.C. to guard the national capitol. From the

---

369 *Ibid.*, may 6, june 3, 1863. (Huntington library).
N.Y. *Times,* apr. 16, 1863. (Huntington library).

time they left camp, their train was cheered all the way to Philadelphia where they arrived at two A.M. Regardless of the very early morning hour, they were served a hearty meal in the Union Volunteer Refreshment saloon by the Quakers. The boys had been on the train for three nights and had had but little sleep so the hospitality of the Friends was greatly appreciated. After breakfast, Major Thompson, their commander, proposed three cheers and a tiger for the citizens of Philadelphia to which the boys responded promptly and vigorously.[370]

Philadelphia lay in the direct route of thousands of soldiers crossing New Jersey, Delaware and Maryland, either going or returning from the front. Many of them were weary, sick or wounded and their condition aroused the sympathy of the wife of a mechanic who shared her coffee with them. Other neighbors joined her and the good work expanded until the Volunteer Refreshment room was opened. A signal gun was fired to let the Quakers know that a regiment had arrived and at all hours of the day or night the women came to cook and serve the soldiers. During the war, the Union Refreshment room alone fed 750,000; supplied lodging for 40,000; and cared for 20,000 wounded in their hospital. The Cooper Refreshment shop opened at the same time and continued to operate until august 1865. Its record of service was equally commendable.[371]

When the Californians reached Washington they were attached to General Samuel Peter Heintzelman's department. They went into camp on East Capitol hill which they described as "a pleasant place in the suburbs where they could look down on the placid waters of the Potomac and the fortifications on its banks."

---

[370] *Alta W. Calif., Str.,* s.f., june 23, 1863. (Huntington library).
[371] Benson J. Lossing, *Pictorial history of the Civil war,* vol. I, p. 576.

After three weeks they were transferred to Fort Stevens, on Brightwood avenue and the Seventh street pike, which was about five miles from the capitol. The fort was built by the troops in 1861 and first named Fort Massachusetts. It was enlarged in '62 and '63 and the name changed to Fort Stevens in honor of General Isaac Stevens who was killed at Chantilly, Virginia. The fortification was comparatively small as the perimeter was less than a quarter of a mile. The abatis surrounding the fort was constructed from felled trees whose sharpened branches faced outward toward the enemy. The cavalry camp near by was known as Camp Brightwood.

The western horsemen soon discovered the lack of cavalrymen among the Union forces as they were kept on the gallop over the roads leading to Washington. Clattering over Chain bridge, they would follow the Leesburg turnpike to scout in Virginia. There was scant welcome for the cavalrymen in Leesburg. The town seemed to be deserted for the Southerners slammed their shutters tight and remained in seclusion until the Westerners left.[372]

The boys were ordered to keep their hands off the property of all Southerners and obeyed orders until they reached the Arlington farm where they found the fine fruit in the orchard too tempting and helped themselves. They camped at the Arlington house which had been taken over by the government at the beginning of the war.

After a 150-mile scout south of the Potomac, they would recross Chain bridge to their camp at Fort Stevens. Chain bridge was a strategic connecting link

[372] *Alta Weekly California (Steamer)*, San Francisco, july 23, 1863. (Huntington library).

between northern supply depots and the Union field armies in the Virginia campaigns. To assure the maximum degree of safety, the planks were removed from the bridge at night during the spring and early summer of 1863.

Early in june the California battalion (companies E, F, L, M, second Massachusetts cavalry) were ordered to join the army of the Potomac at Edwards ferry. Change of command at this time placed them under General George H. Meade who had succeeded General Joseph Hooker.

When General Robert E. Lee's troops crossed the Potomac, june 26, he found Meade prepared to meet them. The Union cavalry of the Potomac, commanded by General Alfred Pleasanton, fought General J. E. B. Stuart's cavalry in the gaps of the Blue Ridge mountains and trailed them north to Gettysburg, the town made famous by the battle and Lincoln's immortal address.

The small group of California horsemen played their tragic part on the field of Gettysburg, july 1-3. That summer month of 1863 was crowded with action for them. Four companies, alone, met the enemy at Ashby gap and lost several of their men. In an engagement with Colonel John Singleton Mosby, partisan rangers, they recaptured thirty-three wagons that he had taken a few days before in one of his frequent raids on the Union lines of communication.

At Coyle's tavern on august 25, thirty of the Californians were attacked by Mosby who was, himself, wounded by William H. Short, company F. At about this time the California hundred (company A, second Massachusetts cavalry) was transferred from their camp near Yorktown to the Union headquarters at

Centerville, Virginia. From here they continued their scouting duty and camped at Fort Ethan Allen to guard the approach to Chain bridge. For a brief time, they camped at Long bridge to keep a watch on possible saboteurs who might block passage over the old mile-long timber structure which passed over two ship channels and extensive mud flats. The bridge was a two-way crossing. One reserved for the use of pedestrians, cattle and horse-drawn vehicles, and the other for the railroad.[373]

While stationed at Centerville in september, one volunteer of the California hundred reported an encounter with Mosby's men. A tin plate on his knee served in lieu of a writing desk as he wrote his news item:

> One hundred Confederate troops under Mosby attacked twenty-four Californians who were bringing a hundred horses into camp. Each led three horses and rode a fourth one when they met Mosby. Thus handicapped, they were obliged to dismount and fight. They heard Mosby say to his cavalrymen, "If they are from New York or Michigan, do not fire." When the identity of the Californians was recognized, Mosby said, "Go in boys! Fight like demons! They are Californians!" [374]

One Californian was killed, ten captured, and seventy-five horses stampeded and lost during this encounter. At other times the Californians were successful and replenished their stock of provisions with captured condensed milk, canned turkey and fruit.

---

[373] Report Maj. D. S. C. Thompson to Brig. Gen. Geo. S. Evans, Adj. Gen. Calif., pub. in Richard H. Orton, *Record of California men in the war reb.,* p. 848-853.

William Gouverneur Morris, Adj. 2nd cav. Calif. vol. and Capt. A.Q.M.U.S., volunteers, *Address delivered before the Society of Calif. Vol.* at its 1st annual celebration at San Francisco, april 25, 1866. Pub. by the society—Commercial Steam Printing, 1866.

[374] *Daily Call,* San Francisco, oct. 11, 1863.

Alertness was the watchword for the Union pickets at their camps at Vienna, Centerville, and Langley during the winter of '63-64. Even so, Mosby's men were able to either sneak past the sentries or capture them. One of the Californians was captured at Langley and died in Libby prison; another was wounded at Vienna; and still another deserted to Mosby's rangers.

Before the arrival of spring, the California cavalry-men were again in their saddles in pursuit of Mosby's men who were proving a serious threat to the Union lines of communication. Railroad tracks leading to Washington were torn up and rolling stock burned; wagon trains captured and fear spread through the countryside. Like a war-cry of the Indians was the blood curdling yell of the Mosby partisan rangers. They were referred to as guerrillas but were organized under what was known as the partisan rangers law passed by the Confederate congress in 1863. They formed part of General J. E. B. Stuart's cavalry force and received the same pay. Nevertheless they were quite independent in their actions and operated under the archaic law, "To the victors belong the spoils." In their "Greenback raid", one hundred seventy thousand dollars was divided among the eighty rangers participating in the attack.[375]

One of the Californians most desperate encounters with Mosby's men was on Dranesville pike, february 22, 1864. Mosby's scouts had discovered the Union cavalrymen the day previous and trailed them quietly all afternoon. At sunrise the next morning Mosby secreted his men at strategic points to block the escape of his enemy. They then emitted their unearthly yells and opened fire. In this battle, Captain J. Sewell Reed

[375] Greenback raid, oct. 14, 1864.

and thirteen of his men were killed. A large number were captured and sent to Andersonville prison, Georgia. Among the prisoners were Captain George A. Manning, company M, and also Lieutenant C. C. Manning, company L. Both of the latter were exchanged in april 1864, fourteen months after their capture.

Captain Reed was buried with military honors from the home of his widow. As a sorrowful reminder of her loss, the surgeon, Charles D. Brown, who embalmed the body, sent Mrs. Reed the bullet that he had removed from the captain's right breast. One of the revolvers, that had been presented to this lost California volunteer, was taken by a Mosby ranger and has since been lost. The other one of the pair was retained by Mrs. Reed.

The rest of the victims of the battle of Dranesville were buried near the Dranesville pike. Exclusive of the government record, J. Henry Rogers has perhaps left the only account of their interment:

> Then laid their burdens down to rest
> Forever, on the green hill's breast.
> The fallen heroes' beds were made
> Beneath a giant pine tree's shade.
> Their comrades fired a farewell shot;
> They raised no cross to mark the spot,
> But high upon the pine tree's trunk
> And deep within its wood, they sunk
> The word *EUREKA* with the number
> Of those who beneath now slumber.
> They carved upon the pine tree's side
> The when and where those heroes died. . .[376]

---

[376] J. Henry Rogers, *The California hundred.*

War. Reb. Ser. I, vol. XXXIII, p. 159-160. Col. John S. Mosby's report to Gen. Lee.

Ibid., vol. LI, Ser. I, pt. I, p. 214-215. Report Maj. Casper Crowinshield.

After the battle of the Wilderness, two companies of the California Battalion were sent as escort to the ambulance train that brought the sick and wounded from that battlefield of may 5-12.

In july the Californians served with General Lew Wallace's forces and took part in his delaying action at Monocacy when General Early's army advanced on Washington. Captain Charles E. Eigenbrodt's company E, held the fords below the Monocacy river and Captain Manning's company M, was placed on Frederick pike. (Captain Manning, himself, was then in Andersonville prison.) Both companies fought until forced up to Fort Stevens on the Seventh street road a few miles from the capitol. There they were engaged in the skirmish line and rifle pits of Fort Stevens, july 11-12, and in front of Fort Reno until the enemy retreated. It was from the parapet at Fort Stevens that President Abraham Lincoln watched this battle between General Ulysses Grant's armies and General Jubal Early's. A tablet marking the spot today bears the inscription, "Lincoln under fire july 12, 1864."

The western cavalrymen marched to Poolsville where they again protected the supply lines until august 9 when they moved to Halltown near Harpers ferry to join the army of Shenandoah under General Philip Henry Sheridan. They were under fire for nineteen days in august. They fought for six days at Opequan and on september 19 took part in the battle of Winchester—the battle commemorated by Thomas Buchanan Read's, *Sheridan's Ride*. They fought at Cedar creek where Early met defeat.

As a part of General Wesley Merritt's division of cavalry, they moved through Ashby gap in the fall to operate against guerrillas east of the Blue Ridge moun-

tains. They scouted through Gordonsville, Charlottesville, Culpepper and Warrenton before returning to
their camp at Winchester.

They marched with Sheridan's army from Winchester to Petersburg in march 1865, participating in
the battles on their 300 mile march. They were present
at the fall of Petersburg and witnessed the meeting of
the generals-in-chief of both armies at Appomattox
court house. They then returned to Petersburg where
they remained until the grand review at Washington
in may.

Few were left to be mustered out as casualties were
high. Many were discharged for disability and others
deserted. Some died in the Confederate prisons—almost
a score died in Andersonville, Georgia; two in Danville, North Carolina; three in Libby, Richmond,
Virginia; six escaped and fourteen others were exchanged.

In memory of these five hundred Californians, three
flags hang in the rotunda of the state capitol at Sacramento. The following letter written by one of the California volunteers at Fairfax court house, july 20, 1865,
tells the story of these flags:

. . . The Bear flag was carried for nearly three years of active
service, including twenty-three general engagements. Under it, three
commanding officers and many comrades have fallen, and now at the
final muster-out and discharge of the Company, the remaining
members present it to our state, California. The accompanying United
States flag was presented by Miss Abbie A. Lord of Charlestown, but
has never been carried upon the field of battle as it was too large for
cavalry horses. It has never been unfurled by the hundred except in
one instance when it was used to enshroud the coffin of our company
commander, Captain J. Sewell Reed. It is the wish of the hundred
that it also be presented to the state. (*Plate* 14).

The colors of the Bear flag are faded and the silk worn and torn to shreds by long service on the field. It was necessary to attach a large blue satin pennant to the staff on which to inscribe the list of battles in which the hundred participated. The pennant was presented to the California men by their commanding officer, Colonel Casper Crowinshield.

The list of battles printed in gold is as follows: South Anna, Dranesville, Aldie, Fort Reno, Rockville, Poolsville, Summit Point, Berryville, Charlestown, Hall Town (four days), Opequan (six days), Winchester, Luray, Waynesboro, Cedar creek, White Oak Road, Dinwiddie Court house, Five Forks, Sailor creek and Appomattox court house.

At Luray, september 24, 1864, twenty-five year old Private Philip Baybutt of the California hundred distinguished himself by the "capture of the Rebel flag" and was awarded the medal of honor, october 19, 1864. The young hero joined the company after its arrival on the Atlantic coast and cited Fall River, Massachusetts as his place of residence.[377]

The flag of the California battalion was presented by Major D. W. C. Thompson just before they left San Francisco and was returned with the Battalion at the close of the war. This flag was saluted by President Lincoln and cheered at receptions and parades in the eastern cities and has been presented to the state by Miss Marian Thompson of Santa Rosa, California.

The story of the service of the battalion is told in letters of red, blue and gold. The blue ground of the flag shows the field of operations. The three upper stripes, their organizations, "California hundred" and "California battalion", enwreathed by green laurel leaves. The white stripes between these two upper red

[377] *Alta Weekly California (Steamer)*, San Francisco, nov. 10, 1865 (written at Fairfax Court house, july 20, 1865, to Adj. Gen. of Calif.) (Huntington library).

Mass. soldiers, sailors and marines in the Civil war, vol VI, p. 230-238, compiled and published by Adj. Gen. Norwood, Mass., 1931.

ones, their numbers—organized october 1862, five hundred mustered in; discharged august 1865, one hundred eighty-two mustered out. The two lower red stripes, the memorable events of which they participated. In the six remaining stripes the fifty battles and skirmishes in which they engaged.[378]

In Capitol park, Sacramento, near Twelfth and L streets, a memorial grove of stately trees reaches ever upward toward the sky as a reminder of the sacrifices of the soldiers of the 1860's.

From the eastern battlefield, young saplings were uprooted and shipped to Sacramento where this memorial grove was dedicated may 1, 1897. A "peace tree", the mulberry, traveled all the way from Appomattox; an oak from Andersonville, Georgia, of prison memories; from Winchester, an elm to remind one of Sheridan's ride on his "steed as black as night"; an elm and a maple from Monocacy. The battlefield of Ball's bluff, where Colonel Edward D. Baker, U.S. senator from Oregon, was killed, supplied a sugar maple tree. A tulip tree that grew at Five Forks was transplanted in this grove together with the red bud, scarlet maple, locust, pitch pine, box elder and others from more than a score of battlefields. Very few of the trees died and when they did they were replaced by new ones.[379]

And there they stand today as though they would offer mute testimony that the wounds left by the conflict between the North and South have been healed.

---

[378] Report Maj. D. W. C. Thompson, *op. cit.,* p. 583. (Orton)

[379] In 1896, Mrs. Eliza H. Waggoner, a member of the Roby Circle no. 2 Ladies of the Grand Army of the Republic, conceived the idea of planting this Memorial grove. The expenses were defrayed by the Ladies of the G.A.R. of Calif. and Nevada and by public subscription.

The Pacific Squadron of 1861-1866

The Pacific squadron of the 1860's played a most important role in world affairs by maintaining peace in the Pacific. Ships of all sea-going nations then sailed the Pacific and dropped anchor in the harbors. Some in pursuit of legitimate commerce, others with ulterior motives. Secretary of the navy, Gideon Welles, 1861-1869, viewed the situation with considerable anxiety and repeatedly directed the commander of the squadron to move his vessels to the ports where international difficulties existed.

How preposterous it would now seem if the secretary of the navy would issue orders to stoke up the furnaces and unfurl the sails of six small wooden vessels and patrol the Pacific ocean. Yet the six sloops-of-war, U.S.S. "Lancaster", U.S.S. "Saranac", U.S.S. "Wyoming", U.S.S. "Narragansett", U.S.S. "St. Marys" and U.S.S. "Cyane" (*Plate 15*) comprised the entire Pacific squadron of 1861.[380]

The total strength of all six represented an insignificant amount of tonnage, horsepower, guns and men in comparison to the fleet of today. The sum of their tonnage was less than seven thousand; the guns numbered about one hundred, and not even one thousand men manned the little fleet. Traveling at the rate of eleven to thirteen knots an hour, they cruised along the coast from San Francisco to Panama; they sailed as far north

[380] Report secy. of navy 1861.
37 Cong. 2 Sess. Sen. Ex. Doc. no. 1, vol. III, pt. 1 (1119)

as Alaska and south to Chili. They visited Hawaii to
guard the whaling fleet. Along the coast of China and
Japan they protected the United States commerce from
piratical Chinese junks. Even Australia and the South
Seas were included in their itinerary.

One half of the vessels were old and had been in
service from twelve to twenty-four years. The u.s.s.
"Cyane" was the oldest and possessed the most illus-
trious and colorful record. This was her third trip to
the Pacific having been present on two different occasions. First, when Commodore Jones prematurely raised
the flag over Monterery in 1842 and again four years
later when formal possession was taken.

It was amazing how much was accomplished with
so little—with only these six small vessels. But the
cooperation of the army with the navy increased the
efficiency of the small fleet. Gideon Welles was well
aware of the defenseless position of the Pacific coast
and sought the assistance of Simon Cameron, secretary
of war. Orders were promptly issued to both army and
navy commanders on the Pacific coast to aid each other
in preventing the Secessionists from gaining a foothold
in Lower California or elsewhere on the Pacific coast.[381]

The shipment East of war materiel had so depleted
the supplies at Mare island and Benicia that great difficulty was encountered in furnishing the essential
equipment for the protection of the West. The Pacific
Mail Steamship company applied to General Edwin V.
Sumner for four 32-pounder guns to be mounted on
their steamers in service between San Francisco and
Panama. General Sumner supplied the guns and ammunition but called on Captain William Gardner,
commanding Mare island, to lend the carriages. In

---

[381] *War. Reb.* Ser. I, vol. L, pt. I, p. 539.

return, General Sumner lent a 24-pounder gun to Mare island and ordered a company of soldiers to guard the powder magazine where but two watchmen stood guard. The soldiers remained on duty there for six months when they were replaced by a company of marines from the U.S.S. "Lancaster", march 14, 1862.[382]

As a further precaution against enemy activities, Commodore J. B. Montgomery ordered the U.S.S. "Wyoming", the U.S.S. "Narragansett" and the U.S.S. "Cyane" to cruise along the coasts of Mexico and California for the protection of the mail steamers and their heavy shipments of gold. Commodore Montgomery in his flagship, U.S.S. "Lancaster", then sailed to Panama to meet dispatches from the Navy department.[383]

The force in the Pacific remained unchanged in 1862 with the exception that the "Wyoming" was detached and sent to the East Indies and Commodore J. B. Montgomery was succeeded by Rear Admiral Charles E. Bell. This decrease in the strength of the squadron, together with the concentration of the fleet on the southern coast, left the Columbia river and the northern coast vulnerable to attack.

The U.S.S. "Shubrick" was then on duty on the northern coast and came to the attention of the public on account of the difficulty over the customhouse at Port Townsend, Washington territory.

In the early part of august 1862, Victor Smith, collector of customs, arrived in the "Shubrick" to take possession of the customhouse at Port Townsend. Lieutenant James H. Merryman, acting collector, declined to turn over the property unless presented with the evidence for so doing.

[382] *Ibid.*, p. 628, 644, 498, 531, 481, 925.
[383] *Ibid.*, p. 539.

The customs collector declined to furnish his papers of authorization but returned to the "Shubrick" where he selected an armed guard and demanded that the customhouse should be given up or it would be entered by force. Lieutenant Merryman was given fifteen minutes to make his decision. Under these circumstances, he turned over the customhouse and papers to Lieutenant Wilson of the "Shubrick" who receipted for the papers and placed them on board.

Much excitement was caused in Port Townsend by the threatening attitude assumed by the cutter as her twelve-pounders were trained upon the port. A warrant was issued for the arrest of Lieutenant Wilson and Victor Smith, but when the United States marshall boarded the "Shubrick" on her return trip, Lieutenant Wilson refused to obey the warrant and sailed away.

A month later the tension appeared to have been relieved as both defendants, Smith and Wilson, consented to undergo a legal investigation for which the warrants of arrest had been issued on august 11.[384]

There was not one fortified point on the Columbia river at this time. Therefore, Brigadier General Benjamin Alvord, commanding the district of Oregon, earnestly requested that an iron-clad be built for service on the northwestern coast.

The Pacific coast alarmists were no doubt justified in their anxiety. For at this time the Confederate forces under General Sibley were already moving up the Rio Grande from Texas; Colonel Baylor had established his government in the Mesilla valley and issued his

---

[384] 35 Cong. 1 Sess. H. Ex. Doc. no. 3, vol. 1 (1127)
War. Reb. Ser. 1, vol. L, pt. 1, p. 535.
Ibid., pt. 11, p. 70-72, 117.
Lewis and Dryden, *Marine history of the Pacific Northwest,* p. 11, 84, 207, 337.

"proclamation"; and both of these Confederate officers were secretly negotiating with the governments of Sonora and Chihuahua to secure their cooperation. The Pacific squadron was alerted and the U.S.S. "St. Marys" ordered to the port of Guaymas to endeavor to secure the neutrality, if not the assistance, of the Mexican government.[385]

The U.S.S. "Saginaw" and the storeship "Farallones" were added to the fleet in 1863. The engine and the boiler for the "Saginaw" were manufactured at the Union Iron works at San Francisco and she was ready to join the Pacific squadron in march. She was scheduled to leave immediately for the Guadalupe islands but the order was soon countermanded as rumors of a conspiracy to attack Mare island had been discovered. However, the rumors proved to be unfounded.[386]

The year 1863 was a year of anxiety for the little squadron of the Pacific, the forts on shore, and the citizens as well. Early in march Captain E. W. Travers discovered a plot to outfit and arm the schooner "J. M. Chapman" which was to be used in the service of the rebellion to cruise on the high seas and commit hostilities upon the citizens, property and vessels of the United States. He informed Adjutant General Colonel Richard Drum who conferred with Lieutenant Commander Paul Shirley of the U.S.S. "Cyane", the revenue officers, and the San Francisco police. A plan was evolved whereby the conspirators could be trapped.

Several months previous, Asbury Harpending, the chief instigator, had gone to Richmond, Virginia, where he received from Jefferson Davis a letter of

[385] *War. Reb.* Ser. I, vol. L, pt. I, p. 1051.
[386] *Ibid.*, pt. II, p. 359, 363-364, 366-367.
Report secy. of navy, dec. 1, 1862.
38 Cong. 1 Sess. H. Ex. Doc. no. 1, vol. IV (1158)

marque and a form of bond with instructions how to use it if any of the prizes were bonded. When Harpending returned to San Francisco, he made arrangements with twenty year old Alfred Rubery, a British subject, to purchase a vessel suitable for their purpose. No doubt the age-old lure of the life of a pirate appealed to this English youth but his enthusiasm exceeded his finances. The drafts drawn by him were not honored and the ownership of a privateer was delayed; yet not for long, as Ridgley Greathouse joined the conspirators and supplied funds to buy the "J. M. Chapman", a swift ninety-ton schooner.

Guns, ammunition and soldiers' uniforms were purchased and packed in cases labeled as oil, merchandise, machinery and quick-silver. Lumber was loaded for berths, a prison room and a lower deck. William C. Law was hired as captain together with a crew of sixteen men. Law was reported to have been employed by the Pacific Mail Steamship company for a brief time. He was also captain of the "Storm Cloud" but his erratic conduct aroused the suspicions of his employers who sent an agent to Valparaiso to relieve him of the command of the vessel for fear he might steal it.

The bill of lading under which Captain Law obtained clearance for the "J. M. Chapman" was necessarily false. He swore that the crew consisted of one captain, one mate, four seamen, and her manifest was quicksilver, merchandise and machinery. The port named for clearance was Manzanillo, Mexico, where he said the men were to engage in mining.

The plans of the pirates were ambitious and extensive. They first considered the island of Cerros as a suitable base for their operations, but decided that Guadalupe island offered greater advantages. Here they planned to land their men, guns and ammunition, then go to Manzanillo, transmit a copy of her crew list to the rebel authorities and return to Guadalupe. Here they would take on board their men, then uniformed, hoist the Confederate flag and proceed on their cruise against the vessels of the United States.

First on their agenda was the capture of one of the Pacific Mail steamers; next they hoped to recover the two million dollar treasure from the S.S. "Golden Gate" which was wrecked off the coast of Mexico near Manzanillo. Then they proposed to cruise down to the Chincha islands and, if their plans were successful, continue to the China sea and Indian ocean.

As they anticipated their booty, they decided how the treasure should be divided. Ridgley Greathouse was to receive the lion's share and the others would share in the following order: first, Asbury Harpending; second, William C. Law; third, Alfred Rubery; and fourth, Lorenzo C. Libby.

While the conspirators were busy with their plans, the custom officers and Lieutenant Commander Paul Shirley of the U.S.S. "Cyane" were keeping a twenty-four hour daily watch on the "J. M. Chapman". On board the steam tug "Anashe", the revenue officers and the San Francisco police kept steam up and fires banked ready for instant service. Nearby the "Cyane" crew watched the unusual commotion on board the "Chapman" and the men coming and going down the wharf all night long before she sailed; saw a lighter draw up beside the schooner and load supplies on board—supplies that had not been manifested by the revenue officers.

It was dawn on march 15, 1863, when the "J. M. Chapman" lifted anchor and sailed slowly away from the wharf. The water was calm, the morning clear and mild. Only Greathouse and Libby were on deck and the vessel looked as innocent and harmless as any craft that ever left the port of San Francisco. When she was about three hundred yards from the dock, two boatloads of armed seamen from the U.S.S. "Cyane" rowed toward the schooner. The steam tug "Anashe" had waited because Captain Law stood on the wharf calling for the "Chapman" to come back for him. Law had spent the night imbibing too freely and was so late that his fellow conspirators left without him. The "Cyane" seamen boarded the "Chapman" and captured her without resistance.[387]

When the schooner was searched her cargo of contraband was soon discovered and the leaders of the conspirators were ironed and placed in solitary confinement at Alcatraz. Sixteen men were found secreted in the hold of the vessel and all were armed with navy revolvers and Bowie knives. On the floor of the cabin was found paper, chewed and torn into tiny pieces. One letter disclosed plans for the capture of the S.S. "Shubrick" but the scheme appeared to have been abandoned. Other papers found in the baggage of Harpending revealed plans for the capture of the United States forts at San Francisco and Alcatraz; a proclamation to the people of California to throw off the authority of the United States; a draft of an oath of fidelity to their cause; and an imprecation of vengeance on all who should prove false. The oath and papers were in the handwriting of Harpending but Rubery admitted helping him.

The conspirators were tried before Judge Stephen J. Fields. Their trial lasted for eight days but it took but

[387] *Alta California,* San Francisco, march 16, 1863.

four minutes for the jury to decide that they were guilty
of treason. Asbury Harpending, Ridgley Greathouse
and Alfred Rubery were each sentenced to ten years in
prison and a fine of ten thousand dollars. The other
prisoners, members of the crew, were discharged upon
taking the oath of allegiance.[388]

Alfred Rubery soon secured his release as President
Lincoln granted him a pardon with the proviso that he
would leave the country thirty days after january 20,
1864, the date set for his release. President Lincoln
explained that his reasons for the pardon were that
Rubery was a subject of Great Britain and but twenty
years old; and furthermore, the pardon had been requested by John Bright, English statesman, and Lincoln
deemed it a mark of respect to the Englishman. His
explanation appears to contain a conciliatory note—or
perhaps a hint of appeasement.

The rest of the traitors were confined at Alcatraz but
a few months as President Lincoln issued his Amnesty
proclamation december 8, 1863 granting full pardon to
all political prisoners upon the condition that they take
and keep the oath of allegiance. Therefore, the traitors
demanded their release from Alcatraz. Under *habeas
corpus* proceedings they were granted trial february,
1864, and given their freedom. Yet it was with the
greatest reluctance that Judge Hoffman did so, for,
said he, "The crime was grave, and Greathouse had
long been a citizen of California." [389]

The schooner "J. M. Chapman" was sold as a war
prize and the money divided between the United States
and the informer, Captain E. W. Travers. The officers
and crew of the U.S.S. "Cyane" objected and brought

---

[388] Sawyer, vol. IV, p. 457.
[389] *Ibid.*, p. 487.

suit for their share of the prize as they were the first to board the "Chapman". The case was decided against the seamen as the judge ruled that the case of the "Chapman" was not piratical in the meaning of the term as defined by the laws of nations. Her crime was treason under the act of august 5, 1861. The third section of that act provided that any person, who supplied information leading to the arrest and conviction of traitors, would be entitled to share equally with the United States in any property so acquired. The crew of the "Chapman" were allowed one month's salary as they were judged innocent of all charges and entitled to their wages.[390]

But at this same time there were other ships anchored in San Francisco harbor, which had come not as enemies, but as friends. Alexander II of Russia sent six warships to visit the Pacific coast to demonstrate his friendship for the United States and his marked respect for President Abraham Lincoln. Between these two men there existed a common bond of sympathy and understanding. Both were opposed to slavery. In 1861 Alexander II freed twenty-three million serfs and less than two years later, Lincoln issued his Emancipation proclamation (january 1, 1863).

While the Russian fleet was anchored in the bay, the United States navy and army officers, the mayor of San Francisco, and many prominent citizens entertained the Russian officers at the Union hall, november 17, 1863.

This friendly gesture on the part of Russia was in direct contrast to that of her neighbor, Japan. An American steamer, the "Pembroke", was fired upon by the Japanese on july 11, 1863, for in spite of their new

---

[390] *Ibid.,* p. 501.

treaty with the United States, they were still suspicious of foreign vessels passing near their shores.

A few days later while the U.S.S. "Wyoming" was cruising through the straits of Shimonoseki, the Japanese land and naval guns opened fire. The "Wyoming" returned the fire and the battle continued for an hour. The Japanese bark, "Daniel Webster", the brig, "Lanrick", were sunk and the steamer "Lancefield" was damaged. All three vessels had been purchased from the United States. The "Wyoming" lost four of her crew and seven were wounded. The sum of $125,000 from the Japanese Indemnity fund was eventually paid to the officers and crew after years of delay and negotiations (march 31, 1874).[391]

The first iron-clad that served in the Pacific was the U.S.S. "Camanche", an Ericsson Monitor of 1857 tons (*Plate* 16). She was built at New York by Francis Secor and when completed, she was disassembled and shipped on board the "Aquila" (*Plate* 17) to San Francisco. The "Aquila" left New York may 29, 1863, and arrived at San Francisco november 10, almost six months en route. The "Aquila" broke from her moorings during a heavy gale on november 16. She was rescued and berthed at the Hathaway wharf, but on the same day, "Camanche" and all, she sank in the mud at the bottom of the bay. Captain Allison of Benicia made an unsuccessful attempt to raise her and after three weeks abandoned his efforts.

The underwriters' agents took over the job of raising the "Aquila" and sent from New York a professional

---

[391] 37 Cong. 2 Sess. Sen. Ex. Doc. no. 15, vol. IV, Report secy. of navy, 1862 (1121)

38 Cong. 1 Sess. H. Ex. Doc. no. 1, vol. IV, Report secy. navy, 1863 (1183)

43 Cong. 1 Sess. H. Report 343, 1874 (1624)

50 Cong. 1 Sess. H. Report 1920, 1888 (2603)

wrecking crew, the Coast Wrecking company, consisting of ten wreckers and four divers under command of Captain Israel E. Merritt. They arrived january 17, 1864, to learn that Charles W. Hathaway and George P. Baker, proprietors of Hathaway wharf, had filed suit for wharfage and storage from november 16, 1863 to january 13, 1864, and had placed an attachment on the "Aquila" and cargo. Peter Donahue gave a bond to release the attachment so that the wreckers could begin work.

All legal entanglements being settled, the contractors constructed a derrick and began removing the cargo before raising the "Aquila". The government property which consisted of about two hundred tons of shot and shells, and two fifteen-inch guns, was landed, cleaned, and sent to Mare island. The winter storms delayed the work somewhat but the last piece of the iron-clad was rescued june 8, 1864.

Peter Donahue, president of the Union Iron works, had contracted with the government to reassemble the "Camanche" and launch her. The original contract for building the iron-clad was for $585,000 in gold or legal tender. When the vessel was assembled at New York $340,000 was advanced. The contractors had given $100,000 cash as security for the fulfillment of their contract and in addition a bond for $400,000. The total insurance on the "Aquila" and cargo was $600,000 of which $340,000 was on the "Camanche" and distributed among twenty-two insurance companies, the policies varying from $5,000 to $35,000. The work of reassembling was begun july 13 and the "Camanche" was finally launched november 14, 1864, one year after her arrival. The presence of the iron-clad in the Pacific allayed the fears of the people and gave assurance of their adequate protection. The board of supervisors of San Francisco city and county passed a resolution (no. 4092) in which they thanked the contractors, Donahue, Ryan and Secor for the completion of the "Camanche".

The "Camanche" continued to make the headlines for more than ten years as repeated attempts were made to collect from the several insurance companies through litigations extending from 1870 to 1880. San Francisco city and county were also involved as $71,166.66 had been paid to Peter Donahue to redeem his note at the Bank of California for $60,000 with interest, which had been given to pay the claim of the wrecking company to eliminate any delay in completing the "Camanche". The insurance policies had been signed over to the board of supervisors with the assurance that the damages would be promptly paid by the various insurance companies. Out of the $60,000 only $7,897.53 was paid.[392]

The mechanized warfare of the new iron-clads called for new methods of defense. So a novel plan for the protection of San Francisco harbor was submitted to Governor Leland Stanford by Adjutant General William C. Kibbe in his report of december 3, 1863. To adequately fortify the harbor it was proposed to construct revolving iron towers at each side of the Golden Gate. These towers to be one hundred feet in diameter and pierced for two tiers of guns with ample space for thirty guns in each tier. Casemated guns were planned for the foundation of the towers. When the towers were completed, massive chains would be laid across the entrance to the harbor. These chains would be drawn

---

[392] *Alta California,* San Francisco, nov. 10, 14, 17; dec. 5, 6, 1863.
Ibid., july 13; nov. 14, 16, 1864.
Bulletin, San Francisco, dec. 5, 1863; jan. 18, 25, 28, 29, 1864.
San Francisco Reports, 1880-1881, 1882-1883. Pub. by George Spaulding.

up by windlasses operated by steam engines. The chains would be designed to check the speed of any enemy vessel and bring it under fire of the guns in the towers. Kibbe contended that if the towers could be built and other approaches to the city fortified, the navies of the world could be kept out of the harbor.[393]

After the capture of the "J. M. Chapman", demands were made on the War department for additional protection for San Francisco harbor. Accordingly Brigadier General René E. De Russy, chief topographical engineer of the department of the Pacific, submitted a plan (june, 1863) for a secondary line of defense which called for fortifications at Fort Point, Lime Point, Alcatraz island, Rincon Point and Yerba Buena island. General De Russy was seventy-three years old at this time and spent the remainder of his life in the construction of the defenses of the harbor.[394]

In the spring of 1864 a conspiracy to capture the California mail steamers was discovered. S. R. Mallory, secretary of the Confederate navy, ordered Captain T. E. Hogg and his command to take passage on board the s.s. "San Salvador" and to capture her after reaching the high seas. Having secured the steamer, he was instructed to arm her and attack the California trade and the whalers in the North Pacific.

Captain Hogg went to Havana and while there the American consul, Thomas Savage, learned about his plans and notified Rear Admiral George F. Pearson at Panama. The passengers boarding the steamers at Panama were carefully watched and when the Hogg party were discovered aboard the s.s. "San Salvador", a force from the U.S.S. "Lancaster" arrested them and

---

[393] Report Adj. Gen. Calif., William C. Kibbe, dec. 3, 1863.

[394] *Professional Memoirs*, vol. VII, 1915, p. 758. Corps of engrs. U.S. army and engr. dept. Pub. bimonthly at Engr. sch. Wash. Barracks, D.C.

brought them to San Francisco. Here they were tried by a military commission and sentenced to be hanged. Later, General Irvin McDowell commuted their sentences to life imprisonment for Captain Hogg and ten years for the others.[395]

To prevent any further attempts to seize Pacific coast shipping, General Irvin McDowell ordered each passenger on board American merchant steamers to deliver every weapon in his possession to the officers of the ship. In order that there would be no evasion of this order, every passenger and his baggage was searched. In addition, all officers were armed for the protection of their ship and themselves.[396]

Sympathy for the resistance of the Mexican republic to the French occupation caused an embarassing situation at San Francisco in the summer of 1864. In april of the same year, Placido Vegas left Mazatlan for San Francisco. He was instructed with a special mission by the Constitutional government of the republic of Mexico and supplied with funds for the purchase of arms and other military supplies. Upon his arrival he professed to have interviewed Governor F. F. Low who expressed his sympathy for the safety of the Mexican nation and offered his personal cooperation. (Governor Low denied the allegation.) Vega also interviewed Thomas Brown, collector and special agent of the U.S. treasury, W. B. Farwell, head of marine office, and Edward F. Beale, corps of U.S. Engineers.

Vega insisted that he faithfully followed the instructions of these officials and did everything with the ut-

395 H. H. Bancroft, *History of California*, vol. VII, p. 297.

39 Cong. 1 Sess. H. Ex. Doc. no. 1, vol. v, Report secy. navy, 1865 (1253)

38 Cong. 2 Sess. H. Ex. Doc. nos. 83, 84, 85, vol. XIV, Report secy. navy, 1864 (1230)

396 *War. Reb.* Ser. I, vol. L, pt. II, p. 911-912.

most caution lest he compromise the neutrality of the United States. General McDowell discovered the plot and the officers engaged in the conspiracy were suddenly relieved from their positions. Cruisers were dispatched in pursuit of Vega's loaded vessel which was overtaken and convoyed to Benicia for safe keeping. A large quantity of arms and munitions were also seized at Half Moon bay after they had eluded the customhouse officers.[397]

Charles James who succeeded Thomas Brown as collector of the port of San Francisco, was the subject of a scathing rebuke from Edward F. Beale. Said he, "I thoroughly appreciate your sensitive and conscientious moral scruples regarding the false oath the captain of a schooner would have to make in order to secure the clearance of his vessel. . . I also question who is entitled to the most respect. He who committed a crime to save a republic, or he who cannot be bullied, wheedled, coaxed, or cajoled into doing so." [398]

Vega repeatedly and earnestly requested General McDowell to release the arms and munitions intended for the Mexican republic. He said: "In regard to my whole conduct, you will be satisfied that I came without disguise of any kind, relying upon the fact that we were defending the same institutions.

"As it was possible at first to send goods by merely taking care that no one should be compromised, and when at a later date, other articles were detained at the customhouse, they were nevertheless placed at my disposal the next day. I gained the greatest confidence and kept on making extensive purchases for cash and on credit, only to see my goods held without knowing

---

397 *Ibid.*, p. 1038-1044.
398 *Ibid.*, p. 1099.

when they would be released. Great expense has been incurred for vessels lying idle and enough has been paid to buy them outright. Even if the cargo is never received I shall have to pay the freight." General McDowell explained that the shipment of arms was a direct violation of Lincoln's order and refused to permit any war materiel to be shipped to Mexico.

In spite of the vigilance of the Pacific squadron and the troops on shore, rumors persisted that privateers were being outfitted at San Francisco. Secretary of State William H. Seward ordered an inquiry by the War department to determine whether or not any vessels were being built to serve as privateers under letters of marque from President Juarez of Mexico, and which would be used in depredations on French commerce.[399]

Before orders reached General Irvin McDowell, he had already seized and held the steamer "Colon" said to have been built for the Peruvian government. The seizure was later approved by the secretary of war and his additional orders provided that all the material for building war marine of every description was required for the use of the United States government, and nothing of the kind could be purchased or taken from the United States, especially on the Pacific coast. Government priority of the 1860's.[400]

The Peruvian government protested against the seizure of the "Colon" and demanded that the vessel be released. The Federal government was slow to act and the order to release the "Colon" was not issued until march 14, 1865, more than six months after the seizure. In the meantime the case had been the subject of an investigation by a grand jury and an opinion

[399] *Ibid.*, p. 1068.
[400] *Ibid.*, p. 948-949, 1105.

rendered that there was no cause for the detention of the "Colon".[401]

While attention was being focused on San Francisco harbor, events of international concern were taking place on the coasts of Mexico and South America. The French fleet had blockaded the Mexican ports but permitted the Pacific Mail Steamship company to use the harbor of Acapulco as an intermediate depot. Rear Admiral Bell found it expedient to station one of the United States men-of-war at that port to protect the property of the company and to assure the safety of the passengers.[402]

On board each steamer there was stationed a detachment of California volunteers. Companies H and K, sixth infantry, were stationed at Benicia barracks at this time and furnished the guard for the steamers "Uncle Sam" and the "Constitution". The volunteers were also detailed to guard the magazine at Benicia and allow no vessel to come within two hundred yards. One evening a schooner anchored about fifty yards off shore. When ordered off, it showed no signs of moving. The guard fired three rounds of ball cartridges at the schooner, forcing her to lift anchor and change her base farther down toward San Francisco.

Whether it was an accident, commercial rivalry, or political differences that caused the S.S. "Yosemite" to ram the S.S. "Washoe", it was the occasion for calling out extra guards from the sixth infantry, California volunteers. The young soldiers stood guard at the Benicia wharf while the boats came and left, but said the volunteer, "There was no disturbance of any kind,

401 *Ibid.*, p. 1161, 1126.
402 38 Cong. 2 Sess. H. Ex. Doc. no. 1, vol. VI, Report secy. navy 1864 (1221)

not the first symptoms of a row." He was probably a bit disappointed that there was no excitement.[403]

About the middle of april 1864, Rear Admiral Bell left Acapulco in his flagship, U.S.S. "Lancaster", and sailed south to Callao where he arrived may 25. Trouble had arisen between Peru and Spain over injuries to Spanish subjects and in retaliation Spain siezed the Chincha islands.

It was imperative that the fleet of the United States vessels engaged in the guano trade on those islands receive adequate protection, so Rear Admiral Bell remained there from may 25 to october 5. He then sailed north to Panama where he was relieved of his command of the Pacific squadron by Rear Admiral George F. Pearson, october 25.

The U.S.S. "Narragansett" cruised to Puget sound, the straits of Juan de Fuca, and to Victoria, where the English authorities representing Queen Victoria, assured the U.S. naval commander that there would be no violation of English neutrality. When the "Narragansett" returned to San Francisco, she was ordered to the Atlantic coast, and the new U.S.S. "Wateree" joined the Pacific squadron, thus maintaining the same strength of the little fleet.

In the spring of 1865 the Pacific coast shipping was again thrown into panic when news arrived about the damage committed by the "Shenandoah". In october 1864, she had sailed from London flying the British flag under the name of "Sea King". A few months later she unfurled the Confederate States flag and sailed as a privateer under the command of James I. Waddell.[404] She destroyed over a million dollars worth of whalers

---

[403] *Tuolumne Courier,* Columbia, july 30, 1864. (County archives, Sonora)

[404] Lt. James I. Waddell C.S.N. surrendered to the British authorities nov. 6, 1865.

and merchant vessels and then sailed for European waters when word was received that the war was over. The U.S.S. "Suwanee" and the U.S.S. "Saranac" of the Pacific squadron were sent in pursuit of the privateer but they were too late—their enemy had fled.

Special precaution was taken by the war department to examine all passports of foreigners arriving at the port of San Francisco. An officer was ordered to examine all passengers and refuse to permit any one to land without a passport. An exception was made regarding passengers coming direct from New York or from Oregon. Those who came from Vancouver island required passports and an officer boarded all vessels at Cape Disappointment to see that this order was enforced.[405]

In 1865 the Pacific squadron was increased to eleven vessels by the addition of the U.S.S. "Powhatan", U.S.S. "Nyack", U.S.S. "Mohongo", U.S.S. "Tuscarora" and the storeship "Fredonia". Secretary of Navy Gideon Welles recommended even greater increase to protect the expanding commerce of the Pacific.

Peace came to the Atlantic seaboard at the close of the war but on the Pacific the sound of the warning of "hands off" and "non-interference" of the Monroe Doctrine was lost in the deafening roar of the French guns at Acapulco and those of the Spanish at Valparaiso and Callao.

By repeated requests and warnings Secretary of the Navy Gideon Welles finally secured six more vessels for the Pacific squadron, raising the number to seventeen vessels in 1866. The fleet was divided into the North Pacific and the South Pacific squadrons. The

405 *War. Reb.* Ser. I, vol. L, pt. II, p. 1158. Gen. Orders no. 308, dec. 29, 1864.

North Pacific squadron embraced the coast of North America and the Sandwich islands (Hawaiian) and was under the command of Rear-Admiral Thatcher who hoisted his flag at San Francisco on august 6, 1866. The following vessels were allotted to his Squadron: U.S.S. "Vanderbilt", flagship, U.S.S. "Pensacola", U.S.S. "Saranac" (temporarily), U.S.S. "Suwanee", U.S.S. "Mohongo", U.S.S. "Jamestown", U.S.S. "Lackawanna", U.S.S. "Mohican", U.S.S. "Resaca" and U.S.S. "Saginaw".

The limits of the South Pacific squadron extended from Panama to Cape Horn and all the way to Australia. The seven vessels, U.S.S. "Powhatan" (flagship), U.S.S. "Tuscarora", U.S.S. "Wateree", U.S.S. "Nyack", U.S.S. "Dacotah", U.S.S. "Farallones", and U.S.S. "Fredonia", assigned to this division, were obliged to cover a wide area, yet they included the trouble spots on their cruises and were at Valparaiso when the Spanish bombarded that city march 31, 1866. They followed the Spanish men-of-war to Callao and stood menacingly near until the Spanish withdrew.

Included in the new arrivals in the Pacific in 1866 was the iron-clad U.S.S. "Monadnock", the first monitor to make the journey around the Horn on her own power, but she was the second one to serve on the Western coast. Three years previous the U.S.S. "Camanche" had made the same journey but she was dismantled and carried aboard the S.S. "Aquila".

The U.S.S. "Vanderbilt", which was presented to the United States by Cornelius Vanderbilt, accompanied the U.S.S. "Monadnock" on her long journey to the Pacifiic and was present at the bombardment of Valparaiso. All the duties of the "Vanderbilt" were not of a belligerent nature for she conveyed Queen Emma on her return journey from San Francisco to Hawaii, october 22, 1866.

In addition to the war-time duties of the fleet, the old vessels aided in ocean surveying to chart their course through the treacherous seas. Through a special act of congress the U.S.S. "Saginaw" was detailed to help the Western Union Telegraph company lay a cable on the northwestern coast.[406]

At the close of the war many of the vessels were sold as surplus property; others were wrecked; some of these small wooden sloops remained afloat for half a century or more.

The U.S.S. "Cyane" was the oldest of the squadron of the 1860's and although she was put out of commission after thirty-four years service, she was not sold until she had reached the half century mark. The selling price of the worthy old sloop was but three thousand dollars which probably represented her value as scrap.

From Canada to Peru lie the wrecks of other vessels of this early Pacific squadron. The U.S.S. "Saginaw" was wrecked on the rocks off Ocean island. She had been stationed at Midway during the improvement of the entrance of the harbor.

Five members of her crew rowed a thousand miles to Kauai island for help. After thirty-one days in their open boat with scant rations and under a tropical sun, they sighted the island. Before they could land, a severe storm capsized their boat and all of the crew except William Halford were drowned. The remainder of the crew stranded on Ocean island were rescued.

The squadron of the Pacific contributed much to the

---

406 39 Cong. 1 Sess. H. Ex. Doc. no. 1, vol. v, Report secy. navy 1865 (1253)
Rear Admiral Dahlgren succeeded Rear Admiral Pearson in command of the South Pacific squadron.

safety of the long Pacific coast line and by close co-operation with the army of the Pacific maintained peace on the western shore.

The Soldiers' Relief Fund

During the first year of the war, California did but little for the relief of the soldiers on the eastern battlefields. No appreciable amount of money was collected by San Francisco or any other Pacific coast city.

Local churches and fraternal organizations supplied kits and other articles for the personal use of the California volunteers stationed in the training camps and small sums were collected for their families where the need was apparent.

In San Francisco the first preliminary meeting to discuss plans for national relief was held in august 1862. When the board of supervisors met september 8, John H. Redington introduced a resolution to call a public meeting on september 10 to increase the relief fund for the benefit of the soldiers. A committee of five was appointed and requested to report on the following day a plan of organization and the names for a permanent state committee. Judge C. Blake was chairman and his colleagues were Eugene Casserly, R. G. Sneath, D. C. McRuer and E. H. Washburn.

By working rapidly, they were ready to report the next evening. They drew up a set of resolutions to serve as the organic law of the San Francisco Committee of the Soldiers' Relief fund and named Mayor H. E. Teschemacher (of San Francisco) as chairman. The other members were William Norris, Henry Seligman, A. L. Tubbs, J. B. Roberts, Peter Donohue, John H. Redington, Horace P. James, James Otis, Herman

Nichols, John R. Risdon, Eugene Sullivan and William Lent. James Otis was appointed treasurer.

The next public meeting was scheduled for september 14 at Platts Music hall. Reverend Thomas Starr King of the Unitarian church of San Francisco, as well as other prominent citizens, was invited to speak. King had already collected small amounts for the National Sanitary commission of which his friend, Henry Whitney Bellows, D.D., was president. The following notice of one of King's meetings was published in the *San Francisco Daily Morning Call* of september 7, 1862: "Natives of Charlestown, Massachusetts, Attention! Ladies and gentlemen born under the shadow of Bunker Hill are invited to attend a meeting at Platts Music hall on monday evening next, september 8, where they will hear some good news from that classic spot. The Reverend Thomas Starr King and other eminent speakers will address the meeting." [407]

From a group of Americans in Victoria, King received one thousand dollars which he publicized to the advantage of the National Sanitary commission. He also succeeded "in shelling off two hundred dollars from the 'Patriotic corn cob' of the Olympic club of gentlemen athletes."

By this time King was well known as a lecturer and pastor since he had lived in San Francisco for more than two years. When he appeared on the platform at the public meeting september 14, he was greeted with enthusiasm from the large audience that crowded Platts Music hall. He began his lecture by saying that he felt as if he would burst because he could not give a million dollars for the Soldiers' Relief fund. . .

---

[407] *The Daily Morning Call*, San Francisco, sept. 7, 9, 10, 11, 12, 13, 1862. Charles J. Stille, *History of the Sanitary commission*, p. 214-215, Lippincott & Co., Philadelphia, Penn., 1866.

He declared that if any one in the audience would loan him that amount, he would contribute it at once and in turn offer his note for security. If afterwards, the lender wished to liquidate the note he might throw it off Meiggs wharf.

King continued his speech by advocating the necessity of all property interests being represented—especially the large corporations. For example, the Ophir Mining company, squatting on government land, should be assessed $100,000 and if they refused to stand for it, King suggested that they be refused the right to work on the people's land. He furthermore said that the music of guineas would cause rejoicing among the angels and Gabriel, himself, might come down to buy five shares in the Ophir lead. In addition, Gould and Curry should be induced to contribute $75,000; the California Steam Navigation and gas and water companies should be urged to pledge a proportionate amount.

He exhorted his listeners to repent their long negligence—to repent in gold and silver as less than $5,000 had been sent east at this time. The response was prompt and generous and by the next steamer day $100,000 was in the hands of Treasurer James Otis.[408]

The Patriotic Relief fund committee met in the mayor's office on september 19 to make its report and to decide how this large contribution should be spent and by what organization. King was present at this meeting and gave a full and interesting description of the plan of operation and the practical results accomplished by the National Sanitary commission.

This organization antedated the American Red Cross

[408] Charles W. Wendte, *Thomas Starr King, patriot and preacher*, p. 162-163. pub. the *Beacon Press*, Boston, Mass., 1921.

by more than twenty years. It was organized in New York in 1861 under the leadership of Dr. Bellows who served as its president until 1865. There were two headquarters—one in New York and the other in Louisville. The board of directors consisted of twenty-one members who looked after the claims and rights of the soldiers, recommended reforms, supported homes for the convalescent, fed and housed others and cared for the homeless.[409]

The San Francisco committee listened attentively to King's report and adjourned until the following day. In the meantime Mayor H. E. Teschemacher telegraphed to President Lincoln asking his advice regarding the best channel through which the San Francisco contribution should be applied. Lincoln conferred with Surgeon General William Alexander Hammond who recommended the National Sanitary commission. Incidently, it was this commission that was instrumental in securing the appointment of Hammond as surgeon general and, no doubt, he was glad to pay off a political debt.[410]

Accordingly, a draft for $100,000 was remitted to Dr. Bellows, president, and George T. Strong, treasurer, National Sanitary commission, New York.[411] So successful was the relief campaign that two weeks later another $100,000 was ready for transmittal. $50,000 of

---

409 *The Daily Morning Call,* San Francisco, sept. 16, 19, 1862.

410 Margaret Leech, *Reveille in Washington, 1860-1865,* Harper & Brothers, New York, London, 1941.

411 Henry Whitney Bellows was born in Walpole, New Hampshire, june 11, 1814. He graduated from Harvard in 1832 and from the Divinity school in 1837; pastor of All Saints church, 1839; editor *Christian Inquirer* and chief founder of that publication. He wrote *Public life of Washington, Relations of Public Amusements to public morality, The old world in its new face, Restatements of Christian doctrines,* and *Treatment of social diseases.*

He supervised the expenditure of five million dollars and distributed supplies valued at fifteen million. *(Encyclopedia Americana)*

this amount was ear-marked for the Western Sanitary commission at St. Louis, a separate and distinct organization.

From every county in the state, from each small village and mining town, thousands of dollars were collected—not in greenbacks but in gold dust and silver. Usually the treasure was melted and cast into bars upon which was stamped the amount and the name of the town whose citizens gave the bullion. It was quite frequently placed on exhibition in San Francisco and in New York.

All sorts of devices were employed to garner in the coin. The San Andreas Sanitary committee owned a little mechanical man which performed for each donor. The rarity of mechanical toys aided in luring the small coins from the inquisitive spectators. For years this little "Sanitary man" has been in the possession of Mrs. Theresa Leonard, a pioneer of San Andreas.

When Sierra county forwarded its contribution to Dr. Bellows, he wrote the committee to thank them for their generous gift. His letter was immediately put up at auction and by repeated sales netted $250. The last man paid $25 and added five dollars more to keep his name out of the paper.

A poor old man of Stockton had no money to offer but he was a cooper so he donated one of his barrels. He hoped that it would bring at least five dollars but he was amazed when it was auctioned off for $175. On the other hand, Captain Weber of Stockton gave sixteen lots in his new subdivision.

Every conceivable method was employed to collect funds. At the election polls in 1863, boxes were conveniently placed to receive the contributions of the voters. As a result, $13,640 in coin and $924 in legal tender was donated to the National Sanitary commission.[412]

By the end of the war California had contributed $1,233,831.31 which was one-fourth of the grand total. Nor was this all. The United States treasurer's report on finances for 1864 reveals the vast amount of treasure shipped from San Francisco within four years' time. On each trip the old "gold steamers" carried a million or more and during these first war years, $173,083,098 left the port of San Francisco. This bullion came from the silver mines of Nevada, the gold mines of California, in fact from all the western states and helped maintain the credit of the United States.[413]

Foremost among all the workers for the soldiers and the Union cause was Thomas Starr King. He traveled over California and as far north as Oregon and Washington, preaching, pleading for the relief of the fighting men and for the preservation of the Union. He was seemingly tireless, yet he overtaxed his strength and died march 4, 1864, before his fortieth birthday.[414]

412 Charles J. Stille, *History of the Sanitary commission,* p. 234, *op. cit.*

In 1841 Capt. Charles M. Weber came to Sutters Fort, California, where he spent some time in the employ of Capt. Sutter. He later settled in Stockton and aided much in its development giving land for streets, channels, and the public square. During the Civil war, Capt. Weber was staunch in his allegiance to the Union and exerted a powerful influence for its cause. He sent to Oregon for timber for a flagpole 124 feet long, which was placed on an island west of his residence. After each Union victory the stars and stripes were always seen waving from the top of the pole, which was visible for miles.

413 38 Cong. 2 Sess. H. Ex. Doc. no. 3, vol. VII, 1864, (1222)

Report of the secretary of the treasury on the finances for the year 1864. Government printing office, Washington, D.C. p. 180-183. Mineral lands and mines of the United States; distribution of the gold product. Treasure sent from San Francisco, p. 184.

414 Thomas Starr King was born in New York City, december 17, 1824. In 1835 he moved to Charlestown, Mass., where his father had been called to preach in the First Universalist church. Young King attended school here and in 1842 was made principal of the Medford grammar school.

After his father died Thomas Starr obtained a position as bookkeeper at

The value and importance of his service has been publicly acknowledged by the people of California by selecting him as one of the two most outstanding men whose statues were placed in Statuary hall, Washington, D.C., in 1931.

A statue of him stands in Golden Gate park, San Francisco; his portrait hangs in the state capitol at Sacramento; a tall tree in Sequoia park bears his name; Mount Starr King towers in Yosemite National park and a peak which was named for him in the White mountains of New Hampshire all testify to the loyalty and appreciation of the American people for the man who lived but to serve.[415]

In Stockton, California, another statue stands as a tribute to one who also proved a friend to the soldiers and engraved in marble are the simple words, "The soldiers' friend," Reuel Colt Gridley.

His method of raising money was perhaps the most unique on record. Just when or why he conceived the idea cannot be determined now. Perhaps it may have been when "Stick to it, Gridley! Never say die!" was shouted by the crowd that had come from the nearby shanties, the tunnels in the hills, and the prosperous stores of Austin, the Reese river mining town. The fifty-pound burden that Gridley shouldered grew heavier with each step on that warm april morning in

---

the Charlestown navy yard so that he might be able to help support his family. At the age of twenty he began to preach and in 1846 he accepted the pastorate at the First Universalist church in Charlestown where his father had served during the last years of his life.

In 1848 he moved to Boston where he continued his religious work from both the pulpit and lecture platform. In 1859 he received a call to the First Unitarian church in San Francisco. Here he spent the remainder of his short life in the service of his church and country.

[415] 72 Cong. 1 Sess. Sen. Ex. Doc. no. 102, vol. XVII, march 1, 1931. (9515) Acceptance and unveiling of statues of Junipero Serra and Thomas Starr King. Proceedings in the Congress and Statuary hall, United States capitol.

1864 for he had walked a long uphill mile to pay off an election bet.

It had been an exciting election in this two-year old town in Nevada. As election day approached, parades grew bigger, speeches more eloquent, while nightly bonfires lured the crowds. Whisky was as free as water and champagne went begging. Merchants closed their stores to participate in the fun and bet on the election.[416]

Reuel Colt Gridley had bet on Colonel David E. Buel, the Democratic candidate for the office of mayor of Austin, but the Republican, Charles Holbrook, was elected so Gridley had to pay off. He had agreed to carry a fifty-pound sack of flour from Clifton to Austin, an uphill mile away. The sack was then to be donated to the Sanitary fund for the benefit of the sick and wounded soldiers.

At the head of Gridley's long procession, rode the brass band playing *John Brown's Body;* next in line were the newly elected Republican officers mounted on western horses that cavorted with each loud blast of the horns; then marched Gridley with his flag-bedecked sack of flour. His teen-age son, Amos, dressed in soldier uniform, walked by his side and following right behind them, were two men. One carried a broom draped in mourning and the other shouldered a long pole from the end of which a large sponge dangled.

With banter and jest, the winners and losers stopped in front of the granite building that housed the Union saloon and the well stocked hardware store of the newly elected mayor, Charles Holbrook. Here with mock ceremony, the sack of flour was delivered to Holbrook, the sponge thrown up, and the broom put away as a symbol of the "clean sweep" made by the Republicans.

416 Election, april 19, 1864. (Sacramento *Union,* april 26, 1864)

The sack of flour was then donated to the local Sanitary committee. Right there it was suggested that the flour be put up at auction. Gridley made the first bid of $200. The flour was sold repeatedly and by the end of the day the Sanitary fund was increased by almost $5,000.

Thus began one of the strangest methods of raising money and perhaps the longest period of existence of an otherwise ordinary sack of American flour. What remains of the flour was presented to the Nevada Historical society in 1914 by Josephine Gridley Wood, daughter of Reuel Colt Gridley, and it is now in the Washoe county building, Reno, Nevada.

It was none other than Gridley, the loser, the Democrat and Southern sympathizer, who gave up his business in Austin and resolved to befriend the soldiers by raising money for the Sanitary fund. He agreed to travel with the sack of flour, pay his own expenses, and auction it off in the neighboring communities.

Virginia City invited him there first. His arrival was publicized by the local newspaper, the *Territorial Enterprise,* where the promising young reporter, Mark Twain, was employed. The sack of flour was auctioned off many times, labeled with the amount of the total sales, and returned to the Sanitary committee to again be sold to the highest bidder.

Enthused by their success, the Virginia City citizens decided upon a mammoth parade to Gold Hill, Silver City and Dayton. With their band leading the procession and the sack of flour in the open barouche, the philanthropists set forth to collect the gold dust and bullion from their fellow miners. The procession increased with each mile as prominent citizens fell into line. Of course, Mark Twain was there as any enterprising reporter should be. The total amount of sales for that eventful day was reported to be in excess of $25,000.[417]

Gridley then headed west for Sacramento where Dr. Henry Whitney Bellows, president of the National Sanitary commission, was scheduled to speak. Elaborate plans had been made for Dr. Bellows's visit. An excursion was planned to Roseville on the newly completed Central Pacific railroad and a semi-holiday was enjoyed by the Sacramentans. At sunrise bells rang and salutes were fired. At eight o'clock the parade formed. Governor Low and Ex-governor Stanford, three hundred "home guards", bands, prominent citizens and plain citizens, and a twelve-pounder field piece named "Union boy", lengthened the line that moved up and down the main streets of the city before assembling at the railroad station. The Central Pacific had granted free transportation for the excursionists but the Sanitary committee collected fares and thereby added $2,683.25 to their fund.

Only six passenger cars were available for the thousands who were eager to experience their first ride on a train. Most of the crowd rode the twenty-three flat cars provided by the railroad. The engine, "Governor Stanford", was coupled on front and the little "Pony, T. G. Judah", was harnessed on the end to give a boost from the rear.

When near Roseville, the connecting rod of the "Governor Stanford" broke but the "Pony" was stout enough to push the train the remainder of the way to Roseville where another engine was attached. But the time was not lost because one of the passengers bor-

417 J. Ross Browne, *Harpers Magazine*, june 1866.
H. H. Bancroft, *History of Nevada, Colorado & Wyoming*, p. 182-183.

rowed a gun and shot a rabbit which he immediately put up at auction. The rabbit sales produced $157.

At the picnic grove, a shooting gallery, beer, ice cream, food, and cigars enriched the Sanitary fund by hundreds of dollars. Strawberries sold from five dollars to ten dollars apiece. A dollar each was charged all those who wished to meet Dr. Bellows and in a short time his hat was heavy with silver dollars.

At two o'clock in the afternoon the train arrived from Folsom and along came Gridley with a negro carrying the now famous sack of flour. He offered the flour for sale and collected $175. However, he won much greater success at the evening meeting at Sacramento where Dr. Bellows lectured. The sack of flour was placed on a table before the speaker and the bidding was spirited. The fund was increased that evening by $2,150 and the total for the day, picnic and lecture, was $10,564.43.[418]

When Gridley arrived in San Francisco with his sack of flour, he proceeded to the Metropolitan theater where he offered it for sale. The bids ranged from five dollars to $500 and the evening's sales amounted to $2,800. Encouraged by the successful sale and resale of his flour, Gridley decided to go to New York where he achieved considerable success. The grand total for this bit of flour has been estimated at $275,000.

When Gridley returned to Austin, Nevada, he found that his business had not prospered during his absence so he went to California where he spent the last years of his short life. He died in 1870 at the age of forty-one.

He had been a great friend to the soldier but it was not until twenty years afterwards that his service received public recognition. In 1886 the Rawlins post of

[418] *Sacramento Union*, Sacramento, may 9, 28, 30, 1864.

the G.A.R., Stockton, erected a monument to Gridley. Funds were obtained by public subscription and a ten-foot marble column, surmounted by a life-size statue of Gridley with a sack of flour by his side, now marks his grave in the Rural cemetery at Stockton. An inscription bears the simple words, "The soldiers' friend".[419]

---

[419] Reuel Colt Gridley was born in Hannibal, Mo. He served in the Mexican war and in 1852, crossed the plains to California. He first lived at San Jose but later moved to Yreka, then to Oroville and at the beginning of the war he owned part interest in a store in Austin, Nev.

After his return from his travels with his sack of flour, he moved to Stockton. His next venture was that of a merchant at Paradise, Stanislaus county, where he also served as postmaster. In 1870 when the railroad was completed to Modesto, he made plans to move his store to a lot he had bought at 8th and H streets.

He died nov. 24, 1870. The following january, Mrs. Gridley moved her store and residence from Paradise to her lot in Modesto. In 1872 she built a two story brick store on her lot. She sold out and retired in 1881. Died 1910.

The Loyal and the Disloyal

Tempers rose and fists went into action when the right of free speech was flagrantly abused by some of the western newspapers. The *Visalia Equal Rights Expositor* was one of the most caustic in its attacks on President Abraham Lincoln. It referred to him as "the cadaverous, long shanked, mule-countenanced rail splitter from Illinois."

One of the first newspapers to be barred from the United States mail was the *Los Angeles Star*. For almost a year, february 1862 until january 1863, this news sheet maintained its circulation without the use of the mail facilities.

The *Visalia Equal Rights Expositor* was denied the use of the mail, september 5, 1862, along with the *Stockton Democrat, Stockton Argus, Placerville Mountain Democrat* and the *San Jose Tribune*. One paper that was completely silenced at this time was the *Democratic Register* owned and published by Joaquin Miller at Eugene, Oregon. He had bought the paper march 15, 1862, and after a brief six months' publication, he was obliged to go out of the newspaper business. The mail was reopened to all western papers january 1863.[420]

The *Visalia Equal Rights Expositor* continued its

---

[420] *War. Reb.* Ser. I, vol. L, pt. II, p. 456-457.
Ibid., pt. I, p. 895-897.
Postmaster general—Papers barred from mail.
37 Cong. 3 Sess. Sen. Ex. Doc. no. 19, 1862. (1149)
Ibid., H. Misc. Doc. no. 16, 1863. (1171)

publication though it was forbidden the use of the mail. Contributions were accepted from its sympathizers among whom were the ladies of the community who collected $300 to keep the paper alive. As an expression of appreciation the *Expositor* published a poem dedicated to the maids and matrons of Tulare.

> Their soft cheeks, how they glow when the news it doth come,
> Of all the brave deeds that our heroes hath done.
> For the cause, all they have, they would freely bestow
> And nightly they pray for old Abe's overthrow.
> Oh, may all the blessings that Heaven can spare,
> Be theirs, the brave wives and maidens of Tulare.[421]

General Wright sought to control these subversive activities by establishing Camp Babbitt near Visalia and stationing there two companies of the second cavalry under command of Captain Moses A. McLaughlin. (october 8, 1862). Apparently the presence of the troops only aggravated the "Secessionists" and they responded with keen and bitter taunts. They called the California volunteers mere hirelings of Lincoln and threatened to shoot the buttons off their uniforms. "The oath of allegiance," they said, "was just a 'gag oath'."

During dress parade at the camp (december 21, 1862) three men from Visalia rode in front of the battalion and cheered for Jeff Davis. They were promptly arrested but this only fanned the flames of the feud between the opposing political parties.[422] On Christmas eve, Captain McLaughlin asked for reenforcements as "the rebels were gathering like locusts." A week later he issued orders for the arrest of the

---

[421] *Quarterly*, California Historical society, vol. XX, p. 154-170, 1941. *The Confederate minority in California*, by Benjamin F. Gilbert in which he quotes from John Jewett Earle Thesis, U.C. Berkeley.

[422] *War. Reb.* Ser. I, vol. L, pt. II, p. 258.

owners and publishers of the *Expositor*. However, on the same day he received a telegram from headquarters with orders to release all political prisoners after they had taken the oath of allegiance. Lovick P. Hall subscribed to the oath and was released but his partner, S. J. Garrison, refused so he was held in jail until he changed his mind.[423]

The *Expositor* continued its publication and explained that the oath which the two partners had taken did not conflict with any sentiments that they had already entertained and announced that the character of their paper would undergo no change. They believed the war was wrong and promised to oppose it with all the zeal they could command.

The majority of the Californians were loyal and thousands of her young men served in the Union armies in the western states and in the East under Grant, Sheridan, Hooker and Meade. California had always been a free state as slavery was prohibited by her constitution. Then, too, this period, 1861-1865, was an era of social reform and temperance. Temperance societies boasted memberships of many thousands of young men and some of the California volunteer companies claimed that every man had signed the "pledge". The Dashaway society of San Francisco (meaning dash away the cup) included in its membership some of the most prominent pioneers. Sunday closing became a law in may 1862 and gambling was prohibited by legislative act april 27, 1863.

Nor were these the only laws passed to aid social reform. To favor the negro and assure more equal rights for him, the School law was amended to permit school trustees to provide schools for the colored chil-

---

[423] *Ibid.*, p. 264, 277.

dren when ten or more of their parents or guardians applied for such service. The expense of such schools was paid from the state school fund. An amendment to an old law passed in 1850 gave the negro the right to testify against a white man when called as a witness. (Approved april 27, 1863.)

But to curb the sudden increase in subversive activities, the public discovered that there were no laws in the California statutes that defined these activities as misdemeanors, felonies or treason and that there were no provisions made for the punishment of these offenders.

A Secret Service fund of $5,000 had been appropriated by the legislature in may 1861, a month after the beginning of hostilities, but this proved inadequate to meet the need. When the fourteenth session of the legislature met in the spring of 1863, the lawmakers speedily passed the necessary laws that would expedite the punishment of the offenders.

To prevent Southern sentiment from gaining influence through the public schools, any teachers who refused to take the oath were denied certificates to teach and furthermore no warrant could be issued to pay their salaries. Any superintendent who failed to comply with this law was liable to a fine not exceeding $500. No attorney was permitted to practice unless he pledged allegiance to the United States and a fine of $1,000 was fixed as penalty if found guilty.

Quite frequently some of the "Secessionists" would raise the flag of the Confederacy, the "bars and stars", over their places of business or a band of horsemen would dash through town with this flag flying, cheering for their favorite hero, and firing shots into the air. Occasionally shots were exchanged but usually there were no casualties.[424] Finally a law was passed, april 20, 1863, prohibiting the display of the flag of the Confederacy and the fine for such offense was placed as $300 and sixty days in jail.

After the capture of the privateer, "J. M. Chapman", in San Francisco bay, march 15, 1863, the legislature passed a law to prevent the arming and equipping of vessels for piratical purposes and fixed the penalty for such crime, imprisonment from five to twenty years or death according to the verdict of the jury. (Approved april 25, 1863.)

But in spite of the laws passed to curb subversive activities, discord and disorder continued. Some of the newspapers continued to attack Lincoln and the government. The *Visalia Equal Rights Expositor,* true to its promise, changed not one iota. However, on march 5, 1863, Hall and Garrison published their last edition. On that date they insulted the California volunteers for the last time when they called them the "California cossacks". The volunteers decided to do something about it. About nine o'clock in the evening seventy or eighty soldiers left Camp Babbitt AWOL and set out for Visalia. They broke the doors and windows of the Expositor building, threw the type, paper and ink into the street and then paraded up the main street shouting, "Where is your Secessionist paper now?" They stopped in front of the *Visalia Delta* and gave three cheers for that news sheet.

A special patrol was immediately sent into town from Camp Babbitt and the Visalia home guards were supplied with arms and ammunition to assist the troops in maintaining order. Quiet prevailed for a few months but when Sergeant Charles C. Stroble, company I,

[424] Sacramento *Daily Union,* april 2, may 16, 1863. (Huntington library).

second cavalry, California volunteers, was shot and killed by James H. Wells, a Secessionist, on august 6, 1863, the patrols were increased and the home guards again called out. Wells was not captured as his friends succeeded in aiding his escape.[425]

This was an election year and ten days after the fatal shooting, Ex-governors Downey and Weller visited Visalia and advised the Southern sympathizers to maintain peace and promised them protection if Downey were successful in the coming election september 2, 1863.[426]

Sectional strife continued in the small town of Visalia. Some of the residents seemed to indulge in the dubious practice of tit-for-tat. If the doors of the Union mens' homes were tarred and feathered by their political adversaries, the Union men in turn applied a liberal coat of tar and feathers to the Southerners' doors.

Old prejudices lingered and old hatreds smoldered to break forth again after the death of Abraham Lincoln. Four of the San Francisco newspapers, the *Democratic Press, News Letter, Occident,* and *Catholic Monitor,* were destroyed by mobs, grieved and infuriated by the death of their president.

Serious trouble between the soldiers and civilians occurred at La Paz on the Colorado in the spring of 1863. Lieutenant Hale and sixteen soldiers sailed from Fort Yuma with government stores for Fort Mojave and on the return trip, they stopped at La Paz. Just at dusk, three soldiers, who had gone ashore, were returning to the boat when they were attacked by an outlaw named Edwards, commonly known as the "Frog". He damned them for being loyal and began firing at the

---

425 *War. Reb.* Ser. I, vol. L, pt. II, p. 341-342, 558.
426 *Ibid.*, p. 572.

unarmed soldiers, killing two of them and wounding the third.[427]

A thorough search of the town was made but the "Frog" could not be found. When the incident was reported to Colonel Ferris Foreman at Drum Barracks, he offered a reward of $500 to any person who would deliver the "Frog", dead or alive, to any post in the district. He ordered the soldiers to shoot down this outlaw whenever or wherever found. For two weeks the colonel advertised his order and promise of reward in the *Los Angeles News,* june 1863.

Captain J. Ives Fitch, then stationed at Mort Mojave, ordered a detachment from his company to La Paz with instructions to capture Edwards who was alleged to be the murderer.[428] This was not the first time that young Edwards had opposed the California volunteers. He was a member of the Showalter party which was captured at Mesa Grande and confined in Fort Yuma. Although he had taken the oath of allegiance upon his release, his pledge was meaningless. Evidently his imprisonment only increased his hatred for the Union and the volunteers.[429]

There is no record available that discloses the capture and punishment of Edwards, the "Frog".

THE UNDERGROUND

While one group openly defied the newly enacted laws of the state, another group went underground. Secret organizations, known as the Knights of the Golden Circle and the Knights of the Columbian Star,

[427] Ferdinand Behn, Co. H, fourth inf.
Truston Wentworth, Co. K, fourth inf.
War. Reb. Ser. I, vol. L, pt. II, p. 460.
[428] *Ibid.,* p. 509.
[429] *Ibid.,* pt. I, p. 37.

caused the civil and military authorities considerable anxiety.

The Knights of the Golden Circle antedated the Ku-Klux Klan by more than a decade. There seems to have been but little similarity in the two organizations except that while the Golden Knights used the word *Circle* in their title, the name Ku-Klux Klan was alleged to be a deliberate corruption of the Greek word *Kyklos* meaning circle. Dr. George L. Beckley first organized the Knights of the Golden Circle in Cincinnati in 1854 for the purpose of filibustering or aiding insurrections in neighboring countries to the south of the United States.

At the beginning of the Civil war this organization championed the Southern cause and within a short time it had burrowed underground in a dozen states. One of their main objectives was to resist the draft, collect arms and ammunition and to respond for duty when called upon. The members pledged, under penalty of death, that they would divulge none of the secrets, the password or the signs.[430]

Reaching California in the early sixties, the organization was nurtured by the Southern sympathizers until they boasted that they had even infiltrated the Union League so that they could learn the plans of that patriotic body. They also enrolled in some of the companies of California volunteers. Their numbers in California have been variously estimated from a few hundred to many thousands. Like most minorities, they held the spotlight.

So secret was this organization that one member knew not what the other one did nor who he was.

---

[430] New York, New Jersey, Maryland, Ohio, Iowa, Illinois, Indiana, Michigan and Missouri.

War. Reb. Ser. III, vol. III, p. 19-20, 62-63, 66-67, 72.

Recognition of fellow-travelers was accomplished by a complicated test involving signs, grips and lengthy questionnaires. They met in private homes, barns, saloons and in the mountains. The badge of the order was a gold circle with a Saint Andrews cross in the center.

Early in the war, Colonel Clarence E. Bennett, with the aid of an accomplice and a bit of conniving, was able to secure a copy of the "pledge" and a set of resolutions explaining the motives of this underground organization. Colonel Bennett was then stationed at San Bernardino where the Knights were reported to be quite active. He forwarded the information he had obtained to General Sumner who at that time was in command of the department of the Pacific.

The Knights expressed the belief that the war had been declared by Lincoln without the consent of either branch of congress and that they, therefore, believed it to be unjust, unholy and iniquitous. They pledged themselves to support the constitution as it then stood and vowed that they would strictly adhere to the decisions of the supreme court of the United States.

They furthermore declared that they would support the Southern confederacy in all their constitutional rights; they denounced the war as unconstitutional as an attempt was being made to deprive the Southerners of their "species of property called slaves."

There pledge was indeed portentous.—"I .... here in the presence of these witnesses, before Almighty God promise and swear that I will not divulge or reveal any of the secrets of this organization to anyone except I know him to be a brother (or to instruct candidates). I furthermore swear that I will obey the proper authorities when ordered to do so, and that I will assist a brother of this institution in his rights, individually or constitutionally, when required to do so. If need be, with my life. All this I solemnly swear to obey under penalty of being shot." [431]

A new order known as the Knights of the Columbian Star gained many members in California during the last years of the war. It was alleged that the old order of the Knights of the Golden Circle controlled the new and that the officers were the same men.

The government detective, Gustav Brown, appointed several assistants and began a vigorous search for the members of this underground organization. Assistant detective Robert Robinson spent the month of august 1864 at Sacramento trying to track down some of the leaders but he reported that it was slow work as the organization was "so cloaked in secrecy that but few members really knew much about it." No large meetings were held—just a few members got together to initiate new ones.

There were three degrees. The members of the first were known as the thirty-three defenders. They pledged not to employ an abolitionist or vote for one. They were obliged to furnish a rifle, a double barrel shotgun, a revolver and a bowie knife as well as a three days' supply for a "hunt".

The second degree was numbered fifty-four and the third one, eighty-two. The pledges of the three degrees were similar but the signs and passwords varied greatly. In giving a sign, a member of the first degree might appear to be patting himself on the back while a member of the second degree would apparently pat himself on the head.

431 *Ibid.,* Ser. I, vol. L, pt. I, p. 556, aug. 6, 1861. Report of Col Bennett to Gen. E. V. Sumner.

To attract the attention of a brother of the first degree, brother number one would fumble with the third button on his coat as though buttoning it. (Orders do not specify what was done if a brother wore a two-button coat.) The brother thus challenged by the coat buttoner would respond by nonchalantly putting his left hand behind him at about waist line level. Then if duly recognized, the two members would start a quiz program.

First brother, "Do you know Jones?"
Second brother, "What Jones?"
First brother, "Preacher Jones."
Second brother, "Yes."

When fully convinced of each other's membership in the Columbian Knights, they would give the password which was spoken word by word alternately by each member. "Death to all traitors."

The greeting sign for members of the second degree involved head work. The first brother would take off his hat with his left hand and then carelessly place his right on the top of his head. The answer was the same. The next test sign required the challenger to rub his lip with forefinger and thumb. The member answering would then place his forefinger and thumb on his stomach. Then the *sacred* password was given. To give the secret grip the members would grip each others wrists instead of their hands. In addition to these there were special signs—danger signs, distress signs, signs for night use and others for horseback riders.[432]

The Knights of the Columbian Star were most active during the 1863 elections but as the Union armies won victory after victory, less and less was heard from the Knights. They and other non-Union men were most

[432] *Ibid.*, pt. II, p. 938-941, 1009, 1018-1019.

active at El Monte, San Bernardino, Los Angeles, San Luis Obispo, Mariposa, Stockton, Sacramento and San Francisco.

No doubt this underground movement gave comfort and aid to the Confederacy but the exact amount is undeterminable. The muster rolls reveal that the men of the military age group in California provided 10% of their numbers for the volunteer army of the Pacific. Surprisingly, 14.4% of the entire population of Stockton enlisted; Los Angeles county which was stigmatized as "the hotbed of secession" contributed 276 men when the city of the Angels numbered 3,854.[433]

Occasionally an over anxious citizen would call for protection from the commander of the department of the Pacific and then discover that the presence of a company of volunteers resulted in the enrollment of new recruits rather than inmates for Alcatraz.[434]

The familiar controversy over the right of free speech and press prevailed during these war years and caused the arrest of men of considerable prominence. Among them was United States Senator William McKendrie Gwin who was taken into custody by General Sumner aboard the s.s. "Orizaba" while both men were en route from California to New York. Evidence against Gwin was insufficient to warrant his detention for very long and after swearing allegiance to his country he was released. Gwin was one of California's first senators and a member of the constitutional convention.

James H. Hardy, judge of the sixteenth district, comprising the counties of Amador and Mariposa, was impeached by the legislature. Among the charges

---

[433] Census, Eighth U.S.

37 Cong. 2 Sess. H. Ex. Doc. no. 116, vol. IX. (1137)

[434] *War. Reb.* Ser. I, vol. L, pt. II, p. 993, 1013-1014.

against him were "huzzas" for Jefferson Davis; a toast, "Here's to Davis and the Confederacy;" and calling the United States flag "an old woman's rag and ought to be torn down." He was found guilty and removed from office.[435]

Another office holder who experienced an encounter with the law was Assemblyman E. J. C. Kewen from Los Angeles. He was first confined at Drum Barracks and then sent to Alcatraz for a brief time. State Senator Thomas Baker of Visalia was also temporarily deprived of his freedom.

Not even the clergy were exempt from arrest. Bishop H. H. Kavanaugh, Methodist South, discovered that the word "South" in the name of his church and some of his sermons aroused suspicions of disloyalty. Dr. William A. Scott prayed for both presidents, Davis and Lincoln, and incurred so much hostility that he resigned from his pastorate at the Calvary Presbyterian church, San Francisco, and left the state.[436]

Judge David Terry's career in California is too well known to consider the details here except to say that he eluded the soldiers on border patrol and escaped to Texas.[437]

The name-calling 1864 election campaign of C. L. Weller, chairman of the state Democratic committee, was branded as "incendiary" then but at present it would be called by another name. His arrest was ordered by the commander of the department of the

---

[435] Calif. Stats. 13 Sess., Senate and Assembly Journals, appendix, 1862. Impeachment of Judge James H. Hardy.

[436] H. H. Bancroft, *History of California*, vol. VII, p. 279, 308.
Daily Alta California, San Francisco, sept. 23, 1861; march 16, 17, 1863.
War. Reb. Ser. I, vol. L, pt. II, p. 918, 920-921.

[437] H. H. Bancroft, *History of California*, vol. VI, p. 724-725, 731-732, 735, 750-751; vol. VII, p. 225.
War. Reb. Ser. I, vol. L, pt. I, p. 490, 499-500, 621-622, 700-701.

Pacific and the orator was given time to reflect in Alcatraz. He was released on $25,000 bond and his oath of allegiance.[438]

However, General Wright was master of every situation and refused to be influenced by local prejudices. He asked the civil officers to arrest and hand over to the military authorities all persons exulting over the death of Lincoln and emphasized the fact that a military force would be sent to make arrests if the civil authority was unable to do it. To ill-advised persons he abruptly told them to attend to their own business and advised them not to try to supervise military affairs. The general furthermore announced that if he would imprison every one whose opinion differed from the federal government there would not be room enough in all the jails and forts.[439]

The general, himself, was not free from criticism which was directed against his farewell address to the people of California. The *Los Angeles News* of july 19, 1864, published a reprint from the *Marysville Appeal* as follows:

The old granny with patriotic buttons on his coat, who has been favored with distinction by the government out of respect for his gray hairs, publishes a farewell address to the people of this state.

We are so well pleased with the announcement of his retirement that our wrath at its unwarranted language is more than appeased. His allusion to the radical press is a direct insult to every Union paper in the state, although only intended for those who have been outspoken in favor of his removal.

There is no distinction in the Union press only as made by the issue whether we should have a live or petrified commander of the department of the Pacific.

But we in common with Union papers feel in too good humor at the retirement of General Wright, old fuss and feathers, to be too

---

[438] *Ibid.*, pt. II, p. 931, 940, 948.
[439] *Ibid.*, p. 1210.

severe. We are willing to attach all his faults to the ravages of time and not to any fault of the old man's heart. He departs and as we say good bye forever, sink all ill will and thoughts of his short comings.

The California legislature, by resolution, may 1861, demonstrated its loyalty to the Union and again in 1864 renewed its declaration of confidence by the endorsement of all the measures of the administration including the abolition of slavery, the confiscation act, conscription law, legal tender, suspension of the writ of habeas corpus and the plan of reconstruction.[440]

In like manner measures for the benefit of the California volunteers were passed. The soldiers were exempted from paying the annual poll tax and, in addition to their regular government salary, the legislature provided five dollars more a month. The following year, a bounty of $160 was granted. This was paid in installments of $40 at the time of enlistment and $20 at the end of each successive six month period of service. To finance these bounties $600,000 worth of 7% bonds were offered for sale. A tax of 12 cents on each $100 worth of property was levied to pay for the interest and redemption of the bonds.[441]

Having legislated for the benefit of the GI of the 1860's, the Sacramento solons did not forget the "officers of the line" as they incurred a great deal of expense

[440] Calif. Stats. 12 Sess., Senate and Assembly joint resolution no. 18, p. 686, may 17, 1861.

Calif. Stats., 14 Sess., Sen. Res. no. 1, Assembly concurring, p. 793, jan. 26, 1863.

Calif. Stats., 15 Sess., Res. no. 15, p. 546-547, jan. 20, 1864.

War. Reb. Ser. I, vol. L, pt. II, p. 756.

[441] Calif. Stats. 14 Sess., chap. 414, p. 662-666, april 27, 1863.

Calif. Stats. 15 Sess., chap. 177, p. 172, march 15, 1864.

Calif. Stats. 13 Sess., p. 205-208, april 12, 1862.

Calif. Stats. 15 Sess., chap. 71, p. 73, feb. 10, 1864.

Calif. Stats., 15 Sess., chap. 442, p. 486-491, april 4, 1864.

War. Reb. Ser. I, vol. L, pt. II, p. 526.

before their companies were mustered in and allowed to draw their pay from the government. Some of the cost was met by private subscription and the rest from the officers' private funds. In recognition of this situation, the legislature appropriated $65,000 so that each and every line officer would receive the same pay and allowances as that received by the federal officers of the same rank then serving in California. This pay was only for the time intervening between the date of receiving their commissions and being mustered in when they would receive their government pay. Five hundred dollar bonds bearing interest at seven per cent were sold to provide the necessary funds.[442]

Although California did not approve of the Legal Tender act, she occasionally managed to profit by its enactment. The legislature passed an act which provided that the sum of $24,260, which had been saved by the exchange of gold for legal tender in payment of the Federal War tax assessed against California, be used as a Military Recruiting fund.

Each company was allotted $898.51. The seven companies, then being recruited to replace those whose term had expired in the first cavalry received $6,289.60. The allowances for the new regiment and battalions were, sixth infantry, $8,985.15; first battalion mountaineers, $5,391.09; and the California native cavalry, $3,594.16.[443]

The legal tender act proved to be a great hardship for the volunteers who were paid in "paper" which they were obliged to exchange for specie at a discount. Their thirteen dollars a month shriveled. General Wright complained that he did not have enough to pay

442 Calif. Stats. 15 Sess., chap. 377, p. 424-427, april 4, 1864.
443 Calif. Stats. 14 Sess., chap. 187, p. 246, april 10, 1863.
U. S. Stats. at Large XII, p. 296-297, 345. (Legal Tender act.)

the board for his wife and himself. He said that he had received orders from Washington to pay the troops half in gold and half in notes but that the order was revoked the following day.[444]

The medical director reported that it was impossible to hire physicians unless authorized to raise their salary to $125 or $150 or gold in equivalent. The contract physicians were then paid $50 a month for a daily visit to the army hospitals.[445]

Again the legislature came to the aid of her volunteers. A resolution was introduced in the assembly to petition congress to raise the pay of the soldiers 30%. The federal lawmakers ignored the suggestion. There were persistent members in the California legislature during the 1860's so another resolution was formulated to ask congress to exempt California from the operation of the Legal Tender law because the state constitution recognized a metallic currency only. The resolution did not receive sufficient support and was rejected.[446]

The Specific Contract act or California "gold law" recognized both notes and specie as lawful money and permitted the people to enter into a contract which stated the *kind of money* by which the obligations would be paid. The court was to enforce such a contract.[447]

The fight began! The paper men called the act the "Shylock" law. The specie advocates swore that the law was unconstitutional. Secretary of the treasury, Salmon P. Chase, said, "I am clearly of the opinion

444 *War. Reb.* Ser. I, vol. L, pt. II, p. 925-926, 303.

445 *Ibid.*, p. 1191.

446 Calif. Stats. 14 Sess., Assembly journal p. 208, feb. 12, 1863.
Calif. Stats. 15 Sess., Sen. and Assembly Res. no. 30, p. 553, april 1, 1864.
Calif. Stats. 15 Sess., Sen. journal p. 287, 1864.

447 Calif. Stats. 14 Sess., chap. 421, p. 687-691, april 27, 1863.
Calif. Stats. 15 Sess., Sen. journal p. 285, feb. 1864.

that the California law is against the national policy
and I shall be much gratified to see that state declare
herself in favor of the currency for the whole people
by its repeal."

The volunteers petitioned the legislature to repeal
the Specific Contract act but without success. The paper
men of both houses could not rally enough support to
defeat the measure and a dual currency remained in
use until the close of the war.

California was not alone in her dilemma of a dual
currency. At Salt Lake, General Connor was called
upon to use his diplomacy to the utmost to control the
unrest and dissatisfaction in the Mormon colony.

The *Deseret News* published a criticism about legal
tender. "Mechanics, laborers, producers and all concerned will understand at a glance that we deem greenbacks the most uncertain in value of all commodities
in their possession and we trust will govern themselves
accordingly lest, though retiring at night with pockets
overflowing with currency, they awake bankrupt."

Nevada also experienced the depressing effect of the
deflated currency and the legislature passed a specific
contract act similar to that of California but Governor
Nye refused to sign it.[448]

California's answer to conscription was to furnish
more volunteers after than *before* the Conscription act
was passed by congress. Three new regiments of infantry, sixth, seventh and eighth, were mustered in and a
fourth, the ninth, was ordered but not enrolled. In
addition to the infantry regiments, the first battalion
mountaineers, six companies, and first battalion native
California cavalry, four companies, were mustered in.
The old regiments were filled up by re-enlistments and

---

[448] *War. Reb.* Ser. I, vol. L, pt. II, p. 889, 893-894, 899, 904, 914.

new recruits. The approximate number enrolled in California before the draft was 7,451 and afterward, 10,000 men, which would make the total 17,000.

Furthermore, the extra five dollars pay allowed the volunteers by legislative act did not apply to any one in California who might be drafted or serve as a substitute for a draftee.

California was not alone among the western states who could prove that their men did not need to be drafted. Governor James W. Nye of Nevada telegraphed the secretary of war to offer a full company of volunteers who would pay all their own expenses from Carson City to New York. Addison C. Gibbs, governor of Oregon, also offered a company of cavalry. The reply from the war department was emphatic—"We do not want to bring troops from the Pacific coast." In the first year of the war, California learned that the war department would not accept volunteers from the Pacific coast. The offers of the second and third regiments and a number of individual companies were refused. The only ones permitted to serve on the eastern front were the five companies that were enrolled in the second Massachusetts cavalry.[449]

---

[449] *Ibid.*, p. 133, 660, 662, 946-947, 949, 1105, 1191, 1208.
Ibid., pt. I, p. 750 (dec. 6, 1861).

Peace

When peace came to the eastern front, unrest entered the camps on the western frontier. The California volunteers impatiently awaited their discharge and return home but they were obliged to remain on duty until the "regulars" arrived from the East.

Opinions were divided as to whether the volunteers should be discharged in the state or territory where they were serving or whether they should be returned to California for mustering out. General Carleton explained to the war department, Washington, D.C., that many of the volunteers had expressed a desire to remain and that they should be allowed to stay if they preferred to do so.

The general further explained:

To compel these men to return over the same desert against their wishes merely to be discharged in California does not seem advisable. Besides we are embarrassed for want of necessary transportation for such movement. Therefore, I beg that they may be discharged here and that necessary funds be sent at once with which to pay them their dues.

Political reasons connected with filling up these rich mineral lands by a hardy population of experienced miners and trained soldiers, who at any time can be called upon to defend the country, whether against the savage within or rebels without its borders, should have great weight with the government.

Such timely forecast will give an impetus to Arizona and New Mexico which will not only be felt by these territories but by the United States at large. For it is to such men that the country must look for the speedy development of the precious metals, now so greatly needed. . . I beg again to urge upon your serious attention the defenseless condition in which this department will be when these troops have been discharged.[450]

The boys came home as their letters testify but congress was slow to act. It was march 1867 when an act was finally passed to pay for the transportation of California and Nevada volunteers to the place of enlistment, such proportionate sum according to distance traveled as had been paid to the troops of the other states similarly situated.[451]

One of the volunteers explains "marching orders":

We have not yet had orders to march or even to get ready to march, although the almost certain prospect is that those of us who are on foot, about forty in number, will start today. Instead of getting the order to march at a certain time, we shall at some time receive the information in some round about way that once upon a time we marched. Things lie around in astonishing profusion and the quarters of company A (first cavalry) look like the last rose of summer.

The last detachment under command of the captain will leave here probably next monday. The lieutenants go with us. Company A feels well, you bet. Whiskey suffered yesterday as it was necessary to offer a sacrifice. Our "pow-wow" is over and we are preparing to "git".[452]

When the volunteers mustered out they received "terminal pay" which had been provided by a special relief fund appropriated by the state legislature, april 27, 1863. According to this act the soldiers received five dollars a month additional to that allowed by the government but this amount was not paid until their honorable discharge. This extra pay was not allowed to any soldier who might be drafted or enlisted as a substitute into the service of the United States. An amend-

[450] 39 Cong. 1 Sess. H. Ex. Doc. no. 138, vol. XVI. (1267)
[451] 40 Cong. 2 Sess. H. Ex. Doc. no. 24, vol. VII, march 2, 1867. (1330)
[452] *Butte Record*, Oroville, april 28, 1866. Letter written at Fort Whipple, march 20, 1866, by W. Y. Bliss, Co. A, first cavalry.

ment passed the next year provided that in case of the death of any soldier, his next of kin would receive the money accrued. Married men were permitted to allot all or part of their monthly "bonuses" to their families during service.

War surplus property plagued the debt ridden government at the close of the war and in spite of all honest efforts to dispose of the firearms, a very small amount was realized from the sales. Hall's old Flintlocks, a thousand of them, sold for $2.25 apiece; French muskets, $1.00 to $1.30; and the Austrian, Prussian, Belgian and Dresden muskets brought about the same price.

American arms brought a higher bid. The top price realized for the Springfield musket was $15.00; Whitney rifles were also valued at $15.00 each; Sharps carbine sold for $5.00; and Colt revolver from $6.00 to $8.00.

Pack saddles seemed to bring a higher price than any other type of saddle, selling for $26.00. Scrap iron was offered for $1\frac{1}{2}$ cents a pound; wrought iron 2 cents; brass $16\frac{1}{2}$ cents and copper $21\frac{1}{2}$ cents.

The volunteers themselves were sold short. There were no GI loans for home building and it was not until seven years after the close of the war that the homestead law was amended to aid the veterans to more speedily acquire a homestead. This act was known as the soldiers' homestead.

It provided that any veteran could have the term of his service, not exceeding four years, deducted from the period of five years residence required under the homestead law. It furthermore provided that the veteran must have served for at least ninety days in the United States army or navy, received his honorable discharge and remained loyal to the government. All were required to live one year on their homesteads and to cultivate and improve them before receiving full title to their land.[453]

No provision had been made for the veterans' employment when they returned, although it was recommended that they seek political offices. A few of them did and creditably served their public. However, in 1891, thirty years after the volunteers enrolled, the legislature passed a veterans' employment act which provided for preferential hiring of honorably discharged Union soldiers, sailors and marines in every state department, public works, offices and all positions of trust or profit in the state. The law furthermore provided that age, loss of limb or other physical impairment, which did not incapacitate, should not disqualify the veterans. No doubt, many of the veterans were too old to work by that time.[454]

Although a national home was established for disabled veterans, march 1865, it failed to meet the need of thousands. Pensions were incredibly small. Even twenty-five years after the close of the war, the pension was but $12.00 a month for those who were unable to perform manual labor to earn their living. A widow was allowed $8.00 a month and an additional $2.00 for each child under sixteen years.

An act to provide for the building and furnishing

---

[453] 42 Cong. 2 Sess. H. Ex. Doc. no. 89 (report for 1871) (1511). Revised Statutes, appendix number one. (2305)

Circular from the General Land Office showing manner of proceeding to obtain title to public lands under the homestead, desert land and other laws, issued january 25, 1904, Government printing office, Washington, D.C., p. 21-24.

42 Cong. 2 Sess. Sen. Misc. Doc. no. 157, vol. II, 1872. (1482)

[454] Calif. Stats. 29 Sess. chap. 212, Assembly bill no. 455, p. 289, march 31, 1891.

of the California Home for Soldiers' Widows and
Orphans and for Army Nurses was passed in 1889 and
the sum of $25,000 appropriated for that purpose. A
two-year continuous residence was required before
admission to the Widows' home would be granted. By
act of congress, august 27, 1888, all states and territories
which had established homes for disabled soldiers and
sailors were allotted $100 a year for each veteran
in such homes. $250,000 was appropriated for that
purpose.

The following year the California state legislature
passed an act to provide for the burial of indigent
ex-Union soldiers, sailors, and marines in California.
Only $50 was allowed for this purpose and that was to
be paid for by the county in which the veterans lived.[455]

Congress also passed an act to mark all the graves of
the soldiers with a suitable headstone. No doubt, it was
then too late, 1888, to locate many of them after a lapse
of a quarter of a century. Many of the graves are unmarked today although the names of these California
volunteers are in the *Roll of Honor* published by the
government printing office, Washington, D.C.

More than five hundred of the young volunteers from
California lie buried either on the field where they fell
or at the many old army posts in all the western states
where they made their last stand. This number does
not include those who died during their service in the
East.[456]

---

[455] Calif. Stats. 28 Sess. chap. 161, Assembly bill no. 50, p. 198, march 15,
1889.

Ibid., chap. 173, Assembly bill no. 604, p. 206-208.

51 Cong. 1 Sess. H. Misc. Doc. no. 77, jan. 1890, vol. IX. (2768)

[456] *Roll of Honor,* Quartermaster general's office, Government printing
office, Washington, D.C., 1867.

Deaths at Calif. Forts, vol. VIII, p. 60; vol. XII, p. 170-173.

Ariz., *Ibid.*, vol. XII, p. 168-173; vol. VIII, p. 119-120.

The veteran commander of the department of the Pacific, through nearly all the trying war years, was one of the many who lost his life. It was july 27, 1865, when General George Wright, with his wife, sailed from San Francisco aboard the s.s. "Brother Jonathan" for Fort Vancouver to assume command of the newly created department of the Columbia. But on the second day of the voyage he was drowned in the wreck of the steamer off the coast near Crescent City, California.

Emory Wing, company C, sixth infantry, California volunteers, was stationed at Camp Lincoln near Crescent City at the time. His letter of august 1, 1865, describes the wreck.

Our flag has been at half-mast yesterday and today for the loss of the Steamship "Brother Jonathan" which was wrecked off the coast near here. . . The vessel left San Francisco on friday, july 27, bound for Portland and Victoria with two hundred fifty passengers, a crew of fifty, and a full load of freight.

They had fair weather friday, but on saturday it began to blow from the northwest and increased to a gale at night. On sunday morning the vessel changed her course nearer the coast in order to

New Mex., *Ibid.*, vol. VIII, p. 121.

Utah, *Ibid.*, vol. XIII, p. 134.

Wyo., *Ibid.*, vol. XII, p. 167.

Idaho, *Ibid.*, vol. VIII, p. 1201.

Wash., *Ibid.*, vol. VIII, p. 126.

Partial list of burials on the field and army posts:

Calif.—Fort Humboldt 11; Fort Gaston 8; Camp Anderson 4; Drum Barracks 26; Fort Yuma 23; Presidio, S.F. 19; Camp Independence 8; Benicia Barracks 19; San Diego 7; Camp Wright, Oak Grove 3; Fort Wright 2.

New Mex.—Fort Craig 19; Fort Sumner 3; Fort Bascom 3; Santa Fe 4; Los Pinos 6; Fort McRae 6; others at Forts Selden, Wingate and Stanton.

Ariz.—Fort Mason 32; Fort Goodwin 12; Tucson 20 (13 marked unknown); Fort Bowie 7; Fort McDowell 6; Picacho 3; others at Fort Mojave, Fort Whipple and temporary camps.

Utah—Camp Douglas 59.

Nev.—Fort Ruby 6; Fort Churchill 6.

Wyo.—Fort Bridger 5.

Idaho—Fort Boise 5; Fort Lapwai 3.

Wash.—Fort Vancouver 5.

escape the heavy seas. When she sighted land and found the seas still rough, she again changed her course toward Crescent City.

Then she struck on a rock and knocked the whole keel off. The swell of the sea raised her bow clear of the rock and then set dead down. . . At this time two guns were fired in quick succession, and a life-boat cleared the ship and came ashore.

The next sea carried the "Brother Jonathan" clear over the rock and her bow went down. The last that was seen of the vessel was her stern, standing straight up in the air. In twenty minutes after striking, everything had gone to eternity.

Nineteen passengers were saved in the only boat that reached the shore. . . A second boat was lowered with about thirty ladies but was upset almost as quick as it touched water. Another boat was swamped under the guards. Then the crew and passengers seemed to become paralyzed and quit trying to save themselves.

Captain De Wolf walked his quarter deck to the last, as cool as if just going to a safe harbor instead of that port whence none return.

General George Wright, his staff and family were on board. The general stood on the quarter deck with the captain as the ship went down. Boats have been out from Crescent City ever since, and people have patrolled the beach for miles up and down, but up to five o'clock this afternoon, nothing, not even a stick of the ill-fated ship has been seen. Fires have been kept burning after night and guns have been fired every hour as signals to those who were out of sight of land. . .

Most of the passengers were in their berths, more or less seasick. One lady who was saved had about as much clothing as Mother Eve before her fall. One of the sailors gave her a pair of pants and a jacket. The survivors were well provided for by the citizens of Crescent City and everything was done that possibly could be to relieve any and every want.[457]

The sea was reluctant to give up its victims. Six weeks later, General Wright's body was recovered at Bay Flat near Shelter Cove, Mendocino county. Funeral services for General and Mrs. Wright were held at San Francisco, october 21. The bodies were then carried by steamer to Sacramento, where they lay

[457] *Weekly Union Record*, Oroville, Butte county, aug. 12, 1865, p. 3, Col. 2-3.

in state in the senate chamber until the military funeral was held at the First Congregational church on Sixth street.

At the old City cemetery, which was donated to Sacramento in 1850 by John A. Sutter, a tall marble shaft marks the resting place of this valiant general and his wife. Here, too, lies his soldier son, Colonel Thomas F. Wright, who was killed in the Modoc war, april 26, 1873.

At the sixteenth session of the state legislature a bill was introduced to authorize an appropriation of $5,000 for the purpose of erecting a monument to General George Wright in the state burial ground. This bill failed to carry and another one was presented at the seventeenth session. The finance committee failed to recommend its passage. Finally Judge Samuel Cross, a relative of General Wright, sponsored an act to permit him to build the monument in the state burial ground. The monument now stands in the Cross family plot and was, no doubt, erected by Judge Cross as there is no record of the legislature having passed a bill for its erection.[458]

The volunteers served without due recognition from their contemporaries; without fan-fare then or since; without adequate pay, medical attention, shelter, food or transportation. Yet it was as great a sacrifice to give one's life in the defense of the western part of the nation as in any other section.

Campaigning in the West was equally as hazardous as in the East. Often the infantrymen were ordered to pursue Indians mounted on tough mustangs. Poorly shod and foot-sore, these soldiers marched hundreds of

[458] Calif. Stats., 16 Sess., Senate bill no. 57—1866.
 Ibid., 16 Sess., Assembly bill no. 153—1866.
 Ibid., 17 Sess., Senate bill no. 389—1868.

miles over the desert without enough water. They plowed their way through snowdrifts until their feet were frozen. They swam the rivers, dodging the broken ice that cut the flesh. Many were drowned in the rivers from the Columbia on the north to the Rio Grande on the southwest; and on the coast, from Humboldt bay to San Diego. The fatalities from arrow wounds were far greater than from bullets—fully sixty per cent of the arrow wounds proved fatal.

Although the service on the western frontier, 1861-1866 has not been publicized during the intervening years, it was then recognized by congress and the general public. The first medal of honor (army) was awarded for distinguished and heroic service on the southwestern frontier. Colonel Bernard J. D. Irwin, medical director, received the award for rescuing sixty men of the seventh U.S. infantry who were trapped in the Chiricahua mountains, Arizona, by Cochise's band of Indians, february 14, 1861. This award focused attention on the soldier so that regardless of the time or place of his heroism, as long as he was offering his life for the protection of his country he deserved to be honored.[459]

Not all the tasks were fighting. They protected and fed the Indians more often than they fought them. The general policy was to remove the Indians from situations detrimental to their peace and general welfare. They were placed on government reservations where they could be taught a better way of life. Unfortunately this ideal has not yet been fully attained.

The volunteers served for but an interlude; they gave their services without a draft; and as Hiram Tuttle,

[459] *Medals of honor of the United States army,* public information division, u.s. printing office 1948.

company K, third infantry, recorded on the last page of his diary, ". . . By losing their lives gave freedom to the thousands of travelers who seek new homes amid the western wilderness."

Bibliography

Bibliography

Manuscripts

AYERS, EDWARD EVERETT. Reminiscences of the far west and other trips. 1861-1918. (Bancroft library, Univ. of Calif.)
> Many interesting experiences as a member of company E, first cavalry, California volunteers, serving in Arizona and New Mexico.

AYERS, JOHN. A Soldier's experience in New Mexico.
> A member of company D, first cavalry, California volunteers, enrolled at Marysville and served for three years. This company enrolled at Marysville maintained a fine three-year record in Arizona, Texas and New Mexico.

BANCROFT, H. H. New Mexican Scraps. (Bancroft library, Univ. of Calif.)
> A collection of news clippings from the early newspapers.

BIDWELL, JOHN. Collection of letters and papers. (Calif. State library)
> Much valuable information is found in this collection.

CHIVINGTON, COL. J. M. Battle of Apache Pass. (Bancroft library, Univ. of Calif.)
> Description of destruction of Sibley's train.

CORNELIUS, THOMAS R. Military Protection of Oregon, Washington and Idaho during the American Civil War Period. 442 pieces. (Huntington library)
> Military correspondence of Cornelius, J. Rinearson, John T. Apperson and other military personnel. Accounts and records of the old military posts. cs 18, 89-92, 95, 151, 156, 158, 166, 171, 174-175, 303, 308, 335, 444, 114.

DAGGETT, JOHN. Daggett Scrap Book. (Calif. State library)
> Newspaper clippings relating to California pioneers.

ELLISON, SAMUEL. History of New Mexico. (Bancroft library, Univ. of Calif.)
> Description of governor's palace and Santa Fe in early sixties.

GILLESPIE, GEORGE A. Several Civil war documents and some relating to the California volunteers. (Huntington library)

HAYES, BENJAMIN IGNATIUS. Scrap Book. (Bancroft library, Univ. of Calif.)

> Judge Hayes' trips through San Diego county and his meeting with the California volunteers at Camp Wright, Oak Grove station.

LIPPITT, FRANCIS J. Co. 2nd. Inf. C.V., Fort Humboldt, California, october 12, 1862, to President Abraham Lincoln. MS (HM 23699) (Huntington library)

McCLEAVE, WILLIAM A. Letters and papers of experiences in Indian wars of the west. (Bancroft library, Univ. of Calif.)

> Loaned to Bancroft library by his son, Dr. Thomas C. McCleave.

OLD BLOTTERS, Account books, Fort Bridger, december 17, 1862 to september 22, 1865. (Bancroft library, Univ. of Calif.)

> Contains a wide range of purchases and prices.

READING, PIERSON BARTON, Biography of, by his daughter Alice M. Reading. (Calif. State library)

RITCH, WILLIAM GILLET. (Huntington library)

Military correspondence, 1861 to 1866 with the civil authorities. RI 1346, 1358, 1409, 1187, 1268, 1254, 1293, 1253.

Oaths of allegiance of civilians and military officers. RI 1200, 1390, 1418, 1444, 1567, 1453.

Gambling and liquor licenses: RI 1220, 1251.

Correspondence between U.S. military officers and Reuben Creel, U.S. counsul at Chihuahua: RI 1258.

Diary of member of company B, New Mexico infantry, under command of Col. C. Carson, august 4-28, 1863: RI 1513.

Memorial to congress from New Mexican legislature regarding General Carleton *et al* claim to portion of Rio Grande grant. RI 1580.

STEARNS, ABEL. Letter from Colonel James H. Carleton to Stearns, august 22, 1861, regarding use of dried beef for California volunteers. (Huntington library)

TUTTLE, HIRAM SINCLAIR. Company K, third regiment infantry, California volunteers, Diary of trip from Benicia to Salt Lake and return, battle of Bear river, escort duty, Mormons, etc. 1862-1865. In possession of his son, H. A. Tuttle, Oakland.

WILSON, BENJAMIN D. Correspondence between Phineas Banning and Benjamin D. Wilson regarding Drum Barracks, Wilmington, january 15; february 4, 13, 19; april 15; may 8, 1873. (Huntington library)

WYCKOFF, CHARLES A. Roster and Journal of company C, seventh

Wyckoff, Chas. A., continued.
infantry, California volunteers, august 13, 1865—march 16, 1866. (Fort Sutter Museum, Sacramento) Presented by Al Wyckoff, Santa Barbara.

United States Government Documents

CALIFORNIA

36 CONG., 2 sess., sen. ex. doc. no. 1, p. 209, vol. II, june 20, 1860. serial 1079.
> Number of federal troops in department of the Pacific placed at 12,984.

37 CONG., 1 sess., ho. misc. doc. no. 20, vol. I, july 19, 1861. serial 1115.
> Volunteer Employment act; pay of volunteers should be same as regular army; that 40c a day allowance for use of a horse furnished by the volunteer.

37 CONG., 2 sess., ho. misc. doc. no. 31, vol. I, january 16, 1862. serial 1141.
> A memorial of 242 negroes in California, petitioning congress to provide means for colonization.

38 CONG., 2 sess., ho. ex. doc. no. 77, vol. XIII, february 28, 1865. serial 1229.
> Report from Stanton regarding the reason the draft was not enforced in Calif.

39 CONG., 1 sess., sen. ex. doc. no. 17, vol. I. serial 1237.
> Passage of u.s. troops through Mexico, 1861.

39 CONG., 1 sess., ho. ex. doc. no. 138, vol. XVI. serial 1267.
> Discharge of California volunteers in Utah, New Mexico and Arizona; payment of mileage to place of enrollment, and retaining of their arms.

40 CONG., 2 sess., ho. ex. doc. no. 24, vol. VII, march 1867. serial 1330.
> Discharge and mileage paid.

40 CONG., 3 sess., ho. misc. doc. no. 54, vol. I, 1868. serial 1385.
> Report of the National Asylum for disabled volunteer soldiers.

51 CONG., 1 sess., ho. misc. doc. no. 77, vol. IX, january 23, 1890. serial 2768.
> National home for disabled volunteer soldiers.

51 CONG., 1 sess., ho. misc. doc. no. 122, vol. IX, february 27, 1890. serial 2768.
> A resolution of inquiry regarding pensions.

PACIFIC COAST DEFENSE

32 CONG., 1 sess., sen. ex. doc. no. 28, vol. VI, 1851-1852. serial 617.
> Lighthouse board recommendations for Pacific coast.

32 CONG., I sess. sen. ex. doc. no. 29, vol. VII, february 1852. serial
618.

Fortifications at San Francisco; estimate for commencement—not less
than $500,000.

32 CONG., 2 sess., sen. ex. doc. no. 42, vol. VII, february 1853. serial
665.

Defense of San Francisco.

33 CONG., I sess., sen. ex. doc. no. 52, vol. VIII, march 1854. serial
698.

California defense of western rivers and harbors.

33 CONG., I sess., ho. ex. doc. no. 113, vol. XIV, june 1854. serial
727.

Further appropriations for lighthouses on Pacific coast.

33 CONG., 2 sess., sen. ex. doc. no. 24, vol. VI, january 1855. serial
751.

Work on San Francisco harbor fortifications.

34 CONG., I sess., sen. ex. doc. no. I, vol. II, part 2, p. 571-572. 1855-
1856. serial 811.

Report of secretary of war regarding Benecia Arsenal.

34 CONG., I sess., sen. misc. doc. no. 10, vol. I, 1855. serial 835.

California request for lighthouses for Crescent City and Trinidad.

35 CONG., 2 sess., ho. ex. doc. no. 65, vol. VII, 1859. serial 1006.

Sites for defense of the north-west coast.

35 CONG., 2 sess., ho. misc. doc. no. 13, vol. I, 1859. serial 1016.

Appropriations for defense of San Diego and San Pedro.

36 CONG., I sess., sen. ex. doc. no. 3, vol. V, p. 286-297, 1860. serial
1027.

Shubrick report on lighthouses of Pacific coast.

36 CONG., 2 sess., sen. ex. doc. no. I, vol. II, p. 253-291, 1859-1860.
serial 1079.

Report of De Russy on Pacific coast fortifications.

37 CONG., 2 sess., sen. ex. doc. no. I, vol. II, p. 32-38, 1861-1862.
serial 1118.

Fortification of Fort Point and Alcatraz.

37 CONG., 2 sess., sen. ex. doc. no. I, vol. III, part I, 1861. serial
1119.

Fortifications at San Francisco.

40 CONG., 2 sess., sen. ex. doc. no. 11, vol. I, 1867-1868. serial 1316.

Controversy between Fremont, Haskell & company and U.S. regarding
the ownership of Point San Jose.

40 CONG., 2 sess., sen. misc. doc. no. 37, vol. I, part 2, 1867-1868.
serial 1319.

Yerba Buena Island and military defense.

42 Cong., 2 sess., sen. misc. doc. no. 161, vol. II, 1871-1872. serial 1482.

California request for the defense of San Diego.

General James H. Carleton

33 Cong., 2 sess., ho. ex. doc. no. 1, p. 33-37, vol. I, part 2, june 1854. serial 778.

Carleton with expedition from Fort Leavenworth to Rocky mountains.

33 Cong., 2 sess., ho. misc. doc. no. 37, p. 296-316, vol. I. Ninth report, Smithsonian Institution, 1855. serial 807.

Carleton's description of ruins of Gran Quivira; recommends pass of Abo for railroad.

36 Cong., 1 sess., sen. ex. doc. no. 42, vol. XI. serial 1033.

Findings of Carleton, who investigated Mountain Meadow massacre.

37 Cong., 3 sess., sen. rept. no. 106, vol. I, february 1863. serial 1151.

Damage to Carleton's property in Albuquerque by Union troops.

39 Cong., 2 sess., ho. misc. doc. no. 16, vol. I, january 1867. serial 1302.

New Mexico protest against acquisition of a portion of Rio Grande Grant by General Carleton et al.

40 Cong., 2 sess., ho. misc. doc. no. 97, vol. II, march 1868. serial 1350.

Confirmation of Rio Grande Grant to Jose Mirabel et al.

42 Cong., 2 sess., ho. misc. doc. no. 181, vol. III, april 1872. serial 1526.

Transcripts of papers, 1795 to 1872, supporting claim of Mirabel.

42 Cong., 3 sess., sen. rept. no. 441, february 1873, vol. I. serial 1548.

Favorable report on Carleton's claim for property damage.

Arizona and New Mexico

37 Cong., 2 sess., ho. ex. doc. no. 11, vol. I, december 1861. serial 1127.

Surrender of Fort Fillmore to the Confederate army.

37 Cong., spec. sess., sen. ex. doc. no. 1, vol. V, maps IVA, IV. serial 1160.

Report from John A. Clark, surveyor general office, Santa Fe.

38 Cong., 1 sess., sen. ex. doc. no. 49, vol. I, june 1864. serial 1176.

Regarding the seizure of Mowry mine, Arizona.

38 Cong., 2 sess., sen. ex. doc. nos. 17, 31, vol. I, february 1865. serial 1209.

Expense of transporting supplies from Fort Leavenworth to the West.

39 Cong., 1 sess., sen. misc. doc. no. 61, vol. I, february 1866. serial 1239.

Resolution by Arizona on termination of the war.

39 Cong., 2 sess., ho. misc. doc. no. 24, vol. I, january 1867. serial 1302.

Proceedings by which town site of Prescott was acquired.

Indian Affairs

31 Cong., 1 sess., ho. ex. doc. no. 17, vol. v. serial 573.

Early report of conditions in Calif. and New Mex.; need of Indians.

33 Cong., 2 sess., sen. ex. doc. no. 78, p. 85, vol. III. serial 760.

Vocabulary of Indians of Southwest.

35 Cong., 1 sess., ho. ex. doc. no. 2, vol. II, part I, p. 561-593, 1858.

Reports on Indians of New Mex. by Carson, Mowry and Collins. serial 942.

35 Cong., 1 sess., ho. ex. doc. nos. 38, 39, 45, vol. IX, 1858. serial 955.

Report of Browne regarding Indians of Wash. and Ore.

35 Cong., 2 sess., sen. ex. doc. no. 32, vol. x, 1859. serial 984.

Wright's campaign against the northern Indians, by John Mullen; with maps.

36 Cong., 2 sess., ho. ex. doc. no. 29, vol. vi, january 1861. serial 1097.

Report on Indians in Oregon.

36 Cong., 2 sess., ho. ex. doc. nos. 24, 31, 33, vol. vi, january 1861. serial 1097.

Indians of New Mexico and Arizona.

36 Cong., 2 sess., ho. ex. doc. no. 46, vol. viii, january 1861. serial 1099.

Massacre of emigrants by Snake River Indians.

36 Cong., 2 sess., ho. ex. doc. no. 52, vol. ix, 1861. serial 1100.

Appeal for relief of destitute Indians.

37 Cong., 2 sess., sen. ex. doc. no. 1, vol. I, p. 624-831. serial 1117.

Summary of report on western Indians by William P. Dole, 1861.

37 Cong., 3 sess., ho. ex. doc. no. 50, vol. II, 1862. serial 1157.

Conditions resulting from occupation of Ariz. and New Mex. by Confederate troops.

38 Cong., 1 sess., sen. misc. doc. no. 127, vol. I, 1864. serial 1177.

Relative to proposed treaty with Indians of Oregon.

38 Cong., 1 sess., ho. ex. doc. nos. 1, 41, 42, vol. III, 1863. serial 1182.

Troubles with the Navajos treaties.

38 Cong., 1 sess., ho. ex. doc. no. 38, vol. ix, 1864. serial 1189.

Condition of Indians in New Mexico.

38 Cong., 1 sess., ho. misc. doc. no. 29, vol. III, 1864. serial 1200.
California petition to move Indians to reservations.

38 Cong., 2 sess., ho. ex. doc. no. 1, vol. V, december 1864. serial
1220.
Condition of Indians of the West.

38 Cong., 2 sess., ho. ex. doc. no. 47, vol. VIII, february 1865. serial
1223.
Request for appropriation for medals for Indian chiefs.

38 Cong., 2 sess., ho. misc. doc. no. 16, vol. I, january 1865. serial
1232.
Indians in Arizona.

39 Cong., 1 sess., ho. ex. doc. no. 1, vol. II, 1865. serial 1248.
Condition of western Indians.

40 Cong., 2 sess., ho. ex. doc. no. 200, vol. XV, march 1868. serial
1341.
Appropriation for Indians of California, 1860 to 1867.

40 Cong., 2 sess., ho. ex. doc. no. 248, vol. XV, 1868. serial 1341,
An agricultural report for Bosque Redondo 1867.

Mexican Affairs

29 Cong., 2 sess., ho. ex. doc. no. 119, vol. IV, august 1846. serial
500.
Gen. Taylor mentions Gen. P. Edward Connor as one of the Texas
rangers.

37 Cong., 2 sess., ho. ex. doc. no. 100, vol. VIII, april 14, 1862. serial
1136.
Foreign powers invading Mexico.

37 Cong., 3 sess., ho. ex. doc. no. 1, vol. I; no. 23, vol V; no. 54, vol.
VI, dec. 1862—mar. 1863. serial 1156, 1161, 1162.
Correspondence concerning the u.s. foreign relations (Mexico).

37 Cong., spec. sess., sen. ex. doc. no. 1, vol. I. serial 1174.
Survey from Tucson to the Gulf of California by Maj. David Ferguson,
1862.

38 Cong., 2 sess., sen. ex. doc. no. 11, vol. I, june 1864. serial 1209.
President Lincoln's message on Mexican affairs.

39 Cong., 1 sess., sen. ex. doc. no. 6, vol. I, january 1866. serial 1237.
The French occupation of Mexico.

39 Cong., 1 sess., sen. ex. doc. no. 17, vol. I, 1865-1866. serial 1237.
Transit of u.s. troops through Mexico.

39 Cong., 1 sess., ho. ex. docs. nos. 13, 20, 31, vol. VII. serial 1255.
Seward's report on the reign of Maximilian in Mexico.

39 Cong., 1 sess., ho. ex. doc. no. 93, vol. XII, feb. 1866. serial 1263.
u.s. recognizes only Republic of Mexico under Juarez; and adheres to
non-intervention policy.

39 CONG., 1 sess., ho. ex. doc. no. 137, vol. XVI, june 1866. serial 1267.

Correspondence between U.S. and Mexico.

39 CONG., 2 sess., ho. ex. doc. no. 8, vol. V, 1866-1867. serial 1287.

President Johnson's message on occupancy of Mexico by U.S. troops.

40 CONG., 1 sess., ho. ex. docs. nos. 30, 31, vol. I, may 1866—july 1867. serial 1311.

Reports from Lewis D. Campbell, U.S. envoy to Mexico, and William H. Seward.

THE PACIFIC SQUADRON

31 CONG., 1 sess., ho. ex. doc. no. 5, vol. III, pt. 1, 1849. serial 569.

Number of vessels in the Pacific squadron.

32 CONG., 1 sess., sen. ex. doc. no. 1, vol. II, pt. 2, 1851. serial 612.

Number of vessels added to U.S. navy, 1851

33 CONG., 1 sess., ho. ex. doc. no. 65, vol. VIII, 1853-1854. serial 721.

Account of the "steam navy".

35 CONG., 1 sess., ho. ex. doc. no. 3, vol. I, 1861. serial 1127.

Port Townsend incident and the U.S.S. "Shubrick".

36 CONG., 1 sess., sen. ex. doc. no. 2, vol. III, 1859-1860. serial 1025.

Emphasizes the small number of vessels in the Pacific squadron. Repair of U.S.S. "Saginaw" at Mare island.

37 CONG., 2 sess., sen. ex. doc. no. 71, vol. VI, july 1862. serial 1123.

Lincoln's message on the steamer "Vanderbilt".

37 CONG., 2 sess., sen. ex. docs. nos. 8, 14, 15, 18, 30, 33, vol. IV. serial 1121.

Doc. no. 15, number of vessels purchased in 1862; other documents about "Trent" affair.

37 CONG., 3 sess., sen. ex. doc. no. 24, vol. I, january 1863. serial 1149.

Exportation of articles of war for use of French army in Mexico.

37 CONG., 3 sess., ho. ex. doc. no. 1, vol. III, 1862-1863. serial 1158.

Conspiracy to capture Mare island.

38 CONG., 1 sess., ho. ex. doc. no. 1, vol. IV, 1863. serial 1183.

Number of vessels in the Pacific; attack on U.S.S. "Wyoming" by Japan; and "J. M. Chapman" affair.

38 CONG., 1 sess., ho. ex. doc. no. 18, vol. VII, 1863. serial 1187.

Claims of American citizens against Peru.

38 CONG., 2 sess., ho. ex. doc. no. 1, vol. VI, 1864. serial 1221.

The blockade of Mexican ports by the French.

38 CONG., 2 sess., ho. ex. docs. nos. 83, 84, 85, vol. XIV, 1864. serial 1230.

Conspiracy to capture Pacific mail steamers.

39 Cong., 1 sess., ho. ex. doc. no. 1, vol. v, 1865. serial 1253.
Plot to capture mail steamers; number of vessels in the Pacific reported
to be only eleven.

39 Cong., 2 sess., ho. ex. doc. no. 1, vol. IV. serial 1286.
Trip of the ironclad u.s.s. "Monadnock" around the Horn.

40 Cong., 2 sess., sen. ex. doc. no. 79, vol. II, 1868. serial 1317.
The discovery and occupation of the island of Midway.

41 Cong., 3 sess., ho. ex. doc. no. 1, pt. 3, vol. III, 1870. serial 1448.
Improvement of harbor at Midway.

42 Cong., 2 sess., ho. ex. doc. no. 1, vol. IV, pt. 3, 1871. serial 1507.
Midway harbor; and wreck of u.s.s. "Saginaw".

43 Cong., 1 sess., ho. rept. no. 343, vol. II, march 1874. serial 1624.
Claims of the crew of the u.s.s. "Wyoming".

50 Cong., 1 sess., ho. rept. no. 1920, vol. XXIX, 1888. serial 2603.
Settlement of claims of crew of the "Wyoming".

50 Cong., 1 sess., ho. ex. doc. no. 1, vol. VIII, pt. 3, 1887. serial 2539.
Sale of condemned vessels at Mare island.

Chapman Treason Case—u.s. circuit court. Lorenzo Sawyer,
vol. IV, p. 457, 487, 501.

Miscellaneous Information

37 Cong., 1 sess., journ. of ho., p. 1-35. serial 1113.
Lincoln's message on state of the nation, 1861.

37 Cong., 1 sess., ho. and sen. joint res. nos. 3, 59, vol. I. serial 1115.
Appointment of a day of prayer; oath of allegiance.

37 Cong., 2 sess., ho. ex. doc. no. 116, vol. IX. serial 1137.
Eighth census of the u.s.

37 Cong., 3 sess., sen. ex. doc. no. 19, vol. I, 1862. serial 1149.
Newspapers barred from u.s. mail.

37 Cong., 3 sess., sen. misc. doc. no. 41, vol. I, march 1863. serial
1150.
Enrollment or conscription act.

38 Cong., 1 sess., sen. ex. doc. no. 41, vol. I. serial 1176.
Veto of Nevada's specific contract act.

38 Cong., 1 sess., ho. ex. doc. no. 45, vol. IX, 1864. serial 1189.
Capt. J. L. Fiske's expedition to Rocky mountains.

38 Cong., 2 sess., ho. ex. doc. no. 3, vol. VII, 1864-1865. serial 1222.
Gold carried on steamers from Pacific coast.

39 Cong., 1 sess., sen. ex. doc. no. 1, vol. I. serial 1237.
Oath of allegiance for civil employees as well as troops.

39 Cong., 1 sess., ho. ex. doc. no. 1, vol. IV, pt. 1, p. 234-235. serial
1251.
Number of desertions, 1861-1865. California's desertions—1,855.

39 CONG., 1 sess., ho. ex. doc. no. 1, vol. v, pts. 1 and 2; appendix
pts. 1 and 2. serial 1249-1252.

> Number of men enrolled in the army.

40 CONG., 3 sess., ho. misc. doc. no. 27, vol. I, january 1869. serial
1385.

> Petition to use Fort Steilacoom for an asylum.

42 CONG., 2 sess., ho. ex. doc. no. 89, vol. VIII, 1871-1872. serial
1511.

> The sale of surplus war property; selling prices.

42 CONG., 2 sess., sen. misc. doc. no. 157, vol. II, 1872. serial 1482.

> Soldiers' Homestead law.

43 CONG., 1 sess., ho. ex. doc. no. 1, vol. I, pt. 2, p. 116, 181, 1873.
serial 1597.

> Land at Wilmington (Drum Barracks) to be reconveyed to original
> owners.

72 CONG., 1 sess., sen. ex. doc. no. 102, vol. XVII. serial 9515.

> Junipero Serra and Thomas Starr King Monument unveiling, 1931.

UNITED STATES Statutes at Large, vol. XII, chap. 32, p. 297, 345,
feb. 25, 1862.

> Issue of U.S. notes and redemption thereof. California tax quota
> $254,538.66.

California Statutes

FOR BENEFIT of California volunteers: recruiting, pay, voting, taxes,
and veterans' benefits.

> 14 Sess. chap. 187, p. 246, april 10, 1863.
> 14 Sess. chap. 355, p. 549-553, april 25, 1863.
> 14 Sess. chap. 414, p. 662-666, april 27, 1863.
> 15 Sess. sen. and assembly res. no. 30, p. 553, april 1, 1864.
> 15 Sess. chap. 71, p. 73, february 10, 1864.
> 15 Sess. chap. 177, p. 172, march 15, 1864.
> 15 Sess. chap. 377, p. 424-427, april 4, 1864.
> 15 Sess. chap. 442, p. 486-491, april 4, 1864.
> 16 Sess. sen. bill no. 57, 1866.
> 16 Sess. assembly bill no. 153, 1866.
> 17 Sess. sen. bill no. 389, 1868.
> 28 Sess. chap. 161, assembly bill no. 50, p. 198, march 15, 1889.
> 28 Sess. chap. 173, assembly bill no. 604, p. 206-208, march 16, 1889.
> 28 Sess. chap. 268, assembly bill no. 281, p. 418, march 19, 1889.
> 29 Sess. chap. 212, assembly bill no. 455, p. 289, march 31, 1891.
> Supreme court of Calif., reports, vol. 26, case 161; vol. 31, case 261.

LOYALTY LAWS and laws to control disloyalty:

> 12 Sess. sen. and assembly joint res. no. 18, p. 686, may 17, 1861.
> 12 Sess. chap. 490, p. 538, may 20, 1861.
> 13 Sess. sen. and assembly journs., appendix, 1862.

Loyalty Laws, continued.

14 Sess. sen. res. no. 1, assembly concurring, p. 793, january 26, 1863.
14 Sess. chap. 264, p. 350, april 20, 1863.
14 Sess. chap. 318, p. 477, april 25, 1863.
14 Sess. chap. 327, p. 490, april 25, 1863.
14 Sess. chap. 365, p. 566-567, april 25, 1863.
14 Sess. chap. 450, p. 727, april 27, 1863.
14 Sess. chap. 498, p. 755, april 27, 1863.
15 Sess. res. no. 15, p. 546-547, january 20, 1864.
15 Sess. chap. 127, p. 115, march 1, 1864.
15 Sess. chap. 192, p. 190, march 18, 1864.
16 Sess. chap. 627, p. 853, april 2, 1866.
17 Sess. chap. 13, p. 8, january 17, 1868.

LAWS REGARDING NEGROES

Calif. State Constitution, art. I, section 18.
5 Sess. chap. 28, p. 31, april 13, 1854.
14 Sess. chap. 70, p. 69, march 18, 1863.
15 Sess. chap. 209, sec. 68, p. 213, march 22, 1864.

CALIFORNIA SPECIFIC CONTRACT ACT

14 Sess. chap. 421, p. 687-691, april 27, 1863.
14 Sess. assembly jour. p. 208, february 12, 1863.
15 Sess. sen. journ. p. 285, february 1864.
15 Sess. sen. journ. p. 287, 1864.

MISCELLANEOUS ACTS:

11 Sess., chap. 161, march 29, 1860.

Plans and specifications for building the state capitol.

13 Sess., chap. 97, p. 90, march 27, 1862.

13 Sess., chap. 357, p. 479, may 2, 1862.

These two measures prohibited the sale of liquor on sunday.

13 Sess., chap. 150, p. 141, april 8, 1862.

Provided for the preservation of newspapers of the state.

13 Sess., chap. 276, p. 309, april 19, 1862.

The contract with P. Edward Connor & George W. Blake for foundation of state capitol cancelled.

14 Sess., chap. 252, p. 328, april 18, 1863.

Name of New San Pedro changed to Wilmington.

14 Sess., chap. 446, p. 723, april 27, 1863.

Gambling prohibited in California.

14 Sess., concurrent res. no. 11, p. 782, february 26, 1863.

Gen. Connor was commended on battle of Bear river.

15 Sess., chap. 277, p. 289-290, april 1, 1864.

Permit granted Phineas Banning to erect a dam on San Gabriel river.

Calif. Constitution, art. XI, sec. 2.

Prohibited dueling and defined penalties.

Newspapers*

IN THE FOLLOWING California newspapers, letters from the California volunteers and other news articles were published:

Alta California, San Francisco. 1861, 1862, 1863, 1865.

Alta Weekly California (Steamer), San Francisco. 1861, 1862, 1863, 1864, 1865.

Amador Weekly Ledger, Jackson. 1862, 1864.

Bulletin, San Francisco. 1863, 1864.

Butte Record, Oroville. 1866.

Calaveras Chronicle, Mokelumne Hill. 1862, 1865.

Daily Morning Call, San Francisco. 1862, 1863.

Humboldt Times, Eureka. 1864.

Los Angeles Semi-Weekly Southern News, Los Angeles. 1861, 1862.

Los Angeles Star, Los Angeles. 1860, 1868, 1873.

Los Angeles Weekly News, Los Angeles. 1865.

Marysville Appeal, Marysville. 1865.

Mountain Messenger, Downieville. 1865.

Pajaro Times, Watsonville. 1863, 1865.

Red Bluff Beacon, Red Bluff. 1861.

Sacramento Union, Sacramento. 1861, 1862, 1863, 1864.

San Francisco Call, San Francisco. 1900.

San Francisco Daily Herald, San Francisco. 1860.

San Joaquin Republican, Stockton. 1862.

San Jose Mercury, San Jose. 1862, 1864.

Shasta Courier, Shasta. 1862, 1865, 1866.

Sierra Democrat, Downieville. 1861, 1862, 1863.

Solano Press, Suisun. 1864.

Stockton Weekly Independent, Stockton. 1862.

Tuolumne Courier, Columbia. 1864, 1866.

Weekly Trinity Journal, Weaverville. 1866.

Weekly Union Record, Oroville. 1865.

Wilmington Journal, Wilmington. 1866.

Yreka Union, Yreka. 1861.

Boston Post, Boston, Mass. 1863, jan. 14, arrival of the California hundred; april 17, arrival of California battalion.

---

* Many were published irregularly and some with slight variations in title.

New York Times, New York. 1863, jan. 4, arrival of California hundred; april 16, arrival of California battalion.

Santa Fe Gazette, New Mexico. October 5, 12, 1867. Erection of a monument to the veterans who served in the west.

National Tribune, Washington, D.C. june 30, 1927. "How California got in the Civil war," George H. Pettis, first lieutenant company K, first infantry, California volunteers. Issues of july 14, 21, 28, tell about war experiences in the southwest.

Union Vedette, Camp Douglas, Salt Lake City. july 20, aug. 11, 1865.

General Works and Periodicals

AMERICAN GUIDE SERIES,—Arizona; Colorado; New Mexico; Washington, City and Capital. Writers program of the work projects administration. (N.Y., v.d.)

AMERICAN HISTORICAL MAGAZINE, february 1886. August Allen Hayes, "California in Civil war, the New Mexican campaign".

AMERICAN JOURNAL of Medical Science, N.S. XLIV, 365-387, 1862. Surgeon J. H. Bill, "Arrow Wounds".

ANNALS OF IOWA, 3rd series, vol. IV, no. 3. Louis Pelzer. "March of the dragoons in Mississippi Valley".

BANCROFT, H. H. History of California, vol. VI, VII.

———————— History of Nevada, Colorado and Wyoming.

BANDEL, EUGENE. Frontier life in the army, 1854-1861. Southwest Historical series, vol. 2. (Glendale, Calif., The Arthur H. Clark Co., 1932)

BARNES, JOSEPH K., et al. Medical and surgical history of the war of rebellion. 3 vols. (Washington, 1870-1888)

BLEDSOE, ANTHONY JENNINGS. Indian wars of the northwest, a California sketch, 1847-1865. (San Francisco, 1885)

BROWNE, J. Ross. Adventures in Apache country. (N.Y., 1869)
    A tour through Arizona and Sonora; silver regions.

CHARLESTOWN (Mass.) directories, 1862-1866.

CLARK, FRANCIS D. The First regiment of New York volunteers. (N.Y., 1882)
    Commanded by Col. Jonathan D. Stevenson, in the Mexican war, service in Upper and Lower California 1847-1848. Names of members and record of survivors and deceased.

CONKLING, ROSCOE P. and Margaret B. The Butterfield overland mail, 3 vols. (Glendale, Calif., The Arthur H. Clark Co., 1947)

Coy, Owen Cochran. The Humboldt bay region, 1850-1875. (Los Angeles, 1929)

———————— Guide to County Archives of California, Sacramento, 1912.

Cremony, John C. Life among the Apaches. (N.Y., 1868)
> Translation of the Apache language; also his experiences with the California volunteers.

Cullum, George Washington. Biographical register of officers and graduates of the u.s. military academy, 2 vols. (N.Y., 1868)
> Biographies of the officers of the army of the Pacific.

DeLong, Sidney R. History of Arizona. (San Francisco, 1905)

Dodge, Grenville M. Battle of Atlanta and other campaigns, addresses, etc. (Council Bluffs, 1911)
> Indian campaigns, campaign in West, block-houses, etc.

Dyer, Frederick H., 7th Conn. Vol. A compendium of war of rebellion. (Des Moines, Iowa)
> From official records of the Federal and Confederate armies.

Edgar, W. F. Report of surgeon, u.s. army, march 1872. Detailed description of many of the western forts.

Ellison, Joseph. California and the nation. (Univ. of Calif., Pubns. in Hist., vol. 16, Berkeley, 1927)
> Chapters 9, 10, 11, are a study of the relations with the federal government.

Farish, Thomas Edwin. History of Arizona. 8 vols. (San Francisco, 1918-1919)
> Vol. IV contains a report of the escape of Governor Ignacio Pesqueira from Sonora. Captain Martin H. Calderwood, California volunteers, furnishes an eye witness account.

Garfielde, Selucius and F. A. Snyder. Compiled laws of the state of California. (Boston, 1853)
> The act respecting fugitives from labor, and slaves brought to this state prior to admission into the Union (passed april 15, 1852) in chap. 65, page 231.

Goodwin, John W. Report to first legislature of Arizona, 1864.
> Report of the military mail express operated by the volunteer soldiers in Arizona, 1861-1864.

Gorley, Hugh Alexander. The loyal Californians of 1861. (War paper no. 12. Commandery of California, military order of loyal legion of u.s.) (San Francisco, 1893)

———————— Selections from his letters and patriotic speeches. (San Francisco, 1876)
> In the latter publication he gives intimate details of his service with the California volunteers.

GUINN, J. M. and George H. Tinkham. History of the state of California and biographical records of San Joaquin county. 2 vols. Los Angeles, 1909)
Biography of Capt. Charles M. Weber in vol. II.

HAFEN, LeRoy R. The overland mail. (Cleveland, The Arthur H. Clark Co., 1926)

HAMMOND, JOHN MARTIN. Quaint and historic forts of North America. (Philadelphia, 1915)

HARPERS NEW MONTHLY Magazine, vol. xxx, 1864-1865. J. Ross Browne, "A tour through Arizona".
Browne meets the California volunteers; sketches of Sylvester Mowry; Fort Tubac, etc.

——————— Vol. LV, june, 1877. William H. Rideing, "The Wheeler survey in Nevada".
The odometer is aptly described by Rideing.

HEITMAN, FRANCIS B. Historical register and dictionary of the United States army, 1789 to 1903. (Washington, 1903)

HITTELL, THEODORE H. History of California. 4 vols. (pub. N. J. Stone & Co., 1897)
Vol. IV contains a review of California specific contract act.

——————— California law statutes, 1850-1864. 2 vols. (San Francisco, 1865)

HUTCHINGS Illustrated California Magazine, vol. II, p. 441, april 1858.
An account of Fort Miller and Millerton.

——————— 1861. James M. Hutchings, "Scenes of Wonder and Curiosity in California".
A description and sketch of Fort Point.

JOHN HOPKINS Hospital Bulletin, vol. XXVII, no. 306, august 1916. Joseph T. Smith, "Review of the life and work of Jonathan Letterman, M.D."

KELLY, HOWARD A., and Walter L. Barrage. Dictionary of American Medical Biography. (N.Y., 1928)

LAND OFFICE, Circular, showing manner of proceeding to obtain title to public lands under the homestead, desert land, and other laws. (Washington, 1904)

LEECH, MARGARET. Reveille in Washington 1861-1865. (N.Y., 1941)
Contains an account of the appointment of Hammond as surgeon general of the U.S. army.

LETTERMAN, JONATHAN. Medical recollections of the army of the Potomac. (N.Y., 1866)
A description of the ambulance corps; hospitals and medical treatment.

LEWIS AND DRYDEN. Marine history of the Pacific Northwest. Edited by E. W. Wright. (Portland, Ore., 1895)
An illustrated review of the maritime industry, with sketches and portraits of marine men.

LOCKWOOD, FRANK C. Pioneer days in Arizona. (N.Y., 1932)
Brief history of the Patagonia or Mowry mine.

LOS ANGELES County Records. Records of deeds, book VI, VII.
Transactions between the government and Phineas Banning and Benjamin D. Wilson in regard to Drum Barracks.

LOSSING, BENSON G. Pictorial history of the Civil war. 3 vols. (Philadelphia, 1866)
The volunteer refreshment room and old signal gun in Philadelphia; sketch of Chain bridge in vol. I. Vol. II contains a sketch of the "Quaker guns".

MACK, EFFIE MONA. History of Nevada, from the earliest times through the Civil war. (Glendale, Calif., Clark, 1936)
Account of Gridley's sanitary sack of flour is given; history of Fort Churchill.

MASSACHUSETTS soldiers, sailors and marines in the Civil war. Compiled and published by the adjutant general, Massachusetts. 8 vols. (Norwood, Mass., 1931)
Vol. VI contains the history of the second Massachusetts cavalry; an important item is the correction of the number of desertions thereby reducing the total by 1,650; another is the winning of the medal of honor by a soldier belonging to the company of the California hundred.

McCLINTOCK, J. H. History of Arizona. 3 vols. (Chicago, 1916)
Biographies of Arizona pioneers in vol. III.

McCORMICK, RICHARD C. Report to the second legislature of Arizona, december 11, 1865.
Account of the establishment of the first post routes in the territory.

McPHERSON, EDWARD, clerk of house of representatives. Political history of the U.S. during the great rebellion. (Washington, 1865)
A classified summary of legislation of the 36, 37, 38 congress. Important executive, judicial, political and military facts of that period.

MEDALS OF HONOR, United States department of the army, public information division. (Washington, 1948)

MEIGGS, M. C. Outline description of U.S. military posts and stations. (Washington, 1871)
From information furnished by division commanders and quartermasters.

MILLER, FRANCIS TREVELYAN, and Robert S. Lanier, editors. Photographic history of the Civil war. 10 vols. (N.Y., 1911-1912)

MORRIS, WILLIAM GOUVERNEUR. Address delivered before the society of California volunteers at its first annual celebration, april 25, 1866.
> Combats with the Indians of Arizona and New Mexico.

MOWRY, SYLVESTER. Arizona and Sonora. (N.Y., 1864)
> Mowry's own version of his arrest and confiscation of his mine.

MUNSEY'S MAGAZINE, vol. XXXII, oct.-march, 1904-1905. "Recollections of a Mosby guerilla", John W. Munson.
> The Dranesville Pike combat, is described on pages 14-16, chapter V.

NATIONAL GEOGRAPHIC MAGAZINE, june 1923; april 1929; march 1930; november 1931; february, april 1935; june 1937; july 1938; april, july 1940; july 1942; june 1947.
> Descriptions of Washington, D.C.

OAKLAND (Calif) directories, 1869-1872.

OCCIDENTAL MEDICAL TIMES, 1893. Henry Gibbons, Jr., "Training of surgeons".
> A comparative study of training in the 1860's and 1890's.

OREGON HISTORICAL QUARTERLY, december 1929. Oscar Winslow Hoop, "History of Fort Hoskins".
> Old Oregon blockhouses and forts.

——————— Vol. VIII. Will J. Trimble, "Soldier of the Oregon frontier".
> Gen. George Wright and Oregon Indian wars.

OVERLAND MONTHLY, vol. I, 1st series, p. 201, 1868. John C. Cremony, "The Apache race".

——————— Vol. V, 1st series, p. 221, 520, 1870. Surgeon George Gwyther, "Our scout to Black canyon".
> A summary of Captain McCleave's campaign; Indian attack on the family of Capt. Albert H. Pfeiffer near Fort McRae, New Mexico.

——————— Vol. VII, 2nd. series, 1886, p. 480-496. Edward Carlson, "Martial experiences of California volunteers".
> Departure of the Shasta volunteers; flood at Sacramento.

PETTIS, GEORGE HENRY. The California column. (Historical society of New Mexico, publications no. 11, Santa Fe, 1908)
> Campaigns and services in New Mexico, Arizona and Texas; sketches of Carleton, and other officers and soldiers.

——————— Frontier service during the rebellion; or, A history of company K, first infantry, California volunteers. (Rhode Island Soldiers and Sailors Historical society. 3d ser., no. 14. Providence, 1885)

PRIESTLEY, HERBERT INGRAM. The Mexican nation. (N.Y., 1923)
    The French occupation of Mexico and the life of Juarez.

PROCEEDINGS of the U.S. Naval Institute, vol. LII, no. 7, dec. 1926.
    p. 2451, 2455-2457. Robert W. Nesser, "Historic ships of the U.S.
    navy".

PROFESSIONAL MEMOIRS. Corps of engrs. U.S. army and engr. dept.,
    vol. VII, 1915, p. 758.
    Biography of Col. René DeRussy, engineer.

QUARTERLY, California Historical society, year 1941, vol. XX, p.
    154-170. "The Confederate minority in California", by Benjamin
    Franklin Gilbert.

QUARTERMASTER MARKING POT, oct. 1925. "Evolution of fortifica-
    tions around San Francisco bay".

RISTER, CARL C. The Southwestern frontier, 1865-1881. (Cleveland,
    The Arthur H. Clark Co., 1928)

ROGERS, FRED B. Soldiers of the overland. (The Grabhorn press, San
    Francisco, 1938)
    Connor and his third regiment of infantry, California volunteers, 1861-
    1866.

ROGERS, J. HENRY. The California one hundred. (San Francisco,
    1865)
    An account in verse of California volunteers in the defense of Washing-
    ton, D.C.

ROLL OF HONOR, 24 volumes. Quartermaster general's office. (Wash-
    ington, 1867)
    Vols. VII, XII, XIII, contain the list of dead from California and names
    the places of burial.

SAN FRANCISCO, board of supervisors. San Francisco municipal
    reports. 1880-1881. (San Francisco, 1881)
    Settlement of the claims involving the U.S.S. "Camanche".

SAWYER, LORENZO. Reports of cases decided in the Circuit and
    District Courts of the U.S. for the Ninth district. (San Francisco,
    1878)
    Case of the "J. M. Chapman" in vol. IV, p. 457, 487, 501.

SHANNON, FRED A. Organization and administration of the Union
    army, 1861-1865. (Cleveland, The Arthur H. Clark Co., 1928)

SHERMAN, EDWIN ALLEN. Fifty years of masonry in California. 2
    vols. illustrated. (San Francisco, 1898)
    Includes biography of Hiram Sinclair Tuttle; his experience with the
    Mormons, and services at the battle of Bear river.

SHUTES, MILTON HENRY. Lincoln and California. (Stanford, 1943)
    Subversive activities in California.

SIMONDS, WILLIAM DAY. Thomas Starr King. (San Francisco, 1917)
His political influence and work with the Sanitary commission.

SPENCER, W. G. *et al.* Hygiene of the U.S. army. (Washington, 1871)
Surgeons report on forts, hospitals, and health of troops.

STILLE, CHARLES J. History of the sanitary commission. (Philadelphia, 1866)
With an accounting of the money donated by California and other western states.

THOMPSON, DEWITT C. California in the rebellion. (War paper no. 8, Commandery of California, Military order of loyal legion of U.S., San Francisco, 1891)

TRANSACTIONS of Kansas State Historical society, vol. VII, 1902, p. 178-180. Address by J. D. Waters, regarding Rev. John A. Anderson.

TRANSACTIONS and reports of Nebraska State Historical society, vol. II, p. 197-229. "History of Powder river expedition", by H. E. Palmer, co. A, eleventh Kansas vol. corps.; paper read before Nebraska Commandery of the Military Order of the loyal legion of U.S., february 2, 1887.

TWITCHELL, RALPH EMERSON. Leading Facts of New Mexican history. 5 vols. (Cedar Rapids, Iowa, 1911-1917)
Vol. II contains many interesting facts of the Civil war period and sketches of leading figures in the political and military field and Indians.

VANDOR, PAUL E. History of Fresno county, with sketches of leading men and women of the county. 2 vols. (Los Angeles, 1919)

WAR OF REBELLION, Compilation of official records of Union and Confederate armies. (Washington, 1897-1900) Ser. I, vols. 3, 4, 9, 15, 26, 33, 34, 41, 48, 50, 51; Ser. III, vols. 3, 4.

WENDTE, CHARLES W. Thomas Starr King, patriot and preacher. (Boston, 1921)
Excerpts from letters in which he tells of his experiences with the California volunteers and especially mentions the "hundred".

WESTWAYS, sept. 1937, vol. XXIX. Franklin Walker, "Bohemian no. 1".
Account of John C. Cremony.

WOODRUFF, CHARLES ALBERT. The Work of the California volunteers as seen by an eastern volunteer. (War paper no. 13, Commandery of California, Military order of loyal legion of U.S., San Francisco, 1893)

WYLLIE, ROBERT E. History and development of medals and decorations of the United States army and navy. (N.Y., 1921)

ZABRISKIE, JAMES A. Address to Arizona pioneers. (in report of board of regents, University of Arizona, Tucson, 1902)

    Personal experiences while serving with the fifth infantry, California volunteers.

Plates

PLATE 2

DRUM BARRACKS, WILMINGTON, CALIFORNIA

The boot camp of the 1860's. Officers quarters as they appear at the present. Photograph by Bill Conway of Long Beach *Press Telegram*.

PLATE 3

LIEUTENANT-COLONEL WILLIAM A. MCCLEAVE
First Cavalry, California Volunteers. By courtesy of
his son, Dr. Thomas C. McCleave, Berkeley.

PLATE 4

WHITE'S MILL, PIMA VILLAGE, ARIZONA

Where McCleave and his men were captured by the Confederates. From photograph by
I. L. Palmer, Descanso, California.

PLATE 5

FORT WHIPPLE, ARIZONA, 1864

Built by California Volunteers. Photograph from *The Argonauts*, by W. E. Wells.

PLATE 6

FORT TUBAC, ARIZONA

Garrisoned by the California Volunteers. From the C. C. Pierce Collection of Historical Photographs.

PLATE 7

"KIT CARSON" AND BRIGADIER GENERAL JAMES H. CARLETON

PLATE 8

FORT CHURCHILL RUINS, NEVADA
From the C. C. Pierce Collection of Historical Photographs.

Plate 9

Patrick Edward Connor
Brevet-major-general U. S. Volunteers
As Brigadier General he commanded the Third regiment,
California volunteers; the Nevada volunteers in the district of
Utah; and also in command of the District of the Plains.

PLATE 10

BLOCKHOUSE AT FORT YAMHILL, OREGON
Courtesy of Oregon Historical Society.

Plate 11

Old Blockhouse, Fort Miller

The site now lies beneath the water impounded by Friant Dam, Fresno County, California. Erected in 1851, the building was constructed without the use of nails.

PLATE 12

FORT YUMA AND COLORADO RIVER
circa 1898

PLATE 13

MEDICINE WAGON

"THE COOLIDGE CART" AMBULANCE WAGON

It was one of this design that was sent to Fort Yuma for use
of the California Volunteers.

PLATE 14

Left: National colors carried by the California Battalion. The names of some of the battles are still discernible. This flag was saluted by Abraham Lincoln.

Upper right: The pennant on which is listed 24 battles in which the Californians fought.

Lower right: The Bear flag carried by the California hundred while serving with the Army of the Potomac and in many battles.

PLATE 15

U. S. S. "CYANE"

which captured the privateer, "J. M. Chapman" in San Francisco Bay. The old sloop-of-war was present at Monterey, 1842 and 1846, at San Diego, 1846; her seamen fought in the Battle of Los Angeles and San Gabriel river.

PLATE 16

THE "AQUILA"

which carried the "Camanche", disassembled, from New York to San Francisco, then sank in San Francisco Bay. From the original sketch at California State library.

PLATE 17

THE U. S. S. "CAMANCHE"

First iron-clad on the Pacific. Through courtesy of Society of California Pioneers.

Index

Index

"ABE": cannon at Volcano (Calif.), 229

Absent ballot (soldiers' ballot): 231; history, note 261

Acapulco: U.S. warship at, 318; 319; bombed by French, 320

"Active", U.S.S.: 40

Adobe ovens: building instructions, 98

Adobe Walls (St. Vrain's Fort): battle, 162-3

Advance guard: 77, 81; Pima village, 88; 94

Agricultural park, Stockton: 34; Camp Halleck, 187-8

Aguanga (Dutchman's): 104

"Alabama" (C.S.A. vessel): 290

Alaska: 302

Albuquerque: 52; abandoned by U.S.A., 60; 67

Alcatraz: photographs, 40; 196, 228; fortification, 234; plot to capture, 308; release of "Chapman" conspirators, 309; 314, 347-9

Alden, Farrelly: U.S. v. consul Mazatlan, 57

Aldie: 299

Alexander II of Russia: frees serfs, 310

Algodones: 104

Allen, Gabriel: wagonmaster, 103

Allen, Lucius H: 283

Allison, ———: 311

Alsea bay: 229

Altar (Mex.): 79, note 131

Alvord, Benjamin: in command Mil. Dist. of Ore., 232; treaty with Nez Percé Indians, 232-3; 236, 304

Amador county: enlistments, 25

Ambulance: 91; tandem, 103; 161;

for Connor's 3rd, 188; 224; description, 267; system, 269; 297

American Journal of Medical Science: arrow wounds, 268

American Red Cross: 326-7

Amyx (Calif. Assemblyman): 69

"Anashe" (tug): 307

Anderson, J. A: Chaplain for Connor's 3rd, 188; biog., note 189; funeral sermon, 195

Andersonville prison: 289; Californians, 296; casualties, 298; oak tree for Memorial Grove, 300

Anesthetics: 267-8

Andrews, George: 77

Andrews, John A: gov. of Mass., 281

Angels Camp: note 142; Calif. vols., 187

"Antelope" (river packet): 251

Antelope Peak: 104

Anthony, Salome: note 68

Antiseptics: 267

Apache canyon: battle of, 65-7; marker, 66; destruction of C.S.A. supply train, 66; 104

Apache Indians: 61, 86, 109; attack Expressman Jones, 116; attack Col. Eyre's advance guard, 117-8; 148; Chief Mangas Coloradas, 150-2; Copper mine Apaches, Mimbres Apaches, 150; six treaties with, 154; 156-7; Mescalero Apaches, 157; campaign against, 157-8; translation by Cremony, 158-9, note 159-60; allies of Calif. col., 160-1; 170, 174, 270; kill Surg. Watson, 271; antelope hunt, 272-3; 276

Apache Pass: 104; attack on Expressman Jones, 115-6; 117; burial
of vols., 118; battle, 120-1; 122;
defense works, 129; Managas
Coloradas wounded, 151; Watson
at Fort Bowie, 271

Appomattox Court House: General
Lee's surrender, 143; 284, 298-9;
"peace" tree for Memorial Grove,
300

"Aquila", s.s.: sinks, 311; raised,
312; 321

Arapahoe Indians: on warpath, 211;
214; defeated, 217; 219

Arcata: 241, 245, 247

Arivaca: 79, 130, *note* 131

Arizona: 19; population, 24; guards,
61; mines, 110; martial law, 110-
3; 265, 269; mustering out of vols.,
355-6

Arizona, Military District of: W.
Ariz., 129, census, 131; Col. West
in command, 134; 135; Gen.
Mason in command, 148; med.
purveyor of, 272; 274

Arizona Miner: 137

Arizona Pioneers' Historical society:
monument in Picacho pass, 92

Arkansas river: 161, 163-4

Arlington house: Calif. Bat. at, 292

Army, Confederate: 20, 22, 40, 52;
3rd reg., 55; retreat, 66-7; 78-86,
88-90; retreat, 92; 94, 99, 104, 113,
115-6; pickets on Rio Grande, 119;
125; sick and wounded, 126; escorted to San Antonio, 127; 154;
threat of 2nd invasion to s.w., 171;
175, 186, 198-200, 270; 44th No.
Car. inf., 288; Stuart's cav., 293;
304

"Army of occupation": on Catalina,
249

Army of the Pacific: 13, 18, 20, 28,
60, 153, 181

Army of the Potomac: 269; McNulty
serves, 273; reviewed by Lincoln,
287; Calif. Bat. joins, 293

Army of the Shenandoah: 297

Army, U.S.: 19, 22; 9th inf., 22; 24;
ordered East, 26; 9th inf., 3rd art.,
26; number, 27; 52; property
burned, 52; 7th inf. surrendered,
53; 56; eastern victories, 60; 1st.,
3rd. cav., 62; 72; defeat at Valverde, 85; 4th and 2nd cav., 107;
125, 154; 5th inf., 161, 174; invasion of Tex., 178; 5th inf. at Franklin, Tex., 183; 187; Fort Vancouver, 220; Cascades, 222; Fort
Colville, 226; 9th inf., 240; medical dept., 266-*note* 266

Arnold, George W: escort to J. Ross
Browne, 133

Arny, W. F. M: 172

Arrow wounds: 227, 266; fatalities,
268; 270, 363

Ashby gap: 293, 297

Aspinwal (Colon): 290

Astoria: 220

Atkinson: Connor at, 186

Auburn: 31, 141, *note* 142

Aurora (Calif.): 258

Austin (Nev.): election, 330-1; 332,
334

Australia: 302, 321

Ayer, Edward Everett: survey to
Gulf of Calif., 130; gift to Newberry library, 130

Aztec Indians: 109

Azul, Antonio (Chief of Pima Indians): San Francisco, 147-8

BAILEY, SANFORD: letter from, 183

Baird, S. M: 175

Baker, Edward D: killed at Ball's
bluff, 300

Baker, George H: sues for wharfage,
312

Baker, Thomas: arrested, 348

Baldwin, Ephriam C: *note* 85, 88

Bale, E: 263

Ballast Point (Catalina Is.): fortification, 249

Ballona creek: 32

Ball's bluff: maple tree for Memorial Grove, 300

Bancroft Library (U.C. Berkeley): MS Cremony's Apache language translation in, 159

Bangor (Calif.): 253

Bank of California (San Francisco): 313

Banning, Phineas: 42; property, 43; water system, 44; 47-8

Bannock Indians: 193

Barr, John: killed in Apache Pass, 120

Barrett, James: 82, *note* 85; death, 88-9; monument, 92

Bartlett, John Russell: gives suit to Mangas Coloradas, 150; Apache translation, 151

Bascom, George N: Fort named, 155

Baybutt, Philip: medal of honor, 299

Baylor, John R: 52-3; proclamations, 53; 54; 61; Fort Fillmore, 79; Mesilla, 80; 81; orders to recruit c.s.a. troops in s.w., 175; 304

Beale, Edward F: 22; surveying party, 102; 315-6

Beall, Benjamin L: 236

Bear Butte: 217

Bear flag: presented to Calif. Hundred, 284; 287-8; preservation, 298-9

Bear Hunter (Indian): Indian chief returns white boy, 193-4; battle of Bear river, 195

Bear river: battle, 194-5; casualties, 195-6; monument to Connor and Calif. vols., 219; 276

Bear Valley: *note,* 142

Beard, ---: supplies beef, 97

Beaver (Utah): 203

Beavers: on Colorado river, 80; 163; trapping at Fort Bridger, 205; trapper at Fort Colville, 226

Beckley, George L: organizes Knights of Golden Circle, 343

Beds: 129; straw for, 227

Bell, Charles E: 57; relieved of command, 303; 318; at Callao, 319

Bellows, Henry Whitney: Pres. of Sanitary Com., 325; biog., *note*

Bellows, Henry W: continued 327; letter auctioned, 328; lectures for funds in the West, 333-4

Bengal fire: 31

Benicia arsenal: 20; lack of defense, 302; Calif. vols. guard, 318

Benicia Barracks: 37, 187, 316; no. Calif. vols. burials, *note* 360

Bennett, Clarence E: 344

Bergmann, E. H: guards Cimarron route, 161

Berkner, Frederick: Mowry sues, *note* 114-115

Bernal heights: 34

Bernal springs: 64

Berryville: 299

Bibles: for Connor's 3rd, 188; for Calif. Hundred, 283

Bidwell, John: 252

Big Horn mountains: 215

Big Jim (Indian): 246

Big Oak Flat: *note* 142

Big Pine: 256, 259

Big Thunder (Indian): 232

Bill, J. H: report on arrow wounds, 268

Bitter springs: 107

Black Bear (Indian): 219

Black canyon: 102; scout to, 274-5

"Black Hawks": 283

Black, Henry Moore: Commands Humboldt Mil. Dist., 247; West Point, 248, *note* 248

Black hills: 216

Black Rock: 253

Blair, (Calif. Assemblyman): 70

Blair, Montgomery: 19, 132

Blair, Ned: stage driver, 198

Blake, C: 324

Bliss, W. Y: letter from, 356, *note* 356

Blockhouses: built by Calif. vols., 241; use of, 265

"Blotters" (cash books): at Fort Bridger, 205-6

Blue Ridge mountains: 293, 297

Blue Slide: 241

Blue Water station: 104

Bond, George W: composer, *note* 51
Bosque Redondo (Indian reservation): 153, 156; res. estab., 157; 158, 170; Indians, 171; removal of Navajos, 171; antelope hunt, 272-3
Boston: entertain Calif. Hundred, 285
Bowery theater (N.Y.): Calif. Bat. entertained, 290
Bowie, George W: 34, 41
Bowie knife: 272, 308
Bradley & Rulofsen: 39
Brady, Peter: 79; Gulf of Calif., 131
Bragg, Braxton: Fort named for, *note* 244
Brehmer's ranch: 241
Bridger, James: guide to Powder R. ex., 215
Bright, John: requests release of Rubery, 309
Broderick, David C: death, 41; duel, *note* 69
"Brother Jonathan", s.s.: 148; wreck, 237, 360-1
Brown, Albert: *note* 214
Brown, Charles D: 296
Brown, Gustav: gov. detective, 345
Brown, Isaac W: 279
Brown, John: of Harper's Ferry, 206
Brown, Mrs. John: Calif. vol. escort to, 206
Brown, Thomas: 315-6
Browne, J. Ross: spec. agt. dept. Int., 133
Bruneau valley: 231, protected, 233
Buckner, Frederick C: 79
Buel, David E: Dem. candidate, 331
Buena Vista, battle of: Carleton participates, 106
Bullion: 328, 332
Bunker Hill Baptist choir: 286
Bunker Hill (Mass.): 325
Burdick, Joseph B: killed, 288
Burke's station: 104

CABORCA: *note* 131
Cady, Albermarle: 236; Camp named for, *note* 263

Cady ranch: site of Camp Cady, 264
Cajon pass: 265
Calaveras county: 141
California: population, 24; military age group, 24, 25; enlistments, 25; 29, 269; protection of coast, 303; slavery prohibited, 338; Knights of the Golden Circle, 343-5; enlistments, 347; Specific Contract act, 352-3; total enlistments, 354
California Battalion: organized, 288; departure, 289; *note* 289; Camp Meigs via New York, 290; East Capitol Hill, 291; Edwards ferry, 293; Gettysburg, 293; Mosby's rangers, 293-6; escorts ambulance train, 297; engagements, 298-9; casualties, 300
California Column: 33, 62; leaves Fort Yuma, 92; officially named, 105; 107, 110-2; hospital fund, 113; 115-7; supply line, 121; order of departure from Tucson, 122, *note* 122; 123, 126-7, 129, 133; prospects, 135; Fort Sumner, 155; 157, 161-5, 171-2; Mex. border, 176-7, 179; 184, 265, 267, 270; pets, 273; 274
"California cossacks": 340
California Highways: "no. 12" (Lockford road), 189
California Home for Soldiers: 359
California Hundred: recruiting, 282; given Bibles, 283; departure, 284; New York, Boston, 285; receives U.S. flag, 286; Gloucester Point, 286; with Army of Potomac, 287; battle South Anna bridge, 288; Mosby's rangers, 293-6; battle of Winchester, 297; engagements, 298-9; casualties, 300
California, Military Department of: 19, 186
California Steam Navigation company: 326
California volunteers: 21; first call, 24, 2nd and 4th inf., 25; 26; number, 26; 9th inf., 27; letters pub-

California volunteers: continued
lished, 28; apply for service in
East, 32; 33; 5th and 3rd inf., 34;
35; 4th inf., 38; 1st inf., 40, 48;
second call, 54; Fort Yuma, 55;
1st cav., 73-4; 4th inf., 75; 77;
haying, 78; 80-1, 83, 85; 1st inf.,
86; mobilized, 96; rations, 97;
cav. walks, 99-100; inf. marches
with knapsacks, 100; 2nd cav. to
So. Calif., 100; 5th inf., 100-1;
prospect, 109-10; 1st inf. praised,
125; no desertions in 5 cos. of 1st
inf., 126; vedettes, 132; 136; build
Fort Whipple, 137-9; build mil.
road, 140; new regiments, 7th and
8th, and veteran inf., 140; bounty,
140-1; relief, 141; postage free,
143; guard Central Overland
mail, 186; leave Stockton, 188; on
the march, 189; 3rd inf. offers to
pay way East, 191; 3rd inf. builds
Camp Douglas, 192; rescue kidnapped boy, 193-4; Fort Bridger,
194; 2nd cav. at battle of Bear
river, 194-5; guard O.M. stages,
200; survey, 201-3; ordered to
prospect, 203-4; burned at O.M.
station, 205; serve in Mil. Dist.
of Plains, 210; horses stolen, 211-
2; note 214; monument at Fort
Douglas, Bear river and Connor
Battlefield park (Wyo.), 219; Fort
Vancouver, 220; on Columbia R.,
221-3; Fort Walla Walla, 223;
224; Fort Colville, 225-6; in Wash.
1st inf., 228; ex. to Coos bay, 229-
30; bounty, 231; 234; Fort Cape
Disappointment, 235-6; Fort Stevens, 236; 238; Humboldt Dist.,
239; build blockhouses, 241; Fort
Bragg, 244; occupy Catalina Is.,
248-9; Fort Crook, 251; Fort
Reading, 253; Owens valley, 254-
60; absent vote, 261; Fort Tejon,
262; Camp Cady, 263; 264; surgeons, 279-80; 281; recruiting for
Mass., 282; guard Benicia arsenal,

Calif. volunteers: continued
303; guard Pacific s.s., 318; Relief
fund, 324; threatened by Secessionists, 337; destroy *Expositor*,
340; 343; exempt from poll tax,
350; Mil. Recruiting fund, 351;
352; oppose "gold law", 353; total
enlistments, 354; offers to serve in
East, 354; muster out, 355; "terminal pay", 356; Soldiers' Homestead law, 357; employment act,
358; 359; total casualties, 359
Callao: 23, 319; bombed by Spanish
fleet, 320; 321
Calloway, William A: 84, *note* 85;
biog. *note* 86; 87-9
Calvary Presbyterian church: 348
"Camanche" ("Comanche"), U.S.S.
(iron-clad): arrives and sinks in
S.F. Bay, 311; raised, 312; cost and
insurance, 312-3; 321
Cameron, Simon: 21, 24, 281, 302
Campo Seco: *note* 143; Calif. vols.,
187
Camps: *Alert*, 34-6; *Anderson*, no.
Calif. vols. burials, *note* 360; *Babbitt*, 261-2; Calif. vols., 337; 340;
Brightwood, Calif. Bat., 292;
Cady, 107; Calif. vols., 262-3;
abandoned, 264; 265, 267; *Carleton* (San Bernardino), 81; *Clarke*,
136; *Douglas*, built by 3rd inf.
Calif. vols., 192; burial of Calif.
vols., 195; 197; surveyors leave,
201; 203; Union *Vedette* published,
206-8; monument to Connor, Calif.
and Nev. vols., 219; no. Calif. vols.
burials, *note* 360; *Downey*, 37;
Surg. Gwyther, 274; *Fitzgerald*
(Los Angeles), 42, 107; Surg.
Letterman, 269; *Floyd*, 191; *Gilmore*, 245; *Grant* (Calif.), 245;
Halleck, 34; 3rd inf. Calif. vols.
train, 187-8; 278; *Independence*,
built by Calif. vols., 254; named,
256; 257-9; abandoned, 261; no.
Calif. vols. burials, *note* 360;
Latham, 32, 41, 255; *Leonard*,

Camps: continued
near Keysville, 260-1; *Lewis,* 65-6; *Lincoln,* 360; *Lyon* (Calif.), 40; built, 241; *Lyon* (Idaho), note 234; *McClellan,* 31; *Meigs* (Mass.), Calif. Hundred at, 285; 286; Calif. Bat. at, 290; *Merritt,* 36; *Mitchell,* 211; *Nicholas,* 163-4; *Sumner,* 40; *Union,* 34, 251, 253; *Watson,* note 234; *Wright* (Oak Grove), establishment, 49; 50; 72-5, 85, 91, 97, 270; no. Calif. vols. burials, note 360

Canada: 19, 221

Cañada de los Ruedas (Wheel Gulch): 162

Cañada del Oro: 109

Canadian river: 162

Canby, Edward R. S: 54-55; in command U.S.A. at Valverde, 59; 60, 62-3, 65-6, 90, 93; news of Cal. column, 115-6, 117, 123, 126; relieved of command in N. Mex., 128

Canby, Mrs. Edward R. S: cares for C.S.A. casualties, 67

Canyon de Chelly: expedition, 167-9

Canyon de los Trizos: 167

Cape Disappointment: 234-235, 320

Cape Horn: 321

Cape Perpetua: 229

Cape San Lucas: 145

Captain George (Indian): peace talk, 257; moves tribe to Sebastian res., 259-60

Carey, A. B: Rio Grande Grant controversy, 173-4

Carleton, Etta: 164

Carleton, Eva: 164

Carleton, James Henry: commands district so. Cal., 42; property burned, 61; 75; commands ex. to Rio Grande, 77; 79-81; orders to McCleave, 84; 85-6, 88; news of defeat, 91; 92; report, 93-4; 96; death of child, 99; 100-1; on the march, 103-5; biog. 105-8; proclaims martial law, 110-13; Mowry

Carleton, James H: continued
sues, 114, note 114-5; 115, 117; orders to Cal. column to leave Tucson, 121-2; "clean up" orders, 124; praised by Cal. vols., 126; 127; in command Mil. Dep. of N. Mex., 128; Fergusson survey, 131; 132; orders to prospect for gold, 135; 137, 151; reply to Doolittle committee, 152-3; 154, 155; Indian policy, 155-7; 158-9; orders guard for Cimarron route, 161-4; prohibits Indian slavery, 165; praises Navajos, 169; orders half rations for vols., 170; report on Bosque Redondo, 171; praise and censure of, 171-3; Rio Grande grant controversy, 173-4; death, 174; concentrates troops on Mex. border, 175; 180, 182, 184, 202, 269, 272; mustering out, 355-6

Carleton, Mrs. James Henry: 163

Carrizo creek: 74, 104, 143

Carson, Christopher "Kit": command New Mex. vols., 157; Fort Stanton, 158; commands guard of Cimarron route, 161-3; commands Navajo campaign, 164-9; biog., note 165

Carson City (Nev.): 24; Morrisites, 198

Carter, W. A: 205

Casa Blanca: 104

Casa Grande: 109

Cascades: Calif. vols., 221-2; note 234

Cassell, Francis M: 279

Casserly, Eugene: 324

Catalina island (Santa): occupation by army, 31; advocated as Ind. res., 248-50; disapproved by Ind. commissioner, 250; surgeon Klunker, 278

Catholic Monitor: destroyed, 341

Cattle: Spanish, 45; army use, 49, 78; jerked beef, 96; price, 97; 99; stolen, 123; escort, 133; 145; stealing, 169; Pesqueira's, 180; stolen, 209; 247

Cedar bluff: 163
Cedar Creek: 284, 297, 299
Cedar (Utah): 203
Census, u.s: 24; Mil. Dist. W. Ariz., 131
Centerville (Va.): Union headquarters, 294; 295
Central Pacific R.R: excursion to Roseville, 333-4; engines "Governor Stanford" and "T. G. Judah (pony)", 333
Cerro Colorado mine (Heintzelman's): confiscated, 79; 130, note 131
Cerros island: 306
Chain Bridge: 292-3; Californians guard, 294
Charcoal: 98
Charlestown (Mass.): entertain Calif. Hundred, 285-6; 325; Starr King, note 329
Charlestown (Va.): 299
Charlie Hostler (Indian): 246
Charlottesville: 298
Chase, Salmon P: opposes Calif. "gold law", 352-3
Chavez, --- (Mexican guide): accompanies Expressman Jones, 115; killed, 116
Chew, John W: beaver trapper, 205
Cheyenne Indians: 163; on warpath, 211
Chico: 252-3
Chihuahua: 54, 151; u.s. consul to, 176; 182-3, 305
Chili: 302
Chili Gulch: Calif. vols. from, 187
China: 302
China Sea: 307
Chincha islands: 307; seized by Spain, 319
Chinese Camp: note 142; Calif. vols. from, 187
Chinese junks: piratical, 302
Chino Ranch: 104
Chino valley (Ariz.): 135-6
Chinook: language, 224
Chiricahua mountains: 363

Chivington, J. M: Chaplain Colo., vols., 62-3; battle reports, 64-6
Christian, Robert A: 279
Christmas: 56; Fort Whipple, 139
Cienega: 104
Cimarron route: 155; protection, 161-4
Cincinnati: 343
City Hall park (N.Y.): Calif. Hundred reviewed, 285
Clark, Cyrus D: 197
Clark, Jonathan: 279
Clearwater river: 232
Clemens, Samuel L. (Mark Twain): 332-3
Clements: site of old Polland house, 189
Coast Wrecking company: raises u.s.s. "Camanche", 312; 313
Cochise (Indian): 363
Cojo, Juan: interpreter, 158
Cole, Nelson: commands right column, note 214; Omaha to Powder R., 216; attacked by Indians, 217-8
Coloma: 29, note 142
"Colonel Wright", s.s: named for Col. George Wright, 223, note 223
"Colon", s.s: built for Pruvian gov., 317-8
Colorado: population, 24; in Mil. Dist. of Plains, 209
Colorado river: 20, 203, 265, 276
Colorado R. Nav. co: 102
Colorado volunteers: 62-3; marched to Fort Union, 64; battles with c.s.a., 64-6; casualties, 65-6; 68, 117, 171
Colt revolver: 41, 160, 252, 272, 286; war surplus, 357
Colt, Samuel: mine confiscated, 79; 139
Columbia: 29, note 142; Calif. vols. from, 187
Columbia, Military Department of: 237, 360
Columbia river: 220-2; defense, 234; shipwreck, 235; 303-4; 362
Columbus (Nebr.): 216

Colusa: 252

Colville, Andrew: *note* 226

Comanche Indians: campaign against, 161-3

Comstock Lode: shipment of bullion, 198

Confederacy: 21; alliance with Mexico, 23, 57; 93; aid, 113, 178, 347; partisan rangers law, 295; toast, 348

Confederate vessels: 20

Confiscation act: 113; 135; Calif. Leg. endorses, 350

"Connecticut", U.S.S., 290

Conness, John: approves Catalina Indian res. plan, 250

Connor Battlefield park (Wyo.): 219

Connor, P. Edward: 34; commands 3rd inf. Calif. vols., 186; Stockton, 187; *note* 187; Camp Halleck, 188; commands Mil. Dist. of Utah, 190; Fort Ruby, 191; 192, 193; Bear river battle, 194-5; 196; colonizer, 197-8; orders Calif. vols. to prospect, 203-4; "war of words" with Mormons, 204-5; stops publication *Vedette*, 207; assigned to command Dist. of the Plains, 208; circular to officers, 210-11; criticized, 213-4; ex. marches, 214; commands west column, *note* 214; battle of Powder river, 215; orders to Cole, 216; 217; battle casualties, 218; returns to Mil. Dept. of Utah, 219; death, 219; 231; treaty with Snake river Indians, 233; 276, 353

Conquest of Mexico: 130

Conrad, George D: 193, *note* 214

Conscription (Enrollment act): suspended in Calif., 140; 141; Calif. Leg. endorses, 350; number of Calif. enlistments after passage of, 353-4

"Constitution", S.S: 288-9; 6th inf. Calif. vols. guard, 318

Constitution of U.S: Resolution to support, 69; 72

Cooke's springs: 104, 116, 123

Cooke's Wells: 104

Coolidge dam: 140

Coolidge, Richard Hoffman: 267, *note* 267

Cooper, James G: 279

Cooper, H. H: miller at Hart's Mill, 126; daughter marries Col. Rigg, 126

Cooper Refreshment room: 291

Coos bay: expedition to, 229-30

Copperheads: 260

Copperopolis: *note* 142

"Corporal Jack": excerpts from letters, 221-6; *note* 226

Coulterville: *note* 142

Coult, Theodore A: *note* 122

Courtright, George S: 161

Covey, E. N: C.S.A. surgeon, 127

Cox, Valentine H: 279

Coyle's tavern: Californians attacked by Mosby's rangers, 293

Craig, Louis S: gives shoes and clothes to Mangas Coloradas, 150

Crazy Woman creek: 215

Creel, Reuben: U.S. consul to Chihuahua, 176; 177-8

Cremony, John C: escorts wagon train, 120-1; *note* 122; raised U.S. flag at Fort Quitman, 128; "kills the moon", 148-9; 155; translates Apache language, 158-9, *note* 159-60; MS translation in Bancroft lib., 159; 263; antelope hunt, 272-3

Crescent City: 239, 243, 360-1

Cross, Samuel: Wright monument in burial plot of, 362

Crowinshield, Casper: 286, 299

Culpepper: 298

Culver City: 42

Cummings, Joseph: Fort named for, 154-5

Curly-headed Tom (Indian): 247

Curtis, James F: en route to Fort Colville, 222-4; 249

Cutter, Abraham: Mowry sues, *note* 114-5

"Cyane", U.S.S: 301; 3rd trip to Pac., 302; 303; captures "Chapman",

"Cyane", U.S.S: continued 305, 307-8; contest "Chapman" war prize, 309-10; sale, 322

"DACOTAH", U.S.S: 321

Dahlgren, John A: note 322

"Daniel Webster" (Japanese bark): sunk by U.S.S. "Wyoming", 311

Danville prison: Calif. vol. deaths in, 298

"Dashaway" (boat): 244

Dashaway society: Ladies, 35; Temperance society, 338

Davis, Jefferson: 90, 125, 179; letter of marque, 304-5; cheers for at Camp Babbitt, 337; toast, 348; prayer for, 348

Davis, Joseph W: 279

Davis, Nelson H: 137, 139; Rio Grande Grant controversy, 173-4

Davis, Nicholas S: note 114; 161

Dayton: "sack of flour" auction, 332

De Russy, René E: 39-40; in charge of Pac. coast defenses, 234; note 234; plan for defense of S.F. bay, 314

De Wolf, ---: capt. of "Brother Jonathan", 361

Dead Man's fork: Indians attack, 211-2

Deans, William C: 279

Delaware: 291

Del Norte county: note 238

Democratic Press: destroyed, 341

Democratic Register: barred from U.S. mail, 336

Democrats: Douglas and Breckinridge, 70

Denver: 62, 207-9; Connor at, 218

Denver, J. W: duel, note 69

Des Moines: Connor at, 186

Deschutes river: 222-3

Deseret News: criticizes Legal Tender act, 353

Desertions: No desertions in 5 cos. of 1st inf. Cal. vols., 126; total desertions, note 126; 212

Dictatorship: of 1860's, 53

Dinwiddie Court house: 299

Displaced persons (Indians): 155-7, 248-50, 260, 363

Dodge, Grenville: 213-4

Dodge, P.O: raises flag, 253

Dole, W. P. (Ind. Com.): 153; disapproved Catalina Is. as Ind. res., 250

"Dollar a year" men: 42

Dominguez, Manuel: 44

Don Pedro's Bar: Calif. vols. from, 187

Dona Ana: 119

Donahue, Peter: reassembles U.S.S. "Camanche", 312; 313, 324

Doolittle, James R: chairman of cong. com. investigation of Indian affairs, 152-3

Dos Palmas: 82

Doty, James D: supt. of Ind. affairs in Utah, 197; treaty with Snake river Indians, 233

Douglas, Charles D: 244

Downey, John G: 24, 37; at Visalia, 341

Downieville: 29, 142, note 142

Downing, B. H: 48

Draft: 25, 140, 141; evaders, 206; no draft west of the Rockies, 363

Dragoon Springs: 104

Drake, Thomas J: Mormons ask resignation, 196

Dranesville: battle of, between Californians and Mosby's rangers, 295-6; 299

Dress parade: 38; Placerville, 189; 190; Camp Babbitt, 337

"Dr. Saw Bones": 267

Drum Barracks (Camp): 41-2; cost, size, 43-4; telegraph terminal, 46; state historical shrine "no. 167", 47; repossesion, 47; sale of buildings, 48; 84-5, 88, 103; Carleton leaves, 104; 142, 145, 170, 249, 254, 262, 342, 348; no. Calif. vols. burials, note 360

Drum, Richard Coulter: 42, 305

Drummed out: 38

Duels: 41, 69; prohibited, *note* 69; duelists, *note* 69; 179

Dutch Flat: 29, 141, *note* 142

EAGLE-OF-THE-LIGHT (INDIAN): 232

Early, Jubal Anderson: attacks Washington, 297

East Indies: 303

Echeverria, Juan (Chief of Maricopa Indians): trip to San Francisco, 148; "kill moon", 148-9

Edwards ferry: 293

Edwards, William (the "Frog"): kills Calif. vols., 341; price on his head, 342

Eel river: 245

Eigenbrodt, Charles S: 289, *note* 289; his co. at Monocacy R., 297

El Dorado canyon: 203

El Monte: 104, 347

El Paso: 90, 124

El Paso del Norte (Mex.): 125, 127; Skillman, 175-6; Juarez, 183

Elections: Calif. state, 230; 247-8, 260; in Austin, 330; 341

Elliott, Stephen E: 279

Elsinore (Laguna Grande): 104

Emancipation proclamation: Lincoln's, 310; Calif. Leg. endorses, 350

Emma, Queen of Hawaii: 321-2

Employment act: for Calif vols., 358

England: warships, 22; Maine boundary dispute, 105; neutrality, 319; flag, 319

Enos, Herbert M: 60, 135

Enrollment act (Conscription): suspended in Calif., 140; 141

Escalante, Manuel: 57-8

Ethnology, Bureau of (Wash. D.C.): 150-1

Eugene (Ore.): pub. of Joaquin Miller's newspaper at, 336

Evans, George S: in command of ex. to Owens valley, 254-60

Execution: at Benicia Barracks, 38-9

"Executive of the Commonwealth": 285

Expedition to Rio Grande: 77; preparation, 96, 100-1; itinerary, 104; 107; order of departure from Tucson, 122, *note* 122; health of troops, 273

Extradition laws: none between U.S. and Mex., 177, 184

Eyre, Edward E: advance guard, 117; meeting with Apache chief, 117-8; vols. killed, 118; raises flag over Fort Thorn, 119; 120-1; 270

FALMOUTH (Va.): army review, 287

Faneuil hall: Calif. Hundred dinner, 285

"Faralones", U.S.S: 305, 321

Farley, C. C: 279

Farmers' Oracle: printed at Springville, Utah, 207

Farwell, W. B: 315

Federal drafts: captured, 53

Ferguson, William L: duel, *note* 69

Fergusson, David: commands Mil. Dist. W. Ariz., 129; survey to Gulf of Calif., 129-31; route, *note* 131; map and census, 131; ordered to Chihuahua, 177

Fiddletown: *note* 142; Calif. vols. from, 187

"Field day": 240

Fields, Stephen J: trial of "Chapman" conspirators, 308-9

"Fighting Parson" (William S. Kidder): at Camp Cady, 263

Filibustering: 343

Fillmore (Utah): 203

First Congregational church (Sacramento): funeral Gen. Wright, 362

First Dragoons: 106

First Presbyterian Church of Stockton: 188

Fisherman's cove at Catalina: 249

Fitch, J. Ives: 342

Five Forks: 299; tulip tree for Memorial Grove, 300

Flag presentation: Shasta, 30-1; Jackson, 33; Sacramento Rangers, 35; Downieville, 35

Flag, preservation of: 33, 298

Flags, U.S: 66, 111; Fort Thorn, 119; 122; Forts Quitman and Davis, 128; Navajo springs, 136; N.Y. vols., 141-6; Sugarloaf Mt., 190; Columbia river steamers, 222; 253, 256; gift to Calif. Hundred, 286; 287; gift to Calif. Bat., 289, 298, 299; Monterey, 302; note 329; slandered, 348

Floods: Sacramento, 32, 34; Benicia Barracks, 37; Fort Yuma, 78; 96, 101; Bosque Redondo, 153; Fort Colville, 227; Fort Vancouver, 231; Humboldt Mil. Dist., 239; Round valley, 244

Florida: 26

Flour: stored at Pima, 85; 88, 97; moldy, 129; 225; Gridley's "sack of flour", 330-4

Foreign affairs: 22, 23, 105, 130, 131, 179, 180, 181, 182, 183, 219, 302, 310, 311, 317, 318, 319, 320

Foreman, Ann. 75-6, marries J. D. Peters, 76; 178

Foreman, Ferris: 75, 178; offers reward for "Frog", 342

Forest Hill: note 142

Forts: Alvord, note 234; Anderson, built, 241; Baker, built, 241; Barrett, establishment, 91-2; 109; Bascom, named for Capt. Bascom, 155; 161, 163; no. Calif. vols. burials, note 360; Bidwell, 238; built, 252; Calif. vols. at, 253; Bliss, 52-5, 66, 124; Calif. vols. at, 175; Boise, 193, 231; new Fort Boise built near old, 233; note 234; no. Calif. vols. burials, note 360; Bowie (for events see Apache Pass), no. Calif. vols. burials, note 360; Bragg, 3rd inf. Calif. vols. at, 187; 238; Calif. vols. arrive, 244; note 244; Breckenridge, 33; Bridger, Calif. vols. at, 194; duty, 205-6; no. Calif. vols. burials, note 360; Buchanan, 33; Cape Disappointment, built, 234; Calif. vols.

Forts: continued

at, 235-6; Churchill, 26, 186; Connor's 3rd at, 190; 198; 255-6; no. Calif. vols. burials, note 360; Colville, 221, 224; Calif. vols. arrive, 225; 226; note 226; theater, 227; 231, note 234; Connor (Idaho) built at Soda Springs, Idaho, 198; 206; Connor (Wyo.), built, 214-5; 217-8; Craig, 19, 52, 54, 58-60, 66, 90, 93, 119, 139; hospital fund, 172; supply base, 177; 268; burial of Watson, 271; 276; no. Calif. vols. burials, note 360; Crook, U.S. troops withdrawn, 250; Calif. vols. at, 251-2; 265; Cummings, named for Maj. Cummings, 154-5; Dalles, Calif. vols. at, 222; 226, note 231, 233; note 234; 235; Davis, 54-5; U.S. flag raised at, 128; 175; U.S. gov. property at, 176; Defiance, 165, 167; Ethan Allen, Californians at, 294; Fauntleroy, renamed Fort Wingate, 155; Fillmore, 52-3, 55, 79, 124, 270; Garland, 275; Gaston, 187, 240, 245, note 245-7; no. Calif. vols. burials, note 360; Goodwin, built by Cal. vols. 139-40; expedition to, 139; 140; no. Calif. vols. burials, note 360; Hall, protection of, 233; note 234; Hoskins, 226; Calif. vols. at, 229; note 229, note 231, note 234; Humboldt, 187, 238; flood, 239; note 239, 242, 244-5, 248, 265; no. Calif. vols. burials, note 360; Jones, 238; Calif. vols. at, 254; note 278; Kearney, 52; Lapwai, 231; built, 232; note 234; no. Calif. vols. burials, note 360; Laramie, 209; troops at, 211-2; 214-5, 217; Larned, 161, 163; Leaton, outlaws, 176; restored as memorial, note 176; Leavenworth, Carleton, 105; 132; Connor, 186; 212, 265; Lyon (Colo.), 63; Marcey, note 360; Mason, death of vols., 144; Cal. vols. at, 179-80; Pesqueira, 180;

Forts: continued
181; no. Calif. vols. burials, *note* 360; *Massachusetts* (Fort Stevens), 292; *McDermitt,* named for Col. McDermitt, 277; *McDowell,* no. Calif. vols. burials, *note* 360; *McLane,* 90; death of Mangas Coloradas, 151; named for Capt. McLane, 154; *McRae,* 276; no. Calif. vols. burials, *note* 360; *Miller,* Calif. vols. at, 254; 262, 265; *Mojave,* 107, 138, 201; survey party arrive, 202-3; 265, 341, 342; no. Calif. vols. burials, *note* 360; *Piute,* 202; description, 264; 265; *Point,* fortification, 234, 314; *Quitman,* 54-6; U.S. Flag raised, 128; 133; *Reading,* built, 253; *note* 253; Calif. vols. at, 254; 265; *Reno,* Californians at, 297, 299; *Ruby,* built by 3rd inf. Calif. vols., 191; 192, 194; no. Calif. vols. burials, *note* 360; *Selden,* no. Calif. vols. burials, *note* 360; *Stanton,* 52-3; named, 154; "Kit" Carson, 158; no. Calif. vols. burials, *note* 360; *Steilacoom,* 226, *note* 231, 234; *Stevens* (Ore.), Calif. vols., 236; *note* 236; *Stevens* (Washington City, D.C.), 284, description, 292; battle of, 297; *Sumner,* built by Cal. col., 155; 156; Capt. Cremony, 158; 160; crop failure, 272; pets, 273; no. Calif. vols. burials, *note* 360; *Sumter,* 19; *Tejon,* 106-7, 240, 259; Calif. vols., 262; 265; Surg. Letterman, 269; *Terwaw,* 187; destroyed by flood, 239; *Thorn,* 55, 58, 93; Eyre raises flag, 119; 122; description, 123; 133, 270; *Tubac,* 143; *Union,* 62-3, 161, 163-4; *Vancouver,* 25, 26; Calif. vols. at, 220-1; *note* 221, 226, 228, 231, 360; no. Calif. vols. burials, *note* 360; *Walla Walla,* Calif. vols. at, 223; 224, 226, 231, *note* 234; *Wallula,* 221, 223; *West,* horses stolen, 274; *Whipple,* 33;

Forts: continued
building of, 135-9; 263; no. Calif. vols. burials, *note* 360; *Wingate,* 33, 135; named for Capt. Wingate, 155; no. Calif. vols. burials, *note* 360; *Wright* (Calif.), built, 244; no. Calif. vols. burials, *note* 360; *Yamhill,* 226; Calif. vols. at, 229; *note* 229, *note* 234; *Yuma,* 20, 34, 74, 77-8, 80; reinforced, 81; 85, 87, 99; supplies forwarded, 100; fortification, 101; water route to, 102; 103-4; Carleton's arrival, 105; 110; Mowry, 114; demobilization center, 145; 265, 267, 270, 278, 341, 342; no. Calif. vols. burials, *note* 360

Fortification bill: defense of Columbia river, 234

Fourth-of-july cove: at Catalina Is., 249

Franklin (El Paso, Tex.): 119, 183

Franklin (Idaho): 195

Fredericks pike: Manning's co. at, 297

"Fredonia", U.S.S: joins Pac. squadron, 320; 321

Freedom: of speech and press, 336, 347-9

French: warships, 22; troops invade Mexico, 130; 131, 179; neutrality laws with U.S., 180; troops at Guaymas, 180; take Native Calif. cav. prisoners, 181; troops, 182; refugees enlist in U.S. army, 183; fleet blockades Mex. ports, 318; bomb Acapulco, 320; sale of French muskets as war surplus, 357

French, Albert H: Escorts C.S.A. prisoners to San Antonio, 127

French Gulch: 30

Frink, (Judge): 71

Frink's Springs: 82

Fritz, Emil: 110, 123

"Frog" (William Edwards): 341-2

"Fuss and feathers": Gen. Wright described as, 349

"GAG OATH": 337
Galisteo: 65
Galveston: battle of, 76
Gambling: license for in Ariz., 112-3; 172; prohibited in Calif., 338
Gardiner's Wells: 104
Garland, John: 106
Garrison, S. J: arrest, 337-8; 340
Gaston, William: Fort named for, note 245
Geleich, Vincent: 279
"Gem" (river boat): 30
"General Jessup": Colo. riverboat, 102
Gerrol, Joseph: original receipt for liquor tax, 172
Gettysburg: 284, Battle of, 293
Gibbs, Addison C: 354
"Gibraltar of Navajodom": 169
Gibsonville: note 142
Gila Bend: 104, 109
Gila City: 78, 104
Gilbert, J. A: duel, note 69
Gilpin, William: govr. of Colo, 62-3, drafts on U.S. treasury, 63
G.I.'s of the 1860's: en route to Tucson, 109; 122, 130; pay of officers, 350-1; 357
Glasby, Almon: trial, 200
Glorieta: 65, 67, 104
Gloucester Point: Calif. Hundred arrive, 286; 287
Gold Hill: "sack of flour" auction, 332
"Gold law": Calif. Specific Contract act, 352
"Gold steamers": 329
"Golden Age", s.s: 284
Golden Gate: 71, 220, 284; Kibbe's plan for defense, 313-4
Golden Gate park: statue of Starr King, 330
"Golden Gate", s.s: sunken treasure of, 307
Goldthwaite, John W: cash subscription, 191
Goodman, Theodore H: letter from, 258

Goodwin, John N: report on vedettes, 132; ar. Navajo springs, 136; 138; Fort named for, 139
Gordonsville: 298
Gould & Curry: 326
Government Corral: 136
Government hole: 202
Government priority: of war materiel on Pac. coast, 317
Government property: 21; guard for, 101; 102; destroyed, 123; captured by C.S.A., 127; at Fort Davis, 176; ordered burned if C.S.A. troops returned, 177; recovered from Mex., 182; stolen, 212; proceeds from sale of "Chapman", 310; on board "Aquila", 312; sale of war surplus, 322, 357
Gran Quivira: Carleton explores, 106
Grand Army of the Republic: 67; Rawlins post, 334-5
Grant, U. S: at Fort Humboldt, note 239, 293, 330
Gray Lady (Navajo): married T. V. Keams, 167
Greathouse, Ridgley: supplies funds, 306; 307-8; conviction and sentence, 309
Greenback raid: 295
Gridley, Amos: 331
Gridley, Reuel Colt: election bet, 330; payoff, 331; travels with "sack of flour", 332-4; total contributions, 334; monument, 335; biog., note 335
Grinnell, ——: supplies beef, 97
Guadalupe: Leaton's hdqrts., 182
Guadalupe Island: 305-7
Guaymas: 22, 57, 81, 101-2; French troops occupy, 180, 182; U.S.S. "St. Marys", 305
Guerra, de la, Antonio Maria: 45
Gulf of California: 101-2; survey to, 129-31, route, note 131
Gulf of Tehauntepec: 289
Gwin, William McKendrie: arrested, 347

Gwyther, George: scout to Black canyon, 274-5; 279

HABEAS CORPUS: 75; for "Chapman" conspirators, 309; suspension, 350
Hail Columbia, Happy Land: 284
Hale, James A: 341
Half Moon bay: munitions siezed, 316
Halford, William: rows 1,000 mi., 322
Hall, Calvin (vedette): 251
Hall, Edward: C.S.A. agent, 176
Hall, James: death, 275
Hall, Lovick P: arrest, 337-8; 340
Halleck, Henry Wager: 173, 191, 243; approved Catalina Ind. res. plan, 250
Halltown: 289, 297, 299
Hammond, William A: recommendation, 327
Ham's Fork: 194
Hancock, Henry: reports on Catalina Is., 249
Handsome Billy (Indian): 246
Handy, John C: 279
Haralson, (Dist. Att'y): 71
Hard tack: 145, 225
Harding, Stephen S: gov. of Utah territory, 196
Hardy, James H: impeachment, 347-8
Hargraves, Joseph P: 135, 137, 165
Harpending, Asbury: receives letter of marque, 305-6; 307; proclamation, 308; conviction and sentence, 309
Harpers ferry: 297
Harper's Magazine: 133
Hart, Simeon: 54-5; aids Confederates, 125; "cotton king", 179
Hart's mill, El Paso (El Molino del Norte): 55; description, 125-6; West's hdqrts., 134; 177
Harvard (Calif.): Camp Cady near, 264
Harwood, Franklin (3rd U.S. art.): 122

Hastings, J. W: 76; scheme to recruit troops for C.S.A. in Cal., 178-9
Hathaway, Charles W: sues for wharfage, 312
Hathaway wharf: 312
Haversack: 100
Hawaiian Islands (Sandwich): 302, 321
Hay: 77-8, 87, 97; haymakers on Central O.M., 211; price, 227
Hayes, Lewis W: 279
Hayes, William W: 279
Heintzelman, Samuel P: Calif. Bat. joins, 291
"Helen Hensley" s.s: 187
Helm, Thomas: 61
Henry, John: killed, 143-4
Henry, John M: 224
Herbert, Philip: 90
Hermosillo: 181
Herrick, Rufus F: 246
Highwaymen: kill and rob vedettes, 132; 198-201
Hill, ---: aids capture of stage robbers, 200
Hobble Creek: 207
Hodges, Preston: convicted, 200
Hoffman, David S: 279
Hoffman, Ogden: trial and release of "Chapman" conspirators, 309
Hogg, T. E: arrest and imprisonment, 314-5
Holbrook, C. E: 279
Holbrook, Charles: Rep. candidate and winner, 331
Home Guards: *note* 284, 333; at Visalia, 340; 341
Hooker, Joseph: army reviewed by Lincoln, 287-8; 293, 338
Hoopa Indians: 246
Hoopa valley: 245-6
Hoover dam: 203
Horn, George H: 279
Horses: Spanish, 45; American, 84; shoes, 98; purchase, 98; stolen, 118; loss during survey, 202-3; burned at O.M. station, 205; stolen, 211-2; Indian horses captured at

Horses: continued
  Powder R., 216; loss, 217; killed, 274; 283; stampeded by Mosby's rangers, 294
Horsetown: 30
Hospitals: description of field hospital, 195; tents used, 266; Letterman, 269; U.S. marine, 270; 277
Howe, Marshall S: commands So. Mil. Dist. of N. Mex., 119
Howitzers, U.S: captured and buried, 67; Fort Yuma, 85; accompany advance guard, 120, 122; Connor's 3rd, 188; at battle of Bear river, 194; 240, 264, 267; "Union Boy", 333
Howland Flat: 142, note 142
Howland, George W: 3rd U.S. cav., 119
Hoyt, Samuel N: 194
Hudson Bay company: 226
Hull, William E: 224
Humboldt county: note 238, 245, 247, 252
Humboldt Indians: plan removal to Catalina Is., 248-50
Humboldt massacre: 192
Humboldt (Nev.): 253
Humboldt, Military District of: 3rd Inf. Calif. vols. in, 187; 188, 228; Lippitt in command, 238; note 238, 241-2; Indian campaign, 243; 244; number of vols., 245; peace with Indians, 246-7; Black in command, 247; Schmidt in command, 248; 250
Hunter, Sherod: march for Tucson, 81; enters Tucson, 82-6; 91; starts for Rio Grande, 92; 110
Hunter's Point: 40
Huntington library (San Marino, Calif.): 172; original of letter to Lincoln, 242; Gwyther's original oaths, 275
Hurdy shop: 38
Hydesville: 241

IDAHO: 34, 234, 236-7, 252-3

"Idaho", s.s: on Columbia river, 222, note 222
Indian express: 97
Indian ocean: 307
Indian policy: of U.S. gov., 155; Carleton's, 155-7; War department's, 156; Wright's, 248-50
Indian troubles: 22
Indian Wells: 104
"Industry" (bark): wreck, 235
Ingraham, Henry M: robs O.M. stage, 199; known as the "Red Fox", 200
Ink powder: 28, 206
Inscription Rock: 166
Interior Department: 133, 152
Intoxicants: sale, 32; license for sale, 112-3; 129, 172; confiscated, 189; price, 227; prohibited on Nez Percé res., 233; "thousand yard whiskey", 243; prohibited, 244; 266; as medicine, 267; free for election campaigns, 331; 356
Iowa: 7th cav., note 214
Iretaba (Chief of Mojave Indians): Washington, D.C., 146; returns home, 147
Iron-clads: 304; Ericsson Monitor, 311; rescued, 312; 313; arrival "Monadnock", 321
"Iron horse": 148
Irwin, Bernard J. D: Medal of honor, 363
Isleta: 176

JACKSON: 33, 141, note 142
James, Charles: 316
James, Horace P: 324
"Jamestown", U.S.S: 321
Japan: 302, 310; treaty with U.S., 311
Japanese Indemnity fund: paid to crew of U.S.S. "Wyoming", 311
Jefferson Barracks: 26; Carleton at, 105
Jenny Lind: Calif. vols. from, 187
Jews: fleeing from Texas, 178
Jimenez, Porfirio: encounter with French troops, 181

"J. M. Chapman" (schooner): conspiracy, 305-10; 314, 340
Joaquin Jim (Indian): in White mountains, 259
John Brown's Body: 331
John Day river: 223; protection, 251
Johnson, George A: 102
Johnson, George Pen: duel, *note* 69
Johnson, Robert S: 271
Johnson's ranch: 65; historical marker, 66
Johnston, Albert Sidney: resignation, 21; 27, 236
Johnston, George: death, 88; monument, 92
Jones, John (expressman): captured, 90; the Paul Revere of the s.w., 115-6; personal narrative, 116; capture at Picacho (on Rio Grande), 116; 123
Jones, Thomas Ap Catesby: 302
Jordan river: 192
Jornada del Muerto (Journey of Death): 33, 59, 124
Joseph (Indian): 232
Juan de Fuca, Strait of: u.s.s. "Narragansett" at, 319
Juarez, Benito Pablo: 82, 90; u.s. recognizes his government, 180; 182; praised by Calif. vols., 183; prophecy of, 185; 317
Judah, Henry Moses: 31-2
Judicial district of California: 4th., Mowry suit filed in, 114

KANSAS: 211; 16th cav., *note* 214
Kauai island: wreck of rescue boat, 322
Kavanaugh, H. H: 348
Keams canyon (Lukadeshjin): inscription on walls, 166-7
Keams, Thomas Varker: Canyon named for, 167
Keaveny, Mrs. Thomas F: 46
Keith, James F: killed, 118
Kelly, William D: killed, 143-4
Kenyon station: 104
Kern river: 260

Kewen, E. J. C: arrest, 348
Keysville: 260-1; marker, *note* 261
Kibbe, William C: plan for Golden Gate defense, 313-4
Kidd, James H: commands left column, *note* 214
Kidder, William S. (Fighting Parson): letter from, 263
Kidnapping: 193-4
"Kill-moon", Captain: Cremony's sobriquet, 148-9
King, Thomas Starr: addresses soldiers, 36; note to Calif. Hundred, 283; praises Calif. Hundred, 285; speech for Soldiers' Relief, 325-6; reports on Sanitary Com., 327; 329; monuments, 330; biog. *note* 329-30
Kinny, M. M: u.s. v-consul at Monterey (Mex.), 177
Kiowa Indians: 163, 174; on warpath, 211
Kirkham, Ralph W: 37
Kirkpatrick, Charles A: 279
Kittridge, Willard: clothing costs, 206
Kittridge, William: at Stanwix, 91; 117; wounded, 118; 270; 280
Klamath county: *note* 238, 247
Klamath river: forests, 239; 245
Klunker, E. A: 278
Klunker, John E: at Catalina Is., 278, *note* 278; 280
Knapp, --- (Judge): 173
Knapsacks: 87, 100
Knights of the Columbian Star: 179; 342; degrees, signs and passwords, 345-6
Knights of the Golden Circle: 179, 342; pledge, password, badge and signs, 343-5
Ku-Klux-Klan: 343

LA LIBERTAD: survey, 129-31, *note* 131
La Paz: 203; Calif. vols. killed, 341-2, *note* 342
La Porte: 142, *note* 142

La Ventana (The Window): Navajo Indian agency, 168

"Lackawanna", u.s.s: 321

Ladies rangers: 76

Laguna Mosca: *note* 131

Lake De Smet 215

Lake Merritt: 37

Lally, F. T: 79

Lambert, John: 139

"Lancaster", u.s.s: 301, 303, 314, 319

"Lancefield", s.s. (Japanese): damaged by u.s.s. "Wyoming", 311

Lane's crossing (Oro Grande): 263

Langley: 295

"Lanrick" (Japanese brig): sunk by u.s.s. "Wyoming", 311

Las Cruces: 119, 124, 157

Las Vegas: 202-3, 265

Latham, Milton Slocum: 41

Law, William C: capt. of "Chapman", 306; 307-8

Lawyer (Indian): chief of Nez Percé Indians, 232-3

"Leather stocking": 241

Leaton, --- (Colonel): attempts to recruit Calif. vols. for Mex., 182

Leaves of absence: curtailed, 21

Ledyard, E. C: letter from, 44-5

Lee, Robert E: 143; crosses Potomac, 293

Leesburg: 292

Legal Tender act: 350; California's profit, 351; 352; disapproval by Mormons, Nevada, 353

Lent, William: 325

Leonard, Mrs. Theresa: owner of "sanitary man", 328

Leonard, William S: death, 88-9; monument, 92

Letterman General hospital: named, 269

Letterman, Jonathan: served in Dep. of Pacific, 268; established ambulance system, 269; biog., *note* 269

Letters, California Vols: 28, 44-5, 83-4, 109-10, 123-4, 125-6, 136; Edgar Pomeroy, 137-8; 143-4; 157-8; Thornton G. Porter, 160-1;

Letters, California Vols: continued 180; Sanford Bailey, 183; Tuttle's diary, 191-2; 207-8; excerpts from "Corporal Jack", 221-6; 235, 239; Lippitt to Lincoln, 242; 243, 246; Ernest M. Woodman, 252-3; 254-5; Theodore H. Goodman, 258; 258-60; William S. Kidder, 263; excerpts, 289-92, 294, 298-300; W. Y. Bliss, 356, *note* 356; Emory Wing, 360-1

Letter of marque: 305-6, 317

Lewis, Charles W: commands 7th inf., 141-3; biog., *note* 142; presents flag to Soc. Stevenson's Calif. Ex. Survivors, 147; at Fort Mason, 179-80; increased guard on Mex. border, 181

Lewis, Micajah G: Fort Bridger, 194

Lewiston: 232

Libby, Lorenzo C: 307-8

Libby prison: 295; Calif. vols. deaths in, 298

Licenses: bars, gambling houses, merchants, 112-3; fines for nonpayment, 113

Lime Point: fortification, 314

Lincoln, Abraham: 23; election, 25; call for volunteers, 29, 52, 54; support, 69; 72, 111, 117; talks to Iretaba, 146-7; appoints Creel consul to Chihuahua, 176; 184, 196; re. firearms to Indians, 210; letter from Lippitt, 242; 252; reviews army, 287-8; 293; at battle of Fort Stevens, 297; salutes Californian's flag, 299; Amnesty proclamation, 309; Emancipation proclamation, 310; bans arms shipment to Mex., 317; 327; name calling of, 336; 337, 340; death, 341; 344; praise, 348; 349

Lippincott, Henry: 280

Lippitt, Francis J: commands Humboldt Mil. Dist., 238; 239, *note* 239; orders forts built, 240; criticized, 241; letter to Lincoln, 242; 243; relieved, 244

Lockford road: 189
London: 115; "Shenandoah" sails from, 319
Lone Palm: 82
Long Bridge: Californians guard, 294
"Loo Choo" (transport) : 26
Looking Glass (Indian) : 232
Lord, Abbie: presents u.s. flag to Calif. Hundred, 286; 298
Los Angeles: 42; description, 45; 347
Los Angeles county: 29; enlistments, 347
Los Angeles News: 342, 349
Los Angeles Star: 46; barred from u.s. mail, 336
Los Pinos: no. Calif. vols. burials, note 360
Louisville: hdqrts. Sanitary Com., 327
Loup river: 216
Low, Frederick F: 27, 315, 333
Lower California: 20; defense, 302
Lower Mission station: 87
Loyalty: of West, 281; of Calif., 338
Loyalty resolution: note 69; 2nd resolution, 350
Ludwig, Mrs. William: 31
Luray: 299
Lynde, Issac: 53

MACHADO, AUGUSTIN: 41
Mackell, W. W: 106
Mad river: 241
Magdalena: 79; Native Calif. cav. at, 181
Magee, John: 73
Magruder, William T: 223-4
Maine: 26
Mallory, S. R: secretary of c.s.a. navy, 314
Maloney, John: killed, 118
Mammoth Tanks: 82
Mangas Coloradas (Red Sleeves): chief of Apache Indians, receives gifts, 150; translates Apache language, 150-1; death, 151-2; 158
Manning, C. C: (Calif. vol.) in Andersonville prison, 296

Manning, George A: (Calif. vol.) 289, note 289; in Andersonville prison, 296-7
Manta: 88; exchanged for provisions, 97
Manzanillo: 289, 306-7
Mare Island navy base: 20; lack of defense, 302; guns, 303; u.s.s. "Saginaw" repaired, 305; 312
Maricopa Indians: 86; chief visits San Francisco, 148
Maricopa Wells: 104, 109
Marin county: 71
Mariposa: 70, 141, note 142; 347
Martial law: in Ariz., 111; in Round valley, 244, note 244
"Mary Ann" (tug): 244
Maryland: 291
Marysville: 141, note 142
Marysville Appeal: 349
Mason, John S: 135; Fort Whipple, 138; commands Mil. Dist. of Ariz., 148
Masons, Free and Accepted: of Santa Fe, 67
Massachusetts: 27; bounty, 281; recruit Calif. vols. for, 282; 53rd reg., 285; 2nd cav., 285, 288; 289; 2nd cav., 293, 354
Maury, Reuben F: 236
Maximilian, Ferdinand (Prince): in Mex., 180; death, 184-5
Maynard, Jesse T: wounded in Apache Pass, 121
Mazatlan: 21, 315
McCabe, F: 166
McCleave, T. C: note 90
McCleave, William A: 81; captured, 83-6, 88-9; personal account of capture, 89-90; release, 92-3; refuses pay, 94; biog., note 94; scout to Black canyon, 274-5
McCormick, Charles: med. inspector Dep. of Pacific, 278
McDermitt, Charles F: death, 277, note 278
McDowell, Irvin: 28, 252; commends Capt. B. West, 263; orders

McDowell, Irvin: continued
to Pacific s.s. co., 315; 316; for-
bids shipment war materiel to
Mex., seizes s.s. "Colon", 317
McDuffie ranch: 71
McGarry, Edward: 193-5
McKee, William H: 280
McKnight, W. L: guards o.m. stages,
200
McKowan, Ned: 90
McLane, George: Fort named for, 154
McLane, Louis: 186; asks guard for
o.m., 200
McLaughlin, Moses: 259; in com-
mand at Camp Babbitt, 337
McNulty, James M: 49, note 122;
services, 271-4; 280
McNulty, John: capt. of s.s. "Idaho",
222
McRuer, D. C: 324
Meade, George H: 293, 338
Mechanical toys: 328
Mechanized warfare: defense
against, 313-4
Medal of honor: to Philip Baybutt,
299; to Bernard J. D. Irwin, 363
Medical colleges: 266
Medical department, u.s. army: per-
sonnel, 266, note 266
Medical supplies: price of, 227; 267
Medicine wagon: 91
Meek, Laura: presents flag, 33
Meiggs wharf: 326
Mellen, Henry B: Fort Crook, 251;
252
Memorial Grove: Capitol Park,
Sacramento, 300, note 300
Mendocino county: note 238, 245, 361
Mendocino Indian reservation: liquor
prohibited, 244
Merritt, Gilbert R: 290
Merritt, Israel E: 312
Merritt, Samuel: 36
Merritt, Wesley: 297
Merryman, James H: Port Towns-
end affair, 303-4
Mesa del Contadera: 59
Mesa Grande: 74, 342

Mesilla: 104; number of Cal. vols.,
122; 124, 132, 157, 304
Mesilla Times: 124
Mesquite beans: food for horses and
men, 98
Messenger, Hiram A: 143; biog.,
note 144
Methodist Episcopal South college:
renamed Wilson college, 48
Methodist South church: 348
Metropolitan theater (S.F.): "sack
of flour" auction, 334
Metropolitan Water & Power com-
pany: line passes Fort Piute, 264
Mexico City: 26
Mexico, Republic of: 19; shipment
of arms, 20; foreign loans, 23;
101; permits u.s. troops to pass
thru, 129-30; invaded by French,
130; protection of coast, 303; neu-
trality, 305; 315-8
Michigan: 6th cav., note 214
Midway island: harbor improve-
ment, 322
Military board of investigation:
Mowry case, 114, note 114
Military Recruiting fund: allotted
for Calif. vols., 351
Military training: 26
Mill creek: 253
Miller, Albert S: Fort named for,
note 254
Miller, Joaquin (Cincinnatus Heine):
pub. of Democratic Register, 336
Millerton: 254
Millerton lake: submerges Fort Mil-
ler and Millerton, 254; 265
Mimbres river: 104, 116
Minerals: prospect for, 109, 110;
135, 203, 204, 232, 233; gold and
silver contributions, 328; output of
western mines, 329; 332; sale for
scrap, war surplus, 357
Minor's ranch: 241
Minstrel show: Fort Bridger, 205
Minter, John S: ranch, 74
Mission Camp: 104
Mission San Xavier del Bac: note 131

Missouri: 2nd art. and 12th cav.,
  note 214
Mitchell, Titus B: 121
Modoc war: Thomas F. Wright
  killed, 362
Mohawk: 104
"Mohican", u.s.s: 321
"Mohongo", u.s.s: joins Pac. squad-
  ron, 320; 321
Mojave Indians: chief visits Wash-
  ington, D.C., 146
Mojave river: protection, 263-4
Mokelumne Hill: 29, *note* 142; Calif.
  vols. from, 187
Mokelumne river: 189
"Monadnock", u.s.s: second iron-clad
  on Pac., 321
Monimann, Theodore: Mowry sues,
  note 114-5
Monocacy river: 297; maple tree for
  Memorial Grove, 300
Monroe Doctrine: 320
Montana: in Mil. Dist. of Plains, 209
Monterey (Calif.) : flag over, 302
Montezuma, Halls of: 182
Montgomery, J. B: orders to protect
  mail s.s., 303
Monuments: State Hist. Shrine no.
  169 at Drum Barracks, 47; marker
  at Apache canyon, 66; Santa Fe,
  67, *note* 68; to Paulino Weaver,
  note 86; to Lt. Barrett and men,
  92; Mountain Meadow, 107; no. 2
  on Mex. boundary, 125; Fort Lea-
  ton, Tex. restored as memorial,
  note 176; 202; to Connor, Calif.
  and Nev. vols., 219; markers, 238;
  marker Fort Crook, 252; marker
  Keysville, *note* 261; Fort Stevens,
  Wash., D.C., 297; Memorial Grove,
  Sacramento, 300; to Starr King,
  330, *note* 330; Gridley and "sack
  of flour", 334-5; to Gen. and Mrs.
  Wright, 362
Moody, W. G: 57-8
Moonlight, Thomas: Indian attack at
Morgan, E. M: 73
  Dead Man's Fork, 211-2

Mormons: 192; ask resignation of
  federal officers, 196; threaten set-
  tlers, 204; disapproval of Legal
  Tender act, 353
Morrisites: settled at Morristown,
  197-8; at Carson City, 198
Morton, Mrs: Indian captive, 211
Mosby, John Singleton: encounter
  with Californians, 293-6
Mother Lode: Calif. vols. from, 141,
  note 142, 187, 229
Mountain battalion: 27, organization,
  244; Whipple commands, 245;
  247; recruiting fund, 351
Mountain Meadow: survey to, 202-3
Mountain Meadow Massacre: 106
Mount Tamalpais: 72
Mowry, Sylvester: mine, 89; arrest-
  ed, property confiscated, 113; Fort
  Yuma, 114; hearing and release,
  114; suit against Carleton, 114,
  note 114-5; Senate investigation,
  114; dies in London, 115; 147
Muddy river: 202-3
Munday, Frederick: 263
Munitions of war: 20; at Mowry
  mine, 113; 302-3; for "Chapman",
  306; 307-8; on board "Aquila",
  312; purchase for Mex., 315-7;
  340; sale of war surplus, 357
Murphys: *note* 142
Murrieta, Joaquin: *note* 187
Mutiny: in Ark. and Mo. troops, 21;
  212

NAPA COUNTY: *note* 238
"Napoleons" (howitzers) : 120, 264
"Narragansett", u.s.s: 301, 303,
  ordered to Atlantic coast, 319
National Sanitary Commission: 325;
  work, 326-7; contribution, 327-8;
  total contribution, 329; "sack of
  flour", 334
Native California cavalry: 27, 45,
  180; deserters held prisoners by
  French, 181; Humboldt Dist., 247;
  Camp Cady, 263; recruiting fund
  for, 351, 353

Navajo Indians: 154, 156-7; campaign against, 160-1, 164-9; radio station KTGM, 168; 170; treaty of 1868, 171; 174; expert bowmen, 268; 272

Navajo springs: 136

Navy department: 303

"Ned Beal" (boat): 249

Negroes: carries "sack of flour", 334; rights and privileges, 338-9

Nelson & Doble: 98

Nevada: 34; disapproval of Legal Tender act, 353

Nevada City: enlistment 25, 142, note 142

Nevada Historical society: 332

Nevada volunteers: guard O.M., 204-5; monument at Fort Douglas, 219; offer to serve in East, 354; mustering out, 355-6

New Eng. Soldiers' Relief Ass'n: entertain Calif. Hundred, 285

New Fort Boise: built, 233

New Jersey: 291

New Mexico, Military Department of: 19, 107; Gen. Canby in command, 117; 119, 127; Gen. Carleton in command, 128, 154; 155; 265; med. inspector of, 272

New Mexico volunteers: 117, 157, 161-9; Gwyther serves with, 275; mustering out, 355-6

New river: 104

New San Pedro (Wilmington): 42-3; named changed, 46

New Year's day: 58; Fort Whipple, 139; Catalina Is. occupied, 249

New York: 22; entertain Calif. Hundred, 285; 311-2, 320; hdqrts. Sanitary Com., 327; bullion exhibited, 328; "sack of flour" auction, 334

New York volunteers: 26; flag of, 142-6

Newberry library (Chicago): E. E. Ayer's gift, 130

Newcomb, --- (interpreter): 117

News Letter: destroyed, 341

Newspapers, California: preservation of, note 28; barred from—reopened to U.S. mail, 336

Nez Percé Indians: treaties, 232-3

Nez Percé reservation: Fort Lapwai built, 232

Nichols, Charles P: 82, note 85

Nichols, Herman: 325

Noble, Herman: 259

Norcross, Daniel: presents Bear Flag to Calif. Hundred, 284

Norris, William: 324

Norton's Wells: 104

"Nyack", U.S.S: joins Pac. squadron, 320; 321

Nye, J. W: 186, 290; vetoes Nev. Specific Contract act, 353; 354

OAK GROVE (CALIF.): 49, 72-3, 85, 104, note 360

Oak Run: 251

Oath of allegiance: 21; Showalter party, 74; 110, 112; Gwyther's original, 275; "Chapman" conspirators, 309; called "gag oath", 337; pub. of Expositor, 338; teachers and attorneys, fines levied, 339; the "Frog's", 342; Gwin's, 347; C. L. Weller's, 349

Oath of fidelity: "Chapman" conspirators, 308

Oath of office: Gwyther's original, 275

Oatman's Flat: hay burned, 87; 104

O'Brien, Charles M: killed in Apache Pass, 120, 123

O'Brien, Michael: 224

O'Campo, Francisco: supplies beef, 97

Occident: destroyed, 341

Occidental Hotel (S.F.): Iretaba registers, 147

Ocean island: U.S.S. "Saginaw" wrecked, 322

"Ocean Queen", S.S: 285, 290

Odometer: 201

Oglesby house: telegraph at, 190

Ohio: 211

Ojo Caliente springs: 276
Old David (Indian): 219
Olympic Club: 325
Omaha: 216
Omaha scouts: *note* 214
Oneida station: 104
Opequan: 297, 299
Ophir Mining company: 326
Oquitoa: *note* 131
Oregon: population, 24; 192-3, 220-1; recruiting vols., 227-8; Calif. vols. four years service in, 228; 234; lack of coastal fortifications, 234; 236-7, 251-2, 320
Oregon, Military Department of: 19; Justus Steinberger in command, 228; 228; Gen. Alvord in command, 232; extent and commanders, 236-7; coast defense, 304
"Oregon", s.s: 40; man overboard, 145
Oregon Steam Navigation company: 231
Oregon volunteers: recruiting vols., 227-8; build Fort Lapwai, 232-3; offer to serve in East, 354
"Orizaba", s.s: 347
Oroville: enlistment, 25, *note* 142
Orton, Richard H: escort duty to Fort Larned, 164; recovers gov. property in Mex., 182
Otis, James: 324-5; Treas., Soldiers' Relief fund, 326
Overland Mail: 20, 24, 49; station, 73; Southern, 77-8; route, 104; buildings used as barracks, 123; 132; moved to Central route, 186; 192, 194; robbery, 198-201; Calif. vols. guard stages, 200, 204; Indians attack station, 205; emigrant, 206; destroyed, 209; 210; Oak Grove station, 270; 281
Owens valley: Indian campaign, 254-60; 262
Owens valley Indians: campaign against, 254-7; receive food and clothing, 258; peace, 259; removal to Sebastian res., 260

Owyhee river: *note* 234; protection, 251-2

PACIFIC COAST: 19, protection, 20; vulnerability, 23; 26, 80; loyal men, 182; fortification, 234; Northwest, 282; lack of defense, 302; alarmists, 304; Russian fleet visits, 310; gov. priority of war materiel, 317; 323
Pacific, Military Department of: 21, 23; size, 27; 105, 112-3, 135, 236, 242, 257, 278
Pacific squadron: 20, 57; description, 301; 317, 319; increase, 320; north and south divisions, 321; duties, 322
"Pacific", s.s: 40, 220
Pacific s.s. company (mail): guard, 20; guns, 302; 303, 306; plot to capture, 307, 314-5; French permit use of Acapulco, 318
Pala Mission: 73-4
Palm Springs (Agua Caliente): 82, 104
Palouse river: 225, 231
Panama: 20, 191, 281, 284, 289-90, 301-2; U.S.S. "Lancaster" at, 303; 321
Panther mountains: 216, 217
Paraje (de Fra Cristobal): 172
Park Barracks (N.Y.): 290
Parry, Isaac: 280
Parvin, Washington L: 74
Pasqual (Yuma chief): 81
Passports: in Mil. Dept. of New Mex., 171; Mex. passports to U.S. officers, 177; for foreigners on Pacific coast, 320
Patagonia mine: 89; seizure, 114
"Patriotic corn cob": 325
Patton, George Jr: *note* 48
Pawnee creek: 164
Pawnee Indians: scouts, *note* 214; Mission, 216
Paymaster: 37-8
Pearson, George F: 314; commands Pacific squadron, 319
Pecos church: 65

Pecos river: 156-7, 160; dam, 170

"Pembroke", s.s: fired on by Japanese, 310

Pemmican: 96-7

"Pensacola", u.s.s: 321

Peralta: 67

Peru, Government of: protests seizure of s.s. "Colon", 317-8; trouble with Spain, 319

Pesqueira, Ignacio: 57-8; protection by Calif. vols., 144; escapes from Sonora, 180

"Petaluma", s.s: 71

Peters, J. D: 76

Petersburg: 298

Petrified trees: 168

Pets: 50; Fort Sumner, 273

Pettis, George H: 123

Pfeiffer, Albert H: 167-8; attacked by Apaches, 275-6

Pfeiffer, Mrs. Albert H. and child: killed by Apaches, 275-6

Phelan, Jeremiah: note 85

Phelps, Edward: 280

Philadelphia: Refreshment rooms, 291

Photographs: Alcatraz and Benicia Barracks, 39; suppression, 40; contract price, 40

Picacho (on Rio Grande R.): Expressman Jones captured, 116

Picacho pass: battle, 88-9, 104; no. Calif. vols. burials, note 360

Pico, José Ramon: encounter with French troops, 181; in Humboldt Mil. Dist., 247-8

Piercy, Charles: quarrel and duel, 70-2; death, 72

Pigeon's ranch (La Glorieta): battle, 65; 67, 91, 104

Pike Peakers: 62, 65

Pima Indians: chief visits San Francisco, 147-8

Pima village: 81, 83-4, 89-92, 99, 104, 109

Pinkney, Joseph C: 226

Pino creek (Prairie Dog): 215

Pinole: 97, 116

Pinos Altos mine: 119, 129

Pioneer race track: 34

Pishon, Nathaniel J: note 85, 87, note 122; ordered to prospect, 135

Pitiquito: note 131

Piute Indians: 269

Piute springs: 202, 264

Placerville: 141, note 142; 3rd inf. Calif. vols. arrive, 189; stage robbers trial, 200; 278

Placerville Mountain Democrat: barred from u.s. mail, 336

Plains, Military District of: 208, extent, 209; 210; order to abolish, 213

Planters hotel, Denver: 218

Platte river: 214, 216

Platt's Music hall: 283; meeting for Soldiers' Relief, 325

Pleasanton, Alfred: 293

Point Isabel: 145

Point Lobos: survey to, 129-30, note 131

Point of Mountain: 104

Political refugees: 181

Poll tax: Calif. vols. exempt, 350

Polland house: site at Clements, 189

Pomeroy, Edgar: letter from 137-8, note 138

Pontoon: of Russian canvas boats, 211

Pony express: 21, 132

Poole, Thomas B: arrested, 199; convicted, 200

Poolsville: 297, 299

Pope, John: orders Dist. of Plains abolished, 213

Port Townsend (Wash.): affair, 303-4

Porter, Thornton G: letter from, 160-1

Portland: 220, 235, 360

Poston mine: 79

Potomac river: 291-2

Poultry stealing: 31, 36, 133

Poverty Bar: Calif. vols. from, 187

Powder river: expedition, 211-8

Powder river expedition: 208; organization, 211-3; four columns,

Powder river expedition: continued 214, *note* 214; battle, 215-6; casualties, 218

"Powhatan", u.s.s: joins Pac. squadron, 320; 321

Prentiss, John H: at Fort Barrett, 91; *note* 122; serves in Mil. Dist. of Ariz., 273-4; 280

Prescott: 132; capital of Ariz., 136-7; Gen. Mason arrives, 138

Prescott, William H: 130; city named for, 137

Presidio (San Francisco): 40, 142; hospital, 269; no. Calif. vols. burials, *note* 360

Presidio del Norte: 178

Price, George F: commands surveying party, 201-3

Prince, --- Major: 106

Prince A. Athearn's ferry: crossing of, 189

Prisoners of war: u.s., 53; c.s.a., 110; c.s.a. escorted to San Antonio, 127; 210

Privateers: 306, 317, 319; laws to prohibit, 340

Proclamations: Baylor, 53; Sibley, 56; Baylor, 61; Carleton, 110-3; Carleton's "clean up" orders, 124; West's orders to farmers, 134; Connor's circular to Mormons, 204; Connor's circular to officers, 210-1; of c.s.a. officers, 305; of "Chapman" conspirators, 308; Lincoln's Amnesty, 309, Emancipation, 310

Providence (Utah): 193

Pueblo Indians: 156

Puget Sound: u.s.s. "Narragansett" at, 319

QUAKERS (FRIENDS): care of Union soldiers, 291

Quincy: *note* 142

Quinn River valley: 277

RAILROAD PASS: 121

Ranchester: Connor Battlefield park near, 219

Rancho Ballona: 41

Rancho de San Pedro: 44

Randle, Peter W: 280

Ranney, --- Constable: wounded, 199-200

Raton pass: 164

Read, Thomas B: 297

Reading, Pierson Barton: 253; Fort named for, *note* 253

Readville (Mass.): Camp Meigs at, 285

Recipe: for bread, 98

Reconstruction: 350

Red Bluff: volunteers, 30; Mrs. John Brown arrives, 206; 251-2

Redington, John H: 324

Redwood creek: 241

Redwood Indians: 246

Reed, J. Sewell: Capt. of Calif. Hundred, 282; receives revolvers and Bear Flag, 283-4; 285-6, 288; killed at Dranesville, 295; burial, 296; 298

Reed, Mrs. J. Sewell and son: 282-4; color bearer, 287-8; 296

Reese river: 330

Regimentation: 171

Reid, Robert K: with Connor's 3rd, 189; at battle of Bear river, 195-6; 276-7; biog., *note* 277; 280

Reily, James: 55; to Mex., 57; letters confiscated, 57; at Tucson, 82; 90; releases McCleave, 93

"Republic", s.s: loss of army supplies, 102

"Resaca", u.s.s: 321

Resignations: restricted, 21

Rhodes, ---: supplies beef, 97

Richmond: 298; Harpending's visit, 305

Ridge route: Fort Tejon ruins, 262

Rigg, Edwin A: 48-50; 72, 73; prescribed oath of allegiance, 74; 75, 77, 79-81, 84, 86, *note* 122; marries Miss Cooper, 125; commands ex. to Fort Goodwin, 139; 140, 172

Rincon Point: fortification, 314

Rinearson, J.S: in command at Fort Lapwai, 232

Ringgold, George: 282

Rio Grande: Hart's mill, 55; C.S.A. 56; 59, 60, 61, 62, 77, 90, 92, 95, 96; retreat C.S.A., 117; capture Jones, 116; 117; Eyre arrives, 119, 120, 121; 123, 124, 125; 133, 175, 176, 178, 270, 271, 363

Rio Grande Grant (Taos): 173-4

Rio Virgin: 202-3

Risdon, John R: 325

Roberts, J.B: 324

Roberts, Thomas L: advance scout, 120

Robinson, Palatine: 79

Robinson, R.L: U.S. consul, 57

Robinson, Robert: ass't detective, 345

Robinson, "Uncle" Jack: 206

Rock springs: 202, 265

Rockville: 299

Rockwell, Porter: Mormon guide, 195

Rogers, J. Henry: quotes from poem by, 282-3, 287-8, 296

Rogue river: 234

Rogue's March: 38

Roll of Honor; Calif. vols. names, 359; burial of vols., *note* 360

Romatke, F.A: 280

Rosebud creek: 214, 216, 217

Roseville: excursion to, 333-4

Round valley: martial law declared, 244, *note* 244

Roundtree, N.L: wagonmaster, 103

Rowe, Edwin A: 256-7

Rubery, Alfred: drafts drawn, 306; 307-8; conviction and sentence, 309

Russia: canvas boats from, 211; serfs freed, 310; fleet on Pacific coast, 310

Ryan, James T: 313

"SACK OF FLOUR" (SANITARY): Gridley's payoff, 330-1; auction, 332-4

Sackett's Wells: 104

Sacramento: enlistments, 141; 251-3; King's portrait in capitol, 330; "sack of flour" auction, 334; 345, 347; Gen. Wright's monument, 362

Sacramento City Cemetery: Gen. Wright's monument, 362

Sacramento river: 30, 251

"Saginaw", U.S.S: repaired at S.F., 305; 321; lays cable on N.W. coast, 322; wreck, 322

Sahuarita: *note* 131

Sailor creek: 299

Salmon Falls: 231; patrol of route, 233; *note* 234

Salmon river: 254

Salt horse meat: 145

Salt Lake (Utah): 24, 106; route to, 107; 186-7; Connor selects site for fort, 191; 3rd inf. arrives, 192; 194, 198, 203, 207; Connor returns, 218; Connor's death, 219; 251, 265, 281

Salton Sea (Dry Lake): 82

San Andreas: *note* 142; Calif. vols. from, 187

San Andreas Sanitary Commission: "sanitary man" collects for, 328

San Antonio: C.S.A. troops from, 55; death of Carleton, 108; C.S.A. sick and wounded escorted to, 127

San Antonio landing, 3)

San Augustin Springs: 53, 157

San Bernardino: 70-1, 81, 344, 347

San Diego: protection, 20; 363; no. Calif. vols. burials, *note* 360

San Elizario: 176, 182

San Felipe: 104

San Francisco: 20, 26, 29, 141, 222, 225-6, 228, 231, 235, 251, 273, 281, 289, 301-2, 305-6; police, 307; plot to capture forts, 308; Russian officers entertained, 310; 313, 315-6, 318; passports examined, 320; com. for Soldiers' Relief fund, 324; contribution, 327; bullion exhibited, 328; "sack of flour" auction, 334; 347, 360

San Francisco Bay: 20, 21, 71; fortification, 234; Russian fleet, 310; U.S.S. "Camanche" arrives and sinks, 311; defense, 313-4; De Russy's plan for defense, 314

San Francisco Bulletin: 57

San Francisco Daily Morning Call: 325

San Gabriel river: 44
San Gorgonio pass: 82
San Joaquin county: 71
San Jose (Calif.): stage robbers arrested, 200
San Jose Tribune: barred from u.s. mail, 336
San Jose (Warner's ranch): valley of, 49, 74
San Juan island: occupation, 23
San Luis Obispo: 347
San Quentin: 71
San Rafael: 71-2
"San Salvador", s.s: capture of Hogg, 314
San Simon: 104, 270
Sandwich islands (Hawaiian): 302, 321
"Sanitary man": collects, 328
Santa Barbara islands: 240
Santa Fe: surrendered to c.s.a., 61; Carleton at, 106; 132; no. Calif. vols. burials, *note* 360
Santa Rita copper mine: 150
"Saranac", u.s.s: 301; pursues the "Shenandoah", 320; 321
Saric: *note* 131
Sasbe (Zazaba): *note* 131
Savage, Thomas: u.s. consul at Havana, 314
Sawyer, Andrew (teamster): wounded in Apache Pass, 120
Schmidt, Albert: killed in Apache Pass, 118
Schmidt, John C: commands Humboldt Mil. Dist., 248
Scott, William A: praise for both presidents, 348
Scott, Winfield: 20-3
"Sea King" (s.s. "Shenandoah"): 319
Sebastian reservation: Owens valley Indians, 259-60
Secessionists: 20, 83; killed, wounded and prisoners at Picacho, 89; 123, 222, 302; threaten Calif. vols., 337; raise "Stars and Bars", 339-40; 341
Secor, Francis: 311, 313
Secret Service fund: 339

Sedden, James A: favors Hastings's scheme, 178-9
Seligman, Henry: 324
"Senator", s.s: 40, 142
Sequoia park: tree named for King, 330
Seranaltin John (Indian): 246; skirmish, 247
Seward, William H: advocates good neighbor policy, 180; foreign policy, 183-4; order of inquiry, 317
Sewing kit: 35, 100
Sharp carbine: 41, 264; sale of war surplus, 357
Sharples, Abram: 280
Shasta: volunteers, 30, 31, 249, 253; 263
Shearer, George: 149
"Shenandoah", s.s. ("Sea King") (c.s.a.): sails from London, 319; in Pacific, 320
Sheridan, Philip H: 183; Californians served with, 297; march, 298; ride of, 300; 338
Sheridan's Ride: 297
Sherman, William T: 183
Shimonoseki, Strait of: battle, 311
Shinn, John B. (3rd u.s. art.): commands battery of artillery, 122; *note* 122
Shirland, Edmond D: raised u.s. flag at Fort Davis, 128; holds Mangas Coloradas prisoner, 151
Shirley, Paul: commands "Cyane", 305; 307
Shoemaker, Francis M: escort to Mrs. John Brown, 206
Short, William H: wounds Mosby, 293
Showalter, Dan: quarrel and duel, 70-2; letter to Ann Foreman, 75-6; 175; letter confiscated, 178; 179
Showalter party: 72-3; capture, 74; imprisonment and release, 75; 342
"Shubrick", u.s.s: 40; Port Townsend affair, 303-4; plot to capture, 308
"Shylock" law: Calif. "gold law", 352

Sibley, Henry H: 52, 54-5; proclamation, 56; letters confiscated, 57; 58; commands c.s.a. at Valverde, 59; 60, 61, 62; retreats, 66-7; 304

Sibley tent: 43

Sierra county: contributions to Sanitary Com., 328

Sierraville: 142

Siletz Blockhouse: Calif vols. at, 229; *note* 234

Silver City: "sack of flour" auction, 332

Sioux Indians: on warpath, 211

"Six horses": 30

Skillman (c.s.a. spy): 75; El Paso, 175-6; 177; killed and mail confiscated, 178

Skobel, C.F. Otto: sketched Fort Miller, 254

Slavery: Carleton prohibits Indian, 165; 310; prohibited in Calif., 338; 350

Slough, John P: 62, 65, 67, 68

Smallpox: in Confederate army, 54

Smith, Albert Y: 193

Smith, Chas. A: *note* 114

Smith, Joseph: 101, 139

Smith R. Indian Res: 242

Smith, Victor: seizes Port Townsend custom house, 303-4

Smithsonian Institution: Carleton's report pub., 106; Cremony's Apache language translation sent, 158-9

Smoke creek: 253

Snake river: 224, 231, 232

Snake River Indians: 193; "talk" with Doty and Connor, 197; treaty, 233

Sneath, R.G: 324

Socorro: 176

Soda lake (Calif.): 263

Soda springs (Calif.): 107

Soda Springs (Idaho): Fort Connor built, 197-8

Soft tack: 225

Soldiers' ballot (absent ballot): 231; history of, *note* 261

Soldiers' bounty: state and federal,

Soldiers' bounty: continued
140-1; Calif. bounty, 231, 350; Calif. bounty denied to draftees, 354; "terminal pay" to Calif. vols., 356

Soldiers' Burial act: by Calif. Leg., 359

Soldier's Farewell: 104

Soldiers' graves marked: act of Congress, 359

Soldiers' hay party: at Fort Bridger, 205

Soldiers' Homestead law: provisions, 357-8

Soldiers' National home: 358-9

Soldiers' pensions: 358

Soldiers' Relief fund: first meeting for, 324; 325; amount collected, 326

Soldiers' Widows, Orphans and Army Nurses Home: 359

Somerset house: stage robbers arrested, 199

Sonoma county: *note* 238

Sonora (Calif.): *note* 142; Calif. vols. from, 187

Sonora (Mex.): troops across, 57, 81; purchase of r.r. right-of-way advocated, 131; Pesqueira flees, 180; 182, 305

"Sonora", s.s: 288

Sopori: *note* 131

Soshone Indians: 193

South America: 318

South Anna: 288, 299

South Seas: 302

Southern California, Military District of: 42; Carleton commands, 107

Southern Pacific r.r: 82, 102, 109

Southwest: c.s.a. victories, 61

Spain: warships, 22; colonies, 23; trouble with Peru, 319; bombs Valparaiso and Callao, 320

Spalding, Zetus N: 277, *note* 277; 280

Specific Contract act: Calif. "gold law", 352-3

Spencer ranch: Skillman captured, 178

Spies: Confederate, 54, 75; 80, 120; 171; 175-6, 178; U.S. 78, 80; U.S. ordered down Rio Grande, 175

Spokane river: 225

"Spot" the ox: epitaph, 45-6

Springfield rifles: 144; sale of war surplus, 357

Springville (Utah): *Farmers' Oracle* printed, 207

Stag dances: 38

Stage robbery: near Placerville, 198-201

Stand by the Flag: 286

Stanford, Leland: orders for Mt. battalion, 244; Kibbe's report, 313-4; 333

Stanton, Edwin M: 114; investigates Powder R. Ex., 212-3; 243

Stanton, Henry W: Fort named for, 154

Stanwix (Grinnell's ranch): skirmish with C.S.A. pickets, 87; Ranch, 104

Staples, Joseph M: killed by robbers, 199

"Stars and Bars" C.S.A: 56; raised at Tucson, 82; 287; captured, 299; 307; flown by "Shenandoah", 319; display prohibited, 339-40

State house (Boston): 285

Stearns, Abel: supplies beef, 97

Steck, M. (Indian agent): expense at Bosque Redondo, 171

Steele, William: 55, 116

Steen, --- Major: 106

Steen's Peak: 104

Steinberger, Justus: recruits vols. in Calif., 228; 236

Stevens, Isaac I: two forts named for, *note* 236, 292

Stevenson, Jonathan D: 26; presents flag to 7th reg., 142

St. Louis: 211; hdqrts. for Western Sanitary Com., 328

"St. Marys", U.S.S: at Guaymas, 57; 301, 305

Stockton: arrival of Connor's reg., 187; 188-9, 277, *note* 277; 328, *note* 329; 330; Gridley's monument, 335; 347

Stockton Argus: barred from U.S. mail, 336

Stockton Democrat: barred from U.S. mail, 336

"Stone Fort" (Putnam's store): Owens lake, 255-6

Stonington: 285

Stoombs, Thomas A: escort duty to Fort Larned, 164

"Stormcloud" (boat): 306

Stroble, Charles C: killed at Visalia, 340-1

Strong, George T: Treas. Nat'l Sanitary Com., 327

Stuart, J.E.B: C.S.A. cav., 293; 295

St. Vrain, --- (trapper): 163

St. Vrain's Fort (Adobe Walls): 162-3

Subversive activities: 337; laws to curb, 339

Sugarloaf mountain: flag raised, 190

Suislaw river: 230

Sullivan, Eugene: 325

Summit Point: 299

Sumner, E.B: 73

Sumner, Edwin V: arrival in S.F., 21; 22, 25; succeeds Johnston, 27; 34, 37, 107, 269; orders guard for Pacific s.s. co., 302; supplies men and guns for Mare Is., 303; 344

Sunday closing law: 338

Surgeons: training, 266; fees, 278; list of Calif. vol., 279-80; salary, 352

Surgery: 267

Surgical instruments: description, 267; gift, 271

Surprise valley: 252

Surveys: to Gulf of Calif., 129-31, route, *note* 131; Salt Lake to Fort Mojave, 201-3; Salt Lake to Denver, 207-8

"Susan Drew" (transport): 26

Susanville: 252

Sutter, John Augustus: 34, *note* 329, 362

Sutterville: 34

"Suwanee", u.s.s: pursues "Shenandoah", 320; 321

"Swan": 30

TACOMA: 234

"Talking wires": 190

Tappan, Samuel F: Colo. vols., 62

Tar and feathers: 341

Taxes: abolished by Sibley, 56; levied by Carleton, 112; paid into hospital fund, 172; receipt for, 172; Federal war, 351

Teal, John: escape from Apaches, 121

Tehama county: 253

Telegraph: 21, 23, 91; flood damage, 101; protection, 186; 190, 192, 194; destroyed, 209; 210

Telegraph City: Calif. vols. from, 187

Temecula: 49, 72-3, 91, 104

Temecula rancho: 73-4

Temescal: 104

Temescal Lusardi canyon: 74

"Terminal pay": for Calif. vols., 356; allotted to families, 357

Terrazas, Luis: gov. of Chihuahua, 177; grants passports to American officers, 177

Territorial Enterprise: 332

Terry, David S: duel, 41, *note* 69; 179, 348

Terry, Mrs. David S: 75

Teschemacher, H.E: 324; telegraphs Lincoln re Sanitary Com., 327

Texans: 19, 79, 90; at Santa Fe, 91; 94, 124-5; second attempt to conquer s.w., 175

Texas: expedition, 21, 22; mounted vols., 57; 127; Jews fleeing, 178; 304

Texas Hill: 104

Texas, Military Department of: 19

Thatcher, H.K: commands North Pac. squadron, 321

The Girl I Left Behind Me: 188

"The Soldiers' Friend" (Gridley): 330-5

Thirteen-mile house: stage robbery, 198-9

"Thomas H. Perkins" (transport): 26

Thompson, D.W.C: commands Calif. Bat., 288; 291; presents flag to Calif. Bat., 299

Thompson, Marian: 299

Thompson, W.A: in charge howitzers, 120; *note* 122

"Tobacco" poker: 38

Tobin, William C: wounded, 89

Todd, Simeon S: 280

Tolman, George B: 280

Tompkins, E.A: 280

Tongue river: 215, 217, 219

Townsend, E.D: 114

Townsend, Hiram: lost at sea, 289

Training camps: location, 33-4

Travers, E.W: discovers "Chapman" conspiracy, 305; reward for capture of "Chapman", 309

Treaties, Indian: Apache, 154; of 1868 with Navajos, 171; Nez Percé, 232-3; Snake river Indians, 233

Trinidad: mail route, 245

Trinity Center: 30

Trinity county: *note* 238, 248

Trinity Indians: 246

Trinity river: 245-6

Tubac: 79

Tubbs, A.L: 324

Tubutama: *note* 131

Tucson: 33, 78-85; 90-1, 99, 104; description, 109-11; survey to Gulf of Calif., 129-31, *note* 131; map, 131; 132; no. Calif. vols. burials, *note* 360

Tuolumne county: 29

Turner, William F: 114

"Tuscarora", u.s.s: joins Pac. squadron, 320; 321

Tuttle, Hiram S: diary, 191; weather report, 192; accomplishment of vols., 363-4

Twain, Mark (Samuel L. Clemens): 332-3

Twiggs, David E: 125

UINTAH: 207

Umpqua river: 230, 234

Uncle Sam: coin, 38; 55; mail, 132-3; crops, 134

"Uncle Sam", s.s: 6th inf. Calif. vols. guard, 318

Uniforms: of Calif. Hundred, 283, 287; of Calif. Hundred and Bat. supplied by citizens, 288-9

Union: 19, 20, 21, 56; victories, 60; 66, 67; resolution to support, 69; opposition, 72; spies, 80; 89, 126; loyalty, 176; 248; candidates, 260; preservation, 281; King lectures, 329; armies, 338; 346; newspapers, 349

Union bay: at Catalina Is., 249

Union Iron works: parts for U.S.S. "Saginaw", 305; 312

Union League: 343

Union Pacific R.R: 264

Union Vedette: published at Camp Douglas, 206-8

Union Volunteer Refreshment room: Calif. Bat. entertained, 291

Unitarian church (S.F.): 35, 325

United States Constitution: opposition, 72

United States consuls: Mazatlan, 57; Chihuahua, 176; Monterey, Mex., 177; Cairo, Egypt, *note* 189; Havana, 314

United States government: 57; neutrality with Mex., 180; neutrality with France, 180; recognizes Rep. of Mex., 180; foreign policy, 183-5; ratifies treaty with Nez Percé Indians, 232; "Chapman" sold as war prize, 309; treaty with Japan, 311; order to release s.s. "Colon", 317; Monroe Doctrine, 320; credit maintained by gold, 329

United States treasurer: ass't at N.Y., 53; receipts from western mines, 329

Updegraff, Joseph: 155, 161

U.S. highways: "no. 85", 66; "no. 101", 35; "no. 70", 140; "no. 50", 190; "no. 91", 203; "no. 87", 215; "no. 101", 230; "no. 91", 264

Utah: population, 24; 34, 204, 209

Utah Lake: 203

Utah, Military Department of: 19; Connor commands, 190; 196, 203-4, 209, 213; Connor returns, 219; 231

Ute Indians: Carson allies, 165

VACA SPRINGS: 104

Vallecita: 77, 104

Valparaiso: 23, 306; bombed by Spanish vessels, 320; 321

Valverde: battleground, 33; battle, 59; casualties, 59-60; 62-3, 85; C.S.A. victory celebrated, 90; 155

Van Dusen river: 241

Van Orman, Zachias: nephew kidnapped, 193; rescued, 194

Van Slyke, T.W: 264

Vance, Lillian: *note* 67

Vancouver island: 320

Vanderbilt, Cornelius: gift of warship to U.S., 321

"Vanderbilt", U.S.S: Escorts U.S.S. "Monadnock" around Horn to S.F., 321

Veck, William S: wagonmaster, 103; freights bricks to Prescott, 138

Vedettes: 73, 122, 129; killed, 132; Tucson to L.A., 132; 3 yrs. service, 133; 143; Fort Crook to Red Bluff, 251; Camp Independence to Aurora, 258

Vegas, Placido: purchases munitions for Mex., 315-7

Vera Cruz (Mex.): Foreign invasion, 23

Victoria (B.C.): U.S.S. "Narragansett", 319; Soldiers' Relief fund, 325; 360

Victoria, Queen of England: 319

Vienna: 295

Virginia City: "sack of flour" auction, 332

Visalia: 29, 257, 262; subversive activities, 337; 340; tar and feathers, 341

Visalia Delta: 340

Visalia Equal Rights Expositor: attacks Lincoln, barred from U.S. mail, 336-7; destroyed by Calif. vols., 340

Vischer, Edward: 190

Vitamins: supplied by wild plants, 97-8

Volcano: 29, *note* 142, 229

WADDELL, JAMES I: commands "Shenandoah", 319-20; *note* 319

Wagon masters: instructions, 99; 103

Wagon trains: Odd Fellows' train, *note* 86; 99, 103; en route to Rio Grande, 120-1, *note* 122; 129; escort, 133; raid, 161; escort, 162-4; Connor's, 188-9; 198; on survey, 202-3; stolen, 209; 211; Cole's, 217; loss, 218; 247; captured by Mosby's rangers, 295

Waite, Charles B: Mormons ask resignation, 196

Walker, Samuel: commands center column, *note* 214; attacked by Indians, 217-8

Walkers pass: 259

Wallace, Lew: Californians served with, 297

War department, U.S: 19, 100, 114; samples of gold ore, 135; 152; Indian policy, 156; 186; uninformed re. Ind. affairs in West, 213; 314, 317; passport orders, 320; refuses to accept vols. from Pac. coast, 354; 355

War materiel: shipment East, 302; government priority, 317

War panic: Pacific coast, 19, 22, 23; Northwest, 304; 312

War songs: volunteer, 50-1

War surplus property: 322; sale, 357

Warner, J.J: 80

Warner, Solomon: 79

Warner's pass: 82

Warners ranch: 48-9, 73-4, 80, 104, 143

Warren, G.K: 216

Warrenton: 298

Washburn, ---: 79

Washburn, E.H: 324

Washington: population, 24; Calif. vols., 221; recruiting vols., 227-8; 234; lack of coastal fortifications, 234; 236-7

Washington (D.C.): protection, 20; 23; 250; Calif. Bat. guard, 290-1; grand review, 298; King in statuary hall, 330, *note* 330

Washington volunteers: 27; recruiting vols., 227-8; Calif. vols. serve in Wash. 1st inf., 228, 230, *note* 231; Fort Lapwai, 232; 236

Washington's birthday: 60

Washoe Co. bldg. (Reno): "sack of flour", 332

"Washoe", s.s: 318

Wassen, Warren (Ind. agent): 256

Watchful waiting: 23

"Wateree", U.S.S: joins Pac. squadron, 319; 321

Waterloo house: 189

Waterman, F.H: 57

Watson, Charles: stage driver, 198-9

Watson, E.L: death, 271; 280

Watsonville: 29; Calif. vols. from, 235

Waynesboro: 299

Weaver, Paulino: 86

Weber, Charles M: gave lots, 328; biog., *note* 329

Weller, C.L: arrested, 348-9

Weller, John B: at Visalia, 341

Welles, Gideon: 301; orders, 302; recommends increase in Pac. squadron, 320

Wellman, Chauncey R: 73-4, *note* 85

Wells Fargo company: robbed, 199

Wells, James H: accused of killing Calif. vol., 340-1

Wentworth, John P.H. (Ind. agent): distributes food and clothing, 258

Weslow, Mrs. Jessie: *note* 86

West, Benjamin R: civil and mil. gov. Catalina Is., 31; *note* 31; takes possession of Catalina Is., 249; builds Camp Cady, 263; 278

West, Joseph R: 41, 77, 91-2, 102; arrests Mowry, 113; Mowry sues, *note* 114-5; *note* 122; 127; commands Mil. Dist. of Ariz., 134; proclamation to farmers, 134; trans. to Mil. Dept. of Ark., 135; 151, 177

West Point: graduates, 26; 113, 248, *note* 248

West Point (Calif.) : Calif. vols. from, 187; stage robbers' hideout, 200

Western Sanitary Commission (St. Louis) : contributions, 328

Western Union Tel. & Tel. co: cable on N.W. coast, 322

Wet-too-law-in (Indian) : accusation against, 232

Whale oil: 145

Wheat: stored at Pima, 85; 97

Wheel Gulch (Cañada de los Ruedas) : 162

Wheeling, William: 78; accompanies Expressman Jones, 115, *note* 115; attacked by Indians and killed, 116; 123

Whipple, Amiel W: 148; explorations and surveys, 151

Whipple, Stephen G: commands Humboldt Mil. Dist., 244-5; biog., *note* 245; peace in Humboldt Dist., 246-7

Whiskeytown: 30

White, Ami: 79; captured, 83, 85

White Mountains (N.H.) : Mt. Starr King, 330

White Oak road: 299

White's mill: gov. supplies, 81; damaged, 83; 89

Whiting, H.R: 67

Wilderness: battle of, 297

William Land park: 34

William Ludwig hotel: 31

Williamson, Jonathan M: Camp Douglas, 195; 280

Williamson, Robert S: 252

Willis, Edward B: 135-8, 165

Wilmington: 85, 103, 262

Wilson, --- Lt: 304

"Wilson A. Hunt", s.s: on Columbia R., 221

Wilson, Benjamin (Benito) D: 42; gift to Methodist college, 48; life saved by Mangas Coloradas, 150

Winchester: 284; battle, 297; 298-300; elm tree for Memorial Grove, 300

Winchester bay (Ore.) : 230

Window Rock (La Ventana) : Navajo Indian agency, 168

Wing, Emory: letter, 360-1

Wingate, Benjamin: Fort named for, 155

Winston, Joseph: wagonmaster, 103

Wolf creek: 215

"Wolf hunting": 241

Wolf, I.H. (vedette) : died in service, 251

Wolf, John: capt. of s.s. "Wilson A. Hunt", 221

Wolfe, ---: tortured, 176

Wood, Erastus W: *note* 114

Wood, Josephine Gridley: gift of "sack" to Nev. Hist. Soc., 332

Woodman, Ernest M: letter from, 252-3

Woods, Eugene H: 280

Wool, John E: Carleton served with, 105-6

Wooster, David: *note* 122; biog., 269-70, *note* 269-70; 280

Wooster, Mrs. David: 270

World War II: 67

Wright, George: commands dept. of Pac., 27, 28; biog., *note* 28; 32, 40, 48-9, 57-8; warns Mex., 58; 60, 74, 96; expense of Rio Grande ex., 98; report on ex., 100-1; 103; 112-3, 128; reply to Doolittle committee, 152; advocates occupation of Guaymas, 182; 186; orders guard on O.M. stages, 200; 234; assigned to Mil. Dept. of Columbia, 237;

Wright, George: continued
  note 238, 240-1, 244; advocates
  Catalina Is. as Ind. res., 248-9;
  orders withdrawal of Calif. vols.
  from Catalina Is., 250; orders
  Calif. vols. to Fort Reading, 253;
  reviews Calif. Bat., 289; 337, 347-
  8; criticism, 349; complains of
  pay, 351; death, 360-1; funeral
  and monument, 362
Wright, Mrs. George: death, 360-1;
  funeral and monument, 362
Wright, Thomas F: son of Gen.
  Wright, 362
Wyckoff, Charles A: journal, 138-9,
  145-6
Wyoming: 34, 219
"Wyoming", U.S.S: 301, 303; to East

Indies, 303; battle with Japan, 311

YAGER, L.J.F: 78; ferry, 79; supplies
  beef, 97
Yankee Doodle: 222, 224
Yaquina bay: 229
Yellowstone river: 217
Yerba Buena island: fortification, 314
Yolo race track: 34
Yorktown: 286, 293
Yosemite National park: Mt. Starr
  King, 330
"Yosemite", S.S: 318
Young, Brigham: summons follow-
  ers, 196
Yreka: 101

ZUNI: 166